TIGER WITH WINGS

China's BRI and Economic Engagement in South Asia

TIGER WITH WINGS

China's BRI and Economic Engagement in South Asia

SANJAY PULIPAKA

Foreword by

James Mayall

Emeritus Professor, University of Cambridge

KW Publishers Pvt Ltd
New Delhi

ISBN 978-81-986658-6-7 Hardback

Published in India by Kalpana Shukla

KW Publishers Pvt Ltd
4676/21, First Floor, Ansari Road
Daryaganj, New Delhi 110 002
Phone : +91 11 43528107
Production : kw@kwpub.in
Marketing : sanjeev@kwpub.in
Website : www.kwpub.in
Cover Design : Anujay Vootla

Printed and Bound in India
Quiinkit Infotech Pvt. Ltd., Gurugram

Dedication

అమ్మ, నాన్న, అన్నయ్య,వదిన, జోష్ మాష్, స్మార్ట్ గర్ల్, మరియు నా స్నేహితులు

James Mayall, Jayaprakash Narayan, Jayne Docherty, Krishnan Srinivasan, and Shakti Sinha

Acknowledgements

This book has evolved over a long time. My work on Myanmar initially prompted me to map Chinese economic engagement in that country. Subsequently, my research interests in South Asian geopolitics led me to explore the growing Chinese presence across the region. I had a wonderful opportunity to work on similar themes as a Senior Fellow at the Nehru Memorial Museum and Library, which is now rechristened as the Prime Ministers Museum and Library. Since then, there has been a prolonged military stand-off between India and China in Ladakh, a notable expansion of Chinese engagement in South Asia, and the emergence of trade as a significant global fault line. I was able to grapple with such complex issues because, over the years, I have been fortunate to interact with numerous scholars, policymakers, journalists, and others in India and several neighbouring countries. I am also grateful to all my teachers and colleagues in various educational institutions and think-tanks, whose encouragement has made this book possible.

Praise for the Book

This is an exceptional work, for its vast scale, conceptual clarity, and logical structure. The treatment of the central theme – the genesis, rationale, evolution, and evaluation of China's Belt and Road Initiative (BRI) – has been handled with in-depth knowledge, considerable sensitivity, and a dispassionate outlook. The author presents a South Asian, not just Indian, perspective on the past performance of BRI in all its critical dimensions. To us accustomed to frequent headlines on BRI, *Tiger with Wings* is a rare scholarly offering that enriches our knowledge and provides an informed view based on quality research. It is a must-read for anyone interested in geo-economics, China, and South Asia today.

Ambassador Rajiv Bhatia
Distinguished Fellow, Gateway House

Sanjay Pulipaka's very scholarly work on the Belt and Road Initiative (BRI) titled Tiger with Wings is essential reading not merely to understand how Beijing sees BRI but also to comprehend the Chinese mind. It is well researched, timely, comprehensive and insightful. It is a must-read for anyone studying China.

Ambassador Gautam Bambawale
Former Indian Ambassador to China and Pakistan
Distinguished Professor, Symbiosis International University

In this broad and deep review and assessment of the impact of the Chinese BRI on all South Asian countries, Sanjay Pulipaka has illuminated and analysed the several impacts of Chinese economic outreach to the region. This book, while based on regional governments' varied experiences with BRI, draws astute implications from the variety of projects, financial arrangements, including indebtedness, and geopolitical realities within the region. Pulipaka also helpfully reflects on the BRI impact on India and its relations with its neighbours. There is no question but that the BRI initiative has had a profound impact in South Asia—and this is the one book, by a distinguished scholar, which describes the reality of BRI and its implications. Highly recommended for both scholars and all those interested in South Asia, including especially diplomats and foreign policy analysts.

A. Peter Burleigh
U.S. Ambassador (Retired)

Sanjay Pulipaka has done a deep dive into China's outward economic strategy and how the country engages in the wider Asian region through the Belt and Road Initiative. It is full of astute observations and provides fresh insight about China's international economic relations. It is an important book!

Fredrik Erixon
Founding Director of the European Centre for International Political Economy (ECIPE)

Sanjay Pulipaka's book is a timely and incisive intervention on a subject that has long demanded deeper regional engagement. With the rare combination of first-hand observations from China and profound expertise in South Asian affairs, he offers a nuanced and authoritative analysis of the BRI in South Asia. This work fills a critical void in the existing discourse and sets a new benchmark for regional scholarship. It is indispensable reading for policymakers, scholars, and strategic thinkers alike.

Sana Hashmi, PhD
Fellow, Taiwan-Asia Exchange Foundation (TAEF)

Tiger with Wings is a timely and insightful analysis of China's expanding footprint in South Asia through the Belt and Road Initiative. For those of us in Japan pursuing deeper engagement with the region under the Free and

Open Indo-Pacific vision, Sanjay Pulipaka's analysis offers valuable lessons on the complex interplay of infrastructure, influence, and sovereignty.

Professor Ken Jimbo

Professor, Keio University / Managing Director, International House of Japan

Sanjay Pulipaka's timely analysis of China's Belt and Road Initiative sheds light on what it actually means for countries which have signed up to the scheme. It was not, what China claimed, an attempt to create a new, more just world order, but a global project designed to enable China to develop its own network of influence. The BRI has created new markets for Chinese goods, ensured a steady supply of minerals, and allowed China to gain control of foreign ports, airports, and other strategically important infrastructure. Pulipaka's study should be read by anyone wanting to understand the ramifications of BRI engagement, and especially how it has affected countries in the region stretching from Afghanistan to Myanmar.

Bertil Lintner

Author of more than twenty books about Asian politics and history.

In Tiger with Wings, Sanjay unpacks the OBOR in the context of history, economy and international relations. He has lucidly brought out the advantages, disadvantages and implications in international relations for China, particularly in South Asia, Afghanistan and Myanmar. This book makes for a very interesting and compelling read. Every China scholar will benefit from this work immensely.

Lt Gen S L Narasimhan, *PVSM, AVSM*, VSM, PhD (Retd)*
Former Member, National Security Advisory Board
Former DG, Centre for Contemporary China Studies

This book is an excellent scholarly work, covering in detail China's external economic engagement strategy. It brings together geopolitical and geoeconomic contours into account, with an interesting analysis on Xi Jinping's pet project, the Belt and Road Initiative. The author's analysis and arguments are interesting, and this book is a reader-friendly one, fitting for all spectrums of society, from business to academia to policy makers.

Dr. Jagannath Panda

Head, Stockholm Center for South Asian and Indo-Pacific Affairs, ISDP, Sweden; and Professor, University of Warsaw

In the timely and pertinent book, 'Tiger with Wings', Sanjay Pulipaka offers a skilful analysis of China's Belt and Road Initiative and its implications for South Asia. Using scholarly precision and geopolitical acumen, Pulipaka demystifies the intricate web of infrastructure projects, strategic ambitions, and economic partnerships that define China's increasing regional influence. This book illuminates how China's initiatives have shaped power dynamics across South Asia, from Sri Lanka to Pakistan to Nepal and Myanmar. Pulipaka's work is an essential reading for policymakers, scholars, and anyone trying to understand the geoeconomic and geopolitical future of one of the most consequential regions in the world.

Dr. Sriparna Pathak
Professor, China Studies and International Relations,
O.P. Jindal Global University

Tiger with Wings by Sanjay Pulipaka is a great scholarly work, providing a comprehensive analysis of China's Belt Road Initiative (BRI) engagement as an instrument of power projection. It critically examines China's rise, and the interface between geopolitics and geoeconomics in the Indian subcontinent, with long-term implications in the balance of power, not just in the region, but in other parts of the world.

Ambassador Preeti Saran (Retired)
Member, UN Committee on Economic,
Social and Cultural Rights, Geneva

Contents

Foreword

In recent years, a new institutional magnet has developed to challenge the framework developed by the United States and its allies after the Second World War. This framework is based on the US dollar and the authority of the Bretton Woods institutions, the IMF and the World Bank, to which should be added the GATT, the forerunner of the World Trade Organisation (WTO), although it was negotiated at a later conference in Havana. The new grouping, the BRICS (Brazil, Russia, India, China, and South Africa), has proved popular amongst countries in the Global South, which are either opposed to, or wary of, the United States' dominance of the world order. Although President Trump has pronounced that the BRICS is dead, this seems unlikely given the revival of interest in pluralism as opposed to the liberal international ideology in world politics. Many of the countries that have either already joined or would like to join the BRICS are already participants in China's Belt and Road Initiative (BRI).

China's revival of the Silk Road concept involved building networks of investment and trade across the world. It was seen as the economic face of China's meteoric rise to world power status, initiated by Deng Xiaoping from 1978 onwards. Although it was much quoted by the media, it was both understudied and poorly understood. With respect to South Asia, this is no longer the case. Sanjay Pulipaka has written a very important book on the subject. *Tiger with Wings* explores China's relations with India, Pakistan, Afghanistan, Myanmar, Nepal, Bangladesh, Sri Lanka, and the Maldives, together with their wider implications in other parts of the world, in detail and in clear accessible prose. While he has no difficulty in agreeing that China's rise has been a game-changer in the region, he is highly sceptical of China's claims to have made a major contribution to the region's development or stability, as indeed of its principled commitment not to interfere in the domestic affairs of other countries.

To some extent, this, no doubt, reflects an Indian perspective. I will return to this issue shortly, but the immediate point to note is that he is extremely fair-minded in spelling out the context within which Chinese-funded projects were agreed upon. His criticisms are mainly the result of his similarly fair-minded analysis of the failure of Chinese assistance to overcome the economic crises in which all the countries he writes about, apart from India, found themselves mired. Given the demographic and geographical dominance of India within the subcontinent, it is unsurprising that the pattern of power politics, with its defining maxim 'the enemy of my enemy is my friend', has always featured prominently in the worldview of its less powerful neighbours.

For Pakistan, its informal alliance with China has been regarded as a central part of its security ever since it was first initiated by Ayub Khan in March 1965. For successive Pakistani governments, the strategic imperative has remained paramount with the Chinese investment in infrastructure being seen as both welcome and important but secondary. In the case of Myanmar and Nepal, their proximity to China would have made it difficult to avoid the inducements to be involved in the BRI even had they wanted to, which seems improbable. For the Maldives and Afghanistan, there was no real conflict with Indian policy, and indeed, Chinese involvement may have acted as a spur to India to increase its own economic contribution to their development.

India is the outlier in Pulipaka's account. It is China's only credible rival for regional influence; it has an approximately two-thousand-mile land border, parts of which are contested with regular skirmishes provoked by one side or the other, some of which have led to fatalities. At the same time, China is India's second most important trade partner while several Chinese companies are also present in India. India is not in danger of being caught in a debt trap like some of the smaller recipients of Chinese trade and investment. Nonetheless, bilateral efforts to reduce India's trade deficit have so far yielded meagre results and have, no doubt, contributed to the growing tension between the two states. Whether their joint membership of BRICS and mutual economic involvement will be sufficient to maintain the present equilibrium remains to be seen. Meanwhile, we must hope that the pattern of conflict and cooperation, checking one another within a single relationship that the Sino-Indian relationship illustrates, can establish itself as part of the new pluralist international order. Anyone wanting to unravel the complexities of China's influence on contemporary world politics should read this book.

James Mayall
Emeritus Professor, University of Cambridge

February 2025

Preface

During one of my visits to China, I attended the renowned Sichuan Opera in Chengdu to watch the actors perform the *Bian Lian* (Face Change). The actor changes his/her face masks at lightning speed, leaving the audience in awe and wonder. The audience cannot afford to get distracted lest they may miss a quick change of mask. With every change of mask, the actor conveys a new mood and a new twist in the plot. Reportedly, the *Bian Lian* technique is a closely guarded secret. Even in China, only a few select artists can perform the art. China's external economic engagement resembles *Bian Lian's* dynamic and multifaceted character. Over the years, Chinese leaders have often articulated concepts such as Panchsheel, the New Type of Great Power Relations, and called for civilisation cooperation based on win-win approaches. Like the masks in *Bian Lian*, the concepts/initiatives are transient, and their sequence/content are defined by the principal actor—the Communist Party of China (CPC).

The fact that many across the world are paying increased attention to Chinese art, culture, politics, and economy indicates China's rise as a major power in global politics. As a rising power, China is using its economic prowess to alter power dynamics in different regions of the world through projects such as the Belt and Road Initiative (BRI). The BRI has attracted considerable international attention because of the ambitious infrastructure projects and massive investments it proposed. While the BRI is a decade-old initiative, it should be noted that China has a long history of robust external economic engagement.

The BRI constitutes one of the important phases in China's external economic engagement. For instance, Chinese leaders invited Soviet specialists to kick-start industrialisation in the 1950s, which indicated their keenness to learn from other countries. However, Sino-Soviet ideological and geopolitical competition ensured that the experiment was short-lived. In the subsequent years, China's gaze turned inwards. Because of the failed policies of the Great Leap Forward and the Cultural Revolution, Chinese society experienced considerable pain and severe economic deceleration.

It was only after the advent of Deng Xiaoping that the CPC sought to balance commitment to ideology with pragmatism. For instance, Deng Xiaoping famously stated, "It doesn't matter whether a cat is black or white, as long as it catches mice." There is a debate as to whether Deng Xiaoping made that statement. Nonetheless, the fact that such a statement was attributed to him indicated that during his tenure, public policy was defined by pragmatism, and foreign capital and technology were solicited. While Deng's reforms were much needed, they resulted in erratic growth and deep inequities, which prompted social unrest and student protests across the country, including the famous Tiananmen Square protests in Beijing. The CPC violently suppressed the student protests, resisted the impulse to return to autarkic economic policies, and persisted with economic reforms. In fact, Deng Xiaoping warned his colleagues, stating, "without implementing reforms and open policy, nothing but death is in store for us ... cadres who don't understand this must replace their brains with better ones." In the subsequent years, China also scaled up its external economic engagement, which is evident in its successful efforts to join the World Trade Organization (WTO) and other regional frameworks during the tenures of Jiang Zemin and Hu Jintao.

Under Xi Jinping's leadership, the BRI was envisaged to address domestic challenges, such as production overcapacities, triggering economic growth in the western provinces, and finding newer investment destinations and consumer markets for Chinese firms. The BRI also had geopolitical goals, such as increasing Chinese influence in different parts of the world, including in South Asia.

South Asia is an India-centric region where the countries share long borders with India but not with each other (except in the case of Afghanistan-Pakistan and Bangladesh-Myanmar). India has close cultural, people-to-people, and robust economic relations with its subcontinental neighbours. Some South Asian countries sought to diversify their partnerships by consolidating their ties with China. However, geographic impediments, such as mountainous terrains and high seas, constrained the Chinese economic engagement with South Asia. With the improvement in construction technologies, these barriers have become relatively easier to surmount. By operationalising massive infrastructure projects, the BRI is attempting to break the insularity of South Asia from China. Almost all South Asian countries signed on to the BRI, except India and Bhutan.

Several economic initiatives and corridors were conceptualised under the BRI framework. The China-Pakistan Economic Corridor (CPEC) is one of the flagship projects of the BRI in South Asia. It is indicative of a robust bilateral relationship rooted in regional geopolitical dynamics. While the leaders on both sides refer to their friendship as 'higher than mountains and sweeter than honey', the relationship is defined by transactionalism. Under the rubric of the CPEC, Beijing participated in the development of infrastructure projects from Kashgar to Gwadar. In return, Chinese defence forces are accessing Pakistan's strategically important ports. The Pakistani establishment sold the CPEC to its citizens as a panacea for all ills. Currently, the country is laden with huge debts that are threatening the stability of the economy. The CPEC has not improved the internal security situation in Pakistan, and the trends point in the opposite direction. Instead of re-examining the master plan, there are plans to extend the BRI into Afghanistan. It is still too early to determine if the Afghan economy will turn around because of increased Chinese engagement.

After proactively participating in various BRI projects, Sri Lanka experienced a severe economic crisis. Unable to repay its debts, Sri Lanka handed over Hambantota port to China on a lease for 99 years. The Chinese investments in the Colombo Port City Special Economic Zone and its attendant institutional frameworks have raised concerns that the primacy of parliamentary scrutiny was undermined. There has been considerable debate as to whether Chinese investments have also contributed to the economic crisis in Sri Lanka. Similarly, in the Maldives, numerous reports suggested that the emergence and consolidation of an authoritarian leadership was largely possible because of Chinese support. There were concerns about the massive debt and lack of transparency in China's loans to the Maldives.

There is growing Chinese influence in Nepal's domestic politics. Until about a century ago, ideas and goods were exported from Nepal to Tibet and to China. Now, the tide has reversed. China was involved in the construction of Pokhara International Airport and a few energy projects. While there is considerable scepticism on the feasibility of the China-Nepal Railway, the project is moving apace in Tibet and has reached towns close to the Nepal border. There are apprehensions that this project may drag Nepal into a debt trap.

On the other hand, Bangladesh thus far has not experienced a severe debt crisis despite growing Chinese engagement. While Beijing is involved in building coal-fired power plants and connectivity projects, there were instances when Bangladesh was reluctant to move forward on Chinese projects, such as the Chittagong deep-sea port project. While there are apprehensions about Chinese projects in the country, the current challenges for Bangladesh's economy are a consequence of the pandemic and a spike in global crude oil prices. It should be noted that Japan is also a major investor in Bangladesh's connectivity and infrastructure projects. The recent political unrest is negatively impacting the economy of Bangladesh and is threatening to undermine regional peace. China has adopted a cautious approach by trying to build bridges with diverse political players in Bangladesh.

The scale of Chinese influence in Myanmar's politics is astounding. The Myanmar-China relationship is often defined as a *'Pauk-Phaw'* (refers to a close and delicate relationship between the lips and the teeth). China has extended support to the Myanmar military on international platforms. Simultaneously, Beijing also enjoys close relations with ethnic armed groups that are contesting the military rule. Thus far, this dual engagement strategy in Myanmar has paid dividends without significant political and economic costs. Because of its influence, China has unprecedented access to Myanmar's natural resources and market. Beijing is also attempting to leverage Myanmar's geostrategic location to its advantage, which is evident in the construction of ports and energy pipelines.

Unlike other South Asian countries, India has not participated in the BRI projects. The Indian government expressed serious concerns that the CPEC goes through sections of the Indian territory of Kashmir, which is currently under the occupation of Pakistan. There was an opinion in India that the BRI was conceived without adequate consultations and that its implementation lacked transparency. While India is encountering persistent grey-zone territorial violations from China, in the realm of bilateral trade, Chinese products are flooding the Indian market. India had a whopping \$85.07 billion trade deficit with China in 2023-2024. The deficit continues to persist despite measures by the Indian government to reduce unhealthy trade dependence on China. It appears that the objective of many BRI projects was to access the Indian market from the neighbouring countries as well. Given the rising friction between China and the leading Western economies, accessing the Indian market assumes greater importance for Beijing.

India has responded to China's BRI through connectivity projects in the neighbourhood. Railway lines and energy pipelines have been operationalised between India and Nepal. Similarly, India is building connectivity networks with Bangladesh, including developing inland waterway infrastructure. Indian firms are involved in developing a terminal in Colombo port. A robust road infrastructure and rail network between the landlocked Afghanistan and the Chabahar port in Iran is also being attempted. In addition, New Delhi is working with like-minded countries, such as Japan and the United States, to improve connectivity infrastructure and trade facilitation in India's neighbourhood. India is also seeking to diversify its trade relations with the West and is advocating the need for diversified supply chains to increase the global economy's resilience.

Interestingly, even after a decade, the concerns about the negative economic consequences of the BRI have not abated. There has been no substantive turnaround in the fortunes of the economies of the BRI-participating countries in South Asia in the past decade. While there is uncertainty regarding harvesting the economic fruits, the geopolitical consequences are evident. Given the robust economic, political, and military cooperation between the two countries, the China-Pakistan relationship resembles an alliance but falls short of it in the absence of an explicit treaty. There is a growing Chinese presence in South Asia's continental domain and the Indian Ocean Region (IOR). Further, Beijing's influence in the domestic politics of South Asian countries is becoming palpable. The pandemic, supply chain challenges, and China's economic crisis are impacting the implementation of the BRI. The growing tension in China's relations with the West, and the US in particular, will prompt Beijing to look more towards developing countries for trade and investment opportunities.

Abbreviations

5PC	Five-Point Consensus
AIIB	Asian Infrastructure Investment Bank
APSEZ	Adani Ports & Special Economic Zone Limited
APTA	Asia-Pacific Trade Agreement
ASEAN	Association of Southeast Asian Nations
BCIM	Bangladcsh, China, India, and Myanmar Economic Corridor
BCPCL	Bangladesh-China Power Company Limited
BDS	BeiDou Navigation Satellite System
BECZ	Border Economic Cooperation Zones
BIMSTEC	Bay of Bengal Initiative for Multi-Sectoral Technical and Economic Cooperation
BLA	Baloch Liberation Army
BOP	Balance of Payments
BPDB	Bangladesh Power Development Board
BRF	Belt and Road Forum
BRI	Belt and Road Initiative
BRICS	Brazil-Russia-India-China-South Africa
CCCC	China Communication Construction Company
CDM	Civil Disobedience Movement
CHEC	China Harbour Engineering Company
CIDCA	China International Development Cooperation Agency
CIPS	Cross-Border Interbank Payment System
CITIC	China International Trust and Investment Corporation

CMC	China National Machinery Import & Export Corporation
CMEC	China-Myanmar Economic Corridor
CNY	Chinese Yuan
CPACDC	China Poverty Alleviation and Cooperation Development Center
CPB	Communist Party of Burma
CPC	Communist Party of China
CPEC	China-Pakistan Economic Corridor
CPFTA	China-Pakistan Free Trade Agreement
CRPH	Committee Representing Pyidaungsu Hluttaw
CSCEC	China State Construction Engineering Corporation
DFQF	Duty-Free-Quota-Free
DSR	Digital Silk Road
ECT	East Container Terminal
ETIM	East Turkestan Islamic Movement
EU	European Union
EXIM	Export-Import
FDI	Foreign Direct Investment
FTA	Free Trade Agreement
FTZ	Free Trade Zones
GDP	Gross Domestic Product
GMCP	Greater Malé Connectivity project
GPS	Global Positioning System
HICDP	High-Impact Community Development Projects
HSR	Health Silk Road
ICT	Information Communication Technologies
CAR	Central Asian Republics
IGETC	Inter-Governmental Economic and Trade Committee
IMEC	India-Middle East-Europe Economic Corridor
IMF	International Monetary Fund
INSTC	International North-South Transport Corridor
ISB	International Sovereign Bonds
ISI	Inter-Services Intelligence
ISKP	Islamic State Khorasan Province
JCC	Joint Cooperation Committee
KMT	Kuomintang

KP	Khyber Pakhtunkhwa
LAC	Line of Actual Control
LDC	Least Developed Country
LMC	Lancang-Mekong Cooperation
LNG	Liquefied Natural Gas
LTTE	Liberation Tigers of Tamil Eelam
MCC	Millennium Challenge Corporation
MDP	Maldivian Democratic Party
MES	Market-Economy Status
MNC	Multinational Corporation
MNDF	Maldives National Defense Force
MOU	Memorandum of Understanding
MW	Megawatt
NDA	Non-Disclosure Agreement
NLD	National League for Democracy
NORINCO	North Industries Group Corporation Limited
NSG	Nuclear Supplier Group
NUG	National Unity Government
NYCDC	New Yangon City Development Company
OBOR	One Belt One Road
OIC	Organisation of Islamic Cooperation
PDF	People's Defense Force
PEACE	Pakistan and East Africa Connecting Europe
PLA	People's Liberation Army
PLI	Production Linked Incentive
PNC	People's National Congress
PoK	Pakistan-Occupied Kashmir
POW	Prisoners of War
PPM	Progressive Party of Maldives
PQEPC	Port Qasim Electric Power Company
PQI	Partnership for Quality Infrastructure
PRC	People's Republic of China
PSX	Pakistan Stock Exchange
RCEP	Regional Comprehensive Economic Partnership
RMB	Renminbi
RMG	Ready-Made-Garment
SAARC	South Asian Association for Regional Cooperation

SEZ	Special Economic Zone
SFF	Special Frontier Force
SLPA	Sri Lanka Port Authority
SOE	State-Owned Enterprises
SPP	State Partnership Programme
SSD	Special Security Division
TAR	Tibet Autonomous Region
THMDCN	Trans-Himalayan Multi-Dimensional Connectivity Network
TTP	Tehreek-e-Taliban Pakistan
UAR	United Arab Republic
UAV	Unmanned Aerial Vehicles
UK	United Kingdom
UN	United Nations
UNHCR	United Nations High Commissioner for Refugees
UNSC	United Nations Security Council
UPI	Unified Payments Interface
US	United States
USAID	United States Agency for International Development
USD	United States Dollar
USIP	United States Institute of Peace
USTR	US Trade Representative
WCT	West Container Terminal
WFP	World Food Programme
WTO	World Trade Organisation

1

Introduction: China's External Economic Engagement—An Overview

Introduction

On September 30, 2024, President Xi Jinping stepped onto the rostrum at the Great Hall of the People in Beijing. Behind the rostrum were huge red flags embossed with '1949–2024', and the audience consisted of senior members of the Communist Party of China (CPC) and foreign dignitaries. President Xi's speech, celebrating the 75th anniversary of the founding of the People's Republic of China (PRC), referred to the 'great rejuvenation of the Chinese nation' and also alluded to 'potential dangers' that confront the nation and the need to 'resolutely overcome unforeseen risks and challenges'.[1] President Xi declared that the CPC had created "twin miracles of rapid economic growth and long-term social stability."[2] The rise of China, which altered the balance of power in world politics, was a consequence of rapid economic growth. The Chinese leadership takes great pride in its economic accomplishments. For instance, President Xi Jinping, speaking at China's National People's Congress in October 2022, proudly announced that "we have won the largest battle against poverty in human history…we have, once and for all, resolved the problem of absolute poverty in China."[3] Terming the Chinese economic growth a "miracle", President Xi declared that "the rejuvenation of the Chinese nation is now on an irreversible historical course."[4]

Over the last three decades, more than 850 million people in China were lifted out of poverty.[5] According to the Chinese authorities, absolute poverty has been eliminated. China's economic growth also increased its military expenditure and external engagement, allowing it to emerge as an important power in global politics. The CPC leadership often states with great pride that "no country has been able to lift hundreds of millions of people out of poverty in such a short time."[6] China today has emerged as a manufacturing hub, the largest trader, the second-largest economy in the world, and a major power in global politics.

For some observers, China's economic growth is a puzzle, as it lacks robust institutional frameworks, such as fully developed autonomous financial markets, required for the success of a market-based economy.[7] Moreover, there is a perception that China has very high levels of corruption, and the actual workings of the CPC are challenging to discern. However, under the CPC's stewardship, China has registered spectacular economic growth in the past three decades. In China's growth story, external economic interactions, which have evolved over many phases, played a significant role.

The Russian Engagement and Failed Experiments

The CPC was formed in 1921, and it emerged victorious after a prolonged civil war with the nationalist Kuomintang (KMT). On October 1, 1949, Mao Zedong stood before the famous Tiananmen Square and announced the formation of the PRC. In addition to the civil war, the establishment of the PRC was preceded by a prolonged struggle against Japanese occupation. Consequently, immediately after its formation, the PRC was plagued by severe poverty, and the state apparatus lacked sufficient resources. To compound the misery, some members of the international community hesitated to bestow formal diplomatic recognition to the PRC. Myanmar and India were some of the first non-communist countries to recognise the PRC. Since its inception, the Chinese government has navigated many such challenges to establish a robust state.

Many continuities and discontinuities mark the Chinese economic success story. While China has registered a quantum leap in its gross domestic product (GDP) in the past seven decades, the economic progress came after experimenting with policies that failed with severe human costs. In the initial years after assuming power, the CPC, under Mao Zedong, made grave mistakes in economic policy. In 1958, Mao Zedong launched the 'Great

Leap Forward' campaign to usher in rapid progress through labour-intensive industrialisation and collectivisation of agricultural farms. Prior to the launch of the Great Leap Forward, Chinese leaders were keen on replicating a Soviet-style industrialisation and requested the Soviet Union to send experts to assist in the planning and implementation of projects in various sectors. As early as 1950, the Soviet Union dispatched experts to assist China in constructing hydroelectric projects at Mao's request.[8] In addition, there was significant military cooperation with Russia, and Moscow shared military advisers, aviation equipment, and naval equipment with China.[9] While Russian experts in Eastern Europe attempted to exert political control, China hosted a large number of 'technical experts'; therefore, their impact on day-to-day politics was minimal.[10] By 1958, over 11,000 Russian non-military experts were working in China.[11] Nonetheless, there was discomfort in some sections of the Chinese leadership with the significant presence of technical experts.

In the subsequent years, as the Sino-Soviet split intensified, there was a rapid reduction in the number of Russian experts working in China. Pankaj Mishra points out that Mao was not merely interested in replicating the Soviet model of industrialisation, but his policies sought to achieve high levels of industrialisation within an exceptionally short duration.[12] The Great Leap Forward policy measures aimed at quick industrialisation resulted in the rapid decline of agricultural productivity and large-scale famine. It is estimated that millions may have perished because of the failed policies. Frank Dikötter, writing in the pages of *The New York Times*, argues that the senior political leadership was fully aware of the growing famine and did not take remedial measures.[13] There was growing discontent, and Mao's leadership was questioned after the failure of the Great Leap Forward. Mao Zedong sought to reinforce his leadership position and called for the Great Proletarian Cultural Revolution in 1966. He argued that capitalist forces had entered the government and society, and therefore, it was important to purge the bourgeois elements. On May 16, 1966, the Central Committee of the CPC issued a circular that called upon party members to "follow Comrade Mao Tse-tung's instructions, hold high the great banner of the proletarian Cultural Revolution, thoroughly expose the reactionary bourgeois."[14] The circular went on to add that the "bourgeoisie who have sneaked into the party, the government, the army, and various cultural circles are a bunch of counter-revolutionary revisionists ... [and] ... once conditions are ripe, they will seize political power and turn the dictatorship of the proletariat into a dictatorship of the bourgeoisie."[15]

Therefore, it became imperative to "expose the reactionary bourgeois stand of those so-called 'academic authorities' who oppose the party and socialism, thoroughly criticise and repudiate the reactionary bourgeois ideas in the sphere of academic work, education, journalism, literature and art, and publishing, and seize the leadership in these cultural spheres."[16] Under the banner of the 'Red Guards', young people were deployed to battle the alleged 'class enemies', who often turned out to be intellectuals, party officials, and people in various authorities. For instance, leading economists, such as Xue Muqiao who was later "widely praised as the architect of China's market transformation", were denounced as 'capitalist-roaders' and were imprisoned.[17] There was a widespread purge of leadership at various levels, and senior political leaders, such as Liu Shaoqi and Deng Xiaoping, became victims. Deng Xiaoping was referred to as 'a restorationist maniac', 'leading capitalist reader', 'old', 'incompetent', and an 'unrepentant capitalist roader'.[18] Liu Shaoqi, a senior leader in the CPC, was labelled as a counterrevolutionary and detained, where he reportedly passed away because of a lack of adequate medical care.[19] The Red Guards became increasingly proactive in targeting the 'class enemies'. To control the Red Guards, many young people were sent to the countryside to work on farms. It is estimated that "16 million young people were sent to the countryside, including Xi Jinping", who later went on to become the president of the country.[20] The Cultural Revolution eliminated Mao Zedong's enemies at the top level of the CPC, and it also percolated to lower levels where many commoners were branded as revisionists or supporters of capitalism and were eliminated or purged from the party. The Cultural Revolution resulted in large-scale violence, and millions suffered. Considerable cultural heritage was also lost as the supporters of the Cultural Revolution were keen on wiping out the four olds—"old things, old ideas, old customs, and old habits."[21] The political uncertainty ushered in by the Cultural Revolution continued until Mao died in 1976. The polity stabilised after Deng Xiaoping came to power in 1977. Instability and imprudent public policies meant that the economic indicators were appallingly low. In 1978, China's GDP was around USD 150 billion, and gross national per capita income was a mere USD 200.[22]

The New Leadership and a Modulated Opening

The emergence of a new leader and the bitter experiences of the failed economic policies of the previous decades created the conditions for a radical rethinking of economic plans. Ideas that invited imprisonment during the

Cultural Revolution were rehabilitated. For instance, writing in the 1950s and 1960s, Sun Yefang sharply criticised setting production output quotas as akin to "make an ox move by lifting its legs" and instead suggested that "stressing profit is more like pulling the ox's nose."[23] Sun Yefang argued that 'socialist profit' differed from 'capitalist profit' as the workers created it for larger social good and public needs.[24] These strands of thinking—profits at the enterprise level—were picked up by other economists after the advent of Deng Xiaoping's regime. Economists such as Xue Muqiao called for fostering the enthusiasm of enterprises and workers and emphasised the role of the market within the rubric of public ownership.[25] More specifically, Xue Muqiao suggested that "every state enterprise should practise independent economic accounting and, in management and operation, enjoy adequate decision-making power, within limits prescribed by law."[26]

Simultaneously, there was a rollback of policies such as the collectivisation of agricultural production. Deng Xiaoping's decollectivisation policy is often credited with invigorating the rural economy. For instance, the Third Plenary Session of the 15th Central Committee of the CPC, held two decades later, noted that "the household contract system with remuneration linked to output, abolition of the people's commune, the breakthrough in the planned economy mould and the development of the socialist market economy have greatly kindled the enthusiasm of hundreds of millions of Chinese farmers and emancipated and developed productive forces, thus bringing historic, tremendous changes to the rural economy and social development."[27] The Third Plenary Session added that "the success of rural reform has been a great victory for Deng Xiaoping Theory."[28] Conversely, Kate Xiao Zhou argues that it was the farmers who went about undermining the collectivisation efforts, and the government subsequently endorsed the movement towards decollectivisation.[29] Either way, the fact that Deng Xiaoping and his colleagues did not stand in the way of change indicated a willingness to chart a new path.

The Chinese leadership had long recognised the need to modernise the economic processes. In fact, Mao Zedong, in his 'Reading Notes on the Soviet Union's Political Economy', observes that "in addition to modernising industry and agriculture, science and culture, we have to modernise national defence."[30] Deng Xiaoping often acknowledged the need for modernisation as an idea emanating from Mao's thinking. However, it is possible that such acknowledgement was aimed at appeasing hardline factions by framing the proposed changes as a continuation of earlier policies. Deng Xiaoping termed his reformist agenda as 'four modernisations' with the following components: (1) modernising agriculture (through mechanisation as well as modernising farming techniques); (2) expanding industry (in addition to focusing on heavy industries, there is also a need to focus on manufacturing consumer goods); (3) developing science and technology (while continuing to focus on primary education, there is also a need to focus on developing higher educational institutions); and (4) upgrading China's defence forces.[31] Deng Xiaoping contended that there are four favourable conditions for the success of his modernisation, which include: 'First, China is a country with vast territory and abundant energy and mineral resources; second, over the past 30 years, [the CPC has] laid a preliminary material foundation for the industry, agriculture, science and technology; third, the Chinese people have the necessary skill set and discipline and are being encouraged to emancipate their minds; and fourth, to realise the four modernisations, [China] must follow the correct foreign policy of opening to the outside world.'[32] The need for correct foreign policy was more of a prescription.

In pursuing reforms, external economic engagement constituted an essential pathway for Deng Xiaoping and his colleagues. China, under Deng Xiaoping, was not afraid to learn the best practices from the world, including from the capitalist countries. Deng Xiaoping called for sending "tens of thousands of students abroad, not just a handful." The policy of encouraging large numbers of young students to study at American universities was initiated in 1978–1979.[33] The objective was to train young people with the necessary skills for China's economic development. There was scepticism about whether the students who travel abroad would return to serve their home country. Deng Xiaoping contended that "even if 5 per cent did not return ... the policy would remain a success."[34] It appears that the policy of sending youngsters abroad for higher education and skill education seems to have paid handsome rewards. According to a *China Daily* report: "More than 70 per cent of presidents of prestigious universities and over 90 per cent of academicians at the Chinese Academy of Engineering and the Chinese Academy of Sciences had studied overseas by the turn of the century ... from 1978 to the end of [2018 about] 5.86 million Chinese studied overseas ... more than 4.32 million completed their studies, and over 3.65 million returned soon after doing so, according to the Ministry of Education."[35] Interestingly, despite a large number of foreign-educated students occupying leadership positions in various sectors, China witnessed very little demand for change in the political process from these segments. However, foreign-educated professionals seem to have increased the efficiency of the communist system.

Since 1978, high-ranking officials have visited different countries to study their economic policies. These studies prompted China to focus on enhancing the productivity of state-owned enterprises by transferring technology, exploiting cheap domestic labour, and enhancing external trade.[36] To attract Foreign Direct Investment (FDI), the Chinese government announced the Open Door Policy with liberal economic incentives, such as special tax provisions, simplifying laws, and enacting new laws to facilitate investment. In this direction, in 1980, China operationalised four special economic zones (SEZs)—Shenzhen, Zhuhai, Xiamen, and Shantou—in the eastern provinces of Guangdong and Fujian provinces.[37] These SEZs picked up momentum and presented a model of economic success. The Chinese government also leveraged the diaspora to attract FDI. There were discussions about whether the SEZ policy went against the grain communist philosophy. Economists such as Xu Dixin argued that the SEZs are not complete free-market zones; instead, they constituted spaces with the presence of State-Owned Enterprises (SOEs), foreign enterprises, and joint ventures with complete state control on "urban planning, distribution of industries and bank loans."[38] For Xu Dixin, the joint ventures, which accounted for a large proportion of firms in the SEZs, constituted "a link between China's state administration and capitalism" and they operated under the control of the state.[39] Moreover, the SEZs played a critical role in China's buying-out strategy, encouraging collaboration with foreign investors to use "their funds, import their technology and learn their managerial skills" to speed up the modernisation drive.[40]

The reform process touched upon many aspects of social life and political processes. It was around 1979 that the one-child policy was announced, premised on the assumption that a reduced population would make it easy to increase per capita income.[41] While the policy may have had beneficial economic outcomes, there were legitimate concerns that it may have resulted in painful choices, such as increased abortions.[42] To strengthen governance, Deng Xiaoping wanted the provinces and municipalities to "be given greater powers of decision in economic planning, finance and foreign trade—always within the framework of a nationwide unity of views, policies, planning, guidance and action."[43] His views implied that provinces and municipalities are free to act as long as they do not deviate from the party line and do not contest the authority of Beijing.

Deng Xiaoping argued that internal economic growth and foreign policy are interlinked. He said that China needed a stable external environment to facilitate domestic economic progress. He rolled back the policy of exporting communism to other countries. In 1979, the United States (US) accorded full diplomatic recognition of China. Subsequently, Deng Xiaoping visited the US, suggesting improved relations between the two countries. During the 1970s, the US and China started coordinating their foreign policies to contain the Soviet Union. The need to contain the Soviet Union disappeared after the late 1980s, and the US became engrossed with the developments in the Middle East. All this provided strategic space for China to pursue its dreams of great power status. Deng Xiaoping's relatively moderate foreign policy also allowed China to access development assistance from countries such as Japan. In fact, Japan emerged as one of the largest sources of development assistance for China in the 1970s and 1980s.[44]

The reformist policies and enhanced external economic engagement resulted in increased foreign investment in the country and relatively more advanced technological inputs into the manufacturing industry. Further, the Chinese were exposed to the Western firms' new managerial techniques/processes. The new policies did produce higher economic growth rates, and they promised significant results in the long run. According to World Bank data, China registered an impressive GDP growth rate of 9 per cent in 1982, 10.8 per cent in 1983, and 15.2 per cent in 1984.[45] So, the early spurt in China's growth rates also came from enhanced economic engagement with the outside world and, more specifically, with the West.

The Crisis and an Opportunity

The opening-up policies and engaging with the West came with certain costs. The reforms, as Vijay Gokhale noted, resulted in ideological contestations between those who emphasised that all 'intellectual output should be evaluated for its ideological merit' and others, such as Hu Yaobang (General Secretary of the Chinese Communist Party), who argued that 'intellectual freedom should not be bridled'.[46] Amid these ideological contestations, 'the idea of electing university student bodies gained ground', and the reluctance of government authorities to concede such demands triggered student protests towards the end of 1986.[47] The scale of demonstrations surprised domestic and international audiences, and there was a debate as to whether the protest constituted a call for democracy.[48] Julia Kwong contends that terming the 1986 student demonstration as a protest for democracy would be inaccurate as these demonstrations had multiple causes, such as demands pertaining to food, lighting regulation, and tuition fees, which varied from university to university.[49] The fact that students in various universities took to the streets at the same time indicates that there were some common grievances. The student protests slowly petered out with a rigorous response from party authorities. The student demonstrations coincided with a more extensive debate on the trajectory of the reform process, giving these protests greater political significance. The response of the authorities demonstrated that while the party leadership was keen on engaging economically with the West, there was little appetite to emulate liberal democratic values and political frameworks.

The reform process also resulted in considerable economic inequity, and there was a general perception that corruption among the party officials had increased. Recognising the growing discontent, a campaign was launched to root out corruption, popularly known as 'tiger-beating in the year of the tiger (*hunian dahu*)'.[50] However, the campaign did not make much headway, as the anti-corruption measures got mired in intra-elite party politics and 'the campaign itself actually netted very few "tigers".[51] On the economic front, by the mid-1980s, it was evident that the story was a mixed bag. A report submitted to the Congress of the US on 'China under the Four Modernizations' observed that "a policy of balanced growth and consumerism was substituted in place of the Stalinist big push development approach."[52] And yet, the same report, while expressing cautious optimism, also noted that the Chinese economy registered a 'strong but erratic economic growth....'[53] The growth rate, which was approximately 8.6 per cent in 1986, increased to 11.7 per cent in 1987, declined marginally to 11.2 per cent in 1988, and then crashed to 4.2 per cent in 1989.[54] Such fluctuations in growth rates were also accompanied by higher inflation, coupled with increased expectations among the citizens. In addition, many communist regimes across the world started to wobble. The emergence of television and relatively enhanced interaction with the outside world fuelled discontent in society as expectations for higher living standards went unmet. If the communist party leadership thought they successfully suppressed students' discontent in 1986–1987, they were proved wrong. The subsiding of the 1986 student protests was only a temporary phenomenon, as the discontent among the youth lurked below the surface.

The discontent spilled onto the streets in April 1989 after the death of the former General Secretary of the CPC, Hu Yaobang. As noted earlier, Hu Yaobang advocated for intellectual freedom, and the party elders criticised him for his lenient approach towards outspoken intellectuals and students during the 1986 protests.[55] Subsequently, Hu Yaobang was forced to resign as Party General Secretary. Hu Yaobang's fearless advocacy for political reforms, his unwillingness to bend to the diktats of the party leaders, and his soft approach towards protesting students were popular among the youth. Immediately after his death, many demanded that he be accorded an appropriate memorial service befitting a tall leader. The memorial service for Hu Yaobang became a site of contestation between the students and the authorities. Thousands of students gathered at Tiananmen Square in Beijing and demanded freedom of the press and immediate political and constitutional reforms.[56] Initially, there was some uncertainty among the CPC leadership on understanding the challenge posed by the protests.[57] However, the Chinese leadership started to perceive the student protests as a clear threat to the four cardinal principles (keep to the socialist road; uphold the dictatorship of the proletariat; uphold the leadership of the Communist Party; and uphold Marxism–Leninism and Mao Zedong Thought)[58] enunciated by Deng Xiaoping a decade before Tiananmen developments. Once the opinion that the student protests presented a systemic challenge to the 'leadership of the CPC and the socialist system'[59] consolidated in party leadership, the authorities deployed the military to disperse the protesting crowds. The use of force resulted in significant casualties. While the official estimates were 241 deaths, others estimated the number to be approximately 2,600.[60]

While the CPC implemented harsh measures to contain the demonstrations in Tiananmen Square and other parts of the country, in the economic realm, the reforms proceeded apace, which has a lot to do with the collapse of the Union of Soviet Socialist Republics (USSR). While Soviet communism collapsed, the CPC in China could hold onto power. Because of the Tiananmen Square protests and the collapse of various communist regimes in different parts of the world, the CPC leadership experienced regime survival anxieties. The collapse of the USSR became a lesson for the CPC in ensuring regime survival. The Chinese leadership thoroughly studied the collapse of the USSR and communism in Eastern Europe. Unlike Mikhail Gorbachev's approach, the CPC did not implement simultaneous political and economic reforms. The CPC did not bring about significant changes in its party organisation or the governmental structure. Instead, it gave greater impetus to free-market economic policies and created the conditions for capitalism to flourish within the one-party rule framework. The CPC focused all its energies on ensuring that it delivered economic progress. Immediately after the collapse of the Soviet Union in 1991, Deng Xiaoping conducted his southern tour in China and instructed party officials to redouble their efforts to promote economic growth and improve people's lives.[61] There was an element of urgency to hasten the economic reform process. Deng Xiaoping warned his colleagues, stating, "without implementing reforms and open policy, nothing but death is in store for us...cadres who don't understand this must replace their brains with better ones."[62] In subsequent years, Deng Xiaoping noted that China's survival after the Tiananmen Square crackdown happened because the CPC implemented economic reforms and promoted robust economic growth. Therefore, the ability to refrain from ideological dogmatism and ushering in pragmatic reforms ensured the survival of the CPC.

State Capitalism and the Western Engagement

Jiang Zemin assumed office in a volatile political context defined by the collapse of the Soviet Union and instability induced by the Tiananmen Square incidents. While Jiang Zemin acquired a reputation for strong-arm tactics against student protestors in Shanghai,[63] his elevation was not based on performance metrics alone. Jiang Zemin was elevated to the high office because he was a compromise candidate and had a reputation for being a dull bureaucrat. However, his tenure was anything but dull. Jiang Zemin deftly managed the power dynamics involving various factions and Deng Xiaoping. It must have been challenging for Jiang Zemin to fill Deng Xiaoping's shoes—more so, given that Deng Xiaoping continued to exert influence behind the scenes even after formally relinquishing office.

Jiang Zemin had a Western education during childhood and became proficient in English.[64] During his visit to the Soviet Union to study the manufacturing sector, Jiang Zemin became proficient in Russian, and in subsequent years, he was an industrial liaison officer in Romania.[65] Given these early experiences, Jiang Zemin acquired a cosmopolitan outlook that influenced his decision-making, and as Lucian W. Pye noted, there was a 'contradiction between Jiang the public man and Jiang the private man ... [that] ... parallels the contradiction between the dullness of official politics under Jiang and the lively pockets of activity in the private sectors of the Chinese economy.'[66] Pye added that Jiang Zemin's regime also witnessed lively intellectual activity, 'especially in China's think tanks and arts and cultural communities'.[67] These contradictions help us understand Jiang Zemin's success in normalising relations with the West after the Tiananmen Square incident. After a severe political crisis, instead of closing the country to external influences, Jiang Zemin pro-actively encouraged external economic engagement in general and, more specifically, nudged China towards greater engagement with the West.

At the 14th National Congress of the CPC in 1992, President Jiang Zemin stated that China's economic restructuring aimed to build a 'socialist market economy'.[68] Building a socialist market economy mandated greater economic engagement with the outside world, and in this direction, Jiang Zemin, at the 16th Party Congress, called for deepening "trade and economic relations with other countries ... [and] ... encouraging more enterprises to engage in foreign trade."[69] A socialist market economy was also premised on widening the base of the CPC by incorporating the business class into the communist party, which was one of the more radical reforms initiated by President Jiang Zemin. While there were murmurs against such a policy within the CPC, Jiang Zemin and other leaders opined that it was more prudent to have the emerging business class working within the party framework than outside it.[70]

Jiang Zemin's tenure also witnessed attempts to integrate the western regions into China's economic growth story. In 1999, President Jiang Zemin called for accelerating the development of western China as it was critical for China's stability and constituted an important component in the 'revitalisation of Chinese people'.[71] While China's 'Go West' policy can be traced back to Mao Zedong and Deng Xiaoping's policies, Jiang Zemin articulated the policy in a specific context. China was about to join as a member of the World Trade Organization (WTO). To compete in the global market and attract investments to all provinces, it was felt that the western provinces would require greater attention.[72] As Long Yongtu, China's Chief WTO negotiator, observed, the western part of China should be allowed to engage with the world "to absorb the inflow of international factors of production and to raise its overall quality through the global exchange of information."[73] In a way, the 'Go West' plan was a precursor to the Belt and Road Initiative (BRI). These initiatives–the Go West plan and accession to the WTO–indicate Jiang

Zemin's stress on increasing the density of external economic interactions. During his tenure, Jiang Zemin's commitment to scale up engagement with the external world was also evident in the Chinese government's successful bid for the Olympics.

Jiang Zemin's 'Three Represents' framework also endorsed enhanced external economic interactions. The Three Represents postulated that the CPC should represent "the orientation of China's advanced culture, focus on advancing productive forces in China, advancing China's culture, and ensuring the fundamental interests of overwhelming majority should guide all policy actions."[74] Yasheng Huang contends that Jiang Zemin's theoretical formulations sought to dilute the focus on the dictatorship of the proletariat and focus more on the Three Represents.[75] By emphasising that the party's objective should be to promote productive forces, the Three Represents validated incorporating the emerging business classes in the governance frameworks and economic engagement with the capitalist countries.

The larger historical context also facilitated the success of Jiang Zemin's policies. With the collapse of the Soviet Union, the United States was no longer worried about a genuine ideological competitor to liberal democracies. Consequently, many multinational corporations (MNCs) were more than willing to engage with communist China. Moreover, the Chinese communist system provided production efficiencies, which many MNCs could not even dream of in liberal democratic countries. Subsequently, the argument that China would witness political liberalisation with economic growth gained credence, and it was repeated ad nauseam. Over time, economic engagement with a communist country acquired political respect, which was not possible during the Cold War. All this facilitated greater economic engagement between the West and communist China.

Wang Xiangwei notes that Jiang Zemin, like his predecessor, was not keen on ruffling feathers on international platforms and summarised "his style of governance as *men sheng fa da cai* (keeping quiet will help you make a fortune)."[76] For Jiang Zemin, the international environment was conducive to facilitating China's rapid economic growth. In his report to the 16th Party Congress, Jiang Zemin noted that "the first two decades of the 21st century is a period of important strategic opportunities, which we must seize tightly and which offers bright prospects."[77] For Jiang Zemin, *men sheng fa da cai* was essential to leverage a favourable geopolitical climate for domestic economic progress. Jiang Zemin placed particular emphasis on strengthening economic relations with the United States.[78] Sustained engagement of the US by the Chinese leadership facilitated the US decision to support the Chinese application for membership in the WTO. There were some apprehensions in the US about letting China become a member of the WTO, which were pushed aside. President Bill Clinton argued that "by joining the WTO, China is not simply agreeing to import more of our products, it is agreeing to import one of democracy's most cherished values, economic freedom."[79] Towards the end of Jiang Zemin's tenure, China became a member of the WTO. The membership facilitated greater Chinese economic engagement with other economies. Jiang Zemin's policies integrated the Chinese economy with the global economy, which was evident in rapidly increasing Chinese exports in the subsequent decade.[80]

In addition to engaging with the big powers, Jiang Zemin also scaled up interactions with continental neighbours. Recognising that the economic progress of China's western provinces is also tied to economic engagement with Central Asian countries, Jiang Zemin visited Uzbekistan, Kyrgyzstan, and Kazakhstan in 1996.[81] In the domestic realm, it was during Jiang Zemin's term that the Great Western Development Strategy (*xibu da kaifa*) was launched. A Leading Group, consisting of the premier, vice premier and seventeen members, was created to implement the strategy by developing reliable infrastructure, creating appropriate policy frameworks to attract investment, and caring for the ecological balance in the region.[82] So, complementary domestic and international policies were implemented to create prosperity in the western regions.

Jiang Zemin's policies created conditions for rapid economic growth in China. With Hu Jintao becoming the General Secretary of the CPC in 2002 and President in 2003, the baton had passed from Jiang Zemin to Hu Jintao. Hu Jintao was a hydroelectric engineer by profession and rose through the ranks of the Chinese Communist Youth League.[83] Interestingly, Hu Jintao was groomed by conservative leaders as well as by leaders with reformist inclinations, such as Hu Yaobang.[84] As the Party Secretary in the Tibetan Autonomous Region, he was known more for his decisive and harsh actions in containing the protests. Swaran Singh notes that Hu Jintao controlled "the rising tide of unrest with a heavy hand (that) established his credentials as one who could coordinate and command men in uniform."[85] As the Party Secretary in Guizhou and Tibet, Hu Jintao acquired a reputation for managing political developments in these provinces. However, during his tenure in Guizhou and Tibet, Hu Jintao did not experiment with new economic ideas.

The challenges confronting Hu Jintao were different from those of his predecessor. When Jiang Zemin assumed office, he was concerned about maintaining the momentum of the reform process. For Hu Jintao, the challenge was dealing with the consequences of rapid economic growth, such as growing inequality in China. Manoranjan Mohanty points out that Hu Jintao identified five imbalances confronting China: "those between economic and social development, rural and urban, inland and coastal, economy and ecology, and domestic and international sectors."[86] To address these challenges, Hu Jintao advanced concepts such as 'building a harmonious society' and 'scientific concept of development'. While the policy framework continued to focus on economic growth, there was a steady expansion of the social safety net by strengthening education, health insurance, social housing and rural pension schemes.[87] The welfare schemes indicated an effort to resolve social conflicts without resorting to destabilising radical political reforms.[88]

The objective of building a harmonious society mandates addressing regional imbalances. Roderick MacFarquhar noted that Hu Jintao and his team's contributions include a 'move away from helter-skelter investment in coastal provinces' to a more balanced developmental approach focusing on central and western China.[89] While the rhetoric about developing the western provinces can be traced to Mao and others, it was during the tenures of Jiang Zemin and Hu Jintao that comprehensive policy frameworks were operationalised. Like Jiang Zemin, Hu Jintao proactively engaged with the Central Asian countries. In 2009, Hu Jintao inaugurated a gas pipeline from Turkmenistan that would traverse Uzbekistan and Kazakhstan before reaching Xinjiang province in China.[90] Jiang Zemin and Hu Jintao emphasised the Shanghai Cooperation Organisation as an important regional platform to engage with Central Asian countries.

The effort to address domestic regional inequities by engaging with the Central Asian countries suggests that foreign policy played a significant role in addressing domestic economic requirements. Wang Jisi noted that the Chinese leadership felt that the foreign policy "must maintain economic construction as its centrepiece, be closely integrated into domestic work and be advanced by coordinating domestic and international situations."[91] Sustained efforts were made to provide new avenues for Chinese products in the external market.

During the first decade of the millennium, China entered into Free Trade Agreements with a host of other countries, such as Chile (2005), and New Zealand (2008).[92] Similarly, ASEAN and China signed agreements, such as Comprehensive Economic Cooperation (2002), Trade in Goods (2004), Trade in Services (2007), and Free Trade Area (2010).[93]

The Rise of Xi Jinping

As Hu Jintao stepped down from office in 2012, there were diametrically opposite assessments of his tenure. There is no denying that in the first decade of the new millennium, China witnessed rapid economic growth and emerged as the second-largest economy in the world. The official media often described Hu Jintao's tenure as a golden decade.[94] However, critics argue that Hu Jintao's term witnessed a significant expansion of the secret police, increased corruption, and mismanagement of the Sichuan earthquake response.[95] In fact, Hu Jintao acknowledged that the 'fight against corruption remains a serious challenge' and went on to add that the CPC is faced with 'unprecedented opportunities for development as well as risks and challenges unknown before'.[96] In addition to growing corruption, the double-digit economic growth started to taper off. It was for the new generation leader, Xi Jinping, to handle the new challenges. Xi Jinping brought in a new leadership style, which was defined by an excessive centralisation of power.

The Chinese leadership acknowledged that reforms needed to address the challenges could be very painful. Prime Minister Li Keqiang noted: "This is a reform targeted at the government itself ... as the government sheds its own powers, vested interests will be upset ... this is not nail-clipping, but taking a knife to one's own flesh ... but however painful it may be, we are determined to keep going until our job is done."[97] Given the scale of economic and governance challenges, one wonders if the party elders felt that the country needed strong leadership. Xi Jinping quickly emerged as a very powerful political player even when compared with the previous presidents. The 19th Party Congress has termed Xi the *core leader,* at par with Mao, Deng, and Jiang.[98] Many opinion articles in the Chinese media justified the elevation of Xi Jinping to the category of *core leader* as necessary to address economic challenges. For instance, an article in the *China Daily* noted the presence of "a pervasive soft resistance–local officials who do not do their job and economic elites who migrate—to the reform process."[99] It is not merely in titular forms that Xi Jinping has emerged as a dominant leader. Various party organs and government institutions are loaded with Xi's allies. Moreover, Xi Jinping is now the president for the third term, which is against the established norms of the party, and he is the chairperson of the Central Military Commission. The president also launched an anti-corruption campaign targeting senior political leaders. There was considerable criticism that the anti-corruption drive also aimed to prevent rival political figures from emerging in the party. It is evident that President Xi has acquired significant control over governance frameworks. In his foreign policy, President Xi Jinping seems to have given up on Deng Xiaoping's dictum of 'keeping a low profile'.[100] Instead, during his tenure, China pursued aggressive territorial assertions in continental and maritime domains. However, Xi Jinping's leadership is getting tested in the economic realm.

Economic Crisis, Excess Capacities, and Enhanced Global Economic Engagement

The Chinese economy is witnessing a severe economic crisis. There are multiple contributing factors to the growth slowdown. It is difficult for the Chinese economy, with a GDP of USD 17.79 trillion (in 2023)[101], to register sustained double-digit economic growth. There are other long-term challenges, such as the ageing population and the need for increased government expenditure towards social security. The 2008 financial crisis sent shockwaves through the global economy, and its repercussions were felt even in China. The structural deficiencies in the Chinese economy came to the fore because of the financial crisis. China's economic growth rate witnessed a spike in 2010, largely due to the stimulus package, further reinforcing the Chinese investment-led growth model. Because of the inherent limitations of the investment-led growth model and the financial crisis, Chinese economic growth started to slow down. There were many reasons which propelled China to indulge in excessive investments. Sustained growth over the years generated market confidence, which prompted further investments. The central, provincial, and regional governments also gave considerable incentives to attract investments. In the rush to promote industrialisation, long-term assessments regarding the viability of investments were not rigorously done. Further, there was a lack of adequate information as much of the information on production was based on estimates. There was always a strong opinion that the growth numbers are inflated. For instance, Wei Chen and Xilu Chen (et al.) argue that the "true growth rate of GDP is probably overstated by almost two percentage points from 2008 to 2016."[102] The lack of appropriate data may have also contributed to erroneous decision-making at various levels. Consequently, there were significant gaps in the policymakers' understanding of excess capacities generated by over-investments.

There was recognition within the Chinese government of the excess capacities that were generated mainly in some critical sectors, such as steel and coal. In 2009, the State Council, in its statement, referred to the overcapacity in some industries.[103] In 2013, the Chinese government came forward with a policy document titled 'Guiding Opinion on Eliminating Severe Excess Capacities' to address the challenges of overcapacity.[104] In the subsequent years, targets for reducing the excess capacities were enunciated. For instance, in 2016, it was stipulated that the steel sector would reduce excess capacities. However, quite often, reaching these targets proved difficult as the provincial and local governments either refrained from implementing the targets or fudged the figures. Such reluctance was understandable, as controlling excess capacities implied the loss of jobs in various sectors. For instance, in December 2017, the Longmay coal mining company announced that it would lay off about one lakh workers, which resulted in unrest in northeastern China.[105] To surmount the possible social unrest, the Chinese government seems to have adopted a twin-pronged strategy, viz., giving substantive severance benefits and consolidating small enterprises into larger conglomerates to ensure efficiencies of scale. For instance, in 2016, Vice-Minister of Industry and Information Feng Fei announced that a special fund of 100 billion yuan would be set up to compensate and facilitate the resettlement of workers.[106] Similarly, attempts were made to consolidate small coal mining companies to ensure economies of scale. It should be noted that merging small firms to create bigger enterprises was also advocated as a part of the reform of state-owned enterprises to make them globally competitive.

To address domestic over capacities, China scaled up its exports to different parts of the world. However, there are concerns that exports driven by overcapacity in China have negative economic implications at the regional and global levels. Many countries are worried that because of industrial overcapacity, Chinese commodities/products are being sold at low prices, which is having a 'distorting and damaging effect on global markets'.[107] For instance, it was reported that China, which accounts for a significant portion of the world's steel output, doubled overseas shipments between 2008 and

2015.[108] Not surprisingly, in December 2017, the United States, the European Union (EU), and Japan issued a sharp statement, emphasising the need to "fight market-distorting trade practices and policies that have fuelled excess production capacity."[109] While the statement did not refer to China directly, it was evident that criticism was being directed towards Beijing. Over the years, Chinese trade representatives have contended that the issue of 'surplus' is being overplayed and referred to numerous measures, such as refraining from approving new steel capacity, shutting down coal mines short on safety standards, and providing adequate financial support for laid-off workers, being instituted to address industrial overcapacities.[110]

Chinese exports have often been subjected to anti-dumping duties in big markets, such as the European Union and the US. Other countries have been able to impose anti-dumping duties on China with relative ease because it has yet to be accorded Market Economy Status (MES) in the WTO. The excess capacities and the substantive presence of SOEs became a bone of contention in granting China MES as per the WTO. As noted, China joined the WTO in 2001, and there was anticipation at that time that the Chinese "economy would be subjected to the rules-based system of the WTO, something which is bound to enhance global economic cooperation."[111] There was also a legitimate concern about whether China could be classified as a market economy. A market economy is one where supply and demand determine the prices. However, in communist countries, the government plays a significant role in determining the prices of various production factors. Given the government's significant influence on production costs within China, there was a genuine apprehension that it would be in a position to dump commodities in other countries. To address such concerns, China agreed to special conditions. According to the 2001 China-WTO agreement, the member countries were allowed to use third-country data for determining the appropriate export price of a commodity from China for 15 years till December 2016. This provision allowed many countries to impose punishing anti-dumping duties on imports from China.

Even after the conclusion of 15 years, many countries were reluctant to grant MES to China. Acquisition of MES by China would have allowed it to export to others with greater intensity and thereby address the problem of domestic excess capacities. However, much to the chagrin of China, important economic players, such as the US and the EU, were unwilling to treat China as a market economy. The US and the EU continue to use the pricing data of third countries to determine the value of the exported goods from China. Further, the US and the EU coordinate their positions on China at the WTO.

In December 2016, the US submitted a 'third-party brief' at the WTO, supporting the European Union's refusal to grant MES to China. The US Trade Representative (USTR), Robert Lighthizer, said a decision in China's favour 'would be cataclysmic for the WTO'.[112] The USTR, in its 2017 Report to Congress On China's WTO Compliance, noted that the 'United States erred in supporting China's entry into the WTO on terms that have proven to be ineffective in securing China's embrace of an open, market-oriented trade regime'.[113] The USTR report listed many issues—investment restrictions, substantial subsidies to its domestic industries, the Made in China 2025 programme, an import ban on remanufactured products, restrictions in government procurement, and lax intellectual property rights—to argue that China remains a state-led economy today.[114] Therefore, according to some countries like the US, China is not eligible for MES in the WTO.

The denial of MES has been a source of much consternation in China. According to a 2016 Chinese news report, "over 80 countries, including Russia, New Zealand, Singapore and Australia, have recognised China's status as a market economy."[115] Among the BRICS countries, India is the only country yet to grant MES to China. India has been non-committal on giving MES to China and sided with the US and the European Union.[116] Bestowing MES to China will make it difficult for India to levy anti-dumping duties on China. In June 2020, China allowed the MES dispute to lapse, thereby losing the dispute to the European Union at the WTO.[117] In the same month, India also rejected the Chinese demand to grant MES.[118] All these developments suggest that the Chinese ability to access big economies is becoming constrained.

As noted, even before the MES dispute, there were growing concerns about China's exporting prowess. The CPC leadership likely anticipated that China's external economic engagement would encounter barriers. Therefore, they created new trade and financial frameworks to ensure that China's external economic engagement continued apace, and the Belt and Road Initiative (BRI) is part of this effort. Interestingly, the Chinese leadership often portrayed the BRI as the revival of the ancient Chinese Silk Road. However, Bertil Lintner marshals considerable evidence to demonstrate that the 'ancient Silk Road' is an invention of more recent times.[119] It should be noted that the 'revival' stemmed from China's contemporary domestic economic imperatives.

Conclusion–The Foundations of the BRI

Over the decades, there have been many shifts in China's external economic engagement. While Mao invited Russian experts to help in various domestic economic projects, the Deng Xiaoping era witnessed the creation of institutional frameworks and policies to attract foreign capital and technology. Despite the student protests and Tiananmen Square incidents, the Chinese leadership persisted with its economic reforms and external economic engagement. At the same time, the CPC made strenuous efforts to refrain from initiating political reforms. During Jiang Zemin and Hu Jinatao's tenure, China successfully leveraged the geopolitical advantages of the post-Cold War era by clocking double-digit economic growth. There was a relative decline in China's economic growth rate in the second decade of the new millennium, and external economic engagement faced new challenges. There was concern among many countries that China deployed unfair trade practices to gain greater market access. Consequently, many countries are now closely monitoring their economic interactions with China. Moreover, Beijing's aggressive foreign policy and territorial assertions prompted many countries to re-evaluate the prudence of deeper economic interactions or engagement with China.

In the domestic realm, the challenges have multiplied. While the greater centralisation of power has provided a semblance of political stability, there is criticism that the leadership did not effectively tackle the structural deficiencies in the Chinese economy. Addressing domestic over-capacities while maintaining a high growth rate proved to be a significant challenge. The anticipated shift from investment-led to consumption-led economic growth is yet to materialise. The Chinese leaders quickly realised they needed enhanced access to international markets to export their domestic surpluses, which laid the foundation for the BRI. The subsequent chapters will tell the story of the BRI, the opportunities it leveraged, the challenges it faced, and the controversies it generated in South Asia.

Notes

1. "A reception to celebrate the 75th anniversary of the founding of the People's Republic of China grandly held in Beijing, Xi Jinping delivers an important speech," *Ministry of Foreign Affairs, The People's Republic of China*, September 30, 2024, https://www.mfa.gov.cn/eng/xw/zyxw/202410/t20241001_11502067.html
2 Ibid.
3. "Transcript: President Xi Jinping's Report to China's 2022 Party Congress," *Asia Nikkei*, October 18, 2022. https://asia.nikkei.com/Politics/China-s-party-congress/Transcript-President-Xi-Jinping-s-report-to-China-s-2022-party-congress

4. Ibid.
5. The World Bank in China. https://www.worldbank.org/en/country/china/overview
6. "Xi declares "complete victory" in eradicating absolute poverty in China," *Xinhua*, February 26, 2021, http://www.xinhuanet.com/english/2021-02/26/c_139767705.htm
7. For example see Suresh Radhakrishnan, "The China puzzle: opportunities for accounting research," *China Journal of Accounting Research* 7, 2014, pp. 1–8. https://www.sciencedirect.com/science/article/pii/S1755309113000282; Stephen S, Roach, "China's growth puzzle." World Economic Forum, February 28. https://www.weforum.org/agenda/2014/02/chinas-growth-puzzle/; Li, Wilson and Tina He. "China puzzle calls for reconstruction of theoretical framework". *China Daily*, March 25, 2014. https://global.chinadaily.com.cn/a/202203/25/WS623d6dd1a310fd2b29e5357d.html
8. "Conversation between A. Vyshinsky and Mao Zedong, Moscow," *Wilson Centre Digital Archive*, January 6, 1950, https://digitalarchive.wilsoncenter.org/document/112676
9. Cable No. 2220, "From Filippov [Stalin] to Mao Zedong," *Wilson Centre Digital Archive*, May 3, 1950, https://digitalarchive.wilsoncenter.org/document/119389
10. Zhihua Shen and Guy Alitto, "A historical examination of the issue of Soviet experts in China: Basic situation and policy changes," *Russian History* 29, 2002, pp. 377–400. https://www.jstor.org/stable/24660793
11. Ibid.
12. Pankaj Mishra, "The hungry years," *The New Yorker*, December 2, 2012, https://www.newyorker.com/magazine/2012/12/10/the-hungry-years
13. Frank Dikötter, "Mao's great leap to famine," *New York Times*, December 15, 2010, https://www.nytimes.com/2010/12/16/opinion/16iht-eddikotter16.html
14 Circular of the Central Committee of the Communist Party of China on the Great Proletarian Cultural Revolution, May 16, 1966, https://www.marxists.org/subject/china/documents/cpc/cc_gpcr.htm
15. Ibid.
16. Ibid.
17. John Gittings, "Xue Muqiao," *The Guardian*, August 17, 2005, https://www.theguardian.com/news/2005/aug/17/guardianobituaries.china
18. Jonathan Kaufman, "Purging the posters," *The New Republic*, February 23, 1980, https://newrepublic.com/article/88352/mao-zedong-communist-china-posters
19. Lowell Dittmer, "Death and transfiguration: Liu Shaoqi's rehabilitation and contemporary Chinese politics." *The Journal of Asian Studies* 40, 1981, pp. 459–460.
20. Austin Ramzy, "China's cultural revolution explained." *The New York Times*, May 14, 2016, https://www.nytimes.com/2016/05/15/world/asia/china-cultural-revolution-explainer.html
21. Tillman Durdin, "China transformed by elimination of 'four olds'." *The New York Times*, May 19, 1971, https://www.nytimes.com/1971/05/19/archives/china-transformed-by-elimination-of-four-olds.html
22. China, The World Bank, 2001, https://data.worldbank.org/country/china?view=chart

23. "A brief introduction to Sun Yefang's economic theory." *Beijing Review*, Vol. 26, No. 24, June 13, 1983, pp. 16-19.
24. Ibid.
25. Xue Muqiao, *China's socialist economy* (Beijing: Foreign Languages Press, 1986)
26. Ibid.
27. "Communique of the Third Plenary of the 15th Central Committee of the CCP from October 12 to 14." *People's Daily*, October 14 http://www.peopledaily.com.cn/english/9810/15/a101.html
28. Ibid.
29. See Katie X Zhou, "*How the farmers changed China: Power of the people*," (Colorado: Westview Press, 1996)
30 "Reading notes on the Soviet text political economy." *Selected Works of Mao Tse-Tung 1961-62*. https://www.marxists.org/reference/archive/mao/selected-works/volume-8/mswv8_64.htm
31. David Mason, "China's four modernizations: blueprint for development or prelude to turmoil?" *Asian Affairs: An American Review* 11, 1984, pp. 47–70.
32. "We can develop a market economy under socialism." *People's Daily*, November 26, 1979, http://en.people.cn/dengxp/vol2/text/b1370.html
33. Dennis Hevesi, "China policy shift on study overseas," *The New York Times*, April 4, 1988, https://www.nytimes.com/1988/04/04/world/china-policy-shift-on-study-overseas.html
34. David Zweig and Stanley Rosen, "How China trained a new generation abroad," *SciDevNet*, May 22, 2003, https://www.scidev.net/global/features/how-china-trained-a-new-generation-abroad/
35. Zou Shuo, "Overseas study no longer only for the elite," *China Daily*, September 19, 2019, https://www.chinadaily.com.cn/a/201909/19/WS5d82e054a310cf3e3556c563_1.html
36. John W Garver, "*China's quest: the history of the foreign relations of the People's Republic of China*," (New York: Oxford Academic, 2016)
37. Y.Y. Kueh, "Foreign Investment and Economic Change in China," *The China Quarterly*, no. 131 (1992), pp. 637–90. http://www.jstor.org/stable/654900
38. Xu Dixin, "Salient feature: state capitalism." *Beijing Review* 27, 1984, pp. 29–31
39. Ibid.
40. Ibid.
41. Malcolm Potts, "China's One Child Policy." *The BMJ*, August 17, 2006, pp. 361–362
42. Anna Fifield, "Beijing's one-child policy is gone. But many Chinese are still reluctant to have more." *The Washington Post*, May 5, 2019, https://www.washingtonpost.com/world/asia_pacific/beijings-one-child-policy-is-gone-but-many-chinese-are-still-reluctant-to-have-more/2019/05/02/c722e568-604f-11e9-bf24-db4b9fb62aa2_story.html
43. Deng Xiaoping, "Emancipate the mind, seek truth from facts and unite as one in looking to the future." *Deng Xiaoping Works*, December 13, 1978, https://www.marxists.org/reference/archive/deng-xiaoping/1978/110.htm
44. Dennis T Yasutomo, "Why aid? Japan as an 'aid great power'." *Pacific Affairs* 62, 1989, pp. 490–503.

45. "GDP growth (annual %)–China,"The World Bank, October 24, 2025 https://data.worldbank.org/indicator/NY.GDP.MKTP.KD.ZG?locations=CN
46. Vijay Gokhale "Tiananmen Square: The Making of a Protest," (Delhi: HarperCollins, 2021), p. 30.
47. Ibid.
48. David A Kelly, "The Chinese student movement of December 1986 and its intellectual antecedents," *The Australian Journal of Chinese Affairs* 17, 1987, pp. 127–142.
49. Julia Kwong, "The 1986 student demonstrations in China: a democratic movement?" *Asian Survey* 28, 1988, pp. 970–985.
50. Stanley Rosen, "China in 1986: a year of consolidation." *Asian Survey* 27, 1987, p. 36.
51. Ibid.
52. For more details see, "The Selected Papers Submitted to the Joint Economic Committee Congress of the United States- Part 1," *Joint Economic Committee US Congress*, August 13, 1982.
53. Ibid.
54. "GDP growth (annual %)–China," The World Bank, October 24, 2025, https://data.worldbank.org/indicator/NY.GDP.MKTP.KD.ZG?locations=CN
55. Yen-Lin Chung, "The ousting of general secretary Hu Yaobang: the roles played by Peng Zhen and other party elders." *China Review* 19, 2019, pp. 89–122.
56. Andrew J Nathan, "The Tiananmen papers." *Foreign Affairs* 80, 2001, pp. 2–48.
57. Alan PL Liu, "Aspects of Beijing's crisis management: The Tiananmen Square demonstration". *Asian Survey* 30, 1990, pp. 505–521.
58. Deng Xiaoping, "Uphold the four cardinal principles," *China Daily*, March 30, 1979, https://www.chinadaily.com.cn/china/19thcpcnationalcongress/2010-10/15/content_29714546.htm
59. "It is necessary to take a clear-cut stand against disturbances." *People's Daily*, April 26, 1989, http://www.tsquare.tv/chronology/April26ed.html
60. "Timeline: what led to the Tiananmen Square massacre," Frontline PBS, June 5, 2019, https://www.pbs.org/wgbh/frontline/article/timeline-tiananmen-square/
61. Zhou Xin, "China's greatest lesson from the Soviet Union's downfall," *South China Morning Post*, September 27, 2022, https://www.scmp.com/comment/opinion/article/3193813/chinas-greatest-lesson-soviet-unions-downfall-economy-key
62. "Foreign policy of the post-Jiang Zemin Era," Institute of Developing Economies, Japan External Trade Organization (IDE-JETRO), 2003, https://core.ac.uk/download/pdf/288464036.pdf
63. John H Maier, "Tiananmen: the view from Shanghai," *Asian Perspective* 14, 1990, pp. 43–67.
64. Andrew, Higgins, "China's former president Jiang Zemin, who ruled after Tiananmen, dies at 96." *The Washington Post*, 2022. November 30, https://www.washingtonpost.com/obituaries/2022/11/30/jiang-zemin-china-dies/
65. David Shambaugh, "China's underestimated leader: the legacy of Jiang Zemin." *Foreign Affairs*, 2022, November 30, https://www.foreignaffairs.com/china/chinas-underestimated-leader
66. Lucian W Pye, "Jiang Zemin's style of rule: go for stability, monopolize power and settle for limited effectiveness," *The China Journal* 45, 2001, pp. 45–51.

67. Ibid.
68. "1992: Socialist market economy," China.org, September 16, 2009, http://www.china.org.cn/features/60years/2009-09/16/content_18535276.htm
69. "Full text of Jiang Zemin's report at the 16th party congress," China.org, November 17, 2002, http://www.china.org.cn/english/2002/Nov/49107.htm
70. Charles Wolf Jr, "China's capitalists join the party." *New York Times*, August 13, 2001, https://www.nytimes.com/2001/08/13/opinion/chinas-capitalists-join-the-party.html
71. Matthew D Moneyhon, "China's great western development project in Xinjiang: economic palliative, or political Trojan Horse," *Denver Journal of International Law & Policy* 31, 2020, pp. 491, https://core.ac.uk/download/pdf/323046873.pdf
72. Heike Holbig, "The emergence of the campaign to open up the west: ideological formation, central decision-making and the role of the provinces." *The China Quarterly* 178, 2004, pp. 335–357, https://www.jstor.org/stable/pdf/20192337.pdf?refreqid=excelsior%3A62c71a9a0bcb40506c5a0bf14c6af693&ab_segments=&origin=
73. Ibid.
74. "Three represents," *China Daily*, July 10, 2007, https://www.chinadaily.com.cn/china/2007-07/10/content_6142053.htm
75. Huang, Yasheng. 2002. "Two cheers for Jiang Zemin's three represents." *Project Syndicate*, November 14, https://www.project-syndicate.org/commentary/two-cheers-for-jiang-zemin-s-three-represents
76. Wang Xiangwei, "As China's legislature opened to elect a new government, it's time to curb the ultra-leftist revival which threatens Xi Jinping's plan to revive the economy and goal of national rejuvenation," *South China Morning Post*, March 6, 2023, https://wangxiangwei.substack.com/p/as-chinas-legislature-opened-to-elect
77. "Full text of Jiang Zemin's report at the 16th party congress," *Xinhua*, November 17, 2002, http://www.china.org.cn/english/2002/Nov/49107.htm#9
78. Stephen McDonell, and Tessa Wong, "Jiang Zemin: Former Chinese leader dies aged 96." *BBC*, November 30, 2022, https://www.bbc.com/news/world-asia-china-63805991
79. Bob Davis, "When the world opened the gates of China." *The Wall Street Journal*, July 27, 2018, https://www.wsj.com/articles/when-the-world-opened-the-gates-of-china-1532701482
80. In 2000, Chinese exports were 250 billion, which increased to 2.5 trillion in 2019. Stephen McDonell, and Tessa Wong, "Jiang Zemin: Former Chinese leader dies aged 96." *BBC*, November 30, 2022, https://www.bbc.com/news/world-asia-china-63805991
81. Sun Zhuangzhi, "The relationship between China and Central Asia." Hokkaido University, 2007, https://src-h.slav.hokudai.ac.jp/coe21/publish/no16_1_ses/03_zhuangzhi.pdf
82. Hongyi H Lai, "China's western development program: its rationale, implementation, and prospects." *Modern China* 28, 2002, pp. 432–466.
83. "Hu Jintao," *China.org*, http://www.china.org.cn/english/PP-e/48915.htm
84. Richard D Ewing, "Hu Jintao: the making of a Chinese general secretary." *The China Quarterly* 173, 2003, pp. 17–34.

85. Swaran Singh, "Hu Jintao's enduring Tibet connection," *IPCS*, November 24, 2002, https://www.ipcs.org/comm_select.php?articleNo=916
86. Manoranjan Mohanty, "'Harmonious society': Hu Jintao's vision and the Chinese party congress." *Economic and Political Weekly* 47, 2012, pp. 12–16. https://www.jstor.org/stable/41720457
87. Christine Wong, "The second decade: the Hu Jintao-Wen Jiabao era." *Plus Ça Change: Three Decades of Fiscal Policy and Central-Local Relations in China*, Lincoln Institute of Land Policy, 2021, pp. 4–11. http://www.jstor.org/stable/resrep43253.5
88. Pin Ho, and Wen Huang, "Hu Jintao: the mysterious man behind China's 'harmonious society'." *CS Monitor*, April 15, 2010, https://www.csmonitor.com/Commentary/Opinion/2010/0415/Hu-Jintao-the-mysterious-man-behind-China-s-harmonious-society
89. Shi Jiangtao, "President Hu Jintao's legacy seen as one of stability but stagnation." *South China Morning Post*, September 7, 2012, https://www.scmp.com/news/china/article/1031120/president-hu-jintaos-legacy-seen-one-stability-stagnation
90. Marat Gurt, "China extends influence into C.Asia with pipeline," *Reuters*, December 14, 2009, https://www.reuters.com/article/china-pipeline-idUKSGE5BD0BQ20091214
91. Jisi Wang, "China's Search for a Grand Strategy: A Rising Great Power Finds Its Way." *Foreign Affairs* 90, no. 2 (2011), pp. 68–79.
92. "New Zealand-China free trade agreement." *New Zealand Foreign Affairs Trade* https://www.mfat.govt.nz/en/trade/free-trade-agreements/free-trade-agreements-in-force/nz-china-free-trade-agreement/overview; "China-Chile FTA," *Ministry of Commerce, PRC*, http://fta.mofcom.gov.cn/topic/enchile.shtml
93. "ASEAN-China free trade area: Building strong economic partnerships," *ASEAN*, https://www.asean.org/wp-content/uploads/images/2015/October/outreach-document/Edited%20ACFTA.pdf; "China-ASEAN FTA," *Ministry of Commerce, PRC*, http://fta.mofcom.gov.cn/topic/chinaasean.shtml
94. Malcolm Moore, "Communist party congress: A decade under Hu Jintao and Wen Jiabao." *The Telegraph*, November 14, 2012, https://www.telegraph.co.uk/news/worldnews/asia/china/9677748/Communist-Party-Congress-a-decade-under-Hu-Jintao-and-Wen-Jiabao.html
95. Ruth Kirchner and Simon Bone, "China's lost decade," *DW*, March 13, 2013, https://www.dw.com/en/looking-back-at-chinas-lost-decade/a-16667956
96. "Full text: Report of Hu Jintao to the 18th CPC National Congress." China.org.cn, November 8, 2012, http://www.china.org.cn/china/18th_cpc_congress/ 2012-11/16/content_27137540.htm
97. "Premier Li Keqiang meets the press," *Ministry of Foreign Affairs, the People's Republic of China*, http://www.fmprc.gov.cn/mfa_eng/wjdt_665385/zyjh_665391/t1247170.shtml
98. Chris Buckley, "Xi Jinping is China's 'Core' leader: Here's what it means," *The New York Times*, October 30, 2016, https://www.nytimes.com/2016/10/31/world/asia/china-xi-jinping-communist-party.html
99. Robert Lawrence Kuhn, "Why China needs Xi Jinping as its core leader," *China Daily*, December 1, 2016, http://www.chinadaily.com.cn/opinion/2016-12/01/content_27540498.htm

100. Huang Youyi, "Context, not history, matters for Deng's famous phrase," *Global Times*, June 15, 2011, https://www.globaltimes.cn/content/661734.shtml
101. "GDP (current US$)–China," *The World Bank*, https://data.worldbank.org/indicator/NY.GDP.MKTP.CD?locations=CN
102. Wei Chen, Xilu Chen, Chang-Tai Hsieh, and Zheng (Michael) Song, "A forensic examination of China's national accounts." *Brookings Papers on Economic Activity*, November 26, 2019, https://www.brookings.edu/bpea-articles/a-forensic-examination-of-chinas-national-accounts/
103. Liu Peng, "China moves to rein in overcapacity," *The Economic Observer*, August 31, 2009, http://www.eeo.com.cn/ens/2009/0910/150693.shtml
104. David Stanway, "China to ban new projects, strengthen market in new overcapacity plan," *Reuters*, October 15, 2013, https://www.reuters.com/article/us-china-overcapacity/china-to-ban-new-projects-strengthen-market-in-new-overcapacity-plan-idUSBRE99E05620131015
105. Jane Perlez and Yufan Huang, "Mass layoffs in China's coal country threaten unrest," *New York Times*, December 16, 2015, https://www.nytimes.com/2015/12/17/world/asia/china-coal-mining-economy.html
106. "The central government took out 100 billion yuan for the relocation of productive workers," *Xinhua News Agency*, February 25, 2016, http://www.gov.cn/xinwen/2016-02/25/content_5046143.htm
107. Chris Buckley and Jane Perlez, "China pushes back against U.S. complaints of industrial overcapacity," *The New York Times*, June 6, 2016, https://www.nytimes.com/2016/06/07/business/international/china-us-economy-overcapacity-complaints.html?_r=0
108. Michael Pooler and Emily Feng, "Steel industry grapples with curse of oversupply," *The Financial Times*, October 29, 2017, https://www.ft.com/content/992ad270-b4d3-11e7-aa26-bb002965bce8
109. Eliana Raszewski, and Luc Cohen, "U.S., EU, Japan slam market distortion in swipe at China," *Reuters*, December 12, 2017, https://www.reuters.com/article/us-trade-wto/u-s-eu-japan-slam-market-distortion-in-swipe-at-china-idUSKBN1E62HA
110. "China to cut overcapacity, help companies out," *Xinhua*, January 8, 2016, http://news.xinhuanet.com/english/2016-01/08/c_134988165.htm
111. "WTO Ministerial Conference approves China's accession." *WTO News*, November 10, 2001. https://www.wto.org/english/news_e/pres01_e/pr252_e.htm
112. David Lawder, "U.S. formally opposes China market economy status at WTO," *Reuters*, December 1, 2017, https://in.reuters.com/article/us-usa-china-trade-wto/u-s-formally-opposes-china-market-economy-status-at-wto-idINKBN1DU2VH
113. United States Trade Representative, "Report to Congress on China's WTO compliance," 2017, https://ustr.gov/sites/default/files/files/Press/Reports/China%20 2017%20WTO%20Report.pdf
114. Ibid.
115. "Still on track for further opening-up," *China Daily*, March 11, 2016, https://www.chinadaily.com.cn/opinion/2016-03/11/content_23820795.htm
116. "India is 'non-committal' about market economy tag for China," *The Hindu*, November 18, 2016, http://www.thehindu.com/business/India-is-%E2%80%

98non-committal%E2%80%99-about-market-economy-tag-for-China/article16667486.ece
117. "China loses WTO dispute over market economy status," *Outlook*, June 21, 2020, https://www.outlookindia.com/newsscroll/china-loses-wto-dispute-over-market-economy-status/1872960
118. Asit Ranjan Mishra, 2020. "India Rejects Market Economy Tag for China," *Mint*, June 18, 2020, https://www.livemint.com/news/world/india-rejects-china-s-demand-to-grant-it-market-economy-status-11592394036306.html
119. Bertil Lintner, "*The End of the Chinese Century?: How Xi Jinping lost the Belt and Road Initiative*," (New Delhi: HarperCollins Publishers, 2024), pp. 1-26.

2

The BRI: Tiger with Wings

Introduction

In September 2013, during his visit to Kazakhstan, Chinese President Xi Jinping called for building the "economic belt along the Silk Road."[1] The announcement came within a few months after Xi Jinping assumed the office of President of the People's Republic of China (PRC). Initially, the reference to the Silk Road was seen as a regional connectivity proposal and as an initiative aimed at burnishing the foreign policy credentials of the new president. However, a month later, in a speech to the Indonesian parliament, President Xi articulated his vision of the Maritime Silk Road of the 21st Century and the need for vigorous cooperation between China and ASEAN countries to develop a maritime partnership.[2] The need for improving connectivity, promoting unimpeded trade, enhancing monetary circulation, and fostering good neighbourly relations were emphasised. President Xi's statements in Kazakhstan and Indonesia unveiled an ambitious and multidimensional connectivity initiative. Subsequently, in 2015, China released a map with the blueprint of connectivity projects under the framework of the One Belt One Road initiative, which was later rechristened as the Belt and Road Initiative (BRI).

The Initiative

The BRI projects, conceived as 'bridges', aimed to connect people, commerce, economies, and ideas across vast geographical expanses. The construct sought to revive old trading routes and create new ones across vast geographies. The grand plan connecting various ports, roads, and rail networks, crisscrossing continents and cutting through natural barriers, such as the Himalayas and expansive oceans, commanded the immediate attention of scholars, diplomats, and policymakers. Interestingly, the continental route was defined as an 'economic belt', and the maritime component was conceptualised as a 'road'.

The ambitious BRI connectivity projects sought to leverage China's core competency in infrastructure building and address domestic industrial overcapacity in sectors such as steel and cement. As noted in the previous chapter, Chinese firms were encouraged to implement the 'going out' (*zou chuqu*) strategy, which mandated increased overseas investments.[3] The BRI sought to consolidate and scale up the 'going out' strategy. A senior Chinese bureaucrat noted that the BRI made China's "internationalisation strategy like a tiger with wings added."[4] In a way, the metaphor of the 'tiger with wings' illustrates how the BRI is perceived both within and outside the country. In China, the 'tiger with wings' has a positive connotation as it implies increased strength and invincibility. However, outside China, the image of a tiger with wings generates considerable anxiety as it may be perceived as a predator with enhanced capabilities.

There was anticipation in China that the BRI would address domestic industrial over capacities and create new markets for Chinese firms. The BRI was also a consequence of the sustained economic growth of China. As prosperity increased in China, labour costs associated with industrial production also increased. Various low-income economies became more attractive destinations for investments because of their lower wages. To meet the twin challenges—increased prosperity resulting in higher wages and competition from other low-income economies—Chinese firms recognised the need to innovate and tap into low-cost labour economies. With robust connectivity networks, the BRI declared an intent to create integrated production networks between China and low-cost labour economies along the BRI route. The need to give a fillip to economic activity in the relatively less prosperous regions of western China and landlocked provinces, such as Yunnan, was also one of the objectives of the BRI. The BRI provided some significant advantages to China. Since the project was conceptualised and substantially funded by Beijing, it is only natural that Chinese companies and related institutions benefitted from this exercise.

The BRI is expansive in its conceptualisation, as it attempted to connect about "55 per cent of world GNP, 70 per cent of the global population, and 75 per cent of known energy resources."[5] As it sought to stitch together diverse regions with rail/road infrastructure spreading across continents, the BRI required significant financial resources. According to Chinese sources, in the past ten years, the BRI "catalysed investment of nearly USD 1 trillion."[6] A Silk Road Fund was created in 2014 to generate financial resources for the BRI. The Asian Infrastructure Investment Bank (AIIB) had a much bigger mandate, and at its inauguration, President Xi Jinping welcomed the "AIIB and other international financial institutions to take part in the building of the Silk Road Economic Belt and 21st Century Maritime Silk Road."[7] A host of other financial institutions, such as the Export-Import Bank of China, China Development Bank, and state-owned banks, were roped in to fund the BRI. However, the BRI turned out to be a constantly evolving process with new projects getting added, some projects getting priority in terms of implementation, and others getting sidelined or discarded. In some instances, projects initiated a few years before the BRI was formally announced were later added to the Belt and Road plan.[8] Consequently, it has been difficult to estimate the precise amount of the total investments under the initiative since its initiation.

The conceptualisation and implementation of the BRI are indicative of the rise of China and presage China's proactive engagement in global politics. Bruno Maçães noted that the BRI indicated China's rise and its capacity to 'remake the world economy and attract other countries to its economic orbit and ideological model'.[9] However, power is not unidirectional; Chinese power projection through the BRI was often contested and modulated. As Daniel Markey observed, the relatively weaker states participating in the BRI also had an agency "to determine political outcomes more than those of the strong."[10] In the past few years, there have been many instances when BRI projects were either rejected by governments or witnessed massive protests from local stakeholders/communities. Nonetheless, it must be noted that the BRI was a physical manifestation of China's global outreach and questioned the notions of geopolitical primacy. For instance, Russia considers Central Asia as a 'near neighbourhood', and India is often seen as the fulcrum of South Asia. The Chinese proactive BRI engagement sought to re-examine such notions of primacy.

There are two components, maritime and continental, to the BRI. The maritime component aimed to connect China with Europe and the South Pacific.[11] The continental route aspired to integrate Western China with

Central Asia and Europe. For the maritime and continental routes, Europe constituted the terminal point. These Eurasian connections are aimed at bringing the Chinese and the European markets closer to each other. Recently, Trans-Eurasian railway connectivity from Chongqing in China to Duisburg in Germany was operationalised.[12] There were concerns regarding the financial viability of transporting goods across continents on a rail network. While sending goods by sea route is about 25 per cent cheaper than sending goods by train, the reduction of transportation time from five weeks to three weeks was perceived as a distinct advantage for the train route.[13] However, the volume of trade by train routes did not pick up to the extent that it impacted the viability of shipping routes. While there were manufacturing units in China's western provinces, much of the manufacturing was on the eastern seaboard, and therefore, using the shipping route was more economical. Not surprisingly, China has emerged as one of the top ship-owning nations, along with Japan and Greece.[14]

Many developing countries were favourably disposed to the BRI. Many developed countries were initially very keen to participate in the BRI. With billions of dollars of proposed investments, many western MNCs hoped that they may get "a piece of action."[15] Many developing countries initially found participation in the BRI attractive, as the Chinese investments did not come with difficult structural reform prescriptions usually associated with Bretton Woods institutions. The BRI investments appeared particularly attractive for countries undergoing a political transition with a weak institutional base. The political leadership in these countries, with a weak institutional and revenue base, needed to demonstrate rapid and tangible developmental outcomes. Chinese-backed infrastructure projects, which are often implemented at great speed, were preferred as they could be showcased in the elections as a symbol of progress that was achieved in a relatively short time. Therefore, the political leadership in many developing countries found Beijing's conditionalities, such as granting contracts to Chinese firms, much more palatable than structural reforms. Further, there were reports that some political leaders favoured the BRI as they received financial support to contest the local elections.[16] In some instances, politicians reportedly received personal loans if state guarantees backed such lending. Whatever the initial triggers for taking part in the BRI, a few years into the project implementation, there were instances when host countries expressed disappointment about the contractual terms or the overall financial viability of the project. Many developing countries had to encounter twin challenges. First, the leadership in many developing countries recognised the need for significant capital infusion to upgrade their physical infrastructure. The capital available with Bretton Woods institutions often came up with painful reform pills. Second, the Chinese were eager to deploy considerable capital, which provided the political leaders with short-term political advantages. However, in the medium and long term, the countries that signed on to the BRI, in many instances, found it hard to face challenges as the contractual terms started to kick in and the debt repayment schedule gained momentum. Consequently, some BRI-participating countries slipped into debt traps. However, Chinese scholars such as Wang Yiwei suggest avoiding a narrow view of debt, "as a certain level of debt can have positive externalities, and the BRI is aimed at building industrial capacity rather than infrastructure only."[17] The issue of BRI indebtedness is not merely a consequence of economic variables. Parker and Chefitz argued that through "debt book diplomacy", China is seeking to achieve strategic goals, such as "projecting power across vital South Asian trading routes, undermining U.S.-led regional opposition to Beijing's contested South China Sea claims, and supporting the PLAN's efforts to break out of the First Island Chain into the blue-water Pacific."[18] While there can be a debate as to whether indebtedness resulted from economic mismanagement or geopolitical strategy, for many countries, the BRI became the tiger they could not dismount without negative consequences.

Some scholars positioned the BRI as the Marshall Plan of Asia.[19] However, there was criticism that the BRI was a far cry from the Marshall Plan because of the indebtedness it generated. The Marshall Plan was operationalised in a specific historical context, which was the end of the Second World War and the advent of the Cold War. The United States of America and other Western leaders were worried about the spread of communist ideology in Europe, which was devastated by the Second World War. To prevent the spread of communist ideology, the US stepped forward with an economic package to quickly rebuild western Europe. On the other hand, the announcement of the BRI happened in a completely different geopolitical context. The collapse of the Soviet Union and the end of the Cold War occurred over two decades before the announcement of the BRI. These developments created new avenues for China to scale up its economic engagement. Lim Tai Wei points out that the "de-Sovietization of Central Asia offered an opportunity for

China to link up with the Central Asian region economically."[20] Moreover, while China was a communist state, there was no ideological contestation on a global scale when the Chinese connectivity plans were articulated. In fact, many argued that China's growth happened mainly due to an authoritarian state's adoption of capitalist principles. Of course, scholars, such as Stephen Harper, argued that China is exporting authoritarian capitalism as a political model.[21] By and large, the academia and policy-making circles of various countries did not see the BRI as an ideological instrument to promote communism in other countries. Instead, even the sharpest critics often defined the BRI as designed exclusively for Chinese economic interests, without appropriate stakeholder consultations, and not as an ideological instrument. However, the experience of the past ten years demonstrates that there are enough examples, as will be reflected in subsequent chapters, to contend that authoritarian regimes received a fillip because of the BRI. The BRI may not have promoted communism, but some authoritarian regimes did find a new lease of life because of increased engagement with China.

It was argued that the BRI was the first worldwide initiative by an 'Eastern' nation ever,[22] and therefore, the initiative was located in the larger East-West divide. It should be noted that an important Asian power—India—stayed out of the BRI. Of course, India has no veto to decide if an initiative is Asian or non-Asian. However, India's non-participation points to the fact that not all countries in the Eastern Hemisphere were comfortable with the lack of transparency of some of the BRI projects. Moreover, there was nothing in the BRI that interrogated the existing world order. The BRI works within the current Westphalian sovereign-state structure and does not seek to create a strong transnational governance framework. In terms of financing, the initiative has not ushered in radically new frameworks that can alter the power balance between the developed western and the developing worlds. Therefore, there is nothing non-western about the BRI in terms of ideas that aim to redesign the world order.

The Precursors

It should be noted that China was not the first to articulate a grand connectivity project in Asia. The BRI had many predecessors, such as the International North-South Transport Corridor (INSTC) and the New Silk Road. The New Silk Road and the INSTC were guided by different geopolitical objectives. The INSTC was announced in 2000 to improve connectivity between India, Iran, and Russia.[23] Subsequently, the INSTC framework expanded to include many other countries, such as the Central Asian Republics (CARs).[24] The North-South corridor was conceptualised to address multiple requirements of its member states. For Russia, the INSTC was supposed to increase access to the Indian Ocean Region. For decades, India had a strong defence partnership with Russia, yet the bilateral economic partnership between the two was not robust. The INSTC was supposed to evolve into a platform for enhanced supply chains between Russia and India. For Tehran, a successful North-South corridor would convert Iran into a connectivity hub between CARs, West Asia, Russia, and India. Like many grand plans, the North-South corridor did not take off as anticipated. Iran and Russia had hostile relations with many Western countries and were often subjected to economic sanctions. The punitive economic measures against Iran and Russia meant that private players from other countries often hesitated to invest as they could be blacklisted in western countries for violating the sanctions. Moreover, India's trade relations gravitated more towards East and Southeast Asian countries and the US. Overall, the geopolitical and geoeconomic climate was not conducive to the success of the INSTC.

Almost a decade after the announcement of the INSTC, on July 20, 2011, US Secretary of State Hillary Clinton called for establishing a New Silk Road in Asia. Speaking in Chennai during her visit to India, alluding to the ancient routes, she said: "Historically, the nations of South and Central Asia were connected to each other and the rest of the continent by a sprawling trading network called the Silk Road. ...Let's work together to create a new Silk Road."[25] Essentially, her plan meant building "highways, railway lines and energy infrastructure from Turkmenistan, through Afghanistan, through Pakistan into India."[26] For Secretary Clinton, the revival of economic activity along the ancient roads from Central Asia to India was critical to combat religious fundamentalism in the region, as well as the Al Qaeda. While Central Asia and India constituted the two ends of the proposed New Silk Road, Afghanistan constituted the core. Secretary Clinton did use various international platforms to popularise her vision of the New Silk Road and often deployed vivid maps to drive home the benefits of the proposed road. For instance, on September 22, 2011, speaking at the New Silk Road ministerial meeting in German House, New York, she noted: "Turkmen gas fields could help meet both Pakistan's and India's growing energy needs and provide significant transit revenues for both Afghanistan and Pakistan ... Tajik cotton could be turned into Indian linens ... Furniture and fruit from Afghanistan could find its way to the markets of Astana or Mumbai and beyond."[27]

While the New Silk Road proposal was ambitious, it had a few challenges. It was also a political/security concept to stabilise Afghanistan. The US spent considerable financial resources on building road connectivity in Afghanistan. According to the 2015 Council on Foreign Relations report, the US spent approximately USD 2 billion to build 1800 km of roads in Afghanistan.[28] However, the expensive road network quickly deteriorated due to sustained insurgency and neglect, as the Afghan authorities lacked the necessary capacity to maintain the network. Among the neighbouring countries of Afghanistan, India stepped in with considerable development assistance. However, India's capacity to wield influence and push for connectivity projects was limited, as it did not have land contiguity with Afghanistan.[29] On the other hand, the other neighbours did not take ownership of the connectivity projects that the US was building either due to lack of resources or serious political differences with Washington DC. As a consequence, the building of road networks became an enterprise of the Americans. Further, the American involvement in Afghanistan was consistently defined by the rhetoric of 'imminent withdrawal'. Such rhetoric might have discouraged entrepreneurs and countries willing to take risks by investing in Afghanistan. More importantly, the imminent withdrawal language also conveyed a message that the US commitment to Central Asia and Afghanistan was suspect. The New Silk Road plan also did not generate an impression that the new connectivity vision had a whole government approach. For instance, President Obama could have made the New Silk Road an important pillar of his pivot to Asia policy. However, no such attempts were made. As a consequence, the plan was perceived as Secretary Clinton's initiative. It quickly faded out of American vocabulary after she demitted the office.

In her articulations, while Secretary Hillary Clinton did mention possible benefits to Pakistan in terms of transit fees, there were considerable benefits for India as well. Probably, such an outcome, without the resolution of the Kashmir issue, might not have been palatable to Pakistan. Further, the Pakistan-China relationship was on an upswing, and there was resentment towards the US among various sections in Pakistan. Given the fact that India was locked in a low-intensity conflict with Pakistan, there were genuine concerns regarding the enhanced economic integration with the Af-Pak region, which continues to be the epicentre of terrorism. Therefore, the Indian government may have hesitated in engaging with the New Silk Road idea. The INSTC and the New Silk Road are but a few examples of grand connectivity conceptualisations. Of course, there are many similarities between the earlier projects and the BRI. And yet, the BRI is also distinct from earlier articulations. The earlier articulations were quite often a single project. On the other hand, the BRI had subsumed multiple projects under its banner. Further, the BRI vision integrated both continental and maritime domains. The US' articulations, such as the Indo-Pacific Economic Corridor, could have done more to inspire confidence in Asia by operationalising a few massive infrastructure projects. On the other hand, the BRI quickly articulated various details about the projects, and finance mechanisms were also specified. Notably, the BRI articulation happened after China had completed a few big-ticket projects, such as the China-Myanmar oil and natural gas pipelines. Therefore, there was very little doubt as to whether the Chinese would complete the projects that have been announced. Unlike the INSTC and the New Silk Road, the geopolitical situation for the Chinese was conducive to the operationalisation of the BRI. The constant friction between Russia and the US and the eastward expansion of NATO implied that Moscow was looking more towards its eastern neighbours for enhanced economic engagement. The CARs were not getting investments from Russia on a scale that would satisfy their infrastructure hunger. Since Russia was experiencing an economic slowdown and was looking more towards China for enhanced economic engagement, Moscow had no option but to countenance the growing Chinese economic presence in the CARs. In South Asia, countries such as Nepal, Sri Lanka, and Bangladesh were looking to reduce their trade dependence on India. In Southeast Asia, Myanmar, Laos, and Cambodia had closer ties with China than with others. Moreover, the US was tied up in two wars (Iraq and Afghanistan), and the domestic opinion called for reduced international commitments. Overall, the geopolitical stage was conducive for China to scale up its economic engagement.

The BRI and its Variants

China scaled up its external economic engagement under the rubric of the BRI by also creating new variants of the Silk Roads. The emergence of the new variants of the Silk Roads was also a consequence of rapid shifts in the global economy. With the growth of Information Communication Technologies (ICT), digital platforms emerged as new frontiers of wealth creation and power projection. Sovereign states, especially the major powers, were rapidly building new digital infrastructures in their territories and in those of others. Expanding digital presence became critical to gaining economic and political leverage in other countries, and the Digital Silk Road became an important platform for such endeavours.

The Digital Silk Road: Even before formally articulating the Digital Silk Road, China was operationalising optical fibre networks linking China with different countries. The Digital Silk Road plan evolved through many iterations, evident in the 2013 and 2015 White Papers, the 13th Five-Year Plan, and the announcement by Xi Jinping in 2016 that China will be a Leading Innovator Worldwide by 2030. It was at the First Belt and Road Forum for International Cooperation (BRF) that Chinese President Xi Jinping called for an "innovation-driven development and [intensified] cooperation in frontier areas such as digital economy, artificial intelligence... so as to turn them into a digital Silk Road of the 21st century."[30] Chinese officials often stated that the Digital Silk Road aims to build a community of common destiny.[31] The Chinese emphasis on playing a proactive role in the global digital economy stems from domestic success. In 2016, the "Chinese digital economy grew at 18.9 per cent and contributed approximately USD 3.35 trillion to the country's economy."[32] Having learnt the tricks of the trade and deploying cutting-edge technologies, Chinese digital companies played a more significant role in the global digital space, and the BRI was the platform through which such ambitions were to be realised. Under the Digital Silk Road rubric, Chinese companies were involved in constructing high-speed broadband networks (including 5G connections) and internet application platforms for public service and applications to ensure the safety of industrial data.[33] Chinese companies emerged as one of the leading network equipment providers. For instance, in 2017, Huawei accounted for 24.4 per cent of the global market share of network equipment, followed by Cisco (18.4 per cent), and Nokia (14.2 per cent).[34] Huawei's share in the global telecommunication equipment market jumped to 28.7 per cent in 2021.[35] Even in 2023, Huawei remained as the top provider of telecom network equipment.[36] This increase in market share happened despite growing concerns about Chinese digital equipment and the reluctance of major markets, such as the United States and India, to use Chinese digital equipment. On the other hand, because of the relatively low prices, the Chinese products are also finding new markets in many developing countries. It was argued that for many low-income countries, Chinese investments in digital infrastructure would enable them to leap-frog into a more advanced telecommunication architecture, which may result in efficiency gains. However, from a Chinese perspective, these infrastructure investments enabled Beijing to access and control digital data, better understand the local markets, and sometimes eliminate competitors.[37]

China's Huawei 5G network forays have attracted global attention and resistance from countries like the US. On the other hand, the Chinese ambition to dominate the undersea communication cable business has gone largely unnoticed. Over the years, Chinese companies have worked with European and American firms to gain knowledge and proficiency in operationalising hi-tech communication projects. Jonathan Hillman noted that the Huawei Marine Networks' joint venture with British Global Marine Systems of Britain enabled China to gain critical knowledge of undersea cable networks.[38] According to the Asia Research Center in Leiden, it is estimated that China will soon own approximately 20 per cent of the world's submarine optical cables.[39] Huawei has reportedly developed technologies to lay submarine cables in some of the deepest parts of the oceans, such as the Challenger Deep in the Pacific Ocean.[40] China's approach to the digital domain was comprehensive. Recognising that the efficiency of various digital platforms was also contingent on location services, the Chinese leadership launched the Space Silk Road.

The Space Silk Road: China has made rapid progress in space-based navigational services in the past two decades. There are a few Global Navigation Satellite Systems , such as the US Global Positioning System (GPS), Russian GLONASS, and the European Union's (EU) Galileo. With its BeiDou Navigation Satellite System, China has entered the elite league of countries that can provide global navigation services.[41] In November 2014, the BeiDou Navigation Satellite System was approved by a UN body for operations, making it the third such system after the GPS and GLONASS.[42] In the same year, as per Chinese news reports, the Russian authorities hinted at the possibilities of collaboration between BeiDou and GLONASS systems with the possible involvement of India.[43] However, such tripartite collaboration did not materialise. Russia and China created a committee in 2014 to take forward the Strategic Satellite Navigation Cooperation.[44] In subsequent years, both countries agreed on the "sharing of Beidou and GLONASS data—as well as the joint development of navigation products."[45]

An important reason for collaborative efforts failing to take off in a substantive manner is that the need to develop an alternative navigation system stemmed from political rather than economic requirements. In 1996, China reportedly fired two missiles across the Taiwan Strait, and the missile failures were attributed to the malfunctioning of the GPS.[46] According to news reports, the BeiDou Satellite (BDS) system was "designed to specify the location to 10 cm of accuracy for military use, compared with GPS's 30 cm."[47] The BDS enabled China to disengage from the US GPS systems. There was always a concern in China that the US could use its GPS as a weapon in times of conflict. With the development of its BDS system, China has ensured that its strategic autonomy is maintained in case of conflict.

The BeiDou project envisaged a three-step process: in the first phase, initiated in 1994 and operationalised in 2000, the BDS system provided services to users in China; in the second phase, which was started in 2004 and completed in 2012, the users in Asia-Pacific were able to access the BDS services; and in the third phase, the BDS system envisaged benefits to global users by the end of 2020.[48] However, six months ahead of schedule, in June 2020, China launched the final satellite of the navigation system, and the BDS system became fully operational on par with other global positioning systems. Referring to the launch of the satellite, the Chinese media noted that "the successful deployment of the BDS constellation indicates that China can independently make breakthroughs in key technologies."[49] Given that the BDS system was developed almost a few decades after the GPS, it is much more advanced in accuracy and other features.[50]

While the military dimension was always evident in the development of the BDS system, the economic spin-offs also assumed significant importance. In November 2022, the BDS started providing regional short-message communication for its users. The BDS was one of the first navigation systems to provide such services.[51] In 2023, Huawei launched a satellite calling feature on its latest phones. China envisaged that the countries participating in the BRI would be encouraged to use the BDS system.[52] The BRI countries that host Chinese critical infrastructure projects, such as railways and energy pipelines, reportedly get subsidised access to BDS Positioning, Navigation, and Timing data.[53]

While the Chinese forays in digital and space domains continued apace, the COVID-19 pandemic generated numerous challenges. There were concerns about the prudence of deep economic integration with China due to the prolonged shutdowns there. The closure of ports, railways, and roads in China had negatively impacted the global economy. There was also disappointment that China was not transparent with the origins of the COVID-19 virus and did not share the related information with the global community in a timely manner. Amid all these challenges, COVID-19 also provided an opportunity for China to scale up its Health Silk Road (HSR).

The Health Silk Road: The HSR was not a consequence of the pandemic and, in fact, predates the pandemic. In 2015, a three-year healthcare cooperation initiative was launched to promote cooperation in the domains of disease prevention, capacity building, health emergency aid, traditional medicine, and health developmental aid.[54] The initiative sought to develop cooperative mechanisms with ASEAN, Arab countries, and Central and Eastern Europe.[55] In 2017, China and the World Health Organisation signed an Memorandum of Understanding (MOU) endorsing "international health regulation and promoting health security on the Silk Road."[56] Initially, there was considerable ambiguity regarding the activities of the HSR. As the pandemic made its presence felt across the world, China saw an opportunity to increase its presence in healthcare and pharmaceutical sectors in other countries under the rubric of the HSR. Broadly, the HSR during the pandemic had the following objectives:

First, through the HSR activities during the pandemic, China sought to shift the discussion away from the origins of the COVID-19 virus and its failure to share information with other governments. Second, China sought to position itself as a friend of many developing countries by proposing to share the vaccines with others. President Xi Jinping often referred to the COVID-19 vaccine as a 'global public good'.[57] Third, the Chinese government sought to use the HSR and vaccine diplomacy to demonstrate the effectiveness of the Chinese governance processes. For instance, the Chinese media often referred to vaccine production and distribution as a consequence of the "strong organising and operating capacity of the Chinese government."[58] Fourth, the HSR was used to promote Chinese vaccines, which were distributed across the world. Pakistan imported vaccine concentrate from CanSinoBio and subsequently processed, packaged, and distributed it as PakVac for local needs.[59] China also signed vaccine production agreements with countries, such as the United Arab Emirates (UAE) and Morocco. Engagement during the pandemic has enabled China to scale up cooperation in domains other than the COVID-19 disease. For instance, China has donated over 100,000 doses of Hepatitis-A vaccines after the 2022 floods in Pakistan.[60] However, the HSR activities encountered significant challenges. There were numerous reports in the international media that the Chinese vaccines were not effective,[61] and there were also reports that unfair prices and non-disclosure agreements were used in the distribution of vaccines to various countries.[62] Despite these concerns, pharmaceutical exports from China witnessed an increase during and immediately after the pandemic,[63] which suggests that the HSR was able to increase the Chinese pharma presence in the global market.

Conclusion

There are many drivers to the BRI. In the realm of domestic politics, the initiative positioned President Xi Jinping as a visionary leader restoring the ancient silk routes, with leadership capabilities to operationalise grand projects. Given the excess production capacities, the BRI became a vehicle to export such overcapacities. The BRI also sought to assert China's preeminence in the immediate and extended neighbourhoods. While the BRI was positioned as an economic project to promote global good, geopolitical objectives were wired into the initiative. The vision statement of the BRI clearly notes that the initiative "embraces the trend towards a multipolar order."[64] The growing Chinese economic presence in Central Asia and South Asia attempted to dilute the primacy of Russia and India, respectively, in these regions. Similarly, Chinese economic activity contested the US hub-and-spoke alliance framework in East Asia, Southeast Asia, and the Pacific.

In the past few years, the BRI did indeed function as a tiger with wings. The Chinese capital, men, and equipment often landed on distant shores to build mega connectivity projects. Sometimes, an increased presence of Chinese personnel at the project sites and contracts to Chinese firms to supply equipment generated discontent among the BRI participant countries. The financing of the BRI projects left much to be desired. Many developing and least developed countries found it difficult to service debt and, in some cases, had to hand over valuable real estate on lease to China. There were a few other challenges with the BRI projects, such as the lack of transparency and consultation. A case in point was the China-Pakistan

Economic Corridor (CPEC) agreement, which was not available for public scrutiny and, therefore, did not witness significant public consultations. In another instance, the Chinese BRI map showed one of the arms of the maritime corridor connecting the Kolkata port in India with other ports in the region. Many in India were mystified as to what might have prompted the Chinese to choose Kolkata port over other ports in India. Further, there was no information as to what plans the Chinese had for the Kolkata port. The Indian government was neither consulted nor informed that the Kolkata port would be on the map of the Maritime Silk Road.

The multiple variants of the Silk Road also point to the Chinese disaggregated strategy of emerging as a leader in a few vital sectors of the global economy. More importantly, the study of the BRI projects highlights the tactics of a rising power to create new political relationships and economic dependencies. The subsequent chapters will examine the themes mentioned above by examining case studies of South Asian countries.

Notes

1. Xi Jinping, "Promote Friendship Between Our People and Work Together to Build a Bright Future," *Ministry of Foreign Affairs,* The People's Republic of China, September 7, 2013, https://www.fmprc.gov.cn/mfa_eng/wjdt_665385/zyjh_665391/t1078088.shtml
2. Speech by Chinese President Xi Jinping to Indonesian Parliament, *ASEAN China Centre,* October 2, 2013, http://www.asean-china-center.org/english/2013-10/03/c_133062675.htm
3. Hong, Eunsuk, and Laixiang Sun. "Dynamics of Internationalization and Outward Investment: Chinese Corporations' Strategies," *The China Quarterly*, no. 187 (2006), pp. 610-34.
4. Keith Bradsher, "U.S. Firms Want in on China's Global 'One Belt, One Road' Spending," *The New York Times,* May 14, 2017, https://www.nytimes.com/2017/05/14/business/china-one-belt-one-road-us-companies.html?searchResultPosition=1
5. Anurag Viswanath, "Reviving the Silk Route via One Belt, One Road," *The Financial Express*, February 29, 2016, http://www.financialexpress.com/article/fe-columnist/reviving-the-silk-route-via-one-belt-one-road/217271/
6. "Chair's Statement of the Third Belt and Road Forum for International Cooperation," *Ministry of Foreign Affairs, The People's Republic of China,* October 18, 2023, https://www.fmprc.gov.cn/mfa_eng/zxxx_662805/202310/t20231020_11164505.html
7. "Asian Infrastructure Investment Bank - Inaugural Meeting of the Board Of Governors," *AIIB,* January 16-17, 2016, https://www.aiib.org/en/about-aiib/governance/board-governors/.content/index/_download/20160816034745788.pdf
8. Stanley Reed, "In Courting Chinese Companies, Britain to Help Fund Planned Nuclear Plant," *The New York Times*, September 21, 2015, https://www.nytimes.

com/2015/09/21/business/energy-environment/britain-says-it-will-aid-planned-nuclear-plant.html.

9. Bruno Maçães, "*Belt and Road: A Chinese World Order*," (London: Hurst & Co., 2018), p. 13.

10. Daniel S. Markey, "*China's Western Horizon: Beijing and the New Geopolitics of Eurasia*," (New York: Oxford University Press, 2020), p. ix.

11. "Chronology of China's Belt and Road Initiative," *Xinhua*, March 28, http://news.xinhuanet.com/english/2015-03/28/c_134105435.htm

12. Nicholas Brautlecht, "Germany Plans to Expand Chinese Rail Link as Xi Visits Duisburg," *Bloomberg*, March 28, 2014, http://www.bloomberg.com/news/articles/2014-03-28/germany-plans-to-expand-chinese-rail-link-as-xi-visits-duisburg

13 Keith Bradsher, "Hauling New Treasure Along the Silk Road," *The New York Times*, July 20, 2013, https://www.nytimes.com/2013/07/21/business/global/hauling-new-treasure-along-the-silk-road.html

14. "China has become the world's second-largest ship-owning nation," *Institute for Shipping Economics and Logistics*, https://www.isl.org/en/news/china-become-the-worlds-second-largest-ship-owning-nation#:~:text=ship%20owning%20nation-,China%20has%20become%20the%20world's%20second%2Dlargest%20ship%2Downing%20nation,capacity%20of%20270%20million%20dwt.

15. Keith Bradsher, "U.S. Firms Want in on China's Global 'One Belt, One Road' Spending," *The New York Times*, May 14, 2017, https://www.nytimes.com/2017/05/14/business/china-one-belt-one-road-us-companies.html?searchResultPosition=1

16. Maria Abi-Habib, "How China Got Sri Lanka to Cough Up a Port," *The New York Times*, June 25, 2018, https://www.nytimes.com/2018/06/25/world/asia/china-sri-lanka-port.html

17 Wang Yiwei, "The Trap of BRI Debt Trap," *CGTN*, March 9, 2019, https://news.cgtn.com/news/3d3d414e34496a4d33457a6333566d54/index.html

18. Sam Parker and Gabrielle Chefitz, "*Debtbook Diplomacy: China's Strategic Leveraging of its Newfound Economic Influence and the Consequences for U.S. Foreign Policy*," (Cambridge, MA: Belfer Center for Science and International Affairs, May 2018), p. 3.

19 See for example Abhishek G Bhaya, "BRI to Lead post-COVID-19 'Marshall Plan' for Global Recovery," *CGTN*, April 11, 2020, https://news.cgtn.com/news/2020-04-11/BRI-to-lead-post-COVID-19-Marshall-Plan-for-global-recovery-Pyun62Fl7y/index.html

20. Lim Tai Wei, "Introduction", in Tai Wei Lim and Katherine Hui-Yi Tseng (edt.) *China's One Belt One Road Initiative* (Shanghai: World Scientific, 2016), p. 3.

21. Halper, Stefan. *The Beijing Consensus*, (New York: Basic Books, 2010).

22. Shichor, Yitzhak. "China's Belt and Road Initiative Revisited: Challenges and Ways Forward," *China Quarterly of International Strategic Studies*, Vol. 4, No. 1, pp. 39-53 (2018), p. 48.

23. "Cross-border Infrastructure: International North-South Transport Corridor (INSTC)," *Asia Regional Integration Centre*, https://aric.adb.org/initiative/international-north-south-transport-corridor

24. "Republic of Azerbaijan, Republic of Armenia, Republic of Kazakhstan, Kyrgyz Republic, Republic of Tajikistan, Republic of Turkey, Republic of Ukraine, Republic of Belarus, Oman, Syria, Bulgaria (Observer)." see "Cross-border Infrastructure: International North-South Transport Corridor (INSTC)," *Asia Regional Integration Centre*, https://aric.adb.org/initiative/international-north-south-transport-corridor
25. Hillary Rodham Clinton, "Remarks on India and the United States: A Vision for the 21st Century," July 20, 2011, *Bureau of Public Affairs*, https://2009-2017.state.gov/secretary/20092013clinton/rm/2011/07/168840.htm
26. Ibid.
27. "Remarks at the New Silk Road Ministerial Meeting." *US Department of State*, September 22, 2011, https://2009-2017.state.gov/secretary/20092013clinton/rm/2011/09/173807.htm
28. James McBride, "Building the New Silk Road," *Council on Foreign Relations*, May 22, 2015, https://www.cfr.org/backgrounder/building-new-silk-road
29. India lost the land contiguity to Afghanistan after its partition in 1947 and Pakistan's subsequent occupation of parts of Jammu and Kashmir.
30. Huang Yong, "Construction of digital Silk Road lights up BRI cooperation," *People's Daily Online*, April 24, 2019, http://en.people.cn/n3/2019/0424/c90000-9571418.html
31. "China, biggest victim of cybercrime, champions 'community of common destiny' in cyberspace," *China Daily*, December 16, 2015, http://www.chinadaily.com.cn/world/2015wic/2015-12/16/content_22727856.htm
32. Andrew Moody and Cheng Yu, "Digital Silk Road forges strong links," *China Daily*, December 5, 2017, http://www.chinadaily.com.cn/business/4thwic/2017-12/05/content_35207841.htm
33. Wang Keju, "Digital Silk Road Strengthens Ties," https://partners.wsj.com/chinadaily/chinawatch/digital-silk-road-strengthens-ties/
34. Wesley Rahn, "Will China's 5G 'digital Silk Road' lead to an authoritarian future for the internet?" *Deutsche Welle*, April 26, 2019, https://www.dw.com/en/will-chinas-5g-digital-silk-road-lead-to-an-authoritarian-future-for-the-internet/a-48497082
35. "Huawei remains top global player in telecom equipment", *China Daily*, March 17, 2022. https://www.chinadaily.com.cn/a/202203/17/WS6232fe2fa310fd2b29e5192d.html
36. "Huawei led worldwide telecom equipment market in 1H23 despite US curbs: Dell'Oro Group," *ET Telecom*, September 13, 2023, https://telecom.economictimes.indiatimes.com/news/telecom-equipment/huawei-led-worldwide-telecom-equipment-market-in-1h23-despite-us-curbs-delloro-group/103627063
37. Tin Hinane El Kadi, "The Promise and Peril of the Digital Silk Road," Chatham House, June 6, 2019, https://www.chathamhouse.org/expert/comment/promise-and-peril-digital-silk-road
38. Jonathan Hillman, "China's global ambitions retrace Britain's imperial past," *The Financial Times*, May 16, 2019, https://www.ft.com/content/58c649f0-771c-11e9-be7d-6d846537acab
39. "China's submarine cable super project shocked Europe and the United States", *Seetao*, July 22, 2022, https://www.seetao.com/details/170609.html

40. Dannie Peng, "China builds a machine capable of laying submarine cables in the Challenger Deep," *The South China Morning Post,* November 25, 2024, https://www.scmp.com/news/china/science/article/3287733/china-builds-machine-capable-laying-submarine-cables-challenger-deep
41. "China's Space Silk Road", *Belt and Road Initiative*, https://www.beltroad-initiative.com/space-silk-road/
42. Bree Feng, "A Step Forward for Beidou, China's Satellite Navigation System," *The New York Times*, December 4, 2014, https://sinosphere.blogs.nytimes.com/2014/12/04/a-step-forward-for-beidou-chinas-satellite-navigation-system/?searchResultPosition=1
43 俄航天署希望与中国互建格洛纳斯和北斗地面站 [The Russian Space Agency hopes to mutually build GLONASS and Beidou ground stations with China], *Sina Military*, May 23, 2014, http://mil.news.sina.com.cn/2014-05-23/0819780906.html
44. "Agreement on China-Russia Intergovernmental Cooperation on Satellite Navigation of Signed in Beijing," *BeiDou Navigation Satellite System*, November 7, 2018, http://en.beidou.gov.cn/WHATSNEWS/201811/t20181113_16594.html
45. John Dotson, "The Beidou Satellite Network and the "Space Silk Road" in Eurasia." *The Jamestown Foundation*, July 15, 2020, https://jamestown.org/program/the-beidou-satellite-network-and-the-space-silk-road-in-eurasia/
46. Kristin Huang, "China's answer to GPS complete as final BeiDou satellite launches," *South China Morning Post*, June 23, 2020, https://www.scmp.com/news/china/science/article/3090186/chinas-global-aspirations-lift-beidou-satellite-launches-orbit
47. Liu Zhen, "BeiDou, China's Answer to GPS, 'Six months Ahead of Schedule' after Latest Satellite Launch," *South China Morning Post*, November 6, 2019, https://www.scmp.com/news/china/military/article/3036529/beidou-chinas-answer-gps-six-months-ahead-schedule-after-latest
48. "Full Text: China's BeiDou Navigation Satellite System," *The State Council Information Office of the People's Republic of China*, June 16, 2016, http://www.scio.gov.cn/32618/Document/1480601/1480601.htm
49. Zhang Fan, "Beidou Navigation Satellite System Mirrors China's Ambition of Independent Innovation," *People's Daily*, July 12, 2020, http://en.people.cn/n3/2020/0712/c90000-9709580.html
50. Ryan Woo and Liangping Gao, "China Set to Complete Beidou Network Rivalling GPS in Global Navigation," *Reuters*, June 12, 2020, https://www.reuters.com/article/us-space-exploration-china-satellite/china-set-to-complete-beidou-network-rivalling-gps-in-global-navigation-idUSKBN23J0I9
51. "China's BeiDou Navigation Satellite System first to provide SMS service: Whitepaper," *The Print,* November 4, 2022, https://theprint.in/world/chinas-beidou-navigation-satellite-system-first-to-provide-sms-service-whitepaper/1198022/
52. Wang Qian, "Beidou Set to Spread its Wings in Region," *China Daily*, May 18, 2013, https://www.chinadaily.com.cn/china/2013-05/18/content_16508460.htm
53. Sarah Sewall, Tyler Vandenberg, and Kaj Malden, "China's BeiDou: New Dimensions of Great Power Competition," *Belfer Center for Science and International Affairs,*

February 2023, https://www.belfercenter.org/sites/default/files/files/publication/Chinas-BeiDou_V10.pdf

54. Kun Tang, Zhihui Li, Wenkai Li, and Lincoln Chen, "China's Silk Road and Global Health," *The Lancet Journal*, December 9, 2017, https://www.thelancet.com/journals/lancet/article/PIIS0140-6736(17)32898-2/fulltext
55. "Major health exchange and cooperation on the Belt and Road Initiative," *China Daily*, December 18, 2015, http://www.chinadaily.com.cn/m/chinahealth/2015-12/18/content_22774412.htm
56. Kun Tang, Zhihui Li, Wenkai Li, and Lincoln Chen, "China's Silk Road and Global Health," *The Lancet Journal*, December 9, 2017, https://www.thelancet.com/journals/lancet/article/PIIS0140-6736(17)32898-2/fulltext
57. Pan Zhaoyi, "Chinese vaccines will be made global public good, says Xi," *CGTN*, May 19, 2020, https://news.cgtn.com/news/2020-05-19/Chinese-vaccines-will-be-made-global-public-good-says-Xi-QCpFSGlL2g/index.html
58. Leng Shumei, "China completes half-year vaccination goal early, will cover as many people as possible in H2," *Global Times*, June 30, 2021, https://www.globaltimes.cn/page/202106/1227529.shtml
59. "Pakistan produces Chinese CanSinoBio COVID vaccine, brands it PakVac," *MINT,* June 4, 2021, https://www.livemint.com/news/india/pakistan-produces-chinese-cansinobio-covid-vaccine-brands-it-pakvac-11622820341931.html
60. "China has donated more than 100,000 doses of hepatitis A vaccines for children and adults to Pakistan," *DAWN,* November 10, 2022, https://www.dawn.com/news/1720072
61. Chao Deng, "Get Vaxxed or Stay Home, Some Local Chinese Governments Say," *The Wall Street Journal*, July 15, 2021, https://www.wsj.com/articles/covid-19-vaccines-are-becoming-mandatory-in-parts-of-china-11626259091
62. Sui-Lee Wee and Benjamin Novak, "Hungary pays big for a Chinese vaccine," *The New York Times,* March 12, 2021, https://www.nytimes.com/2021/03/12/world/hungary-sinopharm-covid.html; see also "Expensive Chinese vaccines stir hornet's nest in Bangladesh, Sri Lanka," *Times of India,* June 1, 2021, https://timesofindia.indiatimes.com/world/south-asia/expensive-chinese-vaccines-stir-hornets-nest-in-bangladesh-sri-lanka/articleshow/83138927.cms; see also "Purchase of Sinopharm Vaccine: Price disclosure sparks confusion," *The Daily Star,* May 28, 2021, https://www.thedailystar.net/frontpage/news/purchase-sinopharm-vaccine-price-disclosure-sparks-confusion-2100137; "China fumes after Nepal's media exposes Sinopharm vaccine procurement price," *The Hindustan Times,* June 20, 2021, https://www.hindustantimes.com/world-news/china-fumes-after-nepal-s-media-exposes-sinopharm-vaccine-procurement-price-101624161782822.html
63. Zhong Nan, "China's Vaccines Exported to Over 40 countries," *China Daily*, June 7, 2021, https://www.chinadaily.com.cn/a/202106/07/WS60bd9074a31024ad0bac410b.html
64. "Full Text: Vision and actions on jointly building Belt and Road," *Xinhua*, April 10, 2017, http://2017.beltandroadforum.org/english/n100/2017/0410/c22-45.html

3

Intimate Souls in a Transactional Relationship

Introduction

The Chinese and Pakistani leaders often describe the relationship between their two countries in colourful phrases. A Chinese diplomat once stated, "China and Pakistan [are] partners with intimate souls ... the friendship between China and Pakistan is indeed as solid as gold and as fragrant as an orchid."[1] Of course, the most well-known phrase describes the China-Pakistan friendship as "higher than mountains and deeper than the oceans", and its coinage is often attributed to the former Pakistani prime minister, Zulfikar Ali Bhutto. It is possible that Bhutto may have used phrases from Christian texts. For instance, a Christian psalm deployed similar imagery by referring to God's love as "higher than the highest mountains and deeper than the deepest ocean."[2] So, it is interesting that leaders of an Islamic republic, in their interactions with atheist communist leaders, deploy a Christian hymn to define their partnership.

In fact, Mao Zedong noted the relationship paradox between China and Pakistan. Interacting with a visiting dignitary from Islamabad, Mao referred to the Chinese commitment to communism, atheism, and dissimilar social systems to demonstrate the contrast between the two countries.[3] Of course, Mao went on to map the similarities in terms of shared colonial subjugation and a desire to live in peace with neighbours, which must have pleased the visiting dignitary.[4] Despite many dissimilarities between the two countries, the leaders on both sides made persistent efforts to build a robust relationship, and they succeeded because of the geopolitical context.

The Early Conversations

In January 1950, Pakistan recognised the People's Republic of China, and the two countries established diplomatic relations a year later. In the 1950s, while both countries explored the possibilities of greater cooperation, the relationship was also marked by hesitations. Responding to a query from Beijing on the pros and cons of allowing Pakistan to open a consulate in Xinjiang, the Xinjiang Foreign Affairs Office, in 1955, noted that such a move may result in "intelligence-gathering activities [and] will also be harmful to the unity of China's minorities.[5]" The concerns that the Chinese leadership now have about the minorities in Xinjiang having transnational connections have a longer historical trajectory dating back to the early 1950s. The hesitation that Pakistan may have noticed in Chinese responses to its attempts to build better relations may have also stemmed from the geopolitical context. Given the Cold War and the ideological divide, Pakistan attempted the complex task of building a strong relationship with China, while being a member of the US alliance framework. In early 1956, talking to Pakistani Ambassador Sultanuddin Ahmad, Chinese Premier Zhou Enlai conveyed his displeasure with Pakistan's participation in the Manila Pact and went on to add that "for friendship's sake, we have not made an issue of mentioning Pakistan by name for disapproval in the newspapers.[6]" The message from the Chinese leadership to their Pakistani counterparts was blunt. Pakistan's diplomats and leaders sought to address the Chinese concerns by arguing that they would not participate in any military activity targeting China. At the same time, the public restraint demonstrated by the Chinese leaders suggests that they valued the relationship with Islamabad.

In their interactions with Manila and Baghdad pact partners, Pakistani leaders also had to address the concerns regarding their relationship with China. Pakistani President Iskander Ali Mirza, in 1956, sought to address such concerns by arguing that developing a close relationship with China benefits the Western alliance. He noted: "If the United States recognised China, it could draw China away from the Russian Communist Party clique, [and] the United States and Britain could influence China to [take] a position more beneficial to the West in international affairs.[7]" So, Pakistani attempts to emerge as a bridge between the US and China started way back in the mid-1950s, well before Kissinger arrived on the scene.

Many early conversations between Beijing and Islamabad focused on security issues. During their interactions, Pakistani leaders often gave lengthy briefings to their counterparts in Beijing on the evolving security dynamic in South Asia. The security-dominated agenda would also witness discussions on trade and economic issues. For instance, in 1956, Pakistani irrigation experts were interested in studying water projects, such as the Xianghongdian Reservoir and the Mozitan Reservoir.[8]

A full-throttle China-Pakistan engagement had to await the resolution of a few niggles in the relationship. These differences pertained to the delineation of the border between the two countries. In response to sporadic border violations by China in 1959, Pakistan President Ayub Khan asserted that "any Chinese intrusion into Pakistani territory would be repelled ... with all the force at her command.[9]" Concerns about Chinese territorial expansion prompted Ayub Khan to explore the possibility of a joint defence pact with India, which was premised on the resolution of "big problems like Kashmir and the canal waters."[10] Ayub Khan's administration hinted that the India-Pakistan joint defence pact could evolve into a regional framework to contain China. There were reports that Pakistan's high commissioner in Delhi reached out to the ambassador of Nepal to explore the possibility of common defence.[11] In response, the Nepal government suggested that such matters be discussed with others, such as India.[12] Given the scale and nature of territorial conflict pertaining to Kashmir, the prospect of an India-Pakistan Joint Defence Pact making progress was limited. Moreover, there was a considerable divergence in the foreign policy postures of India and Pakistan. For instance, responding to a query during a press conference in 1960, Prime Minister Nehru noted that accepting the joint defence proposal of Ayub would result in all kinds of complications, as Pakistan is "tied up with all kinds of military alliances...our basic policy has been not to be so tied up with any military alliance with any country..."[13] Given these divergences of security postures, the probability of operationalising the joint defence pact between India and Pakistan was non-existent. One wonders if Ayub Khan's joint defence proposal with India was aimed at getting a better border deal from the Chinese.

The 1962 India-China war and the 1965 India-Pakistan war created sufficient conditions for the emergence of a strategic partnership between

Islamabad and Beijing. During the 1962 war, the Western powers scaled up their assistance to India without consulting Pakistan. For China, because of the Himalayan conflict with India, it became necessary to quickly iron out wrinkles in its relationship with Pakistan. Through a border agreement in 1963, China and Pakistan announced that the border was delineated between the two countries. New Delhi always asserted that the entire state of Jammu and Kashmir is an integral part of the Indian Union. Therefore, from New Delhi's perspective, through the 1963 Treaty, Pakistan ceded "5180 kms of Indian territory in Shaksgam valley in Pakistan Occupied Kashmir to China."[14] In 1963, Beijing and Islamabad also sought to scale up their trade relations by giving "each other the status of Most Favoured Nation (MFN)"[15] and also concluding an air transport agreement. China-Pakistan bonhomie and attempts at scaling up economic relations did raise eyebrows in Washington DC. The US State Department defined the airline agreement between China and Pakistan as "an unfortunate breach of free world solidarity."[16] From the Pakistani perspective, the growing interest of China in South Asia fundamentally altered the security matrix. The then Pakistan Foreign Minister, Bhutto, observed that a conflict with Islamabad does not involve Pakistan alone, as it will also impinge on the interests of the largest state in Asia.[17] For Islamabad, the 1965 India-Pakistan war further demonstrated the limitations of the US alliance framework. As the war unfolded, the Indian defence forces proved that they had overcome the defeat to the Chinese a few years ago and were contesting Pakistani forces on many fronts. From Islamabad's perspective, the unkindest cut came from the US, which had imposed an "arms embargo on both the warring sides, which hurt Pakistan badly because almost all her weapons were of US origin."[18] A week after the 1965 war ended with a UN-mandated ceasefire, China and Pakistan agreed to build the Karakoram Highway across the high Himalayas.[19] The agreement to build the Karakoram Highway stemmed from the perception in Pakistan and China that their interactions and cooperation should be insulated from other big powers' attitudes/policies (such as the arms embargo).[20] Subsequently, in 1966, China and Pakistan signed an agreement on constructing the China-Pakistan Karakoram Highway. So, the trigger for one of the mega connectivity projects between China and Pakistan was geopolitical concerns and not economic considerations.

As noted earlier, Pakistan often stated that the US and China could work together to alter the balance of power in Asia. The Sino-Soviet border skirmishes in 1969 created conditions for US-China rapprochement. Pakistan carried a message that Beijing was ready to receive the special envoy from the US.[21] A few months later, in 1971, Henry Kissinger transited through Islamabad to reach Beijing to interact with Chinese Premier Zhou Enlai. With Pakistan, China, and the US coming together to pursue their interests in Asia, India entered into a Treaty of Peace, Friendship and Cooperation with the Soviet Union in August 1971. A few months later, the Indo-Pak war resulted in the dismemberment of Pakistan and the emergence of a new nation-state, viz., Bangladesh. It is indeed ironic that such dismemberment occurred precisely when Islamabad's long-cherished dream of the Pakistan-China-US axis came into play. On the other hand, the Beijing-Washington rapprochement facilitated by Islamabad resulted in greater economic engagement between China and the West. A year after Henry Kissinger's furtive visit to Beijing, US President Richard Nixon travelled to China, scaling up the diplomatic relations between the two countries. Probably conscious of Pakistan's contribution to the China-US rapprochement, in 1976, Mao Zedong made it a point to interact with visiting Pakistani Prime Minister Zulfiqar Ali Bhutto despite being unwell, which happened to be his last meeting with foreign dignitaries.[22] The growing trust between the leaders of China and Pakistan created conditions for operationalising major infrastructure projects.

Karakoram Highway: The Prototype

The construction of the Karakoram Highway (from Hongqilafu to Takot) reportedly "lasted 11 years from 1968 to 1979 … [and over] … 22,000 people were deployed to complete the project."[23] Some of the sections of the highway were easy to access from the Chinese side. Pakistan airlifted its workers to Hotan prefecture, and from there, they were transported by the Chinese authorities to work on the various sections of the highway.[24] The treacherous terrain, defined by massive landslides, resulted in numerous fatalities during the construction.[25] Seymour Topping, writing in 1979, gave a graphic account of the human costs incurred during the construction of the Karakoram Highway through very tough terrain and noted that the highway opened a backdoor for the Chinese to access the Arabian Sea and the West.[26] To meet such strategic objectives, the Chinese deployed 9,000–11,000 workers, constructed 80 bridges, and paved 395 miles, and the alignment "was routed through the Khunjerab rather than the Mintaka Pass", as the latter was closer to the Soviet border.[27] There were indeed concerns in the Chinese leadership regarding the high costs of the highway, and yet, they pushed ahead with the project because of its strategic value.[28]

The Karakoram Highway did serve its intended purpose. During the Afghan war, "some Chinese weapons were shipped in convoys along the Karakoram Highway" to the Afghan rebels.[29] So the Karakoram Highway, in its own small way, contributed to the common objective of China, Pakistan, and the US, which was the containment of the Soviet Union. In relative terms, the construction of the Karakoram Highway increased Chinese access to the Wakhan corridor.[30] Improved access to Wakhan was important as there were concerns that the Soviet Union may annex the region as "roads were being built in the corridor towards China and Pakistan."[31] While the Karakoram Highway provided some strategic advantages, China harboured concerns regarding the spread of Islamic fundamentalism from Pakistan into Western provinces of China. For instance, in 1992, after "a failed uprising near Kashgar resulted in 22 deaths, China closed its road links with Pakistan for several months."[32]

For three decades after its construction, the Karakoram Highway was not an all-weather highway, as it was closed every year during the winter from October to May. Moreover, the Pakistan highway segment was relatively more challenging to navigate. Alice Albinia, travelling on the highway in the late 2000s, noted: "In China, the Karakoram Highway is wide, and the traffic moves fast. The moment it crosses into Pakistan, at the peak of the Khunjerab Pass, it becomes an assault course of potholes..."[33] However, the fortunes of the Karakoram Highway started to change with the launch of the Karakoram Road Expansion Project in 2008. As the Karakoram Highway navigated through seismically challenging terrain, landslides created an artificial lake that submerged parts of the Karakoram Highway, which mandated its realignment. The expansion of the highway received funding from China's Export-Import Bank.

While the earlier interactions across the Karakoram Highway were defined by limited people-to-people and economic engagement, there has recently been greater emphasis on enhancing trade relations. However, there has been no dilution in geopolitical dynamics. Reflecting on the Karakoram economic corridor, Senge H. Sering notes: "By approaching Afghanistan through Gilgit-Baltistan rather than Central Asia, China will benefit by avoiding competition with Russia for strategic depth in what Russia considers its near abroad."[34] The Karakoram Highway was, in a way, a prototype of the China-Pakistan Economic Corridor (CPEC). It had all the ingredients of the CPEC—economic, geopolitical, security, and connectivity dimensions. The leaders of both countries were also acutely aware of the importance of the Karakoram since the 1960s. For instance, in 1960, interacting with Chinese Ambassador-designate General Geng Biao, Mao Zedong reportedly counselled him: "Look after Pakistan; it is China's window to the West."[35] Mao's statement was made in a context when the Sino-Soviet split was intensifying, and China had anxieties about the US presence in the first island chain in the Pacific. In addition to providing alternative access to the seas, in the subsequent years, Pakistan also facilitated a dialogue between China and the US. Referring to the long historical trajectory of the conversations about increasing connectivity between the two countries, Sandhya Jain noted that "China's quest for a direct land route to Pakistan was conceived and partially executed by Chairman Mao; President Xi Jinping is trying to complete this agenda."[36]

The China-Pakistan Economic Corridor

The China-Pakistan Economic Corridor (CPEC) is a critical component of the Belt and Road Initiative (BRI), as it fits into Beijing's plans to scale up continental connectivity in Central Asia and beyond. The BRI connectivity was aimed at giving an economic fillip to China's relatively backward western regions. For China, Pakistan is an ideal candidate to scale up economic engagement under the BRI. From a Chinese perspective, compared to other countries on its western frontiers, such as the CARs, Pakistan has a much bigger GDP, territorial area, population, military presence, and capabilities to "become China's voice in the Islamic world."[37] And more importantly, for China, Pakistan would not be just an "economic corridor" but could be a strategic "quasi-alliance" partner in the region.[38]

In May 2013, Chinese Premier Li Keqiang, during his visit to Pakistan, called for enhanced economic interactions and said: "We are ready to work with Pakistan to speed up the project of upgrading the Karakoram Highway, actively explore and develop the long-term plans of building a China-Pakistan economic corridor, expanding our shared interests."[39] The proposed economic corridor was "to be 'four-in-one' corridor covering roads, railways, oil and gas pipelines and fibre optic cables."[40] In July 2013, during the visit of Pakistan Prime Minister Nawaz Sharif to Beijing, both countries agreed to work on the

Long Term Plan for the China-Pakistan Economic Corridor, with a specific focus on projects, such as starting the Fiber Optic Cable line, upgrading the Karakoram Highway, developing industrial parks along the corridor and industrial zones in Gwadar.[41] As a follow-up, the first Joint Cooperation Committee (JCC) meeting was held in Islamabad on August 27, 2013, and the discussions focused on the "Special Fund for Economic Cooperation with Pakistan."[42] A few months later, in February 2014, the second meeting of the JCC was held in Beijing, which focused on development strategies and policy coordination between the two countries.[43]

A year later, the third meeting of the CPEC JCC was held in Beijing, which focused on immediate "short-term projects to be completed."[44] The JCC also acted as a preparatory meeting for Pakistan Prime Minister Nawaz Sharif's visit to Beijing to carry forward the discussion on the economic corridor. In one of his meetings with the Chinese leadership, Nawaz Sharif made the (in)famous gaffe of not being able to complete the rhetorical lines that most Pakistani leaders use to describe their relationship with China, viz., "Our friendship is higher than the Himalayas, deeper than the deepest sea and sweeter than honey." Shehbaz Sharif, the brother of the prime minister, stepped in to complete the sentences. While the gaffe provided some entertainment back home and in the sub-continent, it had no negative impact on the outcome of the visit. After the summit meeting with President Xi Jinping, the Chinese government and companies pledged USD 45.6 billion worth of investments in various infrastructure projects.[45] Pakistan committed to extending cooperation to China on terrorism/extremism-related issues and promised to "resolutely fight the East Turkestan Islamic Movement terrorist forces."[46] While Pakistan was assured about the investments, China received commitments in political and security spheres.

In the run-up to his visit to Pakistan in April 2015, Chinese President Xi Jinping published an article in the *Daily Times* titled 'Pak-China Dosti Zindabad (Long live China-Pakistan friendship)'. It deployed the usual effusive phrases with the president stating: "This will be my first trip to Pakistan, but I feel as if I am going to visit the home of my own brother."[47] Prime Minister Sharif reciprocated in equal measure and said: "You are not just a friend from afar, but one who is so close to our heart."[48] While Pakistan bestowed Xi Jinping with the highest civilian award of Nishan-i-Pakistan, the Chinese government "conferred the Five Principles of Peaceful Coexistence Friendship Award on Pakistani individuals and groups, commending the unremitting contribution they have made to promoting the friendship between the two countries."[49]

During the visit, the CPEC was formally launched. Approximately 51 deals[50] were signed during President Xi Jinping's visit to Pakistan, and of these, at least 30 pertained to the CPEC.[51] President Xi Jinping noted that the CPEC is located at the intersection of the continental and maritime arms of the BRI and called on both countries to ensure greater alignment of "security concerns more closely to strengthen security cooperation."[52] The CPEC would connect Kashgar (China) to Gwadar (Pakistan). The economic corridor, which would span about 3,000 kilometres (1,800 miles), included major cities in Pakistan, such as Karachi, Lahore, and Islamabad. In 2015, Pakistan's Planning and Development Minister, Ahsan Iqbal, announced that there would be three routes: "a western route through Balochistan and Khyber Pakhtunkhwa provinces; an eastern route primarily through Sindh and Punjab provinces; and a central route crisscrossing the country."[53] Initially, it was estimated that the CPEC would cost around USD 46 billion, and much of the funding for this will come from Chinese banks, companies, and government. Approximately USD 33.8 billion was to be invested in the energy projects, and USD 11.8 billion would be invested in the infrastructure projects.[54] At the time of its launch, the total expenditure on the CPEC was equal to approximately "20 per cent of Pakistan's annual GDP and is more than double the total foreign direct investment (FDI) the country has received since 2008."[55] Further, both governments decided to work on quick implementation of 'Early Harvest Projects', and about "USD 15.5 billion worth of coal, wind, solar and hydroelectric power projects" were to be completed expeditiously.[56] Subsequently, the allocation to the Early Harvest Projects was increased to USD 28 billion, of which USD 18 billion was allocated "for power projects and USD 10 billion for rail, road and port infrastructure."[57] An important dimension of the CPEC projects has been the lack of clarity on the exact scale of financial commitments made by the parties involved.

A few weeks after Xi Jinping visited Pakistan, an all-party conference was convened by the Awami National Party to discuss the CPEC proposal, and it called on the government not to change the proposed alignment to the disadvantage of Balochistan and other western provinces.[58] A few days later, at an all-party conference called by the government, Prime Minister Nawaz Sharif announced that the western route of the economic corridor would be constructed first and would receive priority.[59] A few months later, in 2016, Prime Minister Nawaz Sharif inaugurated the Gwadar-Hoshab M8-Road in Balochistan.[60] The road was critical in developing enhanced connectivity between Gwadar and Quetta. Through the inauguration of the highway, Nawaz Sharif sought to demonstrate that the western provinces would also benefit from the CPEC projects. At the inauguration, Nawaz Sharif travelled on the newly constructed road in an open army jeep driven by then Chief of Army Staff General Raheel Sharif, which was interpreted by many as symbolic of the fact that the army is in the driver's seat on CPEC-related matters.

A few months later, a large number of container trucks from China entered Pakistan at the Sost dry port and later proceeded to Gwadar.[61] On their arrival at the Gwadar port, the Chinese ambassador said that the transit of trucks with containers validated the importance of local roads and the "realisation of the concept of one corridor with multiple passages."[62] A Chinese news report credited the Pakistani military with the idea of a trade convoy test run to "examine the road conditions of the route and study the transport costs."[63] As the activities under the CPEC picked up momentum, the costs of implementing the projects also registered an increase. It was at the Sixth JCC meeting held in Beijing towards the end of 2016 that the decision was taken to increase the financial outlay of the CPEC to USD 54 billion, and with the expansion of the list of projects, the 'overall size of the CPEC projects increased to USD 60 billion'.[64]

In early January 2017, a consortium of Chinese companies (the China Financial Futures Exchange, the Shanghai Stock Exchange, and the Shenzhen Stock Exchange) along with two other companies picked up approximately 40 per cent of the stake (about USD 85 million) in the Karachi-based Pakistan Stock Exchange (PSX).[65] Two years earlier, the Islamabad, Karachi, and Lahore stock exchanges were merged into one bourse—the Pakistan Stock Exchange. Reportedly, a British consortium with some local banks was also in the race, but they failed to make it in the final round.[66] The Chinese stake was expected to "bring investment experience, technological assistance and new products" into Pakistan's financial capital markets.[67] Though the acquisition was not formally part of the CPEC, it constituted an important backdrop. The acquisition of stakes in the stock exchange marks the scaling up of financial cooperation from credit cooperation to capital market cooperation.[68] Liang Haiming notes that the objectives that guided the acquisition of stakes in PSX included gaining experience to operationalise national exchanges in various countries, preparing the ground for the creation of regional exchanges, and creating a multi-level financial platform to attract more capital to invest in the Belt and Road developmental initiatives.[69]

In May 2017, Beijing hosted a high-profile diplomatic event on the BRI, which witnessed the participation of "29 foreign heads of state and government leaders."[70] Prime Minister Nawaz Sharif led the Pakistan delegation. At the forum, Pakistan and China agreed on new deals worth USD 500 million pertaining to Gwadar airport, the establishment of the Dry Port, and economic and technical cooperation for the East Bay Expressway.[71] Speaking at the forum, Nawaz Sharif hinted that even India should participate in the CPEC projects, stating: "Let me make it very clear that the China-Pakistan Economic Corridor is an economic undertaking open to *all countries* [emphasis added]. It has no geographical boundaries."[72] Sharif added that Pakistan is "not striving to merely leverage geography for economic prosperity; we are also trying to build a peaceful, connected and *caring neighbourhood* [emphasis added].[73]"

At the 7th JCC in December 2017, Pakistan and China agreed on the CPEC Long Term Plan (LTP) 2014-2030.[74] While both countries agreed on developing the special economic zones, Pakistan was reluctant to facilitate the use of the yuan in the Gwadar economic zone.[75] For China, which wanted to internationalise its currency over time, Pakistan's reluctance to use the yuan in Gwadar port was a setback. By the end of 2017, it became evident that Pakistan's economy was witnessing adverse economic winds, and there was speculation within the country that the government should reach out to the International Monetary Fund (IMF) for a bailout. However, the IMF expressed concerns regarding the financial viability of various CPEC projects.[76] As Pakistan faced a severe balance of payment crisis in mid-2018, there were concerns in the international community that financial support, such as loans, may be used by Pakistan to pay its Chinese debts. For instance, the US Secretary of State, Mike Pompeo, in July 2018, observed: "there's no rationale for IMF tax dollars—and associated with that, American dollars that are part of the IMF funding—for those to go to bail out Chinese bondholders or China itself."[77] There was disappointment within Pakistan's ruling establishment at Pompeo's statements. The Pakistan government argued that the proposed IMF bailout and the CPEC constitute two different spending verticals, and there will be no spillover between the two.[78] However, IMF officials continued expressing apprehensions about the CPEC projects' financial viability. The IMF chief economist reiterated that "it is important that the design of the projects ... be solid and excessive debts which cannot be repaid are avoided."[79] In response to growing demands for transparency on the debt situation, Pakistan's Finance Minister, in October 2018, conceded that Pakistan would share the CPEC debt-related information with the IMF.[80] Pakistan's willingness to discuss the CPEC debt structure also stemmed from the inability to get adequate bailouts from other countries. It is not merely the financial component of the CPEC which was critically examined. Domestic and international observers were also concerned about the proposals for oil pipelines, energy, digital projects, and other components of the CPEC. Pakistan has made persistent efforts to solicit investments from other countries in CPEC-related projects. After assuming office, the Prime Minister of Pakistan, Imran Khan, visited Saudi Arabia and invited Riyadh to invest in the CPEC projects. Imran Khan's diplomatic efforts did bring some cheer, with Saudi Arabia agreeing to a loan of USD 3 billion and a one-year deferred payment facility for oil imports up to USD 3 billion.[81] In 2024, the possibility of Saudi Arabia investing in the energy and transportation sectors of the CPEC received consistent reportage.[82]

During Pakistan's Prime Minister Shehbaz Sharif's visit to China in June 2024, both countries agreed to "jointly develop five major corridors for growth, better life, innovation, green development and openness, with focus on building an upgraded version of the CPEC."[83] Shehbaz Sharif's visit also generated considerable discussion in the media that Pakistan was seeking the support of the Chinese leadership to tide over economic challenges.[84] The CPEC continued to be a platform for high-level engagement between the two countries. China's Premier Li Qiang, during his visit to Pakistan in October 2024, participated in the inaugural ceremony of the New Gwadar International Airport and reiterated China's commitment to upgrade the CPEC.[85] In December 2024, the Pakistan government approved Saudi Arabia's proposal of a "15 per cent investment in the Reko Diq copper and gold mine project."[86] While the Reko Diq is not a flagship project of China-Pakistan cooperation, Saudi investment proposals generated hopes of third-country participation in the CPEC.

Pipelines or Pipedreams

As the CPEC gained prominence, many reports suggested that Chinese investments in Pakistan also aimed to partly address the concerns about excessive dependence on the Straits of Malacca and the South China Sea as transit points for China's energy resources. It was argued that an oil and gas pipeline under the rubric of the CPEC would reduce the distance of "China's energy imports from the Middle East by about 12,000 kms."[87] Such pipelines were to originate from the Gwadar port, which was upgraded with Chinese investments. However, such pipelines are uneconomical as they would have to traverse the high Himalayas, and it is relatively cheaper to carry oil resources by sea. Moreover, there is an opinion in China that there are multiple pipelines in Central Asia, which can be extended to other countries to tap energy resources.[88] Further, it was opined in the Chinese media that an oil pipeline through Pakistan would not address security dilemmas, as the "US and British navies are in control of the Persian Gulf's oil supply, the US Central Naval Command and the Fifth Fleet are based in Bahrain, and the British permanent military base in the port of Mina Salman in Bahrain."[89] These forces can disrupt energy resources even before they can reach Pakistan.

From a Chinese perspective, while the Strait of Malacca may pose security challenges, the projects under the CPEC may not fully address such security concerns. Moreover, a large proportion of China's economic activity will remain on the eastern coast for the foreseeable future. Therefore, meeting the energy requirements of the eastern provinces by sea will remain economical. Not surprisingly, despite media reports that the CPEC was designed to address the Malacca Dilemma, the oil pipeline project across the high Himalayas did not take off in the CPEC framework. However, the construction of the liquefied natural gas (LNG) terminal at Gwadar is eliciting interest. In April 2022, China National Chemical Engineering Construction Company signed an agreement with Daewoo Gas to operationalise its plans to construct an offshore LNG terminal near Gwadar.[90] Reports in 2023 suggested that, in addition to China, Pakistan is keen on inviting Turkmenistan and European countries as energy trade partners and "is seeking gas supplies for Gwadar in an effort to make it an international energy hub … to establish LNG plants and export the fuel."[91]

Corridor of Inequality?

While the Pakistani government was inviting other countries in the region to participate in the CPEC, there was criticism from within that the proposed corridor was not sufficiently inclusive. The CPEC had become a bone of contention in Pakistan. The CPEC has multiple routes: the western route (frontier provinces bordering Afghanistan) and the eastern route (Sindh and Punjab). There was anxiety that the CPEC may get operationalised in the relatively more affluent and politically influential provinces of Punjab and Sind, resulting in the neglect of other areas. For instance, Pakistan Tehreek-e-Insaf (PTI) Chairman Imran Khan, before becoming the prime minister, noted: "We should build a shorter and better route of the CPEC instead of opting for the eastern route, which will create resentment in other provinces against Punjab...."[92] Similarly, in 2016, Khyber Pakhtunkhwa (KP) Chief Minister Pervez Khattak stated: "I warn if the federal government does not address the reservations of KP about the (CPEC) project, then we will take an extreme step ... and you (centre) will see what we are going to do ... build a complete corridor ... we don't need a highway."[93] To address such suspicions, then Pakistan's Prime Minister Nawaz Sharif convened two All Parties Conferences to discuss the CPEC in 2016. In order to generate confidence among the provincial leaders, Prime Minister Nawaz Sharif announced that the western route would be completed by July 2018 and constituted an 11-member committee, headed by him, to hasten the implementation of the CPEC.[94] After becoming the Prime Minister, Imran Khan noted that Pakistan is fortunate to be part of the BRI and added that the western route would trigger prosperity in Balochistan and tribal areas because of growing connectivity with China.[95] While some of the projects pertaining to the western route—the Hakla-DI Khan Motorway, the Hoshab-Gwadar road, the Quetta-Sohrab road, and the Surab-Hoshab road—were completed, as of early 2022, a host of other projects are yet to be completed.[96] The CPEC officials have set a revised deadline of 2024 for the completion of the western route.[97]

Trade

In addition to the impact on regional inequalities, there was an opinion that the China-Pakistan economic engagement did not result in equitable outcomes in the realm of trade. The economic interactions between Pakistan and China did witness an upward trend. However, the asymmetry in the economic power of Pakistan and China also posed a significant challenge to enhanced economic interactions. With a USD 17.79 trillion economy, China is the second-largest economy in the world, and Pakistan's GDP was at USD 337.91 billion, making it the 45th-largest economy in the world in

2023.[98] This asymmetry skewed the trade relations between the countries. For instance, there were concerns in Pakistan that the Free Trade Agreement (FTA) with China did not bring anticipated benefits. The China-Pakistan FTA was signed in 2006, and both countries agreed to bring approximately 35 per cent of tariff lines to zero duty in the first phase of the FTA. After the implementation of the FTA, there was an increase in bilateral trade, resulting from the rise in Chinese exports to Pakistan. For instance, in 2006, Chinese exports to Pakistan amounted to USD 4,664.81 million, and Pakistani exports to China were at USD 915.61 million. However, by 2018, Chinese exports to Pakistan increased to USD 14379.1 million, and Pakistan's exports to China increased marginally to USD 1949.7 million. Reportedly, many Chinese products, such as "tires, tiles and ceramics, polyester staple fibre and synthetic yarn, electronic items, industrial chemicals, amongst many others ... found a competitive position in the Pakistan market only after tariffs were reduced on them."[99] Since the FTA was hurting Pakistan's economy, the modalities for implementing the second phase of the FTA took considerable time to be negotiated.[100] The second phase of the China-Pakistan Free Trade Agreement (CPFTA) was signed on April 28, 2019, and it stipulated that "both countries will liberalise 75 per cent of tariff lines for each other in a period of 10 years by China and 15 years by Pakistan ... and China will immediately eliminate tariffs on 313 most priority tariff lines of Pakistan's export interest."[101] At the time of the signing of the CPFTA, there was a perception in Pakistan that it had received "enhanced and deeper concessions" and import of cost-effective machinery would upgrade domestic industrial production.[102] However, the anticipated positive outcomes from the trade agreement did not materialise. While the overall bilateral trade in 2021 increased to USD 27.8 billion, there is disappointment in Pakistan that its exports to China did not perform well. The trade deficit with China continued to be very high. To overcome these challenges, Pakistan is in conversation with China to enhance the export prospects for select product lines.[103] Further, in February 2022, Pakistan signed a framework agreement on industrial cooperation with China to attract Foreign Direct Investment (FDI) and increase exports.[104] However, Pakistan's Economic Survey 2023-2024 noted that "a significant outflow of USD 173.2 million was observed in January 2024 due to the aggressive pull-out of investment from power projects, mainly by China."[105]

Pakistan's experience demonstrates that enhanced connectivity networks and increased economic interactions alone will not automatically result in positive outcomes for all stakeholders. The asymmetry in economic power between Pakistan and China is benefitting the latter. However, the economic interaction in an asymmetric-set does not always need to be loaded in favour of the powerful. For instance, for Pakistan, the US tends to be the largest export destination. In 2023, Pakistan's exports to the US amounted to USD 4.88 billion, and its imports from the US were around USD 2.04 billion.[106] As of October 2024, Pakistan enjoyed a trade surplus of USD 2.4 billion with the United States.[107] Overall, Pakistan enjoys a trade surplus in its economic interactions with the US. According to the US Trade Representative (USTR), the five largest import categories into the US from Pakistan were: "textile articles, knit apparel, woven apparel, cotton, and leather products."[108] Sectors, such as textiles and knit apparel, generated considerable employment in the country. Unlike in its trade with the US, Pakistan could not find niche areas in its economic interactions with China to ensure equitable outcomes.

Energy

In addition to connectivity projects, the energy sector is one of the most important sub-sets within the CPEC. Energy is essential for faster industrialisation, and Pakistan faced crippling energy shortages.[109] As part of the CPEC, numerous energy projects were conceptualised, including coal, hydro, solar, and wind-based projects.[110] Many countries across the world are moving away from coal-fired power plants. However, Pakistan, which did not have significant coal-based energy generation, shifted to coal-based power plants under the CPEC. This shift towards coal-based production is often criticised for being environmentally unfriendly. However, some in Pakistan argued that these coal-based plants are based on modern technologies and are replacing fuel-oil plants that tend to have higher greenhouse emission rates.[111] The shift towards coal-based power plants also stemmed from the necessity to look for low-cost sources and an eagerness to exploit domestic untapped coal reserves with greater intensity.[112] Some argued that an emphasis on coal-based electricity generation stemmed from a need to diversify the energy base and decrease generation costs.[113] Pakistan's adoption of coal-based power plants was also convenient for Beijing, enabling China to export its excess capacities.

The construction of these power plants was criticised in the same way that Chinese projects are critiqued in other parts of the world. For instance, there was concern that much of the equipment, raw materials, and skilled labour used in the projects' construction came from China.[114] Much of the equipment for these energy projects was procured from Chinese companies because Pakistan did not have the local capacity to supply and render services in this segment.

There are a few challenges that the CPEC coal-fired power plants are facing, which can be understood by examining the Sahiwal and Port Qasim power plants. The construction of the Sahiwal Coal-fired Power Plant (2×660MW) in the Punjab province of Pakistan, initiated in 2015, was completed in less than two years. The plant was a joint venture between Huaneng Shandong Electricity Limited and Shandong Ruyi Group and was built at an estimated cost of USD 1.6 billion.[115] The plant was inaugurated in 2017 and was dubbed "a miracle in the country's history of electric power, with the shortest construction time, largest installed capacity and most advanced technology."[116] The Pakistani officials claimed that the plant is environmentally friendly as it deploys the latest technologies and proposes to use environment-friendly coal.[117] To make the investment profitable, government tax exemptions were provided, reduced import duty was levied on imported machinery, and power producers were reportedly promised that they would be paid based on capacity rather than on actual generation.[118] As a consequence of these provisions and because of the financial crisis, there were instances when the Pakistani government was not able to pay dues to the project developers, threatening the closure of the project.[119] Some of these coal-fired power plants are located very far away from the ports. As a consequence, there are additional costs associated with the transport of coal and ensuring the timely supply of other required materials.[120] In 2024, there were reports of the Sahiwal Coal-fired Power Plant experiencing a critical coal shortage, which prompted the central agencies to request Pakistan Railways to increase the number of freight trains to hasten the transport of imported coal.[121]

Unlike the Sahiwal Coal-fired Power Plant in Punjab, the Port Qasim Coal-fired Power Plant (2×660 MW) is located in Karachi, which is a coastal city with a port. As a consequence, the cost of transportation of imported coal here would be much less compared to that in power plants located in provinces such as Punjab. The project was initiated in 2015 and was completed in 2018, reportedly 67 days ahead of schedule.[122] Reportedly, the cost of the project is around USD 2.09 billion, and in the initial phase 51 per cent was invested by a Chinese firm and 49 per cent by a firm from the Middle East.[123] The Port Qasim Electric Power Company (PQEPC) ran into financial difficulties due to late payment of the arrears by the government of Pakistan. PQEPC

Chairman Sheng Yuming, in May 2019, stated, "We have around USD 150 million late payments now....we are trying our best to generate more power and get more tariff payment timely... we have to import coal from the international market, and also we have to repay the debt to the financing banks."[124] In 2024, the power plant threatened to suspend operations unless the outstanding payments were immediately cleared by the government.[125] Given the dependence on imported coal, the cost of production was subjected to various vagaries, such as the devaluation of the Pakistani Rupee.[126]

The operationalisation of the coal-based power plants resulted in a surge of coal imports into Pakistan. While coal-based power plants may be responsible for a significant chunk of imports, other segments, such as the cement industry, also contributed to the surge in coal imports.[127] Pakistan imported about 3.42m tonnes of coal in 2013, which increased to about 11.2 million tonnes in 2017.[128] By 2021, coal imports surged to around 19 million tons.[129] However, there was a slowdown in the growth of coal imports in 2022. According to a report by S&P Global, Pakistan's power, cement, and steel plants were operating at lower capacities in 2022 because of the increase in global coal prices, which had a negative impact on Pakistan's coal imports.[130] The harsh experiences prompted Pakistan government officials to explore the possibility of reversing coal imports by using more renewable energy resources and domestic coal reserves.[131]

Digital and Space Silk Roads

In addition to the energy sector, China has scaled up its presence in Pakistan's digital landscape. China was the principal mover behind the Pakistan and East Africa Connecting Europe (PEACE) cable project. The project involves an undersea cable from Gwadar in Pakistan to connect with Mombasa in Kenya, Djibouti, Egypt, and Marseille in France. Incidentally, Marseille is also the digital gateway to Europe for Chinese companies, such as China Telecom, China Mobile, and China Unicom.[132] In May 2018, Huawei announced that hydrographic and geophysical surveys were initiated in collaboration with EGS Survey, a United Kingdom-based company.[133]

France's leading telecommunication operator, Orange, collaborated with PCCW Global by supplying and operating a cable land station in Marseille.[134] The participation of a European telecommunication major indicated growing collaboration between European and Chinese firms. The project made quick progress, with Egypt Telecom concluding a landing agreement with PEACE in

May 2019.[135] In March 2020, a survey was conducted for a possible under-sea cable from Mombasa (Kenya) to Perseverance Beach (the Seychelles) as part of the PEACE cable network.[136] By the end of 2022, the PEACE cable network from Karachi (Pakistan) via Egypt to Marseille (France) was completed, and the connection to Kenya was also operationalised.[137] The PEACE submarine cable project is attempting to leverage the possible growth in the economies of African countries by creating the underlying infrastructure that will facilitate enhanced internet usage in the continent. In August 2024, the PEACE cable connecting Singapore and the Seychelles was activated.[138] All these imply that Karachi and Gwadar in Pakistan have emerged as important nodes in the undersea cable networks. However, the PEACE project has yet to significantly alter Pakistan's digital landscape.[139]

Interestingly, Gwadar was also a vital telegraph station on the Indo-European telegraph line of 1865.[140] From Gwadar, an undersea telegraph line was laid up to Bushehr in Iran, and then it moved north towards Tehran and connected Europe and London.[141] The line was opened in 1865, and the first message from London reached Calcutta in only 28 minutes.[142] In 1865, the location of the telegraph station on the Gwadar and Makran coasts led to a dispute regarding the ownership between Persia, the Khan of Kalat, and the Sultan of Muscat. The local communities that were based in and around the telegraph stations or lines did not see a radical improvement in their livelihoods. Similarly, a new fibre-optic cable is transiting through Pakistan today, and the benefit to the local communities is yet to become evident. In contemporary times, higher levels of technical know-how will be required to benefit from big data flowing through these cables.

It should be noted that a fibre-optic cable from Rawalpindi in Pakistan to Khunjerab in Xinjiang was operationalised in 2018.[143] The project was conceptualised in 2007, and approximately 820 kilometres of underground cable was laid.[144] The optic cable line travels further north and connects with Chinese optical fibre lines in Ürümqi in Xinjiang.[145] In 2023, news reports suggested that Chinese firms would be involved in laying the 16,000-km-long fibre-optic cables in Pakistan as a part of the effort to strengthen the digital infrastructure in the country.[146] In 2024, Pakistan Railways signed an agreement with a Chinese firm, providing the latter a right of way on its rail network.[147] In the past few years, China has acquired a robust presence in the operationalisation of Pakistan's internal and also external communication networks. As per the long-term plan for the CPEC, these cable lines will assist in increasing communication between the two countries, ensure reliable connectivity, improve internet penetration, reduce communication costs, and improve connectivity between Pakistan and the Central Asian states.[148]

Currently, Pakistan is connected with over a half-dozen cables, and the majority of the internet load is taken care of by India, the Middle East, Western Europe, and Southeast Asia-Middle East-Western Europe 4.[149] There was a concern among Pakistani military leadership that the many undersea cables in the vicinity were built by a consortium, which included Indian companies, either as partners or shareholders.[150] Therefore, from the perspective of Pakistan's security establishment, connecting with the world through Chinese networks, without the presence of Indian partners, is the most preferred option.

There are concerns that the national security requirements will undermine the rights of citizens in Pakistan. For instance, the Punjab Police Integrated Command, Control and Communication Center Lahore Safe City project was operationalised with Huawei's involvement in January 2018. The project envisaged the provision of "CCTV cameras across the whole city, E-challan and Red Light Monitoring System, and Automatic License Plate Recognition System."[151] There were apprehensions that the CCTV footage was used in a manner that violated the privacy of individuals.[152] There were also reports that a backdoor digital system was created to facilitate "unauthorised access to sensitive information from Lahore's safe-cities surveillance project."[153] However, in a couple of years, it was reported that half of the CCTV cameras were non-functional, as fund crunch impacted the operations.[154] In 2022, both countries launched the China-Pakistan Digital Corridor.[155] According to a Chinese news report, by the end of 2023, the usage of Chinese e-commerce platforms and business-to-business digital platforms also witnessed an increase.[156] In early 2024, both countries signed an agreement that would enable 'China to route its internet traffic through Pakistan'.[157] Given the operationalisation of the PEACE cable, the agreement constituted a logical next step. Overall, China has a significant presence in Pakistan's undersea cable, governmental, business, and other related digital infrastructures.

Further, Pakistan has a growing dependence on China's satellite systems. Pakistan, Thailand, Laos, and Brunei were among the first countries to sign an official cooperation agreement with China on the BeiDou Satellite (BDS) system.[158] According to Chinese reports, Beijing provided Pakistan with BDS infrastructure at subsidised rates.[159] More importantly, Pakistan was among the first to use the BDS system for military purposes. Reportedly, long-range precision weapons, including Shaheen and Hatf missile systems, have been equipped with the BDS navigation chips.[160] There is also considerable discussion as to whether the BDS system has ensured certainty of second-strike capabilities of Pakistan's nuclear weapons, as they are no longer dependent on the GPS.[161] Further, reports suggest that since "BDS-II covers all of India, it will enable Pakistan to achieve greater accuracy in counterforce targeting."[162]

In the coming years, the leverage that the US may have on Pakistan is bound to get further diluted because of various initiatives, such as Pakistan's deployment of the BDS system. The concern in Pakistan that the US could tamper with Pakistan's military GPS signals during a conflict with India was addressed with the BDS system.[163] It is evident that the digital and space silk roads are locking countries such as Pakistan in a tight embrace with China. So, the apparent innocuous economic activities have significant security and defence components. The distinction between civilian and defence technologies is getting erased rapidly. At the same time, Pakistan and China are concerned about providing security to the CPEC projects.

Securing the CPEC

Since its inception, despite strong support from the Pakistan army, providing security to the CPEC projects has often proved to be a difficult enterprise. There have been growing threats to the CPEC projects from various quarters. Pakistani security forces, Chinese personnel, and others have been targeted in the past few years. While in 2015, approximately 25 personnel working on the CPEC were killed, by September 2016, the number increased to 44 deaths and 100 wounded personnel.[164] In May 2016, a Chinese engineer was injured in a bombing in Karachi,[165] and a few months later, two Chinese were killed in Balochistan province.[166] Chinese personnel working at the local language centre in Quetta were abducted in May 2017.[167] All these developments prompted Beijing to scale up and alter its engagement pattern with Pakistan. *The Financial Times*, in February 2018, reported that the Chinese have been "quietly holding talks with Pakistani tribal separatists (Baloch) for more than five years", and the Pakistani officials reportedly welcomed these talks.[168] These talks reportedly aimed to protect Chinese investments in Gwadar and Balochistan. These talks seem to have had little impact, as a few months later, in November 2018, Baloch Liberation Army (BLA) members attacked a Chinese consulate in Karachi.[169] While the attack failed to breach the outer perimeter of the Chinese consulate, it indicated growing boldness in targeting the Chinese in Pakistan. Subsequently, in April 2019, a convoy of 22 vehicles, with some Chinese engineers working on the CPEC projects, was targeted by the BLA with a remote-controlled bomb.[170] A month later, Balochi insurgents targeted the heavily-guarded luxury hotel, Pearl Continental, close to the Gwadar port, which foreign businesspersons, including Chinese, often used.[171] Responding to the attacks, in a Twitter message, the Chinese Embassy noted: "The heroic action of Pakistani Army & law enforcement agencies is highly appreciated ... we express condolences to the families of the security guard who sacrificed his life & two security men who were injured."[172]

In the first few months of 2020, Balochistan insurgents reportedly carried out over "10 attacks, and in 6 of them, they have targeted Pakistani security personnel."[173] In a significant escalation, in June 2020, the BLA attacked the Pakistan Stock Exchange Building in Karachi, resulting in five security personnels' death.[174] As noted earlier, the Chinese had acquired stakes in the stock exchange in Karachi. In July 2021, an attack on a bus at the Dasu Hydro Power Project resulted in the death of 13 people, which included nine Chinese nationals, and injury to 28 others.[175] There was considerable consternation in Beijing with the developments, and Chinese officials joined the investigation process.[176] Subsequently, a Pakistani special Anti-Terrorism Court convicted two people for the terrorist attack.[177] Pakistan reportedly paid USD 11.6 million to the Chinese nationals injured in the attack and to the families of the deceased Chinese.[178] As Krzysztof Iwanek noted, while Pakistan had no legal or financial obligation to pay the compensations, its willingness to do so reflected "the depth of Chinese aggrievement on this occasion."[179] In early 2022, there was a spike in attacks by various insurgent groups. In January 2022, Lahore's Anarkali market witnessed a bomb blast, and there were similar strikes in the Balochistan province.[180] In April 2022, a suicide bomber killed approximately three Chinese nationals and injured another.[181] The BLA claimed responsibility for the attack. The brazen attack in a commercial city in Pakistan demonstrated the volatile security environment in the country. Subsequently, Chinese officials visited Pakistan and stayed back for over two months to assist local security agencies in the investigation process.[182] The fact that the Chinese officials stayed back for a prolonged period indicates Beijing's willingness to deploy a hands-on approach to security incidents. A month later, Pakistani authorities claimed that they had arrested a suicide bomber who was about to target Chinese personnel.[183] In August 2023, the BLA reportedly attacked a convoy carrying Chinese workers, and in the skirmish, two attackers were killed.[184] In November 2023, approximately 14 Pakistani soldiers were killed in an insurgent attack in Gwadar district.[185] In early 2024, two security guards were injured when a bomb went off in Gwadar.[186] In March 2024, in a BLA attack on the Gwadar Port Authority Complex, approximately five security personnel and eight attackers were killed.[187] About a week later, an attack on a convoy resulted in the death of five Chinese nationals in Khyber Pakhtunkhwa.[188]

While the above attacks constitute an example of a few violent incidents, there were many other instances in which personnel working on various CPEC projects were targeted.[189] To meet the security threats pertaining to the CPEC, "a Special Security Division (SSD) comprising 9,000 Pakistan Army soldiers and 6,000 para-military forces personnel" was constituted in 2016.[190] In 2016, the Pakistan Navy constituted Task Force 88 (TF-88), consisting of ships, drones, and other assets to protect the Gwadar port.[191] There were news reports which speculated that the Chinese warships would also contribute to the security of the Gwadar port.[192] In 2018, Pakistan purchased two additional warships with state-of-the-art guns to secure the Gwadar port.[193] With increased attacks in 2019, the Pakistan Army indicated that it would raise another division-size special force to ensure security for the CPEC projects and their personnel.[194] The SSD is tasked with providing protection within and around CPEC projects up to a radius of 5 kilometres.[195] In 2020, there were news reports that a high-security compound was emerging in Gwadar, reportedly aimed at creating a "dual-use economic and military base."[196] By 2024, the construction of the security compound was completed, prompting protests from local fishermen that they may lose access to the sea.[197]

The security incidents prompted Chinese President Xi Jinping to express deep concern and call on visiting Pakistan Prime Minister Shehbaz Sharif to ensure a "reliable and safe environment" for Chinese personnel and organisations working on the CPEC projects.[198] A *Hindustan Times* report in 2023 stated that Chinese officials emphasised the importance of protecting China's personnel and its projects to Pakistan's military leadership.[199] With the deteriorating security situation, there was a greater emphasis on security for Chinese nationals. Efforts were made to ensure that Chinese nationals working on CPEC projects travel in bulletproof vehicles.[200] The advent of the

COVID-19 crisis also increased the challenges for the security of the projects and the personnel working on them. The official communication among the police forces in Punjab suggested that over 10,000 personnel were deployed to provide security to 4,000 Chinese experts.[201] All these developments imply that Pakistan was bearing considerable expenditure in providing security for the CPEC projects. Pakistan will also have to walk a diplomatic tightrope in its response to the developments in Balochistan. While some news reports have indicated that Islamabad "may approach UN Security Council's 1267 Al-Qaeda, Taliban and affiliates committee to brand the BLA a global terrorist organisation", there were concerns within Pakistan if such a diplomatic move would bring greater international attention to the ongoing violence in Balochistan and other parts of the country.[202]

Many members of the Baloch ethnic community opine that the resources of their province are being exploited without any benefit to the local community.[203] They are also deeply concerned that the CPEC projects will fundamentally alter the region's demography to their disadvantage. As Christine Fair notes, "before the expansion of Gwadar, the population of the area was 70,000 ... if the project comes to full fruition, the population would be closer to 2 million—most of whom would be non-Baloch."[204] However, at the moment, these attacks have not deterred the Chinese from investing in the Gwadar port. If the Gwadar port picks up momentum and companies from various countries invest in the port and adjoining areas, there will be a quick change in the city's demographic profile and impact on local livelihoods. There were also concerns that port development activities, such as the construction of perimeter walls, may undermine locals' access to the port. Between 2021-2024 there were massive protests in Gwadar, demanding basic amenities, educational facilities, improved healthcare infrastructure, removal of checkpoints, better employment opportunities for locals, and a ban on Chinese fishing trawlers operating in the region. The protests suggested a lack of confidence in locals that they would benefit from the CPEC projects.[205]

Over the years, there were concerns in India's strategic community that Gwadar's emergence as a naval base for China would alter the security environment in the Arabian Sea and the Gulf of Oman. For instance, Gurmeet Kanwal noted that the conversion of Gwadar port into a naval base implies that India will have to contend with a two-front war and the "Indian Navy would have to contend with a formidable maritime force" and India's trade and energy supplies from the Gulf "will become highly vulnerable to interception."[206] There is a growing presence of Chinese naval vessels in Pakistan's waters, and the maritime cooperation between the two countries is also consolidating. In November 2023, both countries conducted their largest-ever Sea Guardian naval exercises in the northern Arabian Sea, which witnessed the participation of varied Chinese naval platforms.[207]

Conclusion: Economic Crisis and Geopolitical Consequences

In addition to the projects discussed in the preceding sections, several other projects are being operationalised under the CPEC framework. For instance, almost three dozen special economic zones were shortlisted under the CPEC framework.[208] The list of SEZs was subsequently pruned to nine priority projects, which include Moqpondass SEZ in the Gilgit-Baltistan region.[209] There is an opinion in Pakistan that SEZs need to have a more integrated approach involving connectivity and housing and a cluster-based skill-development approach.[210] There is anticipation that implementing the CPEC may enhance agricultural exports with the operationalisation of cold chains and improved supply networks.[211] In the realm of connectivity, a few important railway lines were planned under the CPEC, such as the Karachi-Peshawar railway line. The successful implementation of the railway line would be contingent on the overall security in the region. There were concerns about cost overruns, and Pakistan's Railways Minister, in 2018, suggested reducing the Chinese loans for railway projects from USD 8.2 billion to USD 6.2 billion.[212] Six years later, after much deliberation, the Karachi-Peshawar railway line was deferred as the attempts to 'reduce the cost has made the project unviable'.[213] Similarly, the New Gwadar International Airport, which was reportedly financed by China, is yet to receive significant passengers, and an international news agency observed that "with no passengers and no planes, Pakistan's newest and most expensive airport is a bit of a mystery."[214]

As part of upgrading the urban infrastructure, in 2020, the metro rail in Lahore was operationalised.[215] The metro rail project was initiated under the rubric of the CPEC with a USD 1.6bn loan from China's Exim Bank. Not all projects proposed by various governments are receiving favourable consideration under the CPEC. Karachi Circular Railway, which operated between 1969 and 1999, was incorporated into the CPEC in 2016, yet the anticipated funding did not come through.[216] Towards the end of 2023, there were reports that the China Railway Construction Corporation may build the circular railway project.[217] These initiatives demonstrate that there is considerable diversity in the projects that are being implemented under the rubric of the CPEC.

It has been approximately ten years since the CPEC was launched. In October 2023, Pakistan's caretaker Prime Minister, Anwar ul Haq Kakar, stated that over '50 projects worth $25 billion' were implemented under the CPEC in the past decade.[218] However, it is difficult to ascertain the expenditure incurred for the CPEC projects. The bilateral agreement between China and Pakistan pertaining to the CPEC was not released to the public. Further, there were allegations of a lack of transparency in awarding CPEC contracts and undue concessions to Chinese firms. Consequently, evaluating the CPEC must contend with opacity in the decision-making. Nonetheless, it is possible to deduce broad consequences from implementing the projects under the CPEC.

There was an anticipation in some quarters that the CPEC would bring about a quick improvement in the fortunes of Pakistan's economy. The experience of the past decade belied such expectations. It is essential to recognise that infrastructure investment alone will not immediately result in spectacular economic development. Instead, infrastructure development is a critical variable that needs to be supplemented with other economic interventions. A report by the Asian Development Bank noted that "the CPEC alone will not bring optimal results" and went on to add that "Pakistan needs to increase its tax base."[219] Similarly, a Chinese scholar noted: "Energy and infrastructure investment can indeed boost a country's GDP growth and provide the necessary basic conditions for economic development, but it is not economic development itself. The long-term improvement of Pakistan's national economy depends on whether Pakistan itself can correctly analyse the situation, formulate a sustainable economic plan that is in line with the advantages of domestic resource elements, and continue to promote it effectively."[220] The Pakistani state has not radically changed its economic and public policy frameworks over the past decade. Consequently, mega infrastructure projects were operationalised without appropriate attendant policies to enhance the country's human development index.

Pakistan's hopes of emerging as a major economy with Chinese-backed infrastructure projects are yet to materialise. Instead, Pakistan plunged into an economic crisis. While there was considerable talk about the BRI and its benefits, the Pakistani leadership did not give adequate attention to the country's economic management. Further, a spike in global oil prices and floods in 2022 exacerbated the economic crisis in Pakistan. It is estimated that the floods in Pakistan have affected over 33 million people and have resulted in 1600 fatalities, with the total economic loss estimated at around USD 40 billion.[221] Pakistan experienced severe inflation of around 30 per cent in 2022 and in the first half of 2023.[222] The rise in fuel prices also contributed to increased input costs for various agricultural commodities. The high inflation due to the agricultural crisis triggered a food crisis in the country. The World Food Programme (WFP) designated Pakistan as a 'hunger hotspot of very high concern'.[223] At the various free food distribution centres in the country, there were instances of stampedes resulting in fatalities.[224]

In addition to the food crisis, Pakistan experienced a severe Balance of Payments (BOP) crisis in 2022-2023. In February 2023, Pakistan's foreign exchange reserves tumbled to USD 2.9 billion, and there were concerns about whether Pakistan could pay for energy imports.[225] Pakistan often imports more than it exports, and consequently, experiences a BOP crisis. The enhanced economic engagement with China did not alter Pakistan's trade patterns. The BOP crisis also creates conditions under which Pakistan finds it difficult to service its international debt. A few years before Pakistan's economic crisis grew in intensity, Sushant Sareen referred to Pakistan's growing debt challenge. Sushant Sareen pointed out that even the senior leadership in Pakistan is not exactly certain as to how much money is flowing into the country under the CPEC and the scale of the debt.[226] According to a report from the United States Institute of Peace (USIP), authored by Shahbaz Rana, as of December 2022, Pakistan's external debt and liabilities amounted to approximately USD 126.3 billion.[227] Pakistan's obligations to multilateral institutions have timelines of two or three decades and, therefore, do not constitute a short-term risk. However, the need to service short-term commercial and bilateral debts constitutes an important challenge for Pakistan. While Pakistan 'holds around USD 27 billion of Chinese debt', according to the USIP report, Pakistan will have to repay USD 77.5 billion (between 2023 and 2026) to various creditors, such as Chinese financial institutions, private creditors, and other countries such as Saudi Arabia.[228] Given the scale of debt obligations, there were concerns that Pakistan may default on debt payments. With a Pakistan facing a severe balance of payments crisis, China reportedly rolled over a USD 2 billion loan in March 2023.[229] However, in June 2023, Pakistan's "total debt has increased 34.1 per cent year-on-year."[230]

As the economic crisis deepened, Pakistan desperately awaited an IMF bailout package. After intense negotiations, on June 29, 2023, the IMF extended a USD 3 billion loan as "a nine-month Stand-by Arrangement " to Pakistan.[231] Thus far, Pakistan has received about 24 bailout packages, which attest to persistent economic mismanagement. A few weeks later, Saudi Arabia extended a loan of USD 2 billion.[232] The IMF bailout and the loan from Saudi Arabia gave room for manoeuvre, and Pakistan did not default on its loans. However, there are concerns that Pakistan has slipped into circular debt. Pakistan has been unable to pull itself out of low economic performance. Episodes of foreign exchange crises and less than satisfactory economic growth seem to be a persistent feature of Pakistan's economy. Islamabad often reaches out to other countries such as China and the Middle Eastern countries and multilateral frameworks to overcome the immediate economic crisis. These loans are more like steroidal injections to revive an intensive care unit patient.

In order to get away from circular debt, Pakistan has made efforts to increase FDI inflows into the country. In an effort to attract Chinese investments, Pakistan appointed investment counsellors in China.[233] There were reports which suggested that Chinese firms could be keen on relocating some of their textile industries to Pakistan.[234] Pakistan is one of the leading cotton producers, and it is possible to encourage the textile industry. However, thus far, the plans to foster the textile industry have not materialised as other countries, such as Cambodia, Vietnam, and other Southeast Asian countries, have stronger supply chain networks with China. Countries such as Cambodia and Laos enjoy preferential tariff rates in developed economies because of their Least Developed Country (LDC) status. Therefore, it is not surprising that countries such as Cambodia received more FDI than Pakistan in 2023.[235] A critical reason for the very hesitant FDI inflows was the unstable political situation in Pakistan. Pakistan still has a long way to go in terms of deep structural reforms that need to be ushered in political, social, and economic realms. Enhanced engagement with China cannot be a substitute for major reforms, without which Pakistan will struggle to emerge as a healthy economy.

At a time when considerable political and administrative reforms are needed, the CPEC is generating stress related to federalism and concerns that it is fostering regional inequalities in Pakistan. The creation of the National Coastal Development Authority for the Gwadar port prompted criticism that the limited provincial autonomy of Baluchistan is getting further eroded as the existing regional office is performing similar functions.[236] Similar concerns were expressed regarding the 'China-Pakistan Economic Corridor Authority'. In August 2022, Prime Minister Shehbaz Sharif had, in principle, suggested the 'abolition of the CPEC Authority subject to consent by China'.[237] A separate institutional framework, created through the CPEC Authority Act, was often criticised for stepping into the functional domain of the planning ministry and various line ministries. The proposal to abolish the CPEC Authority was perceived as an attempt to revert 'to the earlier arrangements of routing CPEC projects through concerned ministries'.[238] To ensure that local concerns are heard, Shi Zhiqin and Lu Yang, in their paper for Carnegie Endowment for International Peace, argued that there is a need for China to "abandon its traditional way of dealing only with the Pakistani government and instead get in contact with local communities to accommodate local interests better so that more Pakistani people can benefit from the CPEC."[239] They also stated the need for greater cultural understanding between Pakistan and China at individual and firm levels to successfully implement the CPEC.[240] However, international actors' direct interaction with sub-national units may generate anxiety in Islamabad.

The CPEC has ushered in a fundamental shift in Pakistan's foreign policy. From being an ally of the US, Pakistan is in a quasi-alliance with China. Islamabad's drift away from the US was long in the making. The end of the Cold War altered the geopolitical dynamics and reduced Pakistan's importance to the US. Post-9/11 attacks, Pakistan received renewed attention for the wrong reasons, such as its sympathy for some terrorist groups. Reportedly, after the 9/11 attacks, Richard L. Armitage, then Deputy Secretary of State of the US, told his Pakistani counterparts that they would be bombed to Stone Age if they failed to collaborate with the US in its fight against terrorism.[241] The fact that the US had to coerce Pakistan into accommodating its anti-terror objectives indicated that the congruence of interests between the two declined. While Pakistan collaborated with the US in the war against terror in Afghanistan, Washington long suspected that Islamabad continued to sympathise with the Taliban and other radical elements. The general view that the US did not inform Pakistan of its Operation Geronimo to eliminate Osama bin Laden demonstrated the trust deficit between the two countries. The US withdrawal from Afghanistan in August 2021 improved the Pakistan-US bilateral dynamic, and the Mid-

Level Defence Dialogue picked up momentum.[242] The US increased security cooperation and approved a USD 450 million upgrade for Pakistan's F-16 fighter aircraft in 2022.[243] However, the improved defence dialogue between Islamabad and Washington may not quickly undermine the Pakistan-China strategic partnership for two reasons. First, China has emerged as a principal supplier of weapons for Pakistan. A SIPRI report noted that "China accounted for 51 per cent of Pakistan's arms imports in 2010–14 and for 73 per cent in 2015–19…."[244] Between 2019 and 2023, China accounted for 82 per cent of Pakistan's arms imports.[245] Further, reports suggest that China is involved in developing Pakistan's long-range missile capabilities. In September 2024, the US imposed sanctions on Chinese institutions and companies for assisting Pakistan's ballistic missile programme.[246] Subsequently, the US also imposed sanctions on a few entities in Pakistan to contain the "proliferation threat of Pakistan's long-range missile development."[247] Second, there is an opinion in Pakistan that a close relationship with Washington often results in increased interference of the US in Pakistan's domestic politics. For instance, Imran Khan, in 2022, repeatedly asserted that the US was actively interfering in the domestic politics of Pakistan.[248]

In spite of working closely on regional security issues, Islamabad has not been able to leverage its relationship with the US for Pakistan's economic development. Some reports do suggest that Pakistan tried to procure American investments. For instance, Asif Ali Zardari called on the developed Western countries and the US to assist Pakistan "through massive economic assistance, energy development and greater market access."[249] Zardari's requests did not find a positive reception in Washington, DC. After a lukewarm response from the US, it is possible that Pakistan turned towards China. However, it would be erroneous to think that Pakistan's turn towards China was entirely because of the US neglect. On the contrary, Pakistan wanted large-scale foreign investments without reforming its politics and regional foreign policy posture. With its foreign policy focused on sustained hostility towards India, the security environment in and around Pakistan was always fragile. Additionally, there were always concerns regarding the presence of terrorist infrastructure in the country. Further, as noted above, Pakistan did not demonstrate any genuine inclination towards administrative reforms or decentralisation to improve service delivery. Further, the persistent sectarian violence and terrorism made Pakistan an unattractive destination for the US and other Western investments. Given the volatile security environment and a foreign policy posture that did not allow free trade across Pakistan, only a country motivated by broader geopolitical objectives would consider investing in such an environment. That country was China.

Interestingly, in its approach towards terrorism, unlike others, China's actions suggest that the Pakistani state and associated political apparatus have no role in fostering terrorism. Alternatively, it is possible that China may perceive that the Pakistani state apparatus is not completely innocent on the question of terrorism. Perhaps it is precisely for this reason that Beijing finds it essential to have the Pakistani political and military leadership favourably disposed towards China. Such a favourable disposition ensured Pakistan's silence on Beijing's alleged harsh measures on Muslim minorities living in the western provinces. In 2021, when questioned about the harsh Chinese policies towards the Uyghur Muslims, Pakistan PM Imran Khan stated, "whatever issues we have with the Chinese, we speak behind closed doors … China has been one of our greatest friends to us in our most difficult times."[250] As a country with the capability to export terror to other countries, Pakistan's silence on the Uyghur Muslims is a big gain for China.

The CPEC resulted in the consolidation of the China-Pakistan strategic partnership and greater coordination between the two countries on various international platforms. Because of the CPEC, Mao's vision of a 'window to the west' was operationalised as China could access the Arabian Sea with relatively greater ease than a few decades ago. In addition, many Chinese technicians are working in Pakistan, and reports suggest that some of them could be PLAPeople's Liberation Army (PLA) personnel.[251] There is a growing presence of Chinese vessels in Pakistan's waters in the Arabian Sea. Adversaries of Pakistan planning operations against it will have to factor in the presence of Chinese personnel and platforms in that country. The two countries' army, air force, and naval exercises have acquainted Pakistan with the latest defence technologies, and China has also benefitted by gaining a better understanding of Pakistan's knowledge of Indian defence forces.

In the long run, the CPEC is premised on the belief that enhanced prosperity in Pakistan will have a positive spillover on the overall security situation within the country and the region. For instance, the *Global Times* report notes, "if foreign investment can help reduce poverty and fight terrorism in South Asian countries, it will create a virtuous circle for the development of CPEC."[252] It was assumed that the positive dividends generated by the possible reduction of religious fundamentalism in Pakistan would also be reaped by China and Central Asian countries. As Wang Peng notes, in order to address the challenge of the "three forces of extremism, separatism and terrorism ... joint efforts made by China and Pakistan are not only conducive to maintaining the common security of the two countries but also beneficial for the stability of Central and South Asia."[253] However, the Pakistani government has failed to take adequate actions to dismantle terrorist infrastructure in the country. There is growing exasperation among the countries in the region with Pakistan's policies. In 2024, Iran carried out a missile and drone attack in the Balochistan province of Pakistan to contain the actions of terrorists.[254] According to Shreyas Deshmukh, Iranian attacks demonstrate that "the policies of Pakistan, including harbouring extremist elements, have led to its isolation in the region..."[255] Even the Taliban, which had close relations with Pakistan's security establishment, often criticises Islmabad's regional approach. The growing discord between Pakistan and its western neighbour, Afghanistan, will complicate China's regional connectivity plans.

Notes

1. "Deepening China-Pakistan Friendship and Sharing the Dream of Development," Ambassador Sun Weidong's Speech at National Defence University, *Embassy of the People's Republic of China in the Islamic Republic of Pakistan*, December 14, 2017, http://pk.chineseembassy.org/eng/zbgx/t1219944.htm
2. "Psalm 36: 6-8," *Bible Gateway*, https://www.biblegateway.com/passage/?search=Psalm%2036%3A6-8&version=ERV; also see "Psalm 36," *Bible Gateway*, https://www.biblegateway.com/passage/?search=Psalm%2036&version=NIV
3. Record of Conversation from Chairman Mao's Reception with Pakistani Minister of Commerce Wahid Zaman, Wilson Centre Digital Archive, July 16, 1964, https://digitalarchive.wilsoncenter.org/document/118005
4. Ibid.
5. "Cable from the Xinjiang Foreign Affairs Office to the Chinese Foreign Ministry, 'on the Pros And Cons' of Pakistan Establishing a Consulate in Xinjiang," *Wilson Centre Digital Archive,* October 29, 1955, https://digitalarchive.wilsoncenter.org/document/121722
6. "Abstract of Conversation: Premier Zhou Enlai and Pakistani Ambassador Sultanuddin Ahmad," *Wilson Centre Digital Archive,* January 4, 1956, https://digitalarchive.wilsoncenter.org/document/114840
7. "Cable From The Chinese Embassy In Pakistan, 'Pakistani President's Exclusive Conversation With American Reporters'," *Wilson Centre Digital Archive,* May 17, 1956, https://digitalarchive.wilsoncenter.org/document/114882
8. "Briefing on the Visit to China of Pakistani Prime Minister Suhrawardy (No. 3)," *Compiled by the Office of the State Guest Reception Committee*, Wilson Centre Digital Archive, October 19, 1956, https://digitalarchive.wilsoncenter.org/document/134786

9. Andrew Small, *The China Pakistan Axis: Asia's New Geopolitics*, (New York: Oxford University Press, 2015), p.21
10. "When Nehru rejected Pakistan's Offer of 'Joint Defence' pact against China," *The Week*, May 27, 2020, https://www.theweek.in/news/india/2020/05/27/when-nehru-rejected-pakistan-offer-of-joint-defence-pact-against-china.html
11. "Bi-Weekly Propaganda Guidance Number 23, September 28, 1959," *General CIA Records*, April 23, 1998, https://www.cia.gov/library/readingroom/docs/CIA-RDP78-03061A000100010011-9.pdf
12. Ibid.
13. Madhavan K. Palat, *Selected works of Jawaharlal Nehru, Second Series, Volume Sixty (15 April - 31 May 1960)*, (New Delhi: Jawaharlal Nehru Memorial Fund, 2015), p. 493.
14. "Q.*339 Trans-Karakoram Pass," *Ministry of External Affairs*, Government of India, December 14, 2006, https://www.mea.gov.in/rajya-sabha.htm?dtl/8120/q+339+transkarakoram+pass
15. Zahra Khan Durrani, "Pak-China Trade: Free Trade Agreements," *The Centre for Strategic and Contemporary Research*, September 6, 2018, https://cscr.pk/explore/themes/trade-economics/pak-china-trade-trade-free-trade-agreements/
16. W. M. Dobell, "Ramifications of the China-Pakistan Border Treaty," *Pacific Affairs*, Vol. 37, No. 3 (Autumn, 1964), p. 291.
17. Ibid.
18. Ishfaq Ilahi Chowdhury, "Indo-Pak War 1965: Looking Back 50 Years," *The Daily Star*, September 22, 2015, https://www.thedailystar.net/op-ed/politics/indo-pak-war-1965-146932
19. Wang Ying, 毛泽东与 "中巴全天候友谊"：生前最后一次会见外宾仍不忘询问巴方情况, *People's Daily Online*, August 28, 2017, http://history.people.com.cn/n1/2017/0828/c372327-29499629.html
20. Ibid.
21. "中国与巴基斯坦高层交往的5则小故事", *people.cn*, April 17, 2015, http://politics.people.com.cn/n/2015/0417/c1001-26863311.html
22. 毛主席一生中9个最后一次！看完泪崩, *China Daily*, August 3, 2016, http://www.chinadaily.com.cn/interface/toutiaonew/53002523/2016-08-03/cd_26332818.html
23. "喀喇昆仑公路四十周年特别报道之一：听中巴亲历者讲述四十年前那段感人的筑路历史," *Shanghai Observer*, November 21, 2019, https://www.jfdaily.com/news/detail?id=190038
24. "喀喇昆仑公路—世界上海拔最高的国际公路," *Sina.com*, October 10, 2017, http://blog.sina.com.cn/s/blog_5408ee850102zjdc.html
25. "喀喇昆仑公路四十周年特别报道之一：听中巴亲历者讲述四十年前那段感人的筑路历史," *Shanghai Observer*, November 21, 2019, https://www.jfdaily.com/news/detail?id=190038
26. Seymour Topping, "Karakoram," *The New York Times*, December 2, 1979, p: SM 1
27. Ibid.
28. "喀喇昆仑公路—世界上海拔最高的国际公路," *Sina.com*, October 10, 2017, http://blog.sina.com.cn/s/blog_5408ee850102zjdc.html
29. Jack Anderson and Dale Van Atta, "Afghan Rebel Aid Enriches Generals," *The Washington Post*, May 8, 1987, https://www.washingtonpost.com/archive/

local/1987/05/08/afghan-rebel-aid-enriches-generals/40243b90-55d4-421b-80b7-929c3e4b1075/

30. "The Wakhan Corridor: An Unlikely Afghan-China Link," *National Foreign Assessment Centre*, Central Intelligence Agency, May 1, 1980.
31. Drew Middleton, "Russians in Afghanistan: Forward Base For Region?; Military Analysis," *The New York Times*, July 3, 1982, p. 2.
32. Ziad Haider, "Clearing Clouds Over the Karakoram Pass," *Yale Global Online*, March 29, 2004, https://yaleglobal.yale.edu/content/clearing-clouds-over-karakoram-pass
33. Alice Albinia, "The road between China and Pakistan," *The Financial Times*, July 4, 2009, https://www.ft.com/content/76d57272-6764-11de-925f-00144feabdc0
34 Senge H. Sering, "Expansion of the Karakoram Corridor: Implications and Prospects," *IDSA Occasional Paper No. 27*, September 2012, https://idsa.in/occasionalpapers/ExpansionoftheKarakoramCorridor
35. Munir Akram, "Window to the West," *Dawn*, January 21, 2018, https://www.dawn.com/news/1384310/window-to-the-west
36. Sandhya Jain, "Pakistan, via Ladakh," *The Pioneer*, July 21, 2020, https://www.dailypioneer.com/2020/columnists/pakistan--via-ladakh.html
37. 王鹏Wang Peng, "中巴走廊：何以成为引领"一带一路"的旗舰？," *China Net*, May 11, 2015, http://www.china.com.cn/opinion/think/2015-05/11/content_35539228.htm
38. Ibid.
39. "Li Keqiang urges development of 'China Pakistan economic corridor'," *South China Morning Post*, May 23, 2013, https://www.scmp.com/news/china/article/1244267/li-keqiang-urges-development-china-pakistan-economic-corridor
40. "李克强访巴基斯坦：打造经济走廊寻求双赢合作," *China News Network*, May 24, 2013, http://www.chinanews.com/gn/2013/05-24/4853223.html
41. "Common Vision for Deepening China-Pakistan Strategic Cooperative Partnership in the New Era," *Ministry of Foreign Affairs*, The People's Republic of China, July 5, 2013, https://www.fmprc.gov.cn/eng/wjdt_665385/2649_665393/201307/t20130708_679350.html
42. "中巴经济走廊联委会召开首次会议 [The China-Pakistan Economic Corridor Board held its first meeting]," *Economic and Commercial Office of the Embassy of the People's Republic of China in the Islamic Republic of Pakistan*, Ministry of Commerce of the People's Republic of China, August 29, 2013, http://pk.mofcom.gov.cn/article/jmxw/201308/20130800273313.shtml ;
43. "中巴经济走廊远景规划联合合作委员会第二次会议在京召开 (The second meeting of the Joint Cooperation Committee on Vision of the China-Pakistan Economic Corridor)," *National Development and Reform Commission of the People's Republic of China*, February 19, 2014, http://xwzx.ndrc.gov.cn/xwfb/201402/t20140219_579529.html
44. "Third meeting of JCC on China-Pakistan Economic Corridor held," *The News International*, August 28, 2014, https://www.thenews.com.pk/archive/print/640076-third-meeting-of-jcc-on-china-pakistan-economic-corridor-held

45. "China Commits $45.6 Billion for Economic Corridor with Pakistan," *The Express Tribune*, November 21, 2014, https://tribune.com.pk/story/794883/china-commits-45-6-billion-for-economic-corridor-with-pakistan
46. "Pakistan will help China in fight against Xinjiang militants: Sharif," *South China Morning Post*, November 8, 2014, https://www.scmp.com/news/china/article/1635051/china-says-pakistan-will-help-fight-against-xinjiang-militants
47. "President Xi's Article Published on Pakistani Paper," *China Daily*, April 19, 2015, https://www.chinadaily.com.cn/world/2015xivisitpse/2015-04/19/content_20474266.htm
48. "Pakistan was with us when China stood isolated: Xi Jinping," *The Dawn*, April 21, 2015, https://www.dawn.com/news/1177304/pakistan-was-with-us-when-china-stood-isolated-xi-jinping
49. "Winners of Five Principles of Peaceful Coexistence Friendship Award praise Sino-Pakistani friendship," *People's Daily*, April 30, 2015, http://en.people.cn/n/2015/0430/c98649-8886110.html
50. "Details of Agreements Signed During Xi's visit to Pakistan," *The Dawn*, April 20, 2015, https://www.dawn.com/news/1177129
51. "China, Pakistan ink CPEC, 50 Other Deals on Xi Jinping's Historic Visit," *The Economic Times*, April 20, 2015, http://articles.economictimes.indiatimes.com/2015-04-20/news/61339512_1_china-pakistan-economic-corridor-president-xi-jinping-pok
52. "President Xi's Article Published on Pakistani Paper," *China Daily*, April 19, 2015, https://www.chinadaily.com.cn/world/2015xivisitpse/2015-04/19/content_20474266.htm
53. Daniel S. Markey and James West, "Behind China's Gambit in Pakistan," Council on Foreign Relations, May 12, 2016, https://www.cfr.org/expert-brief/behind-chinas-gambit-pakistan; also see "Ahsan reveals three routes of corridor," *Dawn*, May 15, 2015, https://www.dawn.com/news/1182074/ahsan-reveals-three-routes-of-corridor
54. "China Commits $45.6 Billion for Economic Corridor with Pakistan," *Reuters*, November 21, 2014, http://www.reuters.com/article/2014/11/21/us-pakistan-china-idUSKCN0J51C120141121
55. Aoun Sahi, "The Route Row: Pak-China Economic Corridor," *The News on Sunday*, May 24, 2015, http://tns.thenews.com.pk/the-china-pakistan-economic-route-row/#.VliWNXYrLIV
56. "Economic corridor: Pakistan, China to step up work on framework accord," *The Tribune*, March 13, 2015, http://tribune.com.pk/story/852339/economic-corridor-pakistan-china-to-step-up-work-on-framework-accord/
57. Nasir Jamal, "The cost of CPEC," *The Dawn*, June 21, 2017, https://www.dawn.com/news/1320028/the-cost-of-cpec
58. "Original CPEC Route be Revived, Demands APC," *The News International*, August May 17, 2015, https://www.thenews.com.pk/print/12506-original-cpec-route-be-revived-demands-apc
59. Irfan Haider, "Parties Pledged to take Full Political Ownership of CPEC," *The Dawn*, May 28, 2015, https://www.dawn.com/news/1184733

60. Syed Ali Shah, "Nawaz Inaugurates Gwadar-Hoshab (M-8) portion of the CPEC," *The Dawn,* February 3, 2016, https://www.dawn.com/news/1237192
61. Shabbir Mir, "First Chinese Shipment Rolls into Sost Dry Port in Gilgit Baltistan," *The Express Tribune*, November 1, 2016, https://tribune.com.pk/story/1216912/first-chinese-shipment-rolls-sost-dry-port-g-b
62. "CPEC's Concept of 'One Corridor with Multiple Passages' Realized: Chinese Envoy," *China Daily*, November 14, 2016, http://www.chinadaily.com.cn/world/2016-11/14/content_27367389.htm
63 "让美国人闹吧，中国人静悄悄打通了印度洋出海口," *Sina.com*, November 14, 2016, http://finance.sina.com.cn/roll/2016-11-14/doc-ifxxsmuu5622822.shtml
64. Mehtab Haider, "CPEC soars to Rs5,700 bn," *The News International*, December 30, 2016, https://www.thenews.com.pk/print/175541-CPEC-soars-to-Rs5700-bn
65. "Chinese consortium takes 40 per cent stake in Pakistan's stock exchange," *The Times of India*, January 3, 2017, https://timesofindia.indiatimes.com/world/china/chinese-consortium-takes-40-per-cent-stake-in-pakistans-stock-exchange/articleshowprint/56318175.cms
66. "Consortium of Chinese companies buys stake in Pak bourse," *M&A Critique*, January, 2017, https://mnacritique.mergersindia.com/news/consortium-of-chinese-companies-buys-stake-in-pak-bourse/
67. Dilawar Hussain, "PSX sales 40% stake to Chinese consortium," *Dawn*, August 31, 2020, https://www.dawn.com/news/1304006
68. "巴基斯坦证券交易所股权收购协议签署仪式在卡拉奇举行 [The signing ceremony of the Pakistan Stock Exchange Equity Acquisition Agreement was held in Karachi]," *People's Daily*, January 21, 2017, http://world.people.com.cn/n1/2017/0121/c1002-29039683.html
69. Liang Haiming, "中资收购巴基斯坦交易所的玄机," *finance.sina.com*, December 29, 2016, http://finance.sina.com.cn/zl/china/2016-12-29/zl-ifxzczfc6584583.shtml
70. "Xi elaborates on inspiration behind Belt and Road Initiative," *Xinhua*, May 15, 2015, http://www.xinhuanet.com//english/2017-05/15/c_136285408.htm
71. Kay Johnson, "Pakistan signs nearly $500 million in China deals at Silk Road summit," *Reuters*, May 13, 2017, https://www.reuters.com/article/us-china-silkroad-pakistan/pakistan-signs-nearly-500-million-in-china-deals-at-silk-road-summit-idUSKBN1890KD
72. Atul Aneja, "Nawaz Sharif signals for dialogue with India at BRF summit," *The Hindu*, May 14, 2017, https://www.thehindu.com/news/international/cpec-should-not-be-politicised-says-sharif/article18451116.ece
73. "Prime Minister Nawaz Sharif addresses the Belt and Road Forum in Beijing," *Pakistan-China Institute,* May 15, 2017, http://www.pakistan china.com/mn-news-detail.php?id=NTY5&pageid=news
74. Asia Maqsood, "Takeaways from the 7th JCC meeting on CPEC," *Daily Times*, December 18, 2017, https://dailytimes.com.pk/161894/takeaways-7th-jcc-meeting-cpec/
75. Liu Zhen, "China and Pakistan agree to push forward economic corridor plan after dam deal scrapped," *South China Morning Post*, November 21. 2017, https://www.

scmp.com/news/china/diplomacy-defence/article/2120944/china-and-pakistan-agree-push-forward-economic-corridor

76. Shahbaz Rana, "Sheer size of CPEC portfolio appals IMF," *The Express Tribune*, December 7, 2017, https://tribune.com.pk/story/1578030/1-sheer-size-cpec-portfolio-appals-imf
77. Saeed Shah and Bill Spindle, "U.S. Seeks to Avoid a Pakistan Bailout That Would Repay China," *The Wall Street Journal*, July 31, 2018, https://www.wsj.com/articles/u-s-seeks-to-avoid-a-pakistan-bailout-that-would-repay-china-1533056638
78. Drazen Jorgic, "Pakistan dismisses U.S. concerns about IMF bailout and China," *Reuters*, August 1, 2018, https://www.reuters.com/article/us-pakistan-usa-china/pakistan-dismisses-u-s-concerns-about-imf-bailout-and-china-idUSKBN1KM4BR
79. David Lawder and Yawen Chen, "IMF Says Not Yet Approached by Pakistan for Financial Assistance," *Reuters*, October 9, 2018, https://in.reuters.com/article/us-imf-worldbank-pakistan/imf-says-not-yet-approached-by-pakistan-for-financial-assistance-idINKCN1MJ0AD
80. Dipanjan Roy Chaudhury, "Pakistan to share CPEC debt details with IMF," *Economic Times*, October 16, 2018, https://economictimes.indiatimes.com/news/international/world-news/pakistan-to-share-cpec-debt-details-with-imf/articleshow/66230479.cms
81. Sanaullah Khan, "Saudi Arabia agrees to provide Pakistan $3 billion to address balance-of-payments crisis," *Dawn*, October 25, 2018, https://www.dawn.com/news/1440860/saudi-arabia-agrees-to-provide-pakistan-3-billion-to-address-balance-of-payments-crisis
82. For example, see: "Aramco's $10b refinery project proposed to be included in CPEC," *Profit*, February 16, 2024, https://profit.pakistantoday.com.pk/2024/02/16/saudi-aramcos-10b-refinery-project-is-proposed-for-cpec-inclusion/ ; Matt Harris, "CPEC's Second Phase: A Path To Prosperity And Growth," *CPIC*, April 19, 2024, https://www.cpicglobal.com/cpecs-second-phase-a-path-to-prosperity-and-growth/
83. "Xi Jinping Meets with Pakistan's Prime Minister Muhammad Shehbaz Sharif," *Embassy of the People's Republic of China in the United States of America*, June 7, 2024, http://us.china-embassy.gov.cn/eng/zgyw/202406/t20240611_11424755.htm
84. DP Srivastava, "Sharif in Beijing: In step with China's power game," *The Hindustan Times*, June 10, 2024, https://www.hindustantimes.com/opinion/sharif-in-beijing-in-step-with-china-s-power-game-101718029196404.html
85. "China's Li Qiang vows 'upgraded' Pakistan economic corridor on first visit to Islamabad," *The South China Morning Post*, October 15, 2024, https://www.scmp.com/news/china/diplomacy/article/3282458/chinas-li-qiang-vows-upgraded-pakistan-economic-corridor-first-visit-islamabad
86. Ahmad Ahmadani, "Cabinet approves sale of 15% stake in Reko Diq to Saudi Arabia," *Profit*, December 30, 2024, https://profit.pakistantoday.com.pk/2024/12/30/cabinet-approves-sale-of-15-stake-in-reko-diq-to-saudi-arabia-for-540-million/
87. "China, Pakistan ink CPEC, 50 Other Deals on Xi Jinping's Historic Visit," *The Economic Times*, April 20, 2015, http://articles.economictimes.indiatimes.com/2015-

04-20/news/61339512_1_china-pakistan-economic-corridor-president-xi-jinping-pok

88. Mei Xinyu, "瓜达尔港中巴油气管线可行吗？ (Is the China-Pakistan oil and gas pipeline feasible at The Port of Gwadar?)," *Zhihu.com*, January 15, 2007, https://www.zhihu.com/question/54795199; http://magazine.caijing.com.cn/20161220/4214477.shtml
89. Ibid.
90. "Daewoo Gas signs contract with Chinese company in offshore LNG terminal," *China-Pakistan Economic Corridor*, April 25, 2022, https://cpecinfo.com/daewoo-gas-signs-contract-with-chinese-company-in-offshore-lng-terminal/
91. Zafar Bhutta, "Pakistan invites China, Europe to set up LNG plants," *The Express Tribune,* June 22, 2023, https://tribune.com.pk/story/2422950/pakistan-invites-china-europe-to-set-up-lng-plants
92. "Eastern Route for CPEC May Foster Enmity Between Provinces, warns Imran," *The Express Tribune*, September 30, 2015, http://tribune.com.pk/story/965041/eastern-route-for-cpec-may-foster-enmity-between-provinces-warns-imran/
93. Zulfiqar Ali, "Khattak Threatens 'Extreme Step' over CPEC Project," *The Dawn*, January 01, 2016, http://www.dawn.com/news/1230034
94. "Western Passage of CPEC to be Completed by 2018: PM," *The Express Tribune*, January 16, 2016, http://tribune.com.pk/story/1028326/economic-corridor-pm-sets-2018-deadline-for-western-passage/
95. "CPEC western route to usher in new era of development in Pakistan: PM," *Global Times,* April 29, 2021, https://www.globaltimes.cn/page/202104/1222439.shtml
96. "CPEC western alignment to be completed in 3 years," *Daily Times,* January 26, 2022, https://dailytimes.com.pk/874784/cpec-western-alignment-to-be-completed-in-3-years/
97. Ibid.
98. "Gross Domestic Product 2023," *The World Bank,* July 01, 2024, https://datacatalogfiles.worldbank.org/ddh-published/0038130/DR0046441/GDP.pdf?versionId=2024-07-01T12:42:23.8710032Z
99. Shahid Shah, "Losses prompt Pakistan, China to Revisit FTA," *The News,* September 3, 2015, http://www.thenews.com.pk/print/60093-losses-prompt-pakistan-china-to-revisit-fta
100. Ibid.
101. "Protocol To Amend The Free Trade Agreement Between The Government Of The People's Republic Of China And The Government Of The Islamic Republic Of Pakistan." *Ministry of Commerce, Government of Pakistan,* http://www.commerce.gov.pk/protocol-on-phase-ii-china-pakistan-fta/
102. Khalid Mustafa, "Pak-China FTA-2 to be effective from Jan 1, 2020," *The New International,* December 3, 2019, https://www.thenews.com.pk/print/577808-pak-china-fta-2-to-be-effective-from-jan-1-2020
103. "Pakistan, China may Renegotiate FTA Benefits," *The Express Tribune*, March 10, 2022, https://tribune.com.pk/story/2347206/pakistan-china-may-renegotiate-fta-benefits
104. "Pakistan, China ink framework agreement on industrial cooperation under CPEC," *Dawn,* February 4, 2022, https://www.dawn.com/news/1673244

105. "Pakistan Economic Survey 2023-2024," *Economic Adviser's Wing, Finance Division*, Government of Pakistan, https://finance.gov.pk/survey/chapter_24/Economic_Survey_2023_24.pdf
106. "Trade in Goods with Pakistan," *United States Census Bureau,* December 2024, https://www.census.gov/foreign-trade/balance/c5350.html
107. Ibid.
108. "Pakistan," *Office of the United States Trade Representative*, October 2, 2020 https://ustr.gov/countries-regions/south-central-asia/pakistan#:~:text=U.S.%20%2D%20Pakistan%20Trade%20Facts&text=Goods%20exports%20totaled%20%242.6%20billion%3B%20goods%20imports%20totaled%20%243.9%20billion.
109. "Energy Crisis Deepens as Electricity Shortfall Exceeds 7,000MW," *The News International,* May 31, 2022, https://www.thenews.com.pk/latest/962248-energy-crisis-deepens-as-electricity-shortfall-widens-to-7000mw
110. "Latest Progress on the CPEC," *Embassy of the People's Republic of China in the Islamic Republic of Pakistan*, December 29, 2018, http://pk.chineseembassy.org/eng/zbgx/CPEC/t1626097.htm
111. Dr. Erica Downs, "China-Pakistan Economic Corridor Power Projects: Insights into Environmental and Debt Sustainability," *Center on Global Energy Policy,* Columbia University, October 3, 2019, https://energypolicy.columbia.edu/research/report/china-pakistan-economic-corridor-power-projects-insights-environmental-and-debt-sustainability
112. Rishikesh Ram Bhandary, Kelly Sims Gallagher, "What drives Pakistan's coal-fired power plant construction boom? Understanding the China-Pakistan Economic Corridor's energy portfolio," *World Development Perspectives,* Volume 25, 2022, https://www.sciencedirect.com/science/article/pii/S2452292922000042
113. Dr. Erica Downs, "China-Pakistan Economic Corridor Power Projects: Insights into Environmental and Debt Sustainability," *Center on Global Energy Policy,* Columbia University, October 3, 2019, https://energypolicy.columbia.edu/research/report/china-pakistan-economic-corridor-power-projects-insights-environmental-and-debt-sustainability
114. Sheraz Aziz, "Can China Solve Pakistan's Energy Crisis?" *The Diplomat*, June 12, 2019, https://thediplomat.com/2019/06/can-china-solve-pakistans-energy-crisis/
115. Jacob Mardell and Thomas S. Eder, "The BRI in Pakistan: Too big to fail," *Mercator Institute for China Studies (MERICS*), September 20, 2018, https://merics.org/en/comment/bri-pakistan-too-big-fail
116. "Sahiwal power plant – the first inaugurated CPEC project in Pakistan," *China Daily*, July 19, 2017, https://www.chinadaily.com.cn/m/powerchina/2017-07/19/content_30358906.htm
117. "Feature: CPEC power plant provides clean electricity, green environment to Pakistan," *Xinhua*, August 12, 2019, http://www.xinhuanet.com/english/2019-08/12/c_138302450.htm
118. Amel Ghani, "The High Price of Producing Electricity with Coal," *Herald*, September 26, 2018, https://herald.dawn.com/news/1398670
119. Munawar Hasan, "Sahiwal Coal-Fired Power Plants Feared Closure on Non-Payment of Dues," *The News International*, April 3, 2018, https://www.thenews.

com.pk/print/299722-sahiwal-coal-fired-power-plants-feared-closure-on-non-payment-of-dues

120. Syed Akhtar Ali, "Another imported coal-based plant in Punjab," *The Express Tribune,* July 17, 2017, https://tribune.com.pk/story/1459595/another-imported-coal-based-plant-punjab
121. Mushtaq Ghumman, "Imported coal supply to Sahiwal power plant: CPPA-G asks PR to increase number of freight trains," *Business Recorder,* October 29, 2024, https://www.brecorder.com/news/40329498/imported-coal-supply-to-sahiwal-power-plant-cppa-g-asks-pr-to-increase-number-of-freight-trains
122. "2×660MW Coal-Fired Power Plants At Port Qasim Karachi," China-Pakistan Economic Corridor (CPEC), http://cpec.gov.pk/project-details/1
123. Toh Han Shih, "Chinese firm in US$2.09 billion Pakistan power plant deal," *The South China Morning Post,* April 9, 2015, https://www.scmp.com/business/china-business/article/1761506/chinese-firm-us209-billion-pakistan-power-plant-deal
124. Salman Siddiqui, "CPEC's First Power Project Mired in Financial Difficulties," *The Express Tribune,* May 10, 2019, https://tribune.com.pk/story/1969593/2-cpecs-first-power-project-mired-financial-difficulties/
125. Mushtaq Ghumman, "1,320 MW coal plant: PQEPC threatens to halt operations," *Business Recorder,* October 6, 2024, https://www.brecorder.com/news/40325698/1320-mw-coal-plant-pqepc-threatens-to-halt-operations
126. Salman Siddiqui, "CPEC's First Power Project Mired in Financial Difficulties," *The Express Tribune,* May 10, 2019, https://tribune.com.pk/story/1969593/2-cpecs-first-power-project-mired-financial-difficulties/
127. Javed Mirza, "Pakistan's Coal Imports to Surge to 30 million tons per annum by 2020," *The News International,* January 8, 2019, https://www.thenews.com.pk/print/415916-pakistan-s-coal-imports-to-surge-to-30-million-tons-per-annum-by-2020
128. "Pakistan—the hottest market for South African coal," *Dawn,* February 6, 2018, https://www.dawn.com/news/1387570
129. Sarfraz Ali, "Solving the Energy Crisis is a "Now or Never" for Pakistan: The Future is Thar!" *Daily Pakistan,* April 22, 2022, https://en.dailypakistan.com.pk/22-Apr-2022/solving-the-energy-crisis-is-a-now-or-never-for-pakistan-the-future-is-thar
130. Sarah Matthews and Pritish Raj, "Pakistan's coal crisis prompts industries to shut plants, reduce capacities," *S&P Global,* May 23, 2022, https://www.spglobal.com/commodityinsights/en/market-insights/latest-news/coal/052322-pakistans-coal-crisis-prompts-industries-to-shut-plants-reduce-capacities
131. Stephen Stapczynski and Ismail Dilawar, "Pakistan Plans U-Turn on Fuel Imports After Prices Surge," *Bloomberg,* February 14, 2023, https://www.bloomberg.com/news/articles/2023-02-14/pakistan-turns-to-dirty-coal-from-pricey-lng-reuters-says
132. Yuan Shenggao, "Chinese investment boosts French BRI hub," *China Daily,* November 6, 2019, https://www.chinadaily.com.cn/cndy/2019-11/06/content_37520975.htm

133. "The Marine Survey for Huawei Marine's PEACE Project is Underway," *Huawei Technologies Co*, May 2, 2018, https://www.huawei.com/en/news/2018/5/Huawei-Marine-PEACE-Project
134. "PEACE and PCCW Global signed the LPA with Orange to Land PEACE Cable in France," *PEACE Cable International Network Co. Limited,* September 20, 2019, http://www.peacecable.net/News/Detail/16612
135. See also Winston Qiu, "PEACE Completes Final Splicing to Connect Kenya, Egypt, France and Pakistan," *Submarine Cable Networks,* November 10, 2022, https://www.submarinenetworks.com/en/systems/asia-europe-africa/peace/peace-completes-final-splicing-to-connect-to-kenya-egypt-france-and-pakistan "埃及电信公司签署了价值4500万美元的PEACE电缆系统登陆协议," May 7, 2019, http://www.rfuchina.com/v/201905/0721290.html
136. "Marine survey underway in preparation for Seychelles' second submarine cable," *Seychelles News Agency*, March 3, 2020, http://www.seychellesnewsagency.com/articles/12520/Marine+survey+underway+in+preparation+for+Seychelles%27+second+submarine+cable
137. "PEACE launched Kenya Landing cooperated with Liquid Telecom and Africa Data Centres," *PEACE Cable International Network Co. Limited,* December 4, 2019, http://www.peacecable.net/News/Detail/16615
138. "Project Details," Peace Cable, 2023, http://www.peacecable.net/network; also see Winston Qiu, "China Mobile Activates PEACE Cable Linking Singapore and France," *Submarine Cable Networks,* September 5, 2024, https://www.submarinenetworks.com/en/systems/asia-europe-africa/peace/china-mobile-activates-peace-cable-linking-singapore-and-france
139. "Pakistan's internet capacity to be increased by 96 Tb/s with new submarine cable system," *Dawn*, April 17, 2019, https://www.dawn.com/news/1476691
140. "The Indo-European Telegraph.; Interesting Details of Laying the Line Difficulties with the Natives. The Manufacture of The Cable. Conveying the Cable. The First Station. Among the Arabs. Coming to Terms with the Sheiks. Natural Difficulties. A Surprise. Dangers of Mud. The Last Obstacle," *The New York Times*, March 26, 1865, https://www.nytimes.com/1865/03/26/archives/the-indoeuropean-telegraph-interesting-details-of-laying-the-line.html
141. "The Indo-European Telegraph; Interesting Details of Laying The Line Difficulties With The Natives. The Manufacture of The Cable. Conveying The Cable. The First Station. Among The Arabs. Coming To Terms With The Sheiks. Natural Difficulties. A Surprise. Dangers Of Mud. The Last Obstacle," *The New York Times*, March 26, 1865, https://www.nytimes.com/1865/03/26/archives/the-indoeuropean-telegraph-interesting-details-of-laying-the-line.html
142. "Halfway around the world in 28 minutes," *Siemens,* https://new.siemens.com/global/en/company/about/history/news/indo-european-telegraph-line.html
143. Paran Balakrishnan, "China's digital route to dominance," *The Hindu Business Line*, October 15, 2019, https://www.thehindubusinessline.com/opinion/chinas-digital-route-to-dominance/article29692762.ece
144. "1st land-based China-Pakistan cross-border optical fiber inaugurated," *Xinhua*, July 14, 2018, http://www.xinhuanet.com/english/2018-07/14/c_137322613.htm

145. Simran Taneja, "A complete assessment of the Cross-Border Optical Fibre Cable project under CPEC," *CPEC Portal*, May 18, 2019, http://www.cpecinfo.com/news/a-complete-assessment-of-the-cross-border-optical-fibre-cable-project-under-cpec/NzEyMw==
146. "Chinese firm starts to lay 16,000-km-long fibre-optic cable," *The News*, May 20, 2023, https://www.thenews.com.pk/print/1072079-chinese-firm-starts-to-lay-16-000-km-long-fibre-optic-cable
147. Khalid Hasnain, "Railways signs deals for laying optical fibre on two routes," *The Dawn*, September 4, 2024, https://www.dawn.com/news/1856724
148. Jahanzaib Haque and Qurat ul ain Siddiqui, "Exclusive: The CPEC plan for Pakistan's digital future," *Dawn*, October 1, 2017, https://www.dawn.com/news/1361176
149. Usman Hanif, "Submarine cable fault disrupts internet services in Pakistan," *The Express Tribune*, October 29, 2019, https://tribune.com.pk/story/2519773/submarine-cable-fault-disrupts-internet
150. Jamal Shahid, "Army seeks fibre optic cables along CPEC," *Dawn*, January 25, 2017, https://www.dawn.com/news/1310593
151. "Punjab govt, Huawei inaugurate Lahore Safe City Project," *Pakistan Today*, January 8, 2018, https://www.pakistantoday.com.pk/2018/01/08/punjab-govt-huawei-inaugurate-lahore-safe-city-project/
152. Leo Kelion and Sajid Iqbal, "Huawei wi-fi modules were pulled from Pakistan CCTV system," *BBC*, April 8, 2019, https://www.bbc.com/news/technology-47856098
153. Sarthak Dogra, "Huawei blamed for installing data back door in Pakistan's safe-city project," *India Today*, August 16, 2021, https://www.indiatoday.in/technology/news/story/huawei-blamed-for-installing-data-back-door-in-pakistan-s-safe-city-project-1841625-2021-08-16
154. Asif Chaudhry, "Half of Lahore no more on Safe City radar," *Dawn*, January 13, 2020, https://www.dawn.com/news/1528000/half-of-lahore-no-more-on-safe-city-radar
155. "Pakistan, China jointly agree to launch 3 new corridors besides CPEC," *Business Standard*, October 22, 2002, https://www.business-standard.com/article/international/pakistan-china-jointly-agree-to-launch-3-new-corridors-besides-cpec-122102200486_1.html
156. "Digital Silk Road promotes e-commerce between China, Pakistan," *Xinhua*, September 6, 2023, http://english.scio.gov.cn/beltandroad/2023-09/06/content_112759205.htm
157. Khurshid Ahmed, "China, Pakistan sign agreement to route Internet traffic through Pakistan, generate $400 million revenue," *Arab News*, January 30, 2024, https://www.arabnews.pk/node/2450631/pakistan
158. "Pakistan becomes first foreign country to join satellite navigation system of China," *China Pakistan Economic Corridor*, June 22, 2020, http://cpecinfo.com/pakistan-becomes-first-foreign-country-to-join-satellite-navigation-system-of-china/
159. Sabena Siddiqui, "Pakistan benefits from China's Sat-Nav system," *China.org.cn*, May 23, 2017, http://www.china.org.cn/business/2017-05/23/content_40873203.htm
160. "中国军用北斗进军巴基斯坦大幅提升巴铁战斗力," *GPS Navigation Home*, August 30, 2017, https://www.gpsmap.cc/shiyong/2017/0830/2281.html

161. "北斗导航定位系统让巴基斯坦三军战力脱胎换骨 [Beidou Navigation and Positioning System Renews the Fighting Forces of Pakistan's Three Armies]," Sohu.com, April 25, 2015, https://www.sohu.com/a/12365550_111230
162. Mansoor Ahmed, "Pakistan's Tactical Nuclear Weapons and Their Impact on Stability," *Carnegie Regional Insight*, June 30, 2016, https://carnegieendowment.org/2016/06/30/pakistan-s-tactical-nuclear-weapons-and-their-impact-on-stability-pub-63911
163. 北斗刚完成，巴基斯坦就宣布使用北斗，俄想把格洛纳斯并入北斗网, July 7, 2020, https://baijiahao.baidu.com/s?id=1671525970553369869&wfr=spider&for=pc
164. Syed Raza Hassan, "Attacks have killed 44 Pakistanis working on China corridor since 2014," *Reuters*, September 8, 2016, https://www.reuters.com/article/us-pakistan-china/attacks-have-killed-44-pakistanis-working-on-china-corridor-since-2014-idUSKCN11E1EP
165. Jon Boone, "Chinese Engineer and Driver Injured in Karachi Separatist Bombing," *The Guardian*, May 30, 2016, https://www.theguardian.com/world/2016/may/30/chinese-worker-driver-injured-karachi-bombing-claimed-separatists
166. "Chinese Engineers Killed In Pakistan's Balochistan Province," *Radio Free Europe Radio Liberty*, November 26, 2016, https://www.rferl.org/a/pakistan-chinese-engineers-killed-balochistan/28140991.html
167. Wang Wenwen, "Kidnapping Highlights Risks along China-Pakistan Economic Corridor," *The Global Times*, May 25, 2017, http://www.globaltimes.cn/content/1048723.shtml
168. Farhan Bokhari and Kiran Stacey, "China Woos Pakistan Militants to Secure Belt and Road Projects," *Financial Times*, February 19, 2018, https://www.ft.com/content/063ce350-1099-11e8-8cb6-b9ccc4c4dbbb
169. Asad Hashim, "Gunmen attack Chinese consulate in Karachi," *Al Jazeera*, November 23, 2018, https://www.aljazeera.com/news/2018/11/shots-heard-china-consulate-pakistan-karachi-181123051817209.html
170. Dipanjan Roy Chaudhury, "Baloch Liberation Army attacks Chinese assets for 3rd time since Aug 2018," *The Economic Times*, April 1, 2019, https://economictimes.indiatimes.com/news/defence/baloch-liberation-army-attacks-chinese-assets-for-3rd-time-since-aug-2018/articleshow/68664144.cms
171. Adnan Aamir, "Pakistan insurgent attacks on China project seen to persist," *Nikkei Asian Review*, May 13, 2019, https://asia.nikkei.com/Spotlight/Belt-and-Road/Pakistan-insurgent-attacks-on-China-project-seen-to-persist
172. Salman Masood, "Gunmen Attack Pakistan Hotel Used by Chinese and Vow Further Violence," *The New York Times*, May 11, 2019, https://www.nytimes.com/2019/05/11/world/asia/pakistan-hotel-attack-gwadar.html?searchResultPosition=2
173. Shalinder Wangu and Parth Borah, "Terrorist Attack on Karachi Stock Exchange Marks BLA's Move to Intensify Domain," *News18.com*, July 21, 2020, https://www.news18.com/news/world/terrorist-attack-on-karachi-stock-exchange-marks-blas-move-to-intensify-domain-2726885.html
174. Srijan Shukla, "Baloch Liberation Army, the insurgent group behind Karachi Stock Exchange Attack," *The Print*, June 29, 2020, https://theprint.in/world/

baloch-liberation-army-the-insurgent-group-behind-karachi-stock-exchange-attack/450960/

175. "9 Chinese engineers among 12 killed in 'attack' near Dasu hydropower plant," *Dawn*, July 14, 2021, https://www.dawn.com/news/1635023
176. Niha Dagia, "Terrorists Target Chinese Nationals Working on a CPEC Project," *The Diplomat,* July 19, 2021, https://thediplomat.com/2021/07/terrorists-target-chinese-nationals-working-on-a-cpec-project/
177. "Chinese FM said justice served after Pakistan sentences Dasu terror attackers to death, vowing to invest more to protect overseas Chinese," *The Global Times*, November 15, 2022, https://www.globaltimes.cn/page/202211/1279603.shtml
178. "Pakistan to pay $11.6 million compensation to 36 Chinese victims of hydropower project terror attack," *The Economic Times*, January 22, 2022, https://economictimes.indiatimes.com/news/international/world-news/pakistan-to-pay-11-6-mn-compensation-to-36-chinese-victims-of-hydropower-project-terror-attack/articleshow/89055553.cms?from=mdr
179. "Pakistan to pay compensation for Chinese workers killed in attack," *Nikkei*, January 27, 2022, https://asia.nikkei.com/Spotlight/Belt-and-Road/Pakistan-to-pay-compensation-for-Chinese-workers-killed-in-attack
180. "Lahore Bomb Blast Kills 3, Injures 28 In Busy Market," *NDTV*, January 20, 2022, https://www.ndtv.com/world-news/at-least-3-killed-20-injured-in-powerful-blast-at-pakistans-lahore-market-2719443
181. "Female suicide bomber kills three Chinese teachers and Pakistani at Karachi university," *Reuters*, April 27, 2022, https://www.reuters.com/world/asia-pacific/van-blast-pakistans-karachi-kills-four-2022-04-26/
182. Asif Shahzad and Syed Raza Hassan, "Alarmed by suicide attack, China and Pakistan work together on probe," *Reuters*, October 31, 2022, https://www.reuters.com/world/asia-pacific/alarmed-by-suicide-attack-china-pakistan-join-hands-probe-2022-10-31/
183. "Pak Says It Foiled Suspected Suicide Attack Against Chinese Nationals," *NDTV*, May 16, 2022, https://www.ndtv.com/world-news/pakistan-says-it-foiled-suspected-suicide-attack-against-chinese-nationals-2981677
184. "Pakistan Security Forces Kill 2 after Attack on Chinese Convoy," *Al Jazeera,* August 13, 2023, https://www.aljazeera.com/news/2023/8/13/pakistan-security-forces-kill-two-after-attack-on-chinese-convoy-in-gwadar
185. "14 soldiers killed as terrorists target security forces vehicles in Gwadar, Pakistan," *The Times of India*, November 4, 2023, https://timesofindia.indiatimes.com/world/pakistan/14-soldiers-killed-as-terrorists-target-security-forces-vehicles-in-gwadar-pakistan/articleshow/104959081.cms?from=mdr
186. "2 Security Personnel Injured in Blast in Pakistan's Gwadar," *Xinhua,* February 8, 2024, https://english.news.cn/asiapacific/20240208/b543ab3200f74d56a3842c4937fdbb7f/c.html
187. Adnan Aamir, "Attack in Pakistan's Gwadar strikes near Heart of China's interests," *Nikkei Asia,* March 22, 2024, https://asia.nikkei.com/Politics/International-relations/Attack-in-Pakistan-s-Gwadar-strikes-near-heart-of-China-s-interests

188. Abid Hussain, "Five Chinese nationals among six killed in a suicide bomb attack in Pakistan," *Aljazeera*, March 26, 2024, https://www.aljazeera.com/news/2024/3/26/five-chinese-nationals-killed-in-suicide-bomb-attack-in-pakistan-police
189. "Reuters: Two Killed in Suicide Bombing Targeting Chinese Nationals in Pakistan," *VOANEWS*, August 21, 2021, https://www.voanews.com/a/south-central-asia_two-killed-suicide-bombing-targeting-chinese-nationals-pakistan/6209817.html
190. Raza Khan, "15,000 troops of Special Security Division to protect CPEC projects, Chinese nationals," *Dawn*, August 12, 2016, https://www.dawn.com/news/1277182
191. "Special force set up to guard Gwadar port's sea lanes," *Dawn*, December 12, 2016, https://www.dawn.com/news/1301970
192. "Pakistan and China Boost Security at Gwadar Port," *The Maritime Executive*, December 15, 2016, https://www.maritime-executive.com/article/pakistan-boosts-maritime-security-at-gwadar-port
193. "2 ships sold to Pak Navy for Gwadar security: China," *The Economic Times*, July 13, 2018, https://economictimes.indiatimes.com/news/defence/china-hands-over-2-ships-to-pakistan-navy-for-gwadar-security/articleshow/56560951.cms
194. "Pakistan army plans new unit to protect CPEC projects," *Gulf News*, May 19, 2019, https://gulfnews.com/world/asia/pakistan/pakistan-army-plans-new-unit-to-protect-cpec-projects-1.64050168
195. "15,000 Pak military personnel protecting CPEC," *Press Trust of India (PTI)*, February 21, 2017, http://www.ptinews.com/news/8430735_--15-000-Pak-military-personnel-protecting-CPEC---
196. Kuldip Singh, "China's High-Security Compound at Gwadar: Should India Worry?," *The Quint*, June 8, 2020, https://www.thequint.com/voices/opinion/gwadar-port-china-pakistan-economic-corridor-indian-interests-chinese-army-strategy
197. "Security wall of Gwadar Free Zone North 90pc completed," *Pakistan Today*, July 4, 2023, https://www.pakistantoday.com.pk/2023/07/04/security-wall-of-gwadar-free-zone-north-90pc-completed/
198. "'Deeply concerned' about the security of Chinese people in Pakistan, Chinese President tells visiting Pakistani PM, asks him to speed up projects," *AIR*, November 2, 2022, https://newsonair.gov.in/News?title=%E2%80%9CDeeply-concerned%E2%80%9D-about-the-security-of-Chinese-people-in-Pakistan%2C-Chinese-President-tells-visiting-Pakistani-PM%2C-asks-him-to-speed-up-projects&id=450286
199. Shishir Gupta, "China holds hard talks with Pak generals over CPEC projects security," *The Hindustan Times*, April 27, 2023, https://www.hindustantimes.com/world-news/china-holds-hard-talks-with-pak-generals-over-cpec-projects-security-101682567547495.html
200. "All Chinese CPEC workers in Pakistan to move in bullet-proof cars: report," *The Hindu*, November 26, 2022, https://www.thehindu.com/news/international/all-chinese-cpec-workers-in-pakistan-to-move-in-bullet-proof-cars-report/article66103267.ece
201. Asif Chaudhry, "10,000 Policemen Deputed for Chinese Security 'Vulnerable' to Coronavirus," *Dawn*, January 28, 2020, https://www.dawn.com/

news/1530934/10000-policemen-deputed-for-chinese-security-vulnerable-to-coronavirus

202. Shishir Gupta, "With CPEC in mind, China wants Pakistan to pitch Baloch Outfit as Terror Group in UN," *Hindustan Times*, August 3, 2020, https://www.hindustantimes.com/world-news/with-cpec-in-mind-china-wants-iron-brother-pakistan-to-pitch-bla-as-terror-group-in-un/story-GcOrzYG3gwqqAutSTlPqHL.html
203. "Mapping Militant Organizations: Balochistan Liberation Army," *Stanford University*. Last modified February 2019. https://cisac.fsi.stanford.edu/mappingmilitants/profiles/balochistan-liberation-army
204. C. Christine Fair, "Pakistan Can't Afford China's 'Friendship'," *Foreign Policy*, July 3, 2017, https://foreignpolicy.com/2017/07/03/pakistan-cant-afford-chinas-friendship/
205. Sanjay Pulipaka and Mohit Musaddi, "View: China's economic engagement and protests in three continents," *The Economic Times*, December 24, 2021, https://economictimes.indiatimes.com/news/international/world-news/view-chinas-economic-engagement-and-protests-in-three-continents/articleshow/88476132.cms?from=mdr
206. Gurmeet Kanwal, "Pakistan's Gwadar Port: A New Naval Base in China's String of Pearls in the Indo-Pacific," *CSIS Briefs*, April 2, 2018, https://www.csis.org/analysis/pakistans-gwadar-port-new-naval-base-chinas-string-pearls-indo-pacific
207. Subham Tiwari, "A look at Chinese assets participating in crucial Pakistan naval war game," *India Today*, November 14, 2023, https://www.indiatoday.in/world/story/china-ships-in-pakistan-naval-war-game-a-look-at-chinese-navy-in-pak-2462436-2023-11-13
208. Amir Wasim, "Technical hitches hinder work on economic zones," *Dawn*, August 14, 2019, https://www.dawn.com/news/1499413/technical-hitches-hinder-work-on-economic-zones
209. Khaleeq Kiani, "Chinese experts to visit CPEC Special Economic Zone sites," *Dawn*, July 5, 2017, https://www.dawn.com/news/1343342; also see - "Economic Corridor Development In Pakistan," *ADB*, February 2022, https://www.adb.org/sites/default/files/publication/768396/economic-corridor-development-pakistan.pdf ; also see Mubarak Zeb Khan, "37 special zones to boost production," *Dawn*, February 12, 2017, https://www.dawn.com/news/1314264
210. Taimur Agha, "The power of SEZs," *Dawn*, July 4, 2022, https://www.dawn.com/news/1698131
211. Meng Lingjuan, "Pak-China FTA phase-II to be implemented shortly," *The Express Tribune*, October 7, 2019, https://tribune.com.pk/story/2073582/2-pak-china-fta-phase-ii-implemented-shortly/
212. Mubasher Bukhari, "Pakistan Cuts Chinese 'Silk Road' Rail Project by $2 Billion Due to Debt Concerns," *Reuters*, October 1, 2018, https://www.reuters.com/article/us-pakistan-silkroad-railways/pakistan-cuts-chinese-silk-road-rail-project-by-2-billion-due-to-debt-concerns-idUSKCN1MB2V8
213. Shahbaz Rana, "$6.7b ML-I project 'unviable'," *The Express Tribune*, May 9, 2024, https://tribune.com.pk/story/2465776/67b-ml-i-project-unviable

214. Riazat Butt, "No passengers, no planes, no benefits. Pakistan's newest airport is a bit of a mystery," *AP,* February 24, 2025, https://apnews.com/article/pakistan-china-gwadar-airport-balochistan-militants-81ecfc16827015321183a1f5a52e631d
215. Jamil Bhatti, "Spotlight: Pakistan's First-Ever Urban Train Under CPEC Takes First Test Run," *Xinhua*, December 12, 2019, http://www.xinhuanet.com/english/2019-12/11/c_138622001.htm
216. Adnan Aamir, "Pakistan's stalled China-backed rail project prompts turn to Japan," *Nikkei Asian Review*, October 19, 2019, https://asia.nikkei.com/Spotlight/Belt-and-Road/Pakistan-s-stalled-China-backed-rail-project-prompts-turn-to-Japan
217. "Karachi Circular Railway to be built by CRCC: CM Sindh," *Pakistan Today,* October 18, 2023, https://www.pakistantoday.com.pk/2023/10/18/karachi-circular-railway-to-be-built-by-crcc-cm-sindh/
218. Asif Shahzad, "Pakistan completes projects worth $25 bln under CPEC," *Reuters,* October 18, 2023, https://www.reuters.com/article/idUSL1N3BO0Q0/
219. Khaleeq Kiani, "Without structural reforms, CPEC won't yield results," *ADB*, February 9, 2022, https://www.dawn.com/news/1673012
220. "The Risk Challenges, Strategic Thinking and Suggestions of the China-Pakistan Economic Corridor," *Sohu.com*, May 2, 2016, https://www.sohu.com/a/72956863_389790
221. "Pakistan floods' death toll nears 1,700, puts pressure on fragile economy," *The Hindu*, October 1, 2022, https://www.thehindu.com/news/international/pakistan-floods-death-toll-nears-1700-puts-pressure-on-fragile-economy/article65959347.ece
222. "Pakistan's annual inflation eases to 29.4% in June from May record," *The Times of India*, July 3, 2023, https://economictimes.indiatimes.com/news/international/world-news/pakistans-annual-inflation-eases-to-29-4-in-june-from-may-record/articleshow/101454386.cms
223. WFP and FAO, "*Hunger Hotspots. FAO-WFP Early Warnings on Acute Food Insecurity, the Outlook of June 2023 to November 2023*" (Rome: WFP and FAO, 2023), p. vii.
224. "Stampede at Ramadan food distribution centre kills 11 in Pakistan," *Al Jazeera,* March 31, 2023, https://www.aljazeera.com/news/2023/3/31/stampede-at-food-distribution-centre-kills-11-in-pakistan
225. Aadil Nakhoda, "Explaining Pakistan's Balance of Payments Crisis: A Comparative Analysis," *The Dawn*, April 19, 2023, https://www.dawn.com/news/1745350 ; also see "Pakistan braces for fuel shortages amid liquidity crisis," *Economic Times*, January 31, 2023, https://economictimes.indiatimes.com/news/international/business/pakistan-braces-for-fuel-shortages-amid-liquidity-crisis/articleshow/97487926.cms?from=mdr
226. Sushant Sareen, "Why CPEC could be the end of China-Pakistan relationship," *Observer Research Foundation*, April 27, 2018, https://www.orfonline.org/research/cpec-could-end-china-pakistan-relationship/
227. Shahbaz Rana, "Pakistan's Existential Economic Crisis," *USIP,* April 6, 2023, https://www.usip.org/publications/2023/04/pakistans-existential-economic-crisis
228. Ibid.
229. "China rolls over $2bn loan to Pakistan: Dar," *The Dawn,* March 28, 2023, https://www.dawn.com/news/1745163

230. "Pakistan Government debt swells to 58.6 trillion," *The Hindu,* June 6, 2023, https://www.thehindu.com/news/international/pakistan-government-debt-swells-to-586-trillion/article66936924.ece
231. "IMF Reaches Staff-level Agreement with Pakistan on a US$3 billion Stand-By Arrangement," *IMF,* June 29, 2023, https://www.imf.org/en/News/Articles/2023/06/30/pr23251-imf-reaches-staff-level-agreement-with-pakistan-on-a-us-3-billion-stand-by-arrangement
232. "Pakistan-IMF deal: Dar says Saudi Arabia has deposited $2bn in SBP account," *GeoTv,* July 11, 2023, https://www.geo.tv/latest/498541-pakistan-imf-deal-dar-says-saudi-arabia-has-deposited-2bn-in-sbp-account
233. "Ministry appoints counsellors in China," *Tribune,* July 8, 2021, https://tribune.com.pk/story/2309334/ministry-appoints-counsellors-in-china
234. "China Industries Relocate Elsewhere," *The Express Tribune,* July 10, 2022, https://tribune.com.pk/story/2365457/china-industries-relocate-elsewhere
235. "Foreign Direct Investment, Net Inflows (BoP, current US$)," *World Bank,* 2022, https://data.worldbank.org/indicator/BX.KLT.DINV.CD.WD
236. S. Khan, "Pakistan activists criticize government for new coastal body in Gwadar port," *Deutsche Welle,* 30 October 2019, https://www.dw.com/en/pakistan-activists-criticize-government-for-new-coastal-body-in-gwadar-port/a-51033393
237. Shahbaz Rana, "PM gives nod to abolish CPEC Authority," *Tribune,* August 18, 2022, https://tribune.com.pk/story/2371790/pm-gives-nod-to-abolish-cpec-authority
238. Afshan Subohi, "The controversial disbandment," *DAWN.* August 29, 2022, https://www.dawn.com/news/1707356
239. Shi Zhiqin and Lu Yang, "The Benefits and Risks of the China-Pakistan Economic Corridor," *Carnegie-Tsinghua Centre for Global Policy,* December 21, 2016, https://carnegietsinghua.org/2016/12/21/benefits-and-risks-of-china-pakistan-economic-corridor-pub-66507
240. Ibid.
241. Suzanne Goldenberg, "Bush threatened to bomb Pakistan, says Musharraf," *The Guardian,* September 22, 2006, https://www.theguardian.com/world/2006/sep/22/pakistan.usa
242. Kamran Yousaf, "Pak, US defence dialogue starts today," *The Express Tribune,* February 12, 2023, https://tribune.com.pk/story/2400833/pak-us-defence-dialogue-starts-today
243. "Biden Administration approves $450 million F-16 fleet sustainment programme to Pakistan," *The Hindu,* September 8, 2022, https://www.thehindu.com/news/international/biden-administration-approves-450-million-f-16-fleet-sustainment-programme-to-pakistan/article65864895.ece
244. "Trends in International Arms Transfers, 2019," *SIPRI Fact Sheet,* March 2020, https://www.sipri.org/sites/default/files/2020-03/fs_2003_at_2019.pdf
245. Pieter D. Wezeman, Katarina Djokic, Dr Mathew George, Zain Hussain, and Siemon T. Wezeman, "Trends in International Arms Transfers, 2023," *SIPRI,* March 2024, https://www.sipri.org/sites/default/files/2024-03/fs_2403_at_2023.pdf

246. "US imposes sanctions on Chinese suppliers to Pakistan's ballistic missile program," *Reuters,* September 13, 2024, https://www.reuters.com/world/asia-pacific/us-imposes-sanctions-suppliers-pakistans-ballistic-missile-program-2024-09-12/
247. "U.S. Sanctions on Four Entities Contributing to Pakistan's Ballistic Missile Program," *US Department of State,* December 18, 2024, https://www.state.gov/u-s-sanctions-on-four-entities-contributing-to-pakistans-ballistic-missile-program/
248. Rhea Mogul and Sophia Saifi, "Imran Khan claims there's a US conspiracy against him. Why do so many Pakistanis believe him?" *CNN,* May 27, 2022, https://edition.cnn.com/2022/05/27/asia/pakistan-imran-khan-us-conspiracy-intl-hnk/index.html
249. "Zardari asks US to Plan for Pakistan's Economic Development," *Business Standard,* August 2, 2023, https://www.business-standard.com/article/news-ians/zardari-asks-us-to-plan-for-pakistan-s-economic-development-113080200082_1.html
250. "Axios On HBO: Pakistan Prime Minister Imran Khan on China Clip HBO," *YouTube,* June 21, 2021, https://www.youtube.com/watch?v=YlHPEgE3fjk
251. "Chinese army spotted along Line of Control in Pakistan-occupied Kashmir, say sources," *Times of India,* March 13, 2016, https://timesofindia.indiatimes.com/india/chinese-army-spotted-along-line-of-control-in-pakistan-occupied-kashmir-say-sources/articleshow/51380359.cms
252. Hu Weijia, "Investment can create 'virtuous circle' for CPEC," *Global Times,* February 17, 2019, http://www.globaltimes.cn/content/1139171.shtml
253. Wang Peng, "CPEC key to developing western China and consolidating regional security," *Global Times,* August 26, 2018, http://www.globaltimes.cn/content/1117108.shtml
254. "Iran admits carrying out deadly strike on Pakistan territory," *BBC,* January 17, 2024, https://www.bbc.com/news/world-asia-67999465
255. Shreyas Deshmukh, "Why Iran-Pakistan attacks is unlikely to escalate to war," *Times of India,* January 19, 2024, https://timesofindia.indiatimes.com/world/pakistan/why-iran-pakistan-attacks-is-unlikely-to-escalate-to-war/articleshow/106990899.cms#

4

In Search of Profit Amidst Peril

Introduction

On December 13, 1960, the Chinese news daily, *Renmin Ribao*, in its editorial, noted that the Sino-Afghan Treaty of Friendship and Mutual Non-Aggression had opened a 'new Silk Road'.[1] The editorial went on to add that both countries have "long suffered from imperialist and colonial aggression and oppression" and stressed that the treaty laid the foundation for long-lasting friendship between the "future generations of Chinese and Afghan peoples."[2] The two themes—improved connectivity (Silk Roads) and the need to contest the presence of extra-regional powers—continued to dominate the Chinese policy towards Afghanistan in the subsequent decades as well. However, the emphasis on the two objectives was contingent on the capacities of the Chinese government and the prevalent geopolitical challenges and opportunities at any given time.

The Soviet Union's 1979 invasion of Afghanistan altered the geopolitical landscape on the western boundaries of South Asia. Given the Sino-Soviet rift, Beijing was uncomfortable with Moscow's expanding footprint in its immediate neighbourhood. Because of the Soviet presence, there was a growing strategic convergence between the US and China regarding the developments in Afghanistan. While the US provided significant support to the Mujahideen in their fight against the Soviet Union, Beijing reportedly provided arms and ammunition to the Mujahideen, albeit on a much smaller scale.[3] The withdrawal of the Soviet Union and the consequent consolidation of radical Islamic fundamentalism in Afghanistan coincided with the Uyghur unrest in Xinjiang in China. Uyghur ethnic communities inhabit large tracts of Xinjiang and are predominantly Muslim. Many news reports suggested that China made systematic attempts to dilute the Uyghur ethnic identity, fearing that a secessionist movement may gain momentum.[4] Avinash Godbole and Akash Goud contend that the unrest in Xinjiang in the mid-and-late-1990s got "reinvigorated following the creation of Central Asian states based on ethnic identities after the disintegration of the Soviet Union."[5] While punitive measures were deployed to contain the domestic unrest, China also sought to prevent the consolidation of transnational linkages that could complicate the Uyghur issue. Consequently, in addition to spurring economic growth in Xinjiang, Beijing made persistent efforts to increase engagement with Central Asian and Middle Eastern countries. The BRI became a vehicle to improve economic activity in China's western provinces and engage with countries with significant Muslim populations in Central Asia, the Middle East, and South Asia. The Chinese objective was to access the markets of the countries in its western neighbourhood and develop positive relationships with various regimes to ensure that the spillover of Islamic radicalism into Xinjiang would be minimal or non-existent. As a part of these efforts, China engaged with the principal actors in Afghanistan. Some reports suggest that China had interacted with the Taliban in its earlier incarnation in the 1990s and subsequently "maintained a working relationship with the Taliban as an insurgent group", which laid the foundation for "Beijing's decades-long pragmatic relationship with the Taliban."[6] After all, China and Afghanistan share an approximately 92-kilometre (57-mile) land border, and therefore, as Professor Zha Daojiong noted, Beijing "simply does not have the luxury of pretending that whoever is in charge there is irrelevant."[7]

For China, Afghanistan is of geostrategic importance as it abuts South Asia, Central Asia, and West Asia. China has operationalised various connectivity projects in Central Asia and Pakistan. Further, there is an uptick in China's economic engagement with Iran. However, the political instability in Afghanistan prevented Beijing from operationalising the connectivity projects there. Nonetheless, China, a neighbour and a rising power, made persistent efforts to increase influence among the important stakeholders in Afghanistan. To achieve its objectives, China was "involved in all major dialogue formats related to Afghanistan ... [such as] ... the Istanbul dialogue, and the 'China-Afghanistan-Pakistan' dialogue."[8] In May 2015, Beijing, with support from Pakistani officials, hosted a meeting between the representatives of the Afghanistan government and the Taliban in Urumqi, China. Beijing also scaled up engagement through its special envoy for Afghanistan affairs. Participating in dialogues and facilitating meetings on Afghanistan prompted some to reflect on China's often-stated principle of non-interference in the internal affairs of other countries. Chinese academic Li Xin noted that the Afghan deliberations do not violate the non-interference principle, but China "intends to play a much bigger role in stabilising its western border as the situation deteriorates.... Military intervention is not an option for China, so it can only push for talks among all parties to realise regional peace."[9] The Afghan talks also provided an opportunity for China to position itself as an alternative power to the US in the region. As the Taliban-US talks faltered in 2019, China invited the Taliban leadership to Beijing. For the Taliban, engaging with Beijing provided an opportunity to nudge the US to expeditiously conclude an Afghan peace agreement.[10]

As it became increasingly clear that the US would withdraw from Afghanistan, China scaled up its engagement with the Taliban in close collaboration with Pakistan. In July 2021, during Pakistan's Foreign Minister Makhdoom Shah Mahmood Qureshi's visit to China, both countries issued a press release titled 'China and Pakistan Decide to Launch Joint Actions on Afghan Issue' with an intent to contain the spread of war and combat terrorism, including the activities of the East Turkestan Islamic Movement (ETIM).[11] A month before the complete US withdrawal from Afghanistan, in July 2021, the Taliban Political Commission, headed by Mullah Abdul Ghani Baradar, travelled to Tianjin to meet with Chinese Foreign Minister Wang Yi.[12] This visit indicated the value that the Taliban placed on its relationship with China. Since Abdul Ghani Baradar was a senior leader of the Taliban, the meeting with Wang Yi indicated that the Taliban leadership and China would unhesitatingly interact at the highest level. Wang Yi called on the Taliban to "make a clean break with all terrorist organisations, including the ETIM" and reportedly referred to the Taliban as "an important military and political force in Afghanistan."[13] The Taliban had already stated that it sees China "as a "friend" of Afghanistan and assured Beijing that it would not host Uyghur Islamic militants from the volatile Xinjiang province.[14] The Tianjin meeting, which happened after considerable preparatory work, was perceived by some as a *de facto* endorsement of the Taliban by a major power, viz., China.[15]

Engagement without Diplomatic Recognition

On August 15, 2021, the Taliban took control of Kabul. The Taliban takeover of Afghanistan was quick and dramatic. Leading members of President Ashraf Ghani's government fled the country, and the Afghan Army disintegrated quickly. There was a sense of elation in the Pakistani establishment that their preferred group—the Taliban—had prevailed in the fight with the US. In fact, a few days after the Taliban takeover, Inter-Services Intelligence (ISI) Director General Lt Gen Faiz Hameed visited Kabul and interacted with the Taliban leadership. Lt Gen Faiz Hameed was photographed with a cup of Tea and having a relaxed conversation with people around.[16] The ISI chief told the media not to worry and that "everything will be okay."[17] Nonetheless, there was considerable anxiety in the international community with the return of the Taliban in Afghanistan.

After the withdrawal of the US defence forces, the Taliban took control of Kabul, and many countries shut down their embassies and diplomatic missions and evacuated their personnel. The deteriorating security situation, uncertainty regarding the Taliban's approach towards diplomatic personnel of other countries, and a reluctance to accord diplomatic recognition to the Taliban prompted many countries to do so. However, Beijing's confidence that the Taliban would not undermine Chinese interests prompted it to retain its diplomatic personnel in Kabul. Moreover, the statements from Beijing hinted that the Taliban regime may soon get diplomatic recognition. On August 18, 2021, the Chinese foreign office spokesperson observed that "it is a customary international practice that the recognition of a government comes after its formation."[18] The Taliban spokesperson was also equally enthusiastic about the relationship with China. In early September 2021, the Taliban spokesperson was quoted as saying, "China is preparing to invest in and rebuild Afghanistan.... This is an incredible opportunity ... China is our gateway to markets around the world."[19]

Beijing seized a window of opportunity created by the US withdrawal to scale up its economic and political engagement. China's support to the Taliban became more pronounced. The Chinese official spokesperson stated that "we respect the will and choice of the Afghan people" and went on to add that a "military intervention against a sovereign state in the name of democracy and human rights has ... [caused] ... serious damage to its economic and social development and leading to massive civilian casualties and displacement."[20] While China did not formally recognise the Taliban, its ambassador and other officials regularly met Taliban officials, and the Taliban's office was also opened in Beijing.[21] In March 2022, Chinese Foreign Minister Wang Yi visited Afghanistan and interacted with the Taliban's foreign minister, Amir Khan Muttaqi, and promised to assist in various domains, including medical care and agriculture.[22] The visit by a high-level leader such as Wang Yi was interpreted as growing Chinese comfort with the Taliban regime. China also sought to scale up its engagement with Afghanistan's neighbours by hosting meetings with the foreign ministers of Pakistan, Iran, Russia, Tajikistan, Turkmenistan, and Uzbekistan.[23]

In April 2023, Beijing issued a paper titled "Position on the Afghan Issue', which noted that China would extend cooperation in Afghanistan's reconstruction and counterterrorism activities with a specific focus on ETIM, the fight against narcotics, humanitarian issues, and refugee issues.[24] The position paper also demanded that the US unfreeze Afghanistan's overseas assets and stressed the importance of opposing external interference and infiltration in Afghanistan. Referring to the 'Three Respects and Three Nevers', the position paper noted that China would respect Afghanistan's independence, sovereignty, and territorial integrity and promised to "never interfere in internal affairs, seek selfish interests, and never pursue so-called sphere of influence."[25]

In September 2023, China appointed a new ambassador to Afghanistan, consolidating the diplomatic relations between the two countries. While the Chinese foreign ministry spokesperson noted that the appointment constituted a normal rotation of the ambassador to Afghanistan, the Taliban representatives termed it as a "significant step with a significant message."[26] A few months later, in January 2024, a Taliban representative presented his credentials to President Xi Jinping as the Afghan interim government's ambassador to China.[27] The appointment of ambassadors generated anticipation that China would soon accord formal diplomatic recognition to the Taliban regime. However, the Chinese foreign ministry spokesperson called on the Taliban to "build an open and inclusive political structure, adopt moderate and prudent domestic and foreign policies, firmly combat all forms of terrorist forces, develop friendly relations with other countries, especially with its neighbours, and integrate itself into the international community ... [and added] ... that the diplomatic recognition of the Afghan government in the world will come naturally as the concerns of various parties are effectively addressed..."[28] The statement indicated that China has made diplomatic recognition contingent on the Taliban's reform efforts and its regional posture.

China used the US withdrawal from Afghanistan to criticise the US foreign policy. Speaking at Tsinghua University, Chinese Foreign Minister Wang Yi noted: "As the culprit of the Afghan issue, the United States should take responsible measures to ensure a smooth transition of the Afghanistan situation instead of shifting blame."[29] China sought to portray the withdrawal not just as a failure of the US but as a failure of the concept of Western democracy. Beijing's foreign policy spokesperson argued that the developments in Afghanistan demonstrate that "democracy imposed and transplanted by others will not last or be firm.... Chinese democracy is people's democracy while the US' is money democracy; the Chinese people enjoy substantial democracy while Americans have democracy only in form; China has a whole-process democracy while the US has voting democracy that comes every four years."[30] China also sought to portray the US policies as instrumental in creating obstacles to the reconstruction of Afghanistan by denying necessary financial resources. The Chinese foreign ministry called on the US "to return the assets of Afghan people as soon as possible."[31] It is well known that USD 7 billion in foreign exchange reserves were in the US central bank, and these assets were frozen by the US. In February 2022, United States President Joe Biden signed an order that USD 3.5 billion of the frozen assets would be used to pay the victims of the 9/11 terror attacks, and the remaining USD 3.5 billion would be distributed to various NGOs via the "fund for the Afghan people."[32] In 2024, Yue Xiaoyong, China's special envoy on Afghanistan, criticising Washington's aid plan, called on the US to unfreeze the "Afghan overseas assets and also lift its unilateral sanctions."[33]

The Chinese media was at the forefront of presenting the so-called 'alternative' perspectives.[34] Immediately after the US withdrawal, the Chinese media scaled up its criticism of the US foreign policy. As images of Afghan civilians' desperate attempts to flee their country garnered international attention, the *Global Times* observed that "Afghanistan's recent chaos is directly related to the hasty and disorderly withdrawal of foreign troops."[35] Some Chinese media reports noted that the US and the West created the Afghan crisis, so "the US and its allies should take the most responsibility to resettle refugees from Afghanistan."[36] Further, the Chinese spokesperson noted that a smooth political transition and prevention of a new civil war would "prevent causing a large number of refugees ... [which] is the fundamental way out on this issue."[37] Overall, after the US withdrawal, China advanced a sharp critique of the US policy and engaged the Taliban regime without bestowing diplomatic recognition. Since no major power sought to exert formal diplomatic influence on the Taliban and undermine Beijing's influence, China was in a position to defer formal diplomatic recognition for the Taliban regime. Such a tactic allowed Chinese business firms to have a first-mover advantage with the new regime in Afghanistan. If China had recognised the Taliban, there was a possibility that other countries may follow suit. The increased density of international actors in Afghanistan would mean that there would be greater competition for mining and infrastructure contracts.

Connectivity and Mining for Profit

China has significant capabilities to define the regional context in Afghanistan's immediate neighbourhood. The BRI provided considerable leverage for China in its western neighbourhood and emerged as an important platform for Afghan engagement. Many of the Central Asian countries have deep economic engagement with China. In March 2021, China announced it would invest USD 400 billion in Iran over the next 25 years.[38] Beijing also expressed interest in investing in Chabahar Port.[39] Even if only some portion of the proposed investment materialises, that would still amount to substantive investments from China. Beijing has already made considerable investments in Pakistan. Through the CPEC, China has made rapid inroads in Pakistan's economy. Given the growing Chinese investments in Iran and Pakistan, Afghanistan, which shares borders with these two countries, will acquire relatively more significance in Beijing's calculations. Interestingly, in October 2023, the Taliban attended the third Belt and Road Forum (BRF) without formal diplomatic recognition. The third BRF was one of the first high-level international gatherings in which the Taliban, after taking control of Kabul, were invited to participate. A day after participating in the Forum, the Taliban representatives requested that China allow them to become formal members of the BRI.[40] Since many developed Western countries were reluctant to make substantive investments in Afghanistan, the Taliban eagerly looked towards China for economic engagement under the BRI rubric.

China's attempts at economic engagement in Afghanistan preceded the US withdrawal from Afghanistan. Manoj Kewalramani rightly pointed out that China benefited from the US presence in Afghanistan, as it enabled Beijing "to free-ride in a regional security environment underwritten by

American military power."[41] The US withdrawal altered the balance of power dynamics in the region, and it allowed China to further scale up its presence in Afghanistan. The Mes Aynak mining project, the world's second-largest copper ore project, was awarded to China in 2007, and the project could not take off due to the prevailing security situation.[42] The work on the mining project began in mid-2024, and the Taliban representative for Economic Affairs, Abdul Ghani Baradar, stated that "the time wasted in the implementation of the project should be recuperated with speedy work."[43] The Taliban's intent to quickly operationalise the project, Michael Kugelman notes, was "very much a part of ... [a] ... broader vision that the Taliban have for making Afghanistan a bigger part of connectivity projects spanning South and Central Asia."[44]

Enhanced engagement may enable China to access significant mineral resources, such as rare earth metals. It is estimated that Afghanistan has about "USD1 trillion in untapped mineral deposits, including critical industrial metals such as lithium, iron, copper and cobalt."[45] The prospect of lithium reportedly prompted many Chinese executives to seek exploration rights from the Taliban leaders with promises to build lithium ore processing plants, battery factories, and roads, which would provide considerable local employment.[46] Interestingly, it was the Soviet geologists who discovered lithium in Afghanistan, which was subsequently reiterated by the US Geological Survey teams, and the Chinese firms are now seeking to exploit the resources.[47] A Pentagon internal memo reportedly noted that "Afghanistan could become the Saudi Arabia of lithium", and experts concluded that the resource could "become the backbone of the Afghan economy."[48] While the initial explorations were made by the Soviet Union and subsequently by the US, China may exploit the valuable mineral resources in Afghanistan.

A few months after the Taliban takeover of Kabul, Chinese news reports suggested that there was a spike in Chinese businesspersons visiting Afghanistan, looking for investment opportunities and enhanced trade.[49] About 20 Chinese state-owned and private companies were keen to invest in lithium and other mining projects.[50] News reports also suggested that China reportedly got contracts to build the "China Town Industrial Park" in Kabul, which will be spread over 130 hectares.[51] By mid-2023, over 20 Chinese companies, with an estimated investment of over USD 2 billion, were operating in Afghanistan.[52] In the same year, Fan China Afghan Mining Processing and Trading Co—a joint venture of Chinese and Afghan firms—reportedly promised to invest about USD 350 million.[53] In August 2023, in an attempt to increase revenues, the Taliban awarded mining contracts worth USD 6.5 billion to firms from Britain, China, Iran, and Turkey.[54]

In the realm of oil exploration and extraction, the Amu River basin deal was initially signed by China National Petroleum Corp in 2011 with the previous Afghan regime, which had hoped that revenues from the project would help pay the bills after the US withdrawal.[55] However, the project could not make much progress due to political instability. In August 2022, the Taliban's Minister of Minerals and Petroleum stated that along with Mes Aynak, an oil extraction project in the northern Amu River basin will be developed with Chinese investments.[56] In January 2023, the Taliban signed a 25-year contract with Xinjiang Central Asia Petroleum and Gas Co to extract and develop oil fields in the northern Afghan provinces.[57] In 2024, *Bloomberg* reported that China's Xinjiang Central Asia Petroleum and Gas Co had drilled ten new oil wells, substantially increasing oil production in Afghanistan.[58] Towards the end of 2024, drilling operations were initiated in approximately 18 new oil extraction sites.[59] Furthermore, it appears that the policymakers in Beijing are interested in plugging Afghanistan into energy and other infrastructure networks connecting China, Central Asia, South Asia, and West Asia.[60]

In terms of connectivity infrastructure, the railroad connectivity between Afghanistan and China was operationalised in 2022, with a freight train from Kashgar (China) reaching Hairatan in Afghanistan.[61] The railway from China (Lanzhou transportation hub) will traverse Kyrgyzstan-Uzbekistan before reaching Afghanistan.[62] In 2023, a Chinese official was quoted stating that attempts would be made to "normalise the route for Sino-Afghanistan express service and aim to run four times a month."[63] While the train did not carry goods of high economic value, the development was significant as it suggested possibilities of rail connectivity to a landlocked country. In 2024, Uzbek Railways announced that it had started 'reconstructing the railway line from Hairatan to Mazar-i-Sharif in Afghanistan'.[64] In a significant development, a freight railway line between Nantong (Jiangsu Province, north of Shanghai in China) and Hairatan (Balkh Province of Afghanistan) was operationalised in October 2024.[65] There are proposals to establish a railway line from Uzbekistan to Pakistan via Afghanistan, enabling the Central Asian countries to access the Indian Ocean ports.[66] Reflecting on the Chinese railway projects in the region, Phunchok Stobdan notes that "Central Asia will once become "central" to East and West transit trade … [and] … The Chinese trains will arrive closer to India through the proposed Trans-Afghan Railway."[67] Stobdan also points out that the proposed railway lines and economic corridors will have to surmount numerous challenges, such as the possible spread of radical Salafi ideology, the prevalence of smuggling illicit goods to Russia, and concerns regarding the influx of Chinese migrants.[68]

Similar concerns dominate the conversations on the Wakhan corridor road as well. In early 2024, reports indicated that a 50-kilometre road with a width of five metres was operationalised in the Wakhan corridor, establishing a road connection between Afghanistan and China.[69] The narrow road serves local communities for trade across borders and is not equipped to handle large-scale cargo movement, customs posts, and other trade-related infrastructure. In addition to being of little economic value, Chinese policymakers may be concerned that the road may pose security risks to Xinjiang province.[70] The Wakhan corridor road, at the moment, is not ready for large-scale trade, and yet, it may acquire importance in the coming years. Aarish Khan notes that much of the Afghanistan-China trade happens through ports in Pakistan, and the ease of border trade between Afghanistan and Pakistan is contingent on the security dynamic between Islamabad and Kabul. Therefore, to insulate China-Afghanistan trade from the vagaries of regional geopolitics, the Wakhan corridor road assumes importance.[71] China and Afghanistan also signed an agreement to construct a fibre optic line from Kashgar in China to Faizabad in Afghanistan via the Wakhan corridor.[72] A direct fibre optic line between the two countries may reduce the internet costs in Afghanistan. Unlike physical connectivity projects, operating a fibre optic line is relatively easier, and it may not pose significant security challenges, given China's robust control of the digital information flows on its networks.

In terms of trade relations, after the Taliban takeover, China emerged as the second-largest trade partner of Afghanistan after Pakistan. Afghanistan has been exporting agricultural products, such as almonds, apricots, and pomegranates, to China.[73] Afghanistan's pine nuts have gained popularity in China. Both countries instituted an air corridor to increase the export of these agricultural commodities.[74] Afghanistan also exports animal hair, horsehair yarn, wool, fabric, coins, metals, pearls, and precious stones to China.[75] Because of severe economic stress, Afghanistan could not take advantage of China's zero-tariff rates on 98 per cent of product lines. Overall, China enjoys a positive trade balance and exports numerous products, such as rubber tyres, synthetic filament yarn woven fabric, motorcycles, and cycles, to Afghanistan.[76]

In the realm of humanitarian assistance, within a month of the Taliban taking control of Afghanistan, China provided USD 31 million in emergency aid, which included coronavirus vaccines. After the earthquake in June 2022, China promised about USD 7.5 million worth of emergency humanitarian assistance.[77] Similarly, in 2023, China provided financial and humanitarian assistance to Afghanistan, which included supplies, such as blankets, tents, and medical supplies, to deal with earthquake-related emergencies.[78] Similar aid was extended to conflict-affected Afghans by China through the UN Refugee Agency (UNHCR) in 2024. Overall, China has initiated a full-spectrum economic engagement in Afghanistan, including mining, connectivity infrastructure, improved trade, and financial and humanitarian assistance for emergencies, such as natural disasters.

Conclusion: Perilous Roads into the Heart of Asia

The Chinese policymakers refer to Afghanistan as a "brilliant pearl on the ancient Silk Road" and the "heart of Asia" because of its location.[79] The growing Chinese presence in Afghanistan will alter the balance of power in multiple regions, viz., South Asia, Central Asia, and the Middle East. The consolidation of Chinese influence in Afghanistan may pose significant challenges for India. There is a perception that China has been making persistent efforts to constrain space for India in global and regional frameworks. While China's attempts to prevent India's entry into the East Asia Summit (EAS) forum were unsuccessful, Beijing successfully prevented India's entry into the Nuclear Supplier Group. In the economic realm, structuring the Regional Comprehensive Economic Partnership (RCEP) provisions ensured that India could not participate in the regional economic grouping. China will be able to create a regional economic group involving some Central Asia countries, Afghanistan, Pakistan, and others. The grouping could be structured in a manner (say, free trade provisions and inclusion of transit routes from Pakistan-Occupied Kashmir) that will make it difficult for India to participate in it. India, which is not participating in the RCEP in its east, may also be left out of an economic grouping in its west in the coming years. It would be to Pakistan's advantage if India is not able to participate in the economic frameworks in its immediate western neighbourhood. Therefore, Pakistan's military leaders' reference to a shift from 'geopolitics to geoeconomics'[80] and its collaboration with China may have a more sinister undertone.

In addition to China's economic prowess, permanent membership in the United Nations Security Council, and ability to exert regional influence, the Chinese engagement with the Taliban may also be impacted by ideological elements. Srikanth Kondapalli contends that there are several similarities, such as governance through highly authoritarian and secretive organisational networks.[81] Unlike the erstwhile Soviet Union, China is not interested in exporting atheist communist ideology. On the other hand, some argue that the CPC will likely be more comfortable consolidating the authoritarian state-led economic development model, which some term authoritarian capitalism.[82] In fact, the Chinese leadership and the media are consistently pointing out that "the Afghan situation again proves democracy has no set model and the standard is whether it meets people's needs and expectations."[83] Beijing also hopes that the Taliban leadership will be a rational actor and will prioritise gaining economic benefits from implementing various projects.[84] There is a view among some in China that the Taliban has shown "a very strong willingness to reform.[85]" If the Taliban moderates its stance towards minorities such as Shias and Uzbeks, then there is an added incentive for some neighbouring countries, such as Iran and Uzbekistan, to proactively collaborate in the BRI projects in their neighbourhood, including Afghanistan. However, as of 2024, there was no perceptible shift in the Taliban's approach towards minorities, women and other vulnerable segments.

Pakistan, which has significant influence in its western neighbourhood, is favourably disposed towards China's BRI and economic agenda in Afghanistan. Islamabad hopes to reap the benefits of Beijing's plans to develop infrastructure networks in Afghanistan and Pakistan. In a test run in 2023, a few trucks from China (Kashgar) used the existing CPEC infrastructure to transport goods to Afghanistan via Pakistan.[86] The Pakistani government had invited Turkmenistan to explore the possibility of transporting energy resources to Gwadar port via Afghanistan.[87] There is anticipation in Pakistan that such economic activities will convert Gwadar into an energy hub and make it an attractive investment destination for foreign investors.

Despite the convergences and opportunities, Chinese engagement in Afghanistan, compared to Central Asia, has to transcend a few critical challenges. In Central Asia, China was able to implement the BRI and scale up economic engagement rapidly, as Soviet-built infrastructure provided a base for economic activity.[88] There was no such Soviet-built infrastructure in Afghanistan. Compared to Afghanistan, Central Asia and Pakistan had relatively better state structures to implement large-scale infrastructure projects. On the contrary, in Afghanistan, the state structures are nearly absent, and the country endured decades of civil war, resulting in low human development indices. For Afghanistan to reap the benefits of BRI, big infrastructure projects should be implemented with considerable focus on developing human resources.

In addition, the exploitation of natural resources is happening in the context of the absence of state capacities to handle such processes. Any individual or group that governs Afghanistan will try to leverage natural resources to generate revenues which can be used to ensure regime stability. However, Afghanistan faces significant challenges in implementing such a strategy. Given the absence of an institutional base and lack of capacities, there are questions as to whether Afghanistan can negotiate deals with major powers such as China with profitable revenue-sharing models. Tamim Asey, noted that the Taliban "regime doesn't even have a constitution let alone mining legal framework" and therefore, "the legal-policy framework for the mining sector is not only vague but almost nonexistent."[89] There were multiple concerns about whether the people of Afghanistan would benefit through appropriate resource sharing if the mining contracts were operationalised. Moreover, the presence of armed groups, with a propensity to seek rent either through threat or actual deployment of violence, may find it difficult to give up their existing business model that focuses on immediate gains rather than long-term institution building. Therefore, Afghan negotiators will find it challenging to present a unified front while negotiating with big companies from major powers. China should nudge the Taliban in Afghanistan to build a state apparatus with a modicum of institutional infrastructure.

To a large extent, the success of Chinese projects will be contingent on the overall security situation in Afghanistan and Pakistan. An examination of the joint statements of these countries demonstrates that numerous organisations—such as Al-Qaeda, the BLA, the Eastern Turkistan Islamic Movement (ETIM), Islamic State Khorasan Province (ISKP), Jaish al-Adl, the Tehreek-e-Taliban Pakistan (TTP)—continue to pose significant security threats.[90] In addition, the Taliban is not a homogeneous entity, and there could be quick shifts in its external engagement. In fact, after the US withdrawal, Chinese news reports had anticipated friction between the various factions of the Taliban and also noted that after the consolidation of political power, various elements of the Taliban may no longer see a need to be beholden to Pakistan.[91]

However, the complete fragmentation of the Taliban has not materialised. Further, the emergence of the Islamic State Khorasan (ISKP) points out that there is no guarantee that new transnational terrorist organisations may emerge, which the Taliban and Pakistan may find difficult to control. Further, as noted in the previous chapter, there were multiple attacks on the CPEC projects. And, there were instances when militant groups targeted Chinese personnel working on BRI projects in Pakistan. The security dynamics in Afghanistan and Pakistan are intertwined, and stability in Afghanistan may have a spillover impact on CPEC in Pakistan as well. To ensure the economic viability of the CPEC, Pakistan's leadership will have to work closely with powers that control Afghanistan. However, the Taliban-Pakistan relations have become frosty, with each accusing the other of prompting violence in their country.

Contrary to Pakistan's expectation, the security situation on the Afghanistan-Pakistan border has deteriorated after the Taliban came to power in August 2021. In fact, in November 2023, the Pakistan leadership noted that "since the Taliban government coming into power, Pakistan has witnessed a 60 per cent increase in terrorism-related incidents..."[92] Islamabad often accused the Taliban of failing to reign in terror groups, such as TTP, which were targeting Pakistan.[93] As a retaliation, the Pakistani government initiated the process of deporting 1.6 million Afghan refugees, without government-approved documents, back to their home country.[94] There was considerable disappointment in Kabul that Pakistan, which proactively intervened in Afghanistan for decades and had a fair share of responsibility in contributing to the political instability in the country, decided to send back refugees on short notice without any support. While a Taliban representative stated that "Pakistan should face the consequences of its actions", its spokesperson reportedly noted that Afghans living in Pakistan are not refugees as they live on "Afghan soil since the Durand Line is invalid."[95] There were sporadic border clashes between the Taliban and the Pakistan defence forces. In March 2024, as a response to terrorist attacks, Pakistan carried out airstrikes deep inside Afghanistan, much to the dismay of the Taliban.[96] In December 2024, Pakistan conducted airstrikes deep inside Afghanistan and the Taliban claimed that approximately 46 civilians, mostly women and children, were killed in the attacks.[97] The air raids further deepened the discord between the Taliban and Pakistan. Towards the end of 2024, China's Special Envoy for Afghanistan travelled to Pakistan and Afghanistan and reportedly made efforts to reduce tensions between the two countries.[98] If the Af-Pak discord escalates, Beijing will be forced to reevaluate its strategy of depending on Islamabad to promote its interests in Kabul.

Overall, Beijing's engagement seeks to leverage China's dominant regional presence to increase its presence in Afghanistan. Further, given China's presence in the economies of Afghanistan's neighbours, it has the ability to push them to take coordinated approaches towards the Taliban. Beijing's engagement is premised on the assumption that it can convince the Taliban leadership that their support in containing the terrorism in Xinjiang would result in considerable economic benefits. Beijing is also exerting economic, political, and security influence to ensure that other major powers do not make deep inroads into Afghanistan's economic and political landscape. While engaging the Taliban gives China significant geopolitical benefits, it also comes with substantial reputational costs. In March 2024, the Taliban announced that it would "soon implement the punishment for adultery ... [and] ... will flog women in public ... [and] ... will stone them to death in public."[99] Any country engaging the Taliban will not be able to look the other way when such violent social norms and legal frameworks get implemented.

China will also have to factor in the attitude of the Afghan neighbours to the Taliban rule. There is a discord in Pakistan's relationship with the Taliban. The Taliban has not accepted the Durand Line as the border between Pakistan and Afghanistan. Moreover, Pakistan is undergoing a severe political crisis, as the contest between former Prime Minister Imran Khan and the military shows no sign of an early conclusion. The influence of the Pakistani military in the polity is being contested. While many experts often wonder about the impact of developments in Afghanistan on the Chinese economic engagement and BRI projects in the Af-Pak region, Pakistan is also a variable of political instability.

Since Afghanistan's ethnic diversity spills into the neighbourhood, the Taliban's policies towards minority ethnic groups will elicit a response from the neighbouring countries. Even after a few years of the Taliban rule, as Stanly Johny noted, "there's widespread anger among ethnic Tajiks & Uzbeks towards the Taliban's Pashtun regime."[100] While Tajikistan and Uzbekistan may welcome improved connectivity networks, the ability of the Taliban to build an inclusive governance framework will impact their policies towards Afghanistan. Similarly, Iran will closely monitor the Taliban's attitude toward Shias. The US remains a significant player in Afghanistan as it can influence the sanctions regime targeting the Taliban and can scale up economic engagement. Raffaello Pantucci, writing towards the end of 2023, notes that United States Agency for International Development (USAID) assistance to Afghanistan since the US withdrawal amounted to approximately USD 2 billion.[101] The scale of the aid points to significant financial resources that the US can quickly deploy in Afghanistan if needed. While China has been making rapid strides in its engagement with the Taliban, a modicum of stability in Afghanistan will bring other major powers in search of economic opportunities.

The volatile security situation in Pakistan and Afghanistan has not hindered China from scaling up economic interactions. Multilateral organisations and civil society groups will closely examine Chinese engagement in Afghanistan, a country yet to transition into a post-conflict phase. Thus far, Chinese engagement has not resulted in replicable models of economic engagement that could engender peace in countries experiencing conflict. On the contrary, there is a perception that Chinese engagement threatened the economic stability of countries such as Sri Lanka, which had experienced decades of ethnic conflict.

Notes

1. As cited in "New Stage in Sino-Afghan Friendly Relations," *Peking Review*, December 20, 1960, vol. III, no. 51, p. 19.
2. Ibid.
3. Bonnie Girard, "How 1980 Laid the Groundwork for China's Major Foreign Policy Challenges," *The Diplomat*, September 12, 2018, https://thediplomat.com/2018/09/how-the-1980-laid-the-groundwork-for-chinas-major-foreign-policy-challenges/; also see Justyna Szczudlik-Tatar, "China's Evolving Stance on Afghanistan: Towards More Robust Diplomacy with 'Chinese Characteristics'," *PISM Strategic File*, Vol 22, No.58, October 2014, https://www.files.ethz.ch/isn/184324/PISM%20Strategic%20File%20no%2022%20(58).pdf
4. For example see, Ted Regencia, "What you should know about China's minority Uighurs," *Al Jazeera*, July 8, 2021, https://www.aljazeera.com/news/2021/7/8/uighurs-timeline; also see "Who are the Uyghurs and why is China being accused of genocide?" *BBC*, May 24, 2022, https://www.bbc.com/news/world-asia-china-22278037
5 Avinash Godbole and Akash S Goud, "China's Xinjiang Problem: The 2009 Riots and its Aftermath," *IDSA Issue Brief*, April 20, 2012, https://www.files.ethz.ch/isn/144068/IB_Xinjiang.pdf
6. Ruchi Kumar, "Why has China recognised Taliban's envoy to Beijing?" *South China Morning Post*, February 14, 2024, https://www.aljazeera.com/news/2024/2/14/is-chinas-recognition-of-afghanistan-envoy-a-diplomatic-win-for-taliban

7. Ralph Jennings and Mandy Zuo, "CIIE: China, Afghanistan cultivate deeper ties with agriculture deals," *South China Morning Post*, November 7, 2023, https://www.scmp.com/economy/china-economy/article/3240649/china-afghanistan-cultivate-deeper-ties-agriculture-deals
8. Petr Topychkanov, "Secret Meeting Brings Taliban to China," *Russia & India Report*, May 28, 2015, https://carnegiemoscow.org/2015/05/28/secret-meeting-brings-taliban-to-china-pub-60241
9. Edward Wong and Mujib Mashal, "Taliban and Afghan Peace Officials Have Secret Talks in China," *The New York Times*, May 25, 2015, https://www.nytimes.com/2015/05/26/world/asia/taliban-and-afghan-peace-officials-have-secret-talks-in-china.html
10 "Taliban in China to discuss Afghan peace after US talks collapse," *AlJazeera*, September 23, 2019, https://www.aljazeera.com/news/2019/9/23/taliban-in-china-to-discuss-afghan-peace-after-us-talks-collapse
11. "China, Pakistan agree to launch 'joint actions' in Afghanistan to drive out terrorist forces: Chinese FM," *Indian Express*, July 27, 2021, https://indianexpress.com/article/world/china-pak-agree-to-launch-joint-actions-in-afghanistan-to-drive-out-terrorist-forces-chinese-fm-7423741/#:~:text=China%2520and%2520Pakistan%2520have%2520decided,Foreign%2520Ministry%2520said%2520on%2520Monday.&text=It%2520is%2520necessa
12. "Chinese FM meets with Afghan Taliban's political chief," *Xinhua*, July 28, 2021, http://www.xinhuanet.com/english/2021-07/28/c_1310092289.htm
13. "Wang Yi Meets with Head of the Afghan Taliban Political Commission Mullah Abdul Ghani Baradar," *Ministry of Foreign Affairs*, the People's Republic of China, July 28, 2021, https://www.fmprc.gov.cn/eng/zxxx_662805/202110/t20211026_10058258.html
14 "Afghan Taliban says it sees China as a 'friend', promises not to host Uyghur militants from Xinjiang: Report," *The Economic Times*, July 10, 2021, https://economictimes.indiatimes.com/news/defence/afghan-taliban-says-it-sees-china-as-a-friend-promises-not-to-host-uyghur-militants-from-xinjiang-report/articleshow/84295588.cms?from=mdr
15. Amy Chew, "Boosted by China ties, Taliban now faces tough call on ETIM crackdown," *SCMP*, August 6, 2021, https://www.scmp.com/week-asia/politics/article/3144148/boosted-china-ties-taliban-now-faces-tough-call-etim-crackdown
16. Sajjad Hussain, "'Everything will be Okay': ISI chief in Afghanistan," *The Rediff*, September 5, 2021, https://m.rediff.com/news/report/everything-will-be-okay-isi-chief-in-afghanistan/20210905.htm
17. Naveed Siddiqui, "'Don't worry, everything will be okay': ISI chief during Kabul visit," *The Dawn*, September 4, 2021, https://www.dawn.com/news/1644463
18. "Foreign Ministry Spokesperson Zhao Lijian's Regular Press Conference on August 18, 2021," *Embassy of the People's Republic of China in India*, August 18, 2021, http://in.china-embassy.gov.cn/eng/fyrth/202108/t20210818_8928589.htm
19. "塔利班发言人：中国是主要合作伙伴，是阿富汗通往世界各地市场的门户," *Tencent*, September 2, 2021, https://new.qq.com/rain/a/20210902A08GOO00
20. "Foreign Ministry Spokesperson Zhao Lijian's Regular Press Conference on August 18, 2021," *Ministry of Foreign Affairs, the People's Republic of China*, https://

www.fmprc.gov.cn/eng/xwfw_665399/s2510_665401/2511_665403/202108/t20210818_9170800.html

21. Laura Zhou, "Chinese businesses make headway in Afghanistan despite Beijing's cautious approach to Taliban," *South China Morning Post*, August 28, 2022, https://www.scmp.com/news/china/diplomacy/article/3190469/chinese-businesses-make-headway-afghanistan-despite-beijings
22. "Wang Yi Holds Talks with Acting Foreign Minister of the Afghan Interim Government Amir Khan Muttaqi," *Ministry of Foreign Affairs, the People's Republic of China,* March 25, 2022, https://www.fmprc.gov.cn/eng/zxxx_662805/202203/t20220325_10655541.html
23. "China to host 3rd meeting of foreign ministers of Afghanistan's neighbors," *Hindustan Times*, March 28, 2022, https://www.hindustantimes.com/world-news/china-to-host-3rd-meeting-of-foreign-ministers-of-afghanistan-s-neighbours-101648474441963.html
24. "China's Position on the Afghan Issue," *Ministry of Foreign Affairs, the People's Republic of China*, April 12, 2023, https://www.mfa.gov.cn/eng/wjdt_665385/wsrc_665395/202304/t20230412_11057785.html
25. Ibid.

26 "Taliban gives a warm welcome to China's new ambassador to Afghanistan," *Al Jazeera,* September 13, 2023, https://www.aljazeera.com/news/2023/9/13/taliban-gives-a-warm-welcome-to-chinas-new-ambassador-to-afghanistan

27. "China defends President Xi accepting Afghan Taliban envoy's diplomatic credentials," *Deccan Herald,* January 31, 2024, https://www.deccanherald.com/world/china-defends-president-xi-accepting-afghan-taliban-envoys-diplomatic-credentials-2873328
28. "Foreign Ministry Spokesperson Wang Wenbin's Regular Press Conference on January 31, 2024," *Ministry of Foreign Affairs, the People's Republic of China,* January 31, 2024, https://www.mfa.gov.cn/eng/xwfw_665399/s2510_665401/2511_665403/202401/t20240131_11237282.html
29. "Wang Yi Delivers Keynote Speech at the Opening Ceremony of the 9th World Peace Forum,*" Embassy of The People's Republic of China in The Republic of Kiribati,* July 3, 2021, http://ki.china-embassy.gov.cn/eng/zgyw/202107/t20210704_8893399.htm
30. "Foreign Ministry Spokesperson Hua Chunying's Regular Press Conference on August 20, 2021," *Consulate-General of the People's Republic of China in Gothenburg,* August 20, 2021, http://gothenburg.china-consulate.gov.cn/eng/fyrth/202108/t20210820_8976927.htm
31. Teddy Ng, "China urges US to unlock Afghanistan's frozen assets," *South China Morning Post*, March 31, 2022, https://www.scmp.com/news/china/diplomacy/article/3172573/china-urges-us-unlock-afghanistans-frozen-assets
32. Ibid.

33 Zhao Yusha and Cao Siqi, "China's special envoy on Afghan affairs urges US to unfreeze Afghanistan assets," *The Global Times,* February 20, 2024, https://www.globaltimes.cn/page/202402/1307364.shtml

34 "世界在听：发自阿富汗的"中国声音," *Sohu.com*, August 29, 2021, https://www.sohu.com/a/486380113_115479

35. Liu Xin and Liu Caiyu, "US Leaves Chaos, Destruction in Afghanistan," *The Global Times,* August 31, 2021, https://www.globaltimes.cn/page/202108/1232914.shtml
36. "US can't avoid Afghanistan after creating a mess," *The Global Times*, August 23, 2021, https://www.globaltimes.cn/page/202108/1232247.shtml
37. "Foreign Ministry Spokesperson Hua Chunying's Regular Press Conference on August 20, 2021," *Embassy of the People's Republic of China in India*, August 20, 2021, http://in.china-embassy.gov.cn/eng/fyrth/202108/t20210820_8928591.htm
38. Farnaz Fassihi and Steven Lee Myers, "China, With $400 Billion Iran Deal, Could Deepen Influence in Mideast," *The New York Times*, March 29, 2021, https://www.nytimes.com/2021/03/27/world/middleeast/china-iran-deal.html
39. Sabena Siddiqui, "Can Chinese investment provide boost to Iran's Chabahar port?" *Al Monitor*, May 10, 2021, https://www.al-monitor.com/originals/2021/05/can-chinese-investment-provide-boost-irans-chabahar-port#ixzz7n3vU2ayh; also see: "Iran-China partnership to raise Chabahar port's global status," *Tehran Times*, April 27, 2021, https://www.tehrantimes.com/news/460316/Iran-China-partnership-to-raise-Chabahar-port-s-global-status
40. Joe Cash, "Taliban Says Plans to Formally Join China's Belt and Road Initiative," *Reuters,* October 19, 2023, https://www.reuters.com/world/asia-pacific/taliban-says-plans-formally-join-chinas-belt-road-initiative-2023-10-19/
41. Manoj Kewalramani, "The Future of China's Engagement in Afghanistan," *The Hindustan Times*, September 1, 2021, https://www.hindustantimes.com/opinion/the-future-of-china-s-engagement-in-afghanistan-101630501860368.html
42. "Project to exploit Afghanistan's giant copper deposit languishes," *China Dialogue*, April 25, 2018, https://chinadialogue.net/en/business/10577-project-to-exploit-afghanistan-s-giant-copper-deposit-languishes/
43. "China Starts Work on Afghan Copper Mine Long Stalled by War," *ETEnergyworld,* July 25, 2024, https://energy.economictimes.indiatimes.com/news/power/china-starts-work-on-afghan-copper-mine-long-stalled-by-war/112010684
44. Christina Lu, "China and the Taliban Team Up on Copper," *Foreign Policy,* September 10, 2024, January 2025, https://foreignpolicy.com/2024/09/10/china-taliban-copper-afghanistan-economy-minerals-mes-aynak/
45. Zhou Bo, "In Afghanistan, China Is Ready to Step Into the Void," *The New York Times*, August 20, 2021, https://www.nytimes.com/2021/08/20/opinion/china-afghanistan-taliban.html
46. Gerry Shih and Lorenzo Tugnoli, "Rich lode of EV metals could boost Taliban and its new Chinese partners," *The Washington Post,* July 20, 2023, https://www.washingtonpost.com/world/interactive/2023/ev-lithium-afghanistan-taliban-china/
47. Ibid.
48. James Risen, "U.S. Identifies Vast Mineral Riches in Afghanistan," *The New York Times,* June 13, 2010, https://www.nytimes.com/2010/06/14/world/asia/14minerals.html
49. "Chinese industrial park to be built in Kabul New City," *Global Times*, March 31, 2022, https://www.globaltimes.cn/page/202203/1257334.shtml
50. Ibid.

51. "China seeks to expand business in Afghanistan with "Chinatown industrial park project"," *The Print*, August 26, 2022, https://theprint.in/world/china-seeks-to-expand-business-in-afghanistan-with-chinatown-industrial-park-project/1102363/
52. "Recent Chinese Investment, Contracts Worth $2 Billion: MoIC," *Tolonews,* May 7, 2023, https://tolonews.com/business-183264
53. "China increases Afghanistan investment but faces terrorism challenges," *Business Standard,* July 15, 2023, https://www.business-standard.com/world-news/china-increases-afghanistan-investment-but-faces-terrorism-challenges-123071500042_1.html
54 Ayaz Gul, "Taliban Sign Multibillion-Dollar Afghan Mining Deals," *VoA,* August 31, 2023, https://www.voanews.com/a/taliban-sign-multibillion-dollar-afghan-mining-deals/7249135.html
55. "Afghanistan signs major oil deal with China's CNPC," *Reuters,* December 28, 2011, https://www.reuters.com/article/afghanistan-cnpc/update-1-afghanistan-signs-major-oil-deal-with-chinas-cnpc-idUSL3E7NS40J20111228/
56. "Afghanistan plans to resume Mes Aynak mining and petroleum extraction projects with China soon," *CGTN,* August 27, 2022, https://news.cgtn.com/news/2022-08-27/Afghanistan-plans-to-resume-Mes-Aynak-mining-project-with-China-soon-1cQcnDl48QU/index.html
57. Catherine Putz, "Taliban Settle Oil Deal With Chinese Company," *The Diplomat,* January 6, 2023, https://thediplomat.com/2023/01/taliban-settle-oil-deal-with-chinese-company/
58. Eltaf Najafizada, "China Firm's Crude Output Surges 300% in Taliban-led Afghanistan," *Bloomberg,* December 6, 2023, https://www.bloomberg.com/news/articles/2023-12-06/china-firm-s-crude-output-surges-300-in-taliban-led-afghanistan
59 "Drilling begins on 18 new Amu River Oil wells," *Alemarahe,* November 17, 2024, https://www.alemarahenglish.af/drilling-begins-on-18-new-amu-river-oil-wells/
60. "Will China's latest investment in Afghanistan actually work?" *Al Jazeera,* February 27, 2023, https://www.aljazeera.com/economy/2023/2/27/will-chinas-latest-investment-in-afghanistan-actually-work
61. "Land corridor via rail connects Afghanistan to China as 1st freight arrives," *Global Times,* September 24, 2022, https://www.globaltimes.cn/page/202209/1275988.shtml#:~:text=Land%20corridor%20via%20rail%20connects,1st%20freight%20arrives%20%2D%20Global%20Times&text=Photo%3AXinhua-,The%20land%20corridor%20through%20railroad%20has%20linked%20landlocked%20Afghanistan%20to,northern%20Balkh%20province%20on%20Thursday.
62. "Int'l freight train service launched from China's Gansu to Afghanistan," *Xinhua,* July 7, 2023, http://english.scio.gov.cn/beltandroad/2023-07/07/content_91668103.htm
63. Zhao Ziwen, "China announces land link with Taliban-controlled Afghanistan," *South China Morning Post,* July 6, 2023, https://www.scmp.com/news/china/diplomacy/article/3226822/china-announces-land-link-taliban-controlled-afghanistan
64. "The Uzbek Railways have commenced the reconstruction of the railway line 'Hairatan – Mazar-i-Sharif'," *Railway Supply,* February 2, 2024, https://www.

railway.supply/en/the-uzbek-railways-have-commenced-the-reconstruction-of-the-railway-line-hairatan-mazar-i-sharif/

65 "Taliban Announces Launch of Direct Freight Railway Line Between China & Afghanistan," *Afghanistan International,* October 31, 2024. https://www.afintl.com/en//en/202410314340.

66. Pravesh Kumar Gupta, "A Bleak Future for Trans-Afghan Railway," *The Hindustan Times,* March 19, 2024, https://www.hindustantimes.com/ht-insight/international-affairs/a-bleak-future-for-trans-afghan-railway-101710842519905.html

67. P. Stobdan, "China-Kyrgyzstan-Uzbekistan railway: Could China be at India's border?," *The Indian Express,* January 19, 2024, https://indianexpress.com/article/opinion/columns/china-kyrgyzstan-uzbekistan-railway-could-china-be-at-indias-border-9116257/

68. Ibid.

69. Fidel Rahmati, "Wakhan Corridor officially connects Afghanistan to China: Taliban," *The Khaama Press,* January 16, 2024, https://www.khaama.com/badakhshan-province-officially-connects-afghanistan-to-china-via-wakhan-corridor-official/

70. Zhao Ziwen, "Why China is wary of opening up Afghanistan's new road to Xinjiang," *The South China Morning Post,* January 26, 2024, https://www.scmp.com/news/china/diplomacy/article/3249931/why-china-wary-opening-afghanistans-new-road-xinjiang

71 Aarish U Khan, "The Reality of Afghanistan's Land Link With China," *The Diplomat,* October 9, 2024, https://thediplomat.com/2024/10/the-reality-of-afghanistans-land-link-with-china/

72. "Fiber Optic Network Project to be Completed In 7 Months," *Tolo News,* December 26, 2018, https://tolonews.com/afghanistan/budget/fiber-optic-network-project-be-completed-7-months

73. "China will continue to support Afghanistan as it transitions from chaos to stability: Chargé d'Affaires of Chinese Embassy in Afghanistan," *Embassy of the People's Republic of China in the Islamic Republic of Afghanistan,* August 30, 2023, http://af.china-embassy.gov.cn/eng/sgxw/202308/t20230830_11135538.htm

74. "Air corridor of pine nuts: a bridge of friendship between China and Afghanistan," *Embassy of the People's Republic of China in the Islamic Republic of Afghanistan,* January 11, 2022, http://af.china-embassy.gov.cn/eng/sgxw/202201/t20220111_10480912.htm

75. "China and Afghanistan: Bilateral Trade Relationship and Future Outlook," *China Briefing,* January 10, 2023, https://www.china-briefing.com/news/china-and-afghanistan-bilateral-trade-relationship-and-future-outlook/

76. "China/Afghanistan," *OEC,* https://oec.world/en/profile/bilateral-country/chn/partner/afg

77. "China to offer $7.5 million in emergency humanitarian aid to quake-hit Afghanistan," *Global Times,* June 24, 2022, https://www.globaltimes.cn/page/202206/1268966.shtml

78. "China provides emergency humanitarian assistance to Afghanistan," *Xinhua,* October 12, 2023, https://english.news.cn/20231012/e9cca9b677044c5ea752146a4308a259/c.html

79. "China will continue to support Afghanistan as it transitions from chaos to stability: Chargé d'Affaires of Chinese Embassy in Afghanistan," *Embassy of the People's Republic of China in the Islamic Republic of Afghanistan*, August 30, 2023, http://af.china-embassy.gov.cn/eng/sgxw/202308/t20230830_11135538.htm
80. Arshad Mahmood, "Pakistan's Strategic Shift from Geo-Politics to Geo-Economics," *Pakistan Today*, February 15, 2022, https://www.pakistantoday.com.pk/2022/02/15/pakistans-strategic-shift-from-geo-politics-to-geo-economics/
81 Srikanth Kondapalli, "China and the Taliban – Several Similarities," *Financial Express,* September 15, 2021, https://www.financialexpress.com/business/defence-china-and-the-taliban-several-similarities-2330469/
82. See Stefan Halper, *The Beijing consensus: Legitimizing Authoritarianism in Our Time* (New York: Basic Books, 2012).
83. "Democracy has no single formula and the right to define not monopolized by US and allies," *Global Times*, August 20, 2021, https://www.globaltimes.cn/page/202108/1232042.shtml
84. "一带一路"在塔利班统治下的阿富汗有未来吗?" *manyushijia.com* August 8, 2021, http://www.manyushijia.com/news/show-14128.html
85. "朱永彪谈阿富汗问题（下：对于塔利班，我们心里要"有谱," *The Paper*, August 26, 2021, https://www.thepaper.cn/newsDetail_forward_14209393
86. "New TIR trade route opens connecting China to Pakistan and Afghanistan," *IRU,* September 6, 2023, https://www.iru.org/news-resources/newsroom/new-tir-trade-route-opens-connecting-china-pakistan-and-afghanistan
87. "Pakistan, Turkmenistan ink Joint Implementation Plan for TAPI gas pipeline," *Business Standard,* June 9, 2023, https://www.business-standard.com/world-news/pakistan-turkmenistan-ink-joint-implementation-plan-for-tapi-gas-pipeline-123060900063_1.html
88. Based on multiple interviews.
89. As cited in Zia Ur Rehman, "Afghanistan's $6.5bn mine deals with China, others dig up questions," *Nikkei Asia*, September 17, 2023, https://asia.nikkei.com/Politics/International-relations/Afghanistan-turmoil/Afghanistan-s-6.5bn-mine-deals-with-China-others-dig-up-questions
90. "Joint Statement of the Second Informal Meeting on Afghanistan Between Foreign Ministers of China, Russia, Pakistan and Iran," *Ministry of Foreign Affairs, the People's Republic of China*, April 14, 2023, https://www.fmprc.gov.cn/eng/wjdt_665385/2649_665393/202304/t20230414_11059063.html
91. 阿富汗与中国, https://zhuanlan.zhihu.com/p/382847999
92. "Chose Between Pakistan or Tehrik-E-Taliban Pakistan Says Pakistan Interim PM To The Afghan Interim Government ," *The Khorasan Diary*, November 9, 2023, https://twitter.com/khorasandiary/status/1722149707831759178?s=48
93. "In an Unprecedented move, Pakistan charges Afghan authorities with 'facilitating' militants," *Arab News*, November 8, 2023, https://www.arabnews.com/node/2405231/pakistan
94. Abid Hussain, "As Pakistan deports refugees, tense Afghanistan ties come in sharp focus," *Al Jazeera*, November 7, 2023, https://www.aljazeera.com/news/2023/11/7/as-pakistan-deports-refugees-tense-afghanistan-ties-come-in-sharp-focus

95. "Taliban appeal to Afghan private sector to help those fleeing Pakistan's mass deportation drive," *The Hindu*, November 4, 2023, https://www.thehindu.com/news/international/taliban-appeal-to-afghan-private-sector-to-help-those-fleeing-pakistans-mass-deportation-drive/article67498956.ece; also see Tilak Devasher, Twitter, October 6, 2023, https://twitter.com/tilakdevasher1/status/1710213866720735359?s=61&t=O6GN5wpKRlVGH2grBrh1bA
96. Sumeda, "Why did Pakistan carry out airstrikes in Afghanistan?" *The Hindu*, March 22, 2024, https://www.thehindu.com/news/international/pakistan-airstrikes-afghanistan-taliban-islamabad-terrorism-explainer/article67979105.ece
97. Abid Hussain, "Pakistan Air Strikes in Afghanistan Spark Taliban Warning of Retaliation," *Al Jazeera*, December 25, 2024, https://www.aljazeera.com/news/2024/12/25/pakistan-air-strikes-in-afghanistan-spark-taliban-warning-of-retaliation.
98. Kamran Yousaf, "China pushes to ease Pak-Afghan tensions," *The Express Tribune,* November 25, 2024, https://tribune.com.pk/story/2511744/china-pushes-to-ease-pak-afghan-tensions
99. "Taliban To Resume Stoning Women In Public For Adultery: Report," *NDTV*, March 29, 2024, https://www.ndtv.com/world-news/taliban-says-afghanistans-women-will-be-stoned-in-public-for-adultery-report-5332661
100. Stanly Johny, Twitter, March 25, 2024, https://twitter.com/johnstanly/status/1772121741147463716
101. Raffaello Pantucci, "Afghanistan Shows the Gap between BRI Rhetoric and Reality," *Nikkei Asia,* November 8, 2023, https://asia.nikkei.com/Opinion/Afghanistan-shows-the-gap-between-BRI-rhetoric-and-reality ; also see Katherine Gypson, "US Lawmakers Question Whether Aid Is Benefiting Taliban," *VoA,* January 11, 2024, https://www.voanews.com/a/us-lawmakers-question-whether-aid-is-benefiting-taliban-/7436456.html

5

China and the Emerald Island: Navigating Turbulence

Introduction

During his visit to Sri Lanka in 2014, President Xi Jinping referred to the country as a 'Pearl in the Indian Ocean' and went on to add that the "ship of China-Sri Lanka friendship and cooperation is bound to brave the wind and waves along the magnificent 21st Century Maritime Silk Road."[1] As in the case of Pakistan, even in Sri Lanka, the Chinese leadership deployed soaring rhetoric to define the bilateral relationship. President Xi, in his article for a Sri Lankan newspaper, referred to a Chinese poem—"The ocean is so vast that the fish may leap about happily, and the sky is so high that birds may glide freely"—to describe opportunities that abound Sri Lanka-China partnership.[2] Some Chinese academics often refer to the expedition of Admiral Zheng He to the Indian Ocean Region (IOR), including to Sri Lanka, in the fifteenth century to demonstrate the long-standing historical relations between Colombo and Beijing.[3] In recent times, the Chinese outreach has been defined by Sri Lanka's geopolitical location close to the maritime shipping lines in the Indian Ocean. Moreover, a robust presence in Sri Lanka assumed importance, given the Chinese dependence on energy imports via the Indian Ocean and its growing international trade. Over the years, the changing economic imperatives and geopolitical considerations defined the Chinese-Sri Lanka bilateral dynamic.

Barter Trade and Non-Alignment

Interestingly, while Sri Lanka was one of the early countries that recognised the People's Republic of China in 1950, diplomatic relations were not immediately established. Even in the absence of full diplomatic relations, both countries engaged in path-breaking economic agreements. The historic Sri Lanka-China Rubber-Rice Agreement of 1952 could be characterised as an example of South-South cooperation and was defined by barter trade. The Rubber-Rice Agreement came into play in a specific historical context. Sri Lanka was experiencing an economic crisis, as natural rubber, its principal export, suffered in the global markets due to the introduction of synthetic rubber. Simultaneously, there was a shortage of rice in the global markets. Therefore, Sri Lanka's export earnings declined, making it challenging to fund rice imports at higher prices to feed the nation. On the other hand, Beijing had a surplus of rice and was unable to import rubber from other countries as, on May 18, 1951, the United Nations (UN) imposed an embargo on the shipment of arms and materials of strategic value, which included rubber, to the People's Republic of China and North Korea.[4] The export of rubber to China was curtailed, and there was a glut in the global rubber market, which further contributed to a downward spiral of its prices. All this adversely impacted the rubber farmers in Sri Lanka. While the Americans were willing to buy rubber at global market prices, many in Sri Lanka felt it would result in payments way below the actual price that was prevalent before the imposition of the UN sanctions.[5] A disagreement with the US on the prices and the growing willingness of the Chinese to trade exchangeable surplus commodities paved the way for the Sri Lanka-China 1952 pact. Reflecting on the negotiations, then Sri Lankan Commerce Minister R.G. Senanayake observed that the Chinese side did not indulge in 'haggling on comparatively small points' and instead gave "the impression of being large-minded and forthright in their dealings."[6]

While the Rubber-Rice Agreement, in the long run, laid the foundation for China-Sri Lanka trade, in the short run, it prompted a negative response from the US and the United Kingdom. Both the countries prohibited their vessels from transporting Sri Lankan rubber to China. The US also suspended aid to Sri Lanka in 1952.[7] Howard Wriggins notes that the Rubber-Rice pact had a larger geopolitical message: 'first, it heralded Chinese diplomatic relations with non-Communist states; second, the domestic Left parties in Sri Lanka took credit for protecting the rubber farmers and ensuring the flow of food grains; third, the vision of Asians selling their raw material to other Asian countries, independent of western countries was operationalised; and finally, the western countries despite their opposition to the pact could not do much to prevent the flow of raw materials and food grains.'[8] A few years later, the Rubber-Rice template was deployed in the Ceylon, Japan and Egypt Agreement in 1956, under which "Japan [would] import cotton from Egypt and pay Ceylon in sterling for Egypt's tea imports."[9]

It took almost five more years after the Rubber-Rice Pact to establish diplomatic relations between China and Sri Lanka in 1957, and Chinese Premier Zhou Enlai was the first senior political leader from China to visit the country. Despite harbouring concerns regarding China's Tibet policy, the Sri Lankan leaders were keen on maintaining warm relations and refrained from taking steps that would imperil the relationship. In response to the Chinese incorporation of Tibet in 1959, there were protests by the Buddhist organisation in Sri Lanka, but the Sri Lankan government refrained from giving in to demands to reprimand China on the Tibetan question.[10]

In the subsequent years, Sri Lanka's non-alignment policy ensured cordial relations with China. Sri Lanka's commitment to non-alignment was tested during the 1962 India-China War. Sri Lankan Prime Minister Sirimavo R.D. Bandaranaike took the initiative of convening a meeting in Colombo from December 10 to 12, 1962, with five other non-aligned countries (the United Arab Republic (UAR), Indonesia, Burma, Ghana, and Cambodia) to mediate between the two warring countries. The outcome of the meeting was called the Colombo Conference Proposals, which were placed before the governments of China and India. In fact, Prime Minister Bandaranaike, along with government representatives of the UAR and Ghana, travelled to China and then to India to discuss the proposals. Prime Minister Bandaranaike visited Delhi, and Indian Prime Minister Nehru welcomed the peace efforts and stated: "I can assure you that we, for our part, are eager to take the first and the second and the third step to ensure peace subject naturally to, I say, the honour of our country and the self-respect of our country which we feel have been outraged to some extent."[11] Broadly, the Colombo Conference Proposals suggested a Chinese withdrawal by 20 kilometres as well as the creation of a demilitarised zone in the Western Sector and in the Eastern Sector, "the line of actual control in the areas recognised by both the Governments could serve as a ceasefire line."[12] While the Indian government accepted the proposals, the Chinese government turned them down.[13] Premier Zhou Enlai, in his letter to Prime Minister Bandaranaike, stated: "what the Chinese government has done and is doing actually far exceeds what is required of China by the proposal of the Colombo Conference."[14]

There was an opinion that the non-aligned states (the Colombo Powers) demonstrated an even-handed approach between a leader of the non-aligned group (India) and a member of the Communist bloc (China) and refrained from identifying an "aggressor" and the "defender".[15] At the civic reception for Sirimavo Bandaranaike, Prime Minister Nehru reaffirmed his commitment to non-aligned principles by stating that "this non-alignment is under severe attack ... it is highly important that we stick to our principles and determinedly face the situation. The visit of these representatives has, in fact, strengthened our resolve to adhere to our principles."[16] While the role of the non-aligned countries during the war can be interrogated, Sri Lanka established its credentials in the international community through deft diplomacy. While the Colombo conference proposals did not result in an immediate resolution of the complex India-China boundary dispute, the initiative by Sri Lanka facilitated communication between the two countries at war. A relatively smaller country, Sri Lanka, attempted a mediation between two Asian giants and came out of the process unscathed. Importantly, the Colombo Conference initiative did not undermine Sri Lanka's relations with India or China. While China rejected the Colombo conference proposals, its relations with Sri Lanka were not adversely impacted. An editorial in China's *Renmin Ribao* (1963) newspaper appreciated "the efforts of Ceylon government and other countries which took part in the Colombo Conference."[17] Subsequently, China and Sri Lanka signed an agreement on commercial maritime relations in 1963. During Prime Minister Premier Zhou Enlai's visit to Sri Lanka in 1964, China promised assistance to build an international conference building, which was completed in 1973.[18] The Chinese government also assisted in constructing the Supreme Court building, which was inaugurated in 1988, and a Chinese construction company refurbished the building about two decades later.[19]

With an intent to enhance economic relations, in the 1980s and 1990s, the two countries created frameworks and signed agreements, such as the Sri Lanka-Chinese Joint Commission (1991); Sri Lanka China Business Cooperation Council (1994); China-Sri Lanka Economic and Technical Cooperation Agreement (1994); Letter of Intent for the Development of Trade between China and Sri Lanka (1994); and an agreement on Avoiding

Double Taxation of Income and Preventing Tax Evasion.[20] The bilateral economic interactions picked up momentum in the new millennium, more so after the end of the Civil War.

Sri Lanka endured a brutal civil war for over three decades. The war ended with the defeat of the Liberation Tigers of Tamil Eelam (LTTE) and the death of its leader, Velupillai Prabhakaran, in May 2009. During the final phase of the Sri Lankan government's offensive against the LTTE, China provided fighter jets and other military equipment to Colombo.[21] In 2012, China opposed a US-backed resolution at the United Nations Human Rights Council (UNHRC), calling on Sri Lanka to address human rights violations. The Chinese contention was that "country-specific human rights resolution to impose pressure" would be opposed and "the Sri Lankan government and people are capable of handling their own affairs."[22]

The war resulted in thousands of casualties and considerable destruction of infrastructure. However, despite the civil war, in 2010, Sri Lanka ranked 91 on the Human Development Index, which was relatively better than most of the other countries in the sub-continent, such as the Maldives (107), India (119), Pakistan (125), Bangladesh (129), and Nepal (138).[23] After the end of the civil war, Sri Lanka was eager to make up for the lost time. However, the shadow of the civil war continued to linger. While the Western countries were having serious conversations about the nature of the Sri Lankan offensive against the LTTE, the Chinese government stepped in with the promise of considerable infrastructure investment. As Sri Lanka opened up for Chinese investments, it received military and diplomatic support in return.

Given Sri Lanka's maritime location, China's infrastructure projects focused substantially on transportation infrastructure. Sri Lanka is next to one of the busiest international shipping lines traversing through the IOR. Therefore, developing port infrastructure is critical to ensure the country retains and reinforces its status as a trans-shipment hub. In this direction, constructing new ports and expanding the existing ports were conceptualised in collaboration with China.

Ports, Economy, and Strategy

China Merchants Holdings and Aitken Spence signed an agreement with the Sri Lanka Port Authority (SLPA) to develop the Colombo South Container Terminal in 2011. The agreement stipulated that China Merchants Holdings would hold 55 per cent, Aitken Spence 30 per cent, and SLPA would hold

15 per cent in the joint venture.[24] A year later, Aitken Spence announced that it was selling "its 30 per cent stake in the venture to build Colombo South container terminal" to China Merchants Holdings.[25] It was reported in the media that Aitken Spence withdrew from the joint venture "due to high costs and unreasonable demands."[26] Due to the sale, China Merchants Holdings' share in the joint venture increased to 85 per cent. In 2014, the Colombo South Container Terminal project was completed, with added capacity to service mega container ships.[27]

The Chinese engagement in Hambantota attracted worldwide attention because of the port's geostrategic location and concern that Sri Lanka would have to endure a debt crisis. As early as 2002, the Sri Lankan leadership identified Hambantota port as the core of the Southern Development Program, which aimed to convert the port city into "a garden city like Singapore."[28] In April 2005, the joint communique issued during the visit of Chinese Prime Minister Wen Jiabao to Sri Lanka referred to the possible "development of the Hambantota Bunkering System and Tank Farm Project between the Sri Lanka Ports Authority and the China Huanqiu Contracting and Engineering Corporation."[29] The project did not make progress, as quite often, the discussion about an upcoming port was marked by scepticism as to whether such an endeavour would be financially feasible. Jonathan Hillman at the CSIS noted that there were two feasibility studies—the feasibility study by a Canadian engineering firm, SNC Lavalin, in 2003, which was rejected by the government and a subsequent feasibility study by a Danish consulting firm, Ramboll, in 2006, which was more optimistic on the prospect of a deep-sea port at Hambantota.[30] The second feasibility study gave a fillip to the optimistic discussions on the need to operationalise the Hambantota port. The Joint Press Communique issued during Sri Lankan President Mahinda Rajapaksa's visit to Beijing in 2007 to commemorate 50 years of bilateral diplomatic relations referred to the Hambantota Development Zone and called on the "financial institutions to effectively examine feasibility reports" pertaining to the port project.[31] In March 2007, China and Sri Lanka signed an agreement to construct the Hambantota Port Development project.[32] There was an opinion that Sri Lanka, in its anxiety to get military equipment, had agreed to a financially unviable project. For instance, Jeff M. Smith notes: "in 2007, months before China and Sri Lanka signed their first arms deal, Rajapaksa signed a USD 1 billion deal with a Chinese consortium to construct and operate a new port at Hambantota."[33] Such a coincidence suggests that economic and political considerations were closely intertwined. Like many Chinese projects, the Hambantota Port Phase 1 was implemented expeditiously, and at its inauguration in 2010, President Rajapaksa prophesied that "it is not seawater that will fill this port, but the future prosperity of our nation…from this port will emerge our true economic independence."[34] It was soaring rhetoric, but the developments in the subsequent years threatened to undermine the economic independence of Sri Lanka. The port was supposed to break even and start making money by 2013, but by the end of 2016, it reportedly had losses amounting to USD 3 billion.[35] There was criticism that the award of the project was marked by a lack of transparency. For instance, Vikas Bajaj, writing in the *New York Times,* opined that "Sri Lankan officials have refused to disclose information that would allow analysts to compare China's proposals with those submitted by other bidders."[36] Many argued that the Hambantota port also fuelled Sri Lanka's debt problem. While China "loaned 85 per cent of the finances for the USD 1.5 billion port… The balance was put up by the Sri Lankan government, which borrowed heavily from other sources."[37] As the debt burden mounted, in 2016, the Sri Lankan government sold an 80 per cent stake in a deep-water port to China Merchants Port Holdings Co.[38] The agreement was aimed at helping Sri Lanka overcome a severe debt crisis. The sale of Hambantota port did not dampen Sri Lanka's enthusiasm to participate in the BRI projects. The Sri Lankan prime minister participated in Beijing's 2017 Belt and Road Forum (BRF). Referring to the participation at the BRF, the Chinese Ambassador in Colombo wrote that Sri Lanka's attempts to emerge as a "financing and logistic centre in the Indian Ocean" is in "line with the 21st Century Maritime Silk Road."[39] Meanwhile, towards the end of 2017, Sri Lanka formally handed over Hambantota port to China on lease for 99 years.[40]

There were suggestions that Sri Lanka repay the debt and regain control of the port. In December 2019, reflecting on Chinese management of the Hambantota port, then President Gotabaya Rajapaksa stated that "giving a small loan for investment is a different thing, but giving a strategically important economic harbour is not acceptable….that we should have controlled."[41] However, a few days later, Gotabaya Rajapaksa clarified that he was not interested in "renegotiating the agreement as it is a commercial contract" and added that Hambantota should be like Colombo Port, where the Sri Lankan government controls its security "because it is Sri Lanka's asset."[42] A few months later, a former Sri Lankan official observed that "the perfect circumstance is a return to the norm…We pay back the loan in due course in the way that we had originally agreed without any disturbance at all."[43] However, the Chinese government was reluctant to renegotiate the deal. A senior Chinese government official noted that both countries "will speed up the implementation of cooperation on big economic projects", as per the "existing consensus", which would form the basis for future cooperation.[44] The reluctance to hand back the port to Sri Lanka could have stemmed from the extensive plans the Chinese government may have had for the port. In Chinese media, there were opinions that Hambantota port could be better managed with the infusion of capital and technology and that developing alternative financial streams, such as the oil and gas sector, would add to the project's overall economic viability.[45] There were also proposals to host an industrial park that could become an important hub in the global supply chains and also ensure greater profitability of the port.[46] Hambantota port would also act as a hub between the CPEC and the Bangladesh-China-India-Myanmar (BCIM) economic corridors. Given the port's criticality in the larger Chinese plans for the region, some reports hinted that China might invest more in the port.[47]

Sinopec's Hambantota Port Oil Depot handled its first oil shipment in April 2020.[48] The depot would provide oil supplies to cargo and other ships as well as for Sri Lanka's domestic use.[49] Both countries signed an agreement to build a USD 300 million export-oriented tyre factory close to the Hambantota port.[50] Reportedly, a Chinese industrial group is also constructing 'plug-and-play factories for light industries' near Hambantota.[51] The developments in the recent past suggest that the Chinese are moving ahead with their plans to scale up their economic presence in the port. For these proposals to move forward as envisaged, considerable numbers of skilled human resources would be required. It isn't certain if all such workforce can be procured from Sri Lanka at competitive wages. The port's success will result in demographic shifts in the region abutting the port. If the port fails to take off, despite developing a new industrial zone, it will negatively impact the Hambantota region and Sri Lanka.

Close to Hambantota port, the Mattala Rajapaksa International Airport was also constructed with Chinese assistance. Quite often, the airport was described as "the world's emptiest airport."[52] The airport was built at an estimated cost of USD 209 million, and much of it (USD 190 million) was in the form of loans from China."[53] The airport was built to have a capacity of "one million passengers a year and is expected to handle five million passengers, 50,000 tonnes of cargo and 6,250 air traffic operations per annum by 2028."[54] The airport was supposed to cater to the high-intense activity at Hambantota and the consequent movement of people and goods. However, such grand plans require time to be operationalised, and the activity at the Hambantota port did not take off as anticipated. As a consequence, there was little demand for the airport.

In 2018, there were reports that India, in collaboration with Sri Lanka, would be involved in operating the airport. David Brewster noted that there was speculation that if Hambantota were to evolve into a full-fledged Chinese naval base, it would require maritime air surveillance capabilities and the option of air supplies, which would be denied if India were to control the port.[55] However, Sri Lankan Prime Minister Mahinda Rajapaksa, in July 2020, stated that there were no plans for a joint venture, adding, "...during my recent visit to India ... I told them, please do not take it (airport) ... it is located in my village, and it is only our second international airport ... they (India) heeded our request, so we were able to save it."[56] So it is not certain if India has given up interest in managing the airport given its strategic significance. Subsequently, during the pandemic, the Mattala Rajapaksa International Airport was used to bring back stranded Sri Lankans from different parts of the world.[57] By early 2023, while there was some increase in the number of passengers utilising the airport,[58] the Sri Lankan government continued to make the airport financially viable by seeking foreign direct investment in aviation-related ventures, such as repair and overhaul facilities and logistic services.[59] As the airport continued to make losses, in 2024, the Sri Lankan government reportedly handed over the airport operations for 30 years to Indian and Russian firms.[60]

Energy and Expressways

There were Chinese investments in the energy sector as well. In 2006, China National Machinery Import and Export Corporation won the bid to operationalise a coal-fired power plant in Norochcholai, Sri Lanka. India's National Thermal Power Corporation's bid for the power plant was unsuccessful.[61] The power plant would run on imported coal, and China's Export Import (EXIM) bank provided the loan to construct the power plant.[62] The coal was to be imported from Indonesia and subsequently, from South Africa and Russia. This raised concerns about the increase in costs for transporting coal, which may get passed on to the customers.[63] The power plant was operationalised in 2011 and often encountered technical problems. According to reports, between its operationalisation in March 2011 and August 2012, the power plant had to be shut down at least five times due to technical issues.[64] As the power plant accounted for a substantial percentage of total power generation, the government agencies had to impose power cuts across the country.[65] By 2022, the breakdowns were reportedly so frequent that the power plant was often referred to as "always breakdown."[66] Sri Lankan news reports pointed out that the government was spending considerable amounts on repair and maintenance services.[67]

Chinese firms were involved in constructing the Colombo-Katunayake Expressway, which was opened in 2013.[68] The 25.8 km expressway between Bandaranaike International Airport and Colombo City was operationalised to reduce the travel time for locals and tourists, and the project conceptualised the development of nearby towns into economic centres.[69] The EXIM Bank of China provided USD 248.2 million, out of a total expenditure of USD 292 million, as a loan towards the project's construction.[70]

Chinese firms also constructed the Southern Expressway, which connects Colombo, Galle, and Matara. The project was initiated in 2011, and by 2014, the Colombo to Matara segment was open to the public.[71] The expressway was further extended to connect to Hambantota as well. The project involved "USD 1.9 billion of concessional loan from Export-Import Bank of China."[72] Various Chinese companies, such as the China State Construction Engineering Corporation, China National Aero-Technology International Engineering Corporation, and China Harbour Engineering Company (CHEC), were involved in the project.[73] In early 2020, President Gotabaya Rajapaksa inaugurated the Palatuwa to Barawakumbuka segment of the expressway.[74] The project is based on the premise that Chinese projects, such as the Colombo Port City and Hambantota Port, would be stitched together by the expressway, making it easy for the movement of goods as well as people. As the then Sri Lanka premier noted, the expressway "will connect lives, livelihoods and boost economic activity."[75] Chinese firms may construct other projects, such as the New Kelani Bridge elevated highway.[76]

Real Estate

Chinese firms reportedly were also involved in the real estate sector, such as "a four-tower structure with 602 luxury apartments", named Astoria.[77]

The construction of Astoria was operationalised by the Aviation Industry Corporation of China, a mega-corporation owned by the Chinese government, with many subsidiary companies, which specialise in a range of industries from trade and logistics to real estate and hotel management.[78] The China State Construction Engineering Corporation Limited was the main contractor for the real estate project.[79]

The CHEC Port City Colombo (Pvt) Ltd, a subsidiary of China Communication Construction Company (CCCC) and the Sri Lanka Port Authority, was involved in an ambitious venture to build the Colombo Port City Project. The project involved construction on reclaimed land from the sea at an estimated cost of "USD 1.4 bn invested by CCCC subsidiary China Harbour."[80] Quite often, the new city plans are presented to domestic populations with images of the city skyline resembling New York. Even in the case of Colombo Port City, the image presented for public consumption consists of a city gleaming with skyscrapers made of glass. Given the climatic conditions of Colombo, skyscrapers made of glass and steel are anachronistic, but that's the image of progress that sells in subcontinental politics. There is anticipation that the Colombo Port City Project will provide "a nearby solution to the expenses of operating in Singapore and may attract back office functions from Singapore to Sri Lanka."[81] It is anticipated that the city development project will create some 83,000 direct and many more indirect jobs.[82] The project is expected to attract USD 13 billion as investment once it is completed.[83] The project fits into the larger trend in politics worldwide, where many political leaders would like to leave a lasting legacy in terms of building a new city. Astana and Naypyitaw are but a few examples. However, the Colombo Port City project extends an existing city on reclaimed land. The prospect of the project ending up with desolate streets looks minimal at the moment unless sustained efforts are made to make the new city desolate.

The Colombo Port City project went through many twists and turns. The agreement was first signed in 2014, and President Maithripala Sirisena's government suspended the project in 2015. However, realising that the cost of compensation to be paid was onerous, the project was restarted under a new agreement.[84] The new agreement awarded "CCCC a minimum of 110 hectares of land out of a total 269 hectares that have been reclaimed from the sea… [but did] … not to grant the freehold on 20 hectares of land to the Chinese firm."[85] In July 2020, the Sri Lankan government announced many tax incentives.[86] The project witnessed considerable discussion as to whether the new city should be a "separately governed entity" with relaxed taxation procedures to attract investments.[87]

In May 2021, the Sri Lankan parliament enacted the Colombo Port City Economic Commission Bill.[88] The Colombo Port City SEZ, which a Chinese company is operating, aims to promote trade, banking, financial, and BPO (business process outsourcing) services, and residential and entertainment facilities.[89] However, there were apprehensions that the legislation has created an alternative governance framework by empowering a commission (consisting of five to seven members) to make all-important decisions regarding the port city.[90] The President appointed the members of the commission. The Sri Lankan government contended that the commission would facilitate quick decision-making and faster project implementations.[91] However, there were concerns that the new institutional framework would undermine parliamentary scrutiny and centralise decision-making in the hands of the President. Referring to the project, India's Ministry of External Affairs 'noted the concerns' raised and added that "we expect Sri Lanka will remain mindful of our excellent bilateral cooperation, including for mutual security in our shared environment, which includes the maritime domain."[92] The Colombo Port City project raised numerous questions about its financial viability, political accountability, and environmental impact.

From a Sri Lankan perspective, the attempt to evolve as a financial hub also stems from the recognition that Indian trade accounts for a dominant proportion of the trade at Colombo port. Indian transhipment amounted to approximately 45 per cent of Colombo port's total container trans-shipment volume.[93] India is developing its port facilities and is also relaxing the "cabotage laws enabling the foreign-flagged vessels to carry coastal cargo in India."[94] These measures, in the long run, may reduce the importance of Colombo as a trans-shipment hub for India. In such an instance, from a Sri Lankan perspective, it becomes imperative to ensure that Colombo Port diversifies its trade and economic portfolio. However, economic engagement with China did not result in resilient economic interactions with the outside world. Instead, there is a strong opinion that Sri Lanka plunged into an economic crisis because of its economic engagement with China.

The Economic Crisis

Sri Lanka's 2022 economic crisis was a long time in the making. Over the past few years, the Sri Lankan government made a series of imprudent economic decisions. Such decisions include implementing tax cuts that undermined revenue collections and an overnight ban on importing non-organic fertilisers on very short notice, which dented food production in the country.[95] The agrarian crisis was so grave that the Indian government airlifted nano-nitrogen fertilisers to be distributed to Sri Lankan farmers.[96] Other international developments, such as a dramatic fall in tourist inflows due to the pandemic, ensured that the revenues and employment associated with the tourism sector were negatively impacted. Further, the Russia-Ukraine conflict and rising fuel prices resulted in a spike in oil prices.

Consequently, Sri Lanka had to spend its precious foreign exchange reserves on securing energy resources. The foreign exchange crisis prompted Sri Lanka to cut down imports of vital commodities, such as food and medicines, resulting in soaring inflation and a dramatic fall in the value of the Sri Lankan rupee.[97] The economic crisis pushed the foreign ministry to temporarily shut down its "missions/posts in Abuja (Nigeria), Frankfurt (Germany) and Nicosia (Cyprus) to conserve the country's much needed foreign reserves and minimise expenditure."[98]

Since Sri Lanka had to spend precious forex reserves on purchasing oil, it resulted in a decline in the value of the Sri Lankan rupee, and the subsequent spike in debt payments created the necessary conditions for a perfect storm in the Sri Lankan political and economic realms. On the domestic front, Sri Lanka faced many challenges, such as unemployment, reduced food production, severe inflation, energy shortages, and daily blackouts, which prompted spontaneous and massive protests in the country in early 2022. The protesting crowds attacked government buildings and residences of the ruling political leadership. As a result, the government was paralysed, and President Rajapaksa had to flee the country.

As Sri Lanka plunged into an economic crisis, the role of Chinese loans in engendering the economic crisis was one of the dominant themes of discussion. For instance, in July 2022, Samantha Power, Administrator of USAID, noted that China's 'opaque loan deals' with high interest rates contributed to Sri Lanka's financial crisis.[99] The Chinese Foreign Office immediately argued that while China extended preferential loans with low interest rates, it was the US interest rate hike and 'manipulation of the credit rating [of Sri Lanka that] seriously undermined Sri Lanka's financing credibility.'[100] Despite such forceful contestation from the Chinese diplomats, there were numerous arguments that debt to China played an important role in Sri Lanka's economic crisis.

However, there was no clarity on the scale of the Chinese share in Sri Lanka's international debt. According to news reports, the percentage share of the Chinese debt ranged from 10 per cent to 20 per cent.[101]

There was an opinion that excessive spending on infrastructure projects contributed to the economic crisis. Arai Etsuyo contends that Sri Lanka started to raise finances by issuing International Sovereign Bonds (ISB) from the global financial markets to fund its share in various infrastructure projects that were getting built in collaboration with China.[102] So, while the formal Chinese loans were around 10 per cent-20 per cent, the need to be a shareholder in massive infrastructure projects that China was constructing prompted Sri Lanka to become indebted by issuing ISBs. Consequently, Sri Lanka's overall international debt witnessed a dramatic increase. Moreover, Sri Lanka refrained from raising funds from formal multilateral institutions, such as the World Bank and the International Monetary Fund (IMF), as they would demand rigorous financial viability evaluation of the proposed infrastructure projects. Instead, the Sri Lankan government generated resources from the international financial markets. Unlike international financial institutions, the space for renegotiation or restructuring the debt tends to be very limited for ISBs. So overall, there was a deleterious impact of Chinese-funded projects as they pushed Sri Lanka into unhealthy borrowing behaviour. As Sri Lanka slipped into a severe economic crisis, China promised additional loans to Sri Lanka and refrained from calling off the debts, as it would result in similar demands from other BRI participant countries. Various mechanisms, such as currency swap agreements,[103] were of little use to Sri Lanka in preventing its slide into a severe economic crisis. Towards the end of 2022, China was one of the largest bilateral lenders to Sri Lanka, and much of this constituted market borrowings from various Chinese financial institutions.[104] In 2024, Sri Lanka reached a debt restructuring agreement with China and other countries, which enabled the rescheduling of bilateral loan payments to foreign countries until 2028.[105]

The Security Dynamic

The growing economic interactions were supplemented by enhanced defence and military cooperation between India's neighbours and China. As Shantanu Roy-Chaudhury noted, "in 2007, the then-President Mahinda Rajapaksa's visit to China led to a USD 37.6 million deal to purchase Chinese Jian-7 fighter jets, anti-aircraft guns, JY-11 3D air surveillance radar, armoured personnel carriers, and other weaponry."[106] In the subsequent years, Sri Lanka purchased weapon systems, such as light transport aircraft, trainer aircraft, and a frigate from China.[107] In addition to the procurement of weapons, the Chinese naval vessels' frequent port calls in Sri Lanka attracted much international attention. In 2014, a Chinese submarine (Changzheng-2), as well as a warship (Chang Xing Dao), docked at the Port of Colombo, and a few weeks later, another Chinese submarine made a port call as well.[108] From an Indian perspective, the concerns that the Chinese economic relationship with Sri Lanka will have political and security ramifications were validated. The Chinese Defence Ministry spokesman clarified that the submarine docked in Colombo "on its way to and back from the mission area, the submarine made technical docking in Sri Lanka twice, and it is a quite common practice for submarines of world navies to dock at certain ports and conduct replenishment."[109] In a similar vein, a Sri Lankan official noted that "this is nothing unusual … since 2010, 230 warships have called at Colombo port for various countries on goodwill visits and for refuelling and crew refreshment."[110] Such statements may not have addressed India's concerns. However, in 2017, when a Chinese submarine requested permission to dock at the Colombo Port, the Sri Lankan authorities refused to grant such access.[111]

As the Hambantota port became operational, there was speculation that China would use the port as a naval base. The then Sri Lankan Prime Minister Ranil Wickremesinghe was quick to refute such statements and reiterated that "there are no foreign naval bases in Sri Lanka," and added that some people are "seeing imaginary Chinese Naval bases in Sri Lanka … whereas the Hambantota Port is a commercial joint venture…."[112] Interestingly, in 2018, the Sri Lankan government decided to shift its Southern Command naval base from Galle to Hambantota.[113] The objective of such a move was probably to ensure greater surveillance of the activities at the Hambantota port. Despite the repeated denials from senior leadership, the perception that the port would be used for military purposes persisted.

In a significant development, a Chinese satellite tracking ship, Yuan Wang 5, docked in Hambantota port in August 2022.[114] Yuan Wang 5, which also has the ability to track intercontinental ballistic missiles, reportedly arrived at the port for replenishment purposes. The initial news reports suggested that Sri Lanka may not permit the Chinese ship to dock. Subsequently, the Sri Lankan authorities allowed the ship to dock in the port. However, the port call happened amid the India-China standoff in Ladakh. A few months later, another satellite and ballistic missile tracking ship, Yuan Wang 6, entered the Indian Ocean Region.[115] While the vessel operated in the Lombok Straits, far away from Sri Lanka, its presence suggests a pattern of growing Chinese naval presence in the region. The visit of the satellite tracking ship constitutes one more episode of civilian infrastructure being used by Chinese military platforms. There was also an increase in Chinese research vessels and fishing boats operating close to India's exclusive economic zone. According to reports, "over 600 Chinese fishing vessels are in the IOR beyond India's Exclusive Economic Zone every year from 2015 to 2019... there are also four to six Chinese research vessels known to be ... operating in the IOR."[116] In March 2023, a Chinese research vessel, Hai Yang Shi You, was spotted in the Bay of Bengal close to the Indian coast.[117] In January 2024, Sri Lanka barred the Chinese research vessel, Xiang Yang Hong 03, from accessing its ports as a part of its moratorium "on foreign research ships entering its waters for a year."[118] In December 2024, President Anura Kumara Dissanayake's government announced that a national policy on permitting foreign research vessels will be formulated.[119]

A host of Chinese economic activities are raising security concerns in India. There were reports about Chinese investments in the sea cucumber hatchery in the Jaffna region in northern Sri Lanka.[120] The harvested sea cucumber is exported mainly to China and other countries, such as Singapore and Taiwan.[121] While sea cucumber harvesting may have created some local employment, there is also criticism that it has negatively impacted "traditional fishermen who harvest prawns for a living" and "poses a severe threat to the region's long-term environmental sustainability."[122] It was reported that a Chinese firm was shortlisted to construct renewable energy wind farms on three islands near the Jaffna peninsula.[123] Given the proximity of these islands to India, the possible presence of Chinese nationals at these islands was construed as a security threat for India, and the local Tamil population also expressed apprehensions. Subsequently, this project was handed over to an Indian company. Indian security agencies have reportedly noted that China is scaling its surveillance capabilities in northern Sri Lanka by "deployment of Hi-tech gadgets such as satellites, drones and other communication equipment."[124]

There is a perception in India that China is also scaling up its diplomatic engagement in northern Sri Lanka. In December 2021, Chinese Ambassador

Qi Zhenhong visited the northern province, which has a significant Tamil majority population. During his visit, he interacted with various government officials, donated water purification plants, fishing gear, laptops, and books to the Jaffna public library, and visited Chinese-funded projects in the region.[125] At the Adam's Bridge (Ram Sethu), the Chinese Ambassador reportedly stated: "This is the End, but also the Beginning."[126] The Chinese Ambassador's statements could be interpreted as the Chinese intention to scale up its presence in the Jaffna peninsula, which is very close to the southern tip of India.

Conclusion: Asymmetry and Economic Engagement

There are elements of cooperation between the two countries, such as Sri Lanka donating human eye corneas, that go beyond the concerns of geopolitics and economics. News reports in 2022 estimated that in Sri Lanka, with a population of 22 million, over 15 million people have signed up for eye donation.[127] Sri Lanka is one of the leading donors of cornea in the world, and it has a long history of cornea donation rooted in Sri Lanka's Buddhist traditions of *dana*.[128] Since 1967, China and Sri Lanka have been cooperating in the realm of cornea donation, and in the recent past, "around 1,500 corneas are flown to China for transplant annually, and China is the second-largest recipient of cornea donations from Sri Lanka."[129] Such donations, which improve the lives of people with visual challenges, should have generated considerable goodwill in China for Sri Lanka.

However, in international politics, 'goodwill' tends to have little currency, and power dynamics define the conduct of nation-states. In case of asymmetry in power relations, countries with relatively lesser power resources often play by the rules of the powerful. For instance, during the pandemic, countries with vaccine- manufacturing capacities often tried to define not only the price of vaccines but also the procurement procedures in other countries. As the COVID infection rate picked up momentum, like many countries in Asia and beyond, the Sri Lankan government also worked to strengthen its healthcare infrastructure by ensuring a constant supply of vaccines and other medical equipment. In the process, Sri Lanka signed a Non-Disclosure Agreement (NDA) with Sinovac.[130] However, there was considerable criticism regarding the NDA, and the Chinese Embassy in Colombo pointed out that such agreements are common and unwarranted shrill discourse would undermine the procurement processes.[131]

The power asymmetry in the China-Sri Lanka relationship and its impact on Colombo's decision-making process was also evident during the fertiliser dispute. Towards the end of 2021, Sri Lanka and China were embroiled in an ugly spat over organic fertilisers. The Sri Lankan government reportedly ordered organic fertilisers from a Chinese firm. However, the Sri Lankan government rejected 20,000 tons of fertiliser dispatched by the Chinese firm due to the alleged presence of harmful bacteria. The firm responded by stating that the rejection of the order resulted in reputation damage and called for punitive economic measures, such as restricting tea imports from Sri Lanka.[132] As the crisis escalated, the Commercial High Court of Sri Lanka barred the "People's Bank from making any payments under the letter of credit".[133] In response, the Chinese government blacklisted the People's Bank for failing to honour the commitments made.[134] In November 2021, Chinese foreign ministry spokesperson Wang Wenbin noted that "China attaches great importance to the quality of its exports" and added that "the fertiliser had passed tests of third-party agencies assigned by the Sri Lankan side before shipping."[135] The Chinese firm subsequently filed a lawsuit in Singapore against the Sri Lankan government for failing to adhere to the contractual obligations. However, before the visit of then China's Foreign Minister Wang Yi, in January 2022, the Sri Lankan government settled the USD 6.9 million fertiliser bill with the Chinese firm.[136]

The asymmetric power dynamic is also impacting Sri Lanka's engagement with other external players. For instance, in 2019, an MOU was signed with India and Japan for the construction of the East Container Terminal (ECT). However, two years later, in early 2021, the Sri Lankan government cancelled the deal for the construction of the ECT. The Sri Lankan government stated that it would develop the ECT on its own. The ostensible reason for the cancellation was the opposition from the local trade unions. There was speculation that the ECT deal with India and Japan was cancelled because the terminal was adjacent to the Chinese-constructed jetty. Subsequent reports stated that the Sri Lankan government "decided to rope in China Harbor Engineering Company to construct the second phase of the Colombo Port's East Container Terminal (ECT)."[137] In response to growing criticism, India was asked to invest in the West Container Terminal (WCT) by the Sri Lankan government.[138] In September 2021, India's Adani Ports & Special Economic Zone Limited (APSEZ) signed an agreement with John Keells Holdings and the Sri Lanka Ports Authority (SLPA) to develop the Colombo

Port's Western Container Terminal. While John Keells and the SLPA will hold 34 per cent and 15 per cent stake, respectively, the Adani group will have a majority share of 51 per cent.[139] A year later, the APSEZ started the dredging for the construction of the WCT.[140] In November 2023, the US International Development Finance Corporation (DFC) declared its intent to invest USD 553 million in Port of Colombo's West Container Terminal.[141] While commercial considerations drove the DFC investment, many interpreted it as a measure to counter the Chinese influence in Sri Lanka.[142] In a related development, the Sri Lankan cabinet formally announced that it would work with India to develop the Trincomalee oil tank farm in January 2022.[143] The Indian government would upgrade approximately 61 tanks on a lease, the Ceylon Petroleum Corporation would upgrade 24 tanks, and the Lanka IOC would upgrade about 14 tanks.[144] In November 2023, the Indian Finance Minister, during her visit to Sri Lanka, participated in commissioning two oil tanks in Trincomalee.[145] The upgrade of the oil farm will strengthen the bilateral relationship between the two countries and enable Sri Lanka to mitigate an economic crisis induced by fuel shortages in future.

India reiterated its role as a first responder in the region by supporting Sri Lanka in mitigating the adverse consequences of the economic crisis. India provided loans worth USD 968 million in 2022 to enable Sri Lanka to overcome economic challenges.[146] While there was a perception that Chinese lending pushed Sri Lanka into a financial crisis, Indian lending aimed to pull Colombo out of a financial crisis. The Indian government stepped in with wide-ranging policy initiatives, including currency swaps and credit lines. India has assisted Sri Lanka by extending "USD 4 billion in terms of credits and rollovers to help Sri Lanka get through an economic crisis."[147] India and Japan acted in tandem to help Sri Lanka overcome the crisis. While India shipped 9000 metric tons of milk powder, rice, and life-saving medicines, Japan provided USD 1.5 million for essential food supplies, which the United Nations World Food Programme (WFP) would supply.[148] Subsequently, in 2023, Japan committed an additional USD 6.6 million to the WFP to meet the food and nutritional requirements of the poor in Sri Lanka.[149]

Towards the end of 2023, the EXIM Bank of China and the Sri Lankan government agreed on a debt restructuring deal, which possibly included extending the tenure and reducing the interest rates.[150] While the details were not immediately available, reports suggested that the China EXIM Bank and Sri Lankan government were "actively working on formalising and implementing the agreed parameters of the debt treatment."[151] Despite the unwillingness of Beijing to waive off the debt and the growing interest of other powers to scale up interactions with Colombo, Sri Lanka refrained from disengaging or scaling down its economic engagement with China. In fact, in the midst of growing concerns about the Chinese-funded projects, there were news reports that Chinese firms would be investing in logistics[152] and the retail fuel market in Sri Lanka.[153] During Sri Lankan President Ranil Wickremesinghe's 2023 visit to China to attend the third Belt and Road Forum for International Cooperation, , both sides agreed to "make every effort to push forward the Colombo Port City and Hambantota comprehensive development project."[154] In November 2023, Sinopec's proposal to construct a USD 4.5 billion oil refinery in Hambantota was approved by the Sri Lankan government.[155] The need to complete the existing projects prompted Sri Lanka to continue its engagement with China. In Sri Lanka-China's bilateral dynamic, economic interactions are also a consequence of geopolitical considerations. For China, the massive infrastructure projects were subject to considerable international opprobrium for engendering the economic crisis in Sri Lanka. And yet, China is moving forward with existing projects and contemplating new investments. China has gained a presence in vital ports, such as Colombo and Hambantota. In addition, there is an increased Chinese naval presence in the Indian Ocean and in the Bay of Bengal. Furthermore, Chinese business firms have attempted to establish enterprises in the strategically important Jaffna peninsula. The economic interactions have provided a platform for Beijing to scale up its engagement with Sri Lanka's political elite. Such friendships or familiarity will prompt continued economic exchanges between the two countries. Other countries are competing for various projects in the island nation in a context wherein Chinese firms have now established strong relationships across the administrative hierarchy in Sri Lanka.

Sri Lankan President Anura Kumara Dissanayake sought to address Indian concerns regarding the growing Chinese presence in his country. In December 2024, President Dissanayake chose India over China for his first foreign visit. During the three-day visit, he assured the Indian leadership "that Sri Lanka will not permit its territory to be used in any manner inimical to the security of India as well as towards regional stability."[156] For Sri Lanka, India is the most proximate neighbour and source of significant investment. During Sri Lanka's economic crisis, India extended "assistance of USD 4 billion in various kinds of aid in 2022 and 2023" and also restructured the debt.[157]

Unlike India, China is not a close neighbour. Nonetheless, the rubber-rice trade and Sri Lankan diplomacy during the India-China war point to the long history of Colombo's engagement with Beijing. While China is not a new element in Sri Lankan foreign policy, the scale and intensity of economic interactions have significantly increased recently. Sadly, Sri Lanka was not able to leverage its relationship with China for rapid economic progress, and it appears that Beijing has benefitted more than Colombo. The balance may further tilt in favour of Beijing if Sri Lanka agrees to a Free Trade Agreement (FTA) with China. Sri Lankan authorities should study the experience of other countries in South Asia, such as Pakistan, before implementing an FTA with China. The Sri Lankan negotiating team may be apprehensive, given the asymmetry in the economic power between the two countries and the substantive diversity of the Chinese export basket. A similar asymmetric power dynamic also impacted the China-Maldives' economic engagement.

Notes

1. "Xi Jinping, 'Let us become partners in pursuit of our dreams'," *Daily News*, September 16, 2014, https://mfa.gov.lk/exclusive-xi-jinping-president-peoples-republic-of-china-to-daily-news-readers-let-us-become-partners-in-pursuit-of-our-dreams/
2. "Xi Jinping, 'Let us become partners in pursuit of our dreams'," *Daily News*, September 16, 2014, https://mfa.gov.lk/exclusive-xi-jinping-president-peoples-republic-of-china-to-daily-news-readers-let-us-become-partners-in-pursuit-of-our-dreams/
3. Sun Guangqi, "Zheng He's Expeditions to the Western Ocean and His Navigation Technology," *The Journal of Navigation*, Vol. 45, No. 3, September 1992, pp. 329–343.
4. United Nations High Commissioner for Refugees. "Additional Measures to Be Employed to Meet the Aggression in Korea (Resolution Adopted on the Report of the First Committee)." *Refworld*. Last modified September 15, 2020. https://www.refworld.org/docid/3b00f07f20.html.
5. Li Chang, "Ceylon's Trade with Communist China," *Far Eastern Survey*, Vol. 22, No. 6 (May, 1953), pp. 70-72.
6. Nihal Mallikaaratchi, "66th anniversary of SL–China Rubber-Rice Pact," *Sunday Times* (Sri Lanka), January 6, 2019.
7. S.U. Kodikara, "Major Trends in Sri Lanka's Non-Alignment Policy after 1956," *Asian Survey 13*, no. 12 (1973), p. 1126.
8. Wriggins, W. Howard, "Ceylon: Dilemmas of A New Nation," (New Jersey: Princeton University Press), pp. 403-410.
9. "Ceylon's Tea, Egyptian Cotton, Japan's Sterling in 3-Way Deal," *The New York Times*, October 13, 1956, p. 25.

10. C. F. Amerasinghe, "Legal Relations Between Ceylon and the People's Republic of China 1949-1971," *Malaya Law Review*, Vol. 16, No. 1 (July 1974), p. 89.
11 Madhavan K. Palat, "*Selected works of Jawaharlal Nehru, Second Series Volume Eighty (1 December 1962–31 January 1963)*," (New Delhi: Jawaharlal Nehru Memorial Fund, 2019), pp. 413-415.
12 Ibid., p. 786.
13 Ibid., p. 432.
14. "Premier Chou En-Lai Responds to Madame Bandaranaike," *Peking Review*, February 1, 1963, Vol. VI, No. 5, p. 11.
15 Michael Brecher, "Non-Alignment Under Stress: The West and the India-China Border War," *Pacific Affairs*, Vol. 52, No. 4 (Winter, 1979-1980), p. 629.
16 Ibid., n. 11, p. 417.
17 "Welcome to the Peaceful Efforts of the Colombo Conference," *Peking Review*, February 1, 1963, Vol. VI, No. 5, p. 12.
18 《人民日报》刊登驻斯里兰卡大使吴江浩署名文章《友好的故事说不完, *Embassy of the People's Republic of China in the Democratic Socialist Republic of Sri Lanka*, June 6, 2013
19. "Sri Lanka's Supreme Court Refurbishment Completed, says Chinese Embassy," *Ada Derana*, July, 21, 2015, http://bizenglish.adaderana.lk/sri-lankas-supreme-court-refurbishment-completed-says-chinese-embassy/
20. "五、斯里兰卡与中国的经贸关系," *Ministry of Commerce of the People's Republic of China*, http://history.mofcom.gov.cn/?bandr=sllkyzgdjmgx
21. Hannah Gardner, "China's Aid Revealed in Sri Lanka's Victory Parade," *The National*, June 9, 2009, https://www.thenationalnews.com/world/asia/china-s-aid-revealed-in-sri-lanka-s-victory-parade-1.556125
22. Ananth Krishnan, "China Backs Sri Lanka on UNHRC Resolution," *The Hindu*, March 22, 2012, https://www.thehindu.com/news/international/china-backs-sri-lanka-on-unhrc-resolution/article3088478.ece
23. United Nations Development Programme, "*Human Development Report 2010 – The Real Wealth of Nations: Pathways to Human Development*," (New York: United Nations Development Programme, 2010), p. 142.
24. "Sri Lanka enters in to a US$500 million BOT agreement with China Merchants Holdings to upgrade Colombo South Container Terminal," *Embassy of Sri Lanka in Beijing*, August 12, 2011, https://mfa.gov.lk/sri-lanka-enters-in-to-a-us500-million-bot-agreement-with-china-merchants-holdings-to-upgrade-colombo-south-container-terminal/
25. "Aitken Spence Confirms Sell-Out From Port venture," *Daily Financial Times*, January 24, 2012, http://www.ft.lk/front-page/aitken-spence-confirms-sell-out-from-port-venture/44-67966
26. "Sri Lanka's Aitken Spence sells port stake to China Merchants," *Reuters*, January 23, 2012, https://in.reuters.com/article/srilanka-port-spence/sri-lankas-aitken-spence-sells-port-stake-to-china-merchants-idINL4E8CN4PO20120123
27 Asian Development Bank, "Sri Lanka: Colombo Port Expansion Project," Completion Report-Project Number: 39431-013, July 2015, https://www.adb.org/sites/default/files/project-document/162329/39431-013-pcr.pdf

28. Ravi Ladduwahetty, "Hambantota Port Will Attract 36,000 Ships Annually—Ananda Kularatne," *Daily News*, June 18, 2002, http://archives.dailynews.lk/2002/06/18/bus04.html
29. B. Raman, "Gwadar, Hambantota and Sitwe: China's Strategic Triangle," *C3S India*, March 6, 2007, https://www.c3sindia.org/geopolitics-strategy/gwadar-hambantota-sitwe-chinas-strategic-triangle/
30. Jonathan Hillman, "Game of Loans: How Chia Bought Hambantota," *CSIS Briefs*, March 2018, https://csis-website-prod.s3.amazonaws.com/s3fs-public/publication/180717_Hillman_GameofLoans.pdf?bjj0dzdfO5jaedmhoC2Eq7pC6cknyvEz
31. "Joint Press Communique of the People's Republic of China and the Democratic Socialist Republic of Sri Lanka," Ministry of Foreign Affairs, the People's Republic of China, September 22, 2020, https://www.fmprc.gov.cn/mfa_eng/wjdt_665385/2649_665393/t303108.shtml.
32. Uditha Kumarasinghe, "Major Development Drive with Hambantota Port Project," *Daily News*, March 13, 2007, https://archives.dailynews.lk/2007/03/13/news02.asp
33. Jeff M. Smith, "China's Investments in Sri Lanka," *Foreign Affairs*, May 24, 2016, https://www.foreignaffairs.com/articles/china/2016-05-23/chinas-investments-sri-lanka
34. B. Muralidhar Reddy, "Phase 1 of Hambantota Port Opened," *The Hindu*, August 15, 2010, https://www.thehindu.com/news/international/Phase-1-of-Hambantota-port-opened/article16133123.ece
35. "Hambantota Augury," *The Indian Express*, December 18, 2017, https://indianexpress.com/article/opinion/editorials/hambantota-augury-sri-lanka-china-port-4987382/
36. Vikas Bajaj, "India Worries as China Builds Ports in South Asia," *The New York Times*, February 16, 2010, https://www.nytimes.com/2010/02/16/business/global/16port.html.
37. "Hambantota Augury," *The Indian Express*, December 18, 2017, https://indianexpress.com/article/opinion/editorials/hambantota-augury-sri-lanka-china-port-4987382/
38. Gordon Fairclough and Uditha Jayasinghe, "Sri Lanka to Sell 80% Stake in Strategically Placed Harbor to Chinese," *The Wall Street Journal*, December 8, 2016, https://www.wsj.com/articles/sri-lanka-to-sell-80-stake-in-strategically-placed-harbor-to-chinese-1481226344.
39. Yi Xianliang, "A Brilliant Future for China-Sri Lanka Cooperation under the "Belt and Road" Initiative," *Embassy of the People's Republic of China in Sri Lanka*, May 16, 2017, http://lk.china-embassy.gov.cn/eng/xwdt/201706/t20170616_1374499.htm#:~:text=The%20participation%20of%20Sri%20Lankan,Initiative%20and%20the%20summit%2C%20itself.
40. Kiran Stacey, "China signs 99-year lease on Sri Lanka's Hambantota port," *Financial Times*, December 11, 2017, https://www.ft.com/content/e150ef0c-de37-11e7-a8a4-0a1e63a52f9c
41. "Sri Lanka President Gotabaya's Remarks on Hambantota Port Quoted out of Context: PM Mahinda," *The New Indian Express*, December 10, 2019, https://www.newindianexpress.com/world/2019/dec/10/sri-lanka-president-gotabayas-remarks-on-hambantota-port-quoted-out-of-context-pm-mahinda-2074080.html

42. “Sri Lanka Not to Renegotiate Hambantota Port Agreement with China: President,” *Xinhua*, September 22, 2020, https://www.xinhuanet.com/english/2019-12/20/c_138646092.htm
43. Anusha Ondaatjie and Asantha Sirimanne, “Sri Lanka Wants to Undo Deal to Lease Port to China for 99 Years,” *Hindustan Times*, July 31, 2020, https://www.hindustantimes.com/business-news/sri-lanka-wants-to-undo-deal-to-lease-port-to-china-for-99-years/story-iH9W5T4vaGf6PSajTLUUyK.html
44. “China, Sri Lanka to Accelerate Implementation of Cooperation on Big Economic Projects,” *Xinhua*, September 22, 2020, https://www.xinhuanet.com/english/2019-12/02/c_138600489.htm
45 一签就是99年！斯里兰卡的这个港口被中国承包了，*Zhihu.com*, January 16, 2020, https://zhuanlan.zhihu.com/p/101382298
46 Ibid.
47 “斯里兰卡汉班托塔港,” *Guangming Daily*, January 26, 2018, http://news.gmw.cn/2018-01/26/content_27458405.htm?from=search
48 “中国石化斯里兰卡汉班托塔港油库投运（图片新闻,” *People's Daily*, April 13, 2020, http://paper.people.com.cn/zgnyb/html/2020-04/13/content_1981832.htm
49 “中斯合营汉班托塔港启动燃料油加油业务,” *People's Daily*, April 8, 2020, http://world.people.com.cn/n1/2020/0408/c1002-31664821.html
50. “斯里兰卡拟在汉班托塔投资3亿美元建轮胎厂,” *Economic Daily*, September 4, 2020, http://intl.ce.cn/specials/zxgjzh/202009/04/t20200904_35673745.shtml; “Sri Lanka, China sign 300 mln USD investment agreement to manufacture tires in Hambantota,” *Xinhua*, November 21, 2020, http://www.xinhuanet.com/english/2020-11/21/c_139531446.htm
51. “Sri Lanka China-backed port's plug-and-play factories almost ready,” *Economy Next*, December 22, 2022, https://economynext.com/sri-lanka-china-backed-ports-plug-and-play-factories-almost-ready-107322/
52 For example see, Brook Larmer, “What the World's Emptiest International Airport Says About China's Influence,” *The New York Times*, September 13, 2017. https://www.nytimes.com/2017/09/13/magazine/what-the-worlds-emptiest-international-airport-says-about-chinas-influence.html.
53. Wade Shepard, “The Story Behind the World's Emptiest International Airport,” *Forbes*, May 30, 2016, https://www.forbes.com/sites/wadeshepard/2016/05/28/the-story-behind-the-worlds-emptiest-international-airport-sri-lankas-mattala-rajapaksa/#94222dd7cea2
54. “Despite Oppn Protests, Sri Lanka to Hand over Loss-making Airport to India,” *Business Standard,* October 2, 2020, https://www.business-standard.com/article/current-affairs/despite-oppn-protests-sri-lanka-to-handover-loss-making-airport-to-india-118071801501_1.html
55. “Why India is Buying the World's Emptiest Airport,” *The Interpreter*, July 14, 2018, https://www.lowyinstitute.org/the-interpreter/why-india-buying-world-s-emptiest-airport
56. “Lanka PM Says India Heeded His Request Not to Seek Joint Venture to Run Mattala Airport,” *Outlook*, July 10, 2020, https://www.outlookindia.com/newsscroll/lanka-pm-says-india-heeded-his-request-not-to-seek-joint-venture-to-run-mattala-airport/1891827

57. "Celebrating of Ten years since the first Commercial Flight with 108 Passengers from USA to Mattala Rajapaksa International Airport (18th March 2013-2023)," *Ceylon Digest*, March 14, 2023, https://www.ceylondigest.com/celebrating-of-ten-years-since-the-first-commercial-flight-with-108-passengers-from-usa-to-mattala-rajapaksa-international-airport-18th-march-2013-2023/
58. "MRIA facilitates over 11,000 tourist arrivals in February," *Adaderana,* March 6, 2023, https://www.adaderana.lk/news/88864/mria-facilitates-over-11000-tourist-arrivals-in-february
59. Namini Wijedasa, "Extensive moves to resuscitate MRIA," *The Sunday Times*, January 8, 2023, https://www.sundaytimes.lk/230108/news/extensive-moves-to-resuscitate-mria-507850.html
60. Heena Sharma, "Sri Lanka leases Chinese-built Mattala Rajapaksa Int'l Airport to Indian, Russian firms amid debt woes," *WION*, April 26, 2024, https://www.wionews.com/south-asia/sri-lanka-leases-chinese-built-mattala-rajapaksa-intl-airport-to-indian-russian-firms-amid-debt-woes-715433
61. "NTPC loses Puttalam Project To China," *The Financial Express*, February 15, 2006, https://www.financialexpress.com/archive/ntpc-loses-puttalam-project-to-china/147973/
62 "Coal Power Plant Project, Infrastructure Unit, Department of Foreign Aid and Budget Monitoring," *Ministry of Plan Implementation, Government of Sri Lanka*, July 27, 2006, https://web.archive.org/web/20091122150502/http://www.fabm.gov.lk/downloads/Norochcholai.pdf
63. Chris Kamlendran, "Another Controversy Over Coal Shipment: Why From Russian Port?" *The Sunday Times*, December 7, 2014, http://www.sundaytimes.lk/141207/news/another-controversy-over-coal-shipment-why-from-russian-port-131634.html ; also see Pavani Hapuarachchi, "Sufficient Coal imported to run Norochcholai: CEB," *News First*, May 3, 2022, https://www.newsfirst.lk/2022/05/03/sufficient-coal-imported-to-run-norochcholai-ceb/
64. "Sri Lanka Extends Daily Power Cut as Chinese Plant Fails Again, *Reuters*, August 13, 2012, https://in.reuters.com/article/srilanka-power/sri-lanka-extends-daily-power-cut-as-chinese-plant-fails-again-idINDEE87C0AC20120813
65. "China-Built Power Plant Resumes in Sri Lanka," *Xinhua*, 12 September 2012, http://www.chinadaily.com.cn/bizchina/2012-09/12/content_15752874.htm
66. "Chinese-built coal power plant and associated technical and environmental issues," *Colombo gazette*. September 7, 2022, https://colombogazette.com/2022/09/07/chinese-built-coal-power-plant-and-associated-technical-and-environmental-issues/
67. "Norochcholai Coal Power Plant: Maintenance and repairs only by Chinese," *The Morning*. January 30, 2022, https://www.themorning.lk/norochcholai-coal-power-plant-maintenance-and-repairs-only-by-chinese/
68. "President opens Chinese-funded Katunayake Expressway," *Daily Financial Times,* October 28, 2013, http://www.ft.lk/article/206440/President-opens-Chinese-funded-Katunayake-Expressway
69. "E03-Colombo-Katunayaka Expressway (CKE)," Road Development Authority Sri Lanka, 2020, http://www.exway.rda.gov.lk/index.php?page=expressway_network/e03

70. Dreher, A., Fuchs, A., Parks, B.C., Strange, A. M., & Tierney, M. J. (2017). "Aid, China, and Growth: Evidence from a New Global Development Finance Dataset," *AidData* Working Paper #46. Williamsburg, VA: AidData.
71. "China Exim Bank loans Sri Lanka 180 million USD for second stage of Southern Highway project," *AidData,* 2017. Global Chinese Official Finance Dataset, Version 1.0, https://china.aiddata.org/projects/38337.
72. Li Ping, "Extended Highway in Southern Sri Lanka Brings Roads, Hearts Closer," *China Daily*, October 3, 2018, https://www.chinadaily.com.cn/a/201810/03/WS5bb4a258a310eff3032809e3_1.html
73. "Spotlight: Expressway Built Amid COVID-19 Outbreak Connects Cities, Supply Chains in Sri Lanka," *Xinhua*, March 4, 2020, https://www.xinhuanet.com/english/2020-03/04/c_138842227.htm
74. "Sri Lanka : President Opens Southern Expressway Extension Linking Colombo to Hambantota-Mattala for Public," *Colombo Page*, February 23, 2020. https://www.colombopage.com/archive_20A/Feb23_1582473171CH.php
75. "BRI Builds Solidarity Amid COVID-19 Pandemic," *China Daily*, April 28, 2020, https://www.chinadaily.com.cn/a/202004/28/WS5ea7a043a310a8b241152410.html
76. "Cabinet approval sought to suspend land acquisition for elevated expressway," *The Sunday Times*, April 2, 2023, https://www.sundaytimes.lk/230402/news/cabinet-approval-sought-to-suspend-land-acquisition-for-elevated-expressway-516307.html
77. "AVIC International launches real estate project in Sri Lanka," *Xinhua*, October 11, 2014, https://www.chinadaily.com.cn/business/2014-10/11/content_18723091.htm
78. "AVIC Signs on Top Contractor for Astoria Luxury Condominium Completion," *Daily Mirror*, May 7, 2015, https://www.dailymirror.lk/71513/avic-signs-on-top-contractor-for-astoria-luxury-condominium-completion.
79. "The Element of Success Behind AVIC Astoria," *Astoria*, January 23, 2018, https://www.astoria.lk/element-success-behind-avic-astoria/.
80. Michael Safi, "Sri Lanka's 'new Dubai': Will Chinese-built City Suck the Life out of Colombo?" *The Guardian*, February 3, 2020, https://www.theguardian.com/cities/2018/aug/02/sri-lanka-new-dubai-chinese-city-colombo
81. Chris Devonshire-Ellis, "Colombo Port City Turns Into Belt & Road Initiative Cash Cow For Investors," *Silk Road Briefing*, August 12, 2020, https://www.silkroadbriefing.com/news/2020/08/11/colombo-port-city-turns-into-belt-road-initiative-cash-cow-for-investors/
82. Shiran Illanperuma , "Xinhua Headlines: 6 Years On, Colombo Port City Set to Boost Sri Lanka's Economic Growth," China.org.cn, September 28, 2020, https://www.china.org.cn/world/Off_the_Wire/2020-09/26/content_76754608.htm
83. "Port City to Give New Facelift to Colombo," CHEC Port City Colombo, June 12, 2018, https://www.portcitycolombo.lk/press/2018/06/12/port-city-to-give-new-facelift-to-colombo.html
84. ShiharAneez and Ranga Sirilal, "Sri Lanka to Allow Chinese Port City Project After Delay," *Reuters*, January 12, 2016, https://www.reuters.com/article/sri-lanka-china-portcity-idUSL3N14W42G20160112

85. "Sri Lanka Says Chinese Firm Drops Claim over Colombo Port City's Delay," *Reuters*, August 2, 2016, https://in.reuters.com/article/sri-lanka-china-portcity/sri-lanka-says-chinese-firm-drops-claim-over-colombo-port-citys-delay-idINKCN10D18B
86. Chandani Kirinde, "Govt. Unveils Tax Breaks for Colombo International Financial Centre," *Daily Financial Times*, July 29, 2020, https://www.ft.lk/front-page/Govt-unveils-tax-breaks-for-Colombo-International-Financial-Centre/44-703848
87. Shihar Aneez, "Sri Lanka to Offer Tax Breaks for Project Involving China-backed Port City," *Reuters*, October 25, 2017, https://in.reuters.com/article/sri-lanka-china-portcity/sri-lanka-to-offer-tax-breaks-for-project-involving-china-backed-port-city-idUSL4N1N02MD
88. "Colombo Port City Economic Commission Act", https://www.portcitycolombo.lk/downloads/economic-commission-law.pdf
89. "Building a World Class City for South Asia", https://www.portcitycolombo.lk/about/
90. Meera Srinivasan, "Sri Lankan parliament passes controversial Bill on China-backed Port City," *The Hindu*, May 20, 2021, https://www.thehindu.com/news/international/sri-lankan-parliament-passes-controversial-bill-on-china-backed-port-city/article60682827.ece
91. "Members appointed to Colombo Port City Economic Commission…," *Presidential Secretariat Press Release*, June 1, 2021, https://www.presidentsoffice.gov.lk/index.php/2021/06/01/members-appointed-to-colombo-port-city-economic-commission/
92. "Transcript of Virtual Weekly Media Briefing by the Official Spokesperson," *Ministry of External Affairs*, June 17, 2021, https://mea.gov.in/media-briefings.htm?dtl/33927/Transcript_of_Virtual_Weekly_Media_Briefing_by_the_Official_Spokesperson_June_17_2021
93. P. Manoj, "Adani Ports Eye Colombo Box Transhipment Pie with Government Backing," *Business Line*, https://www.thehindubusinessline.com/companies/adani-ports-eye-colombo-box-transhipment-pie-with-government-backing/article31980337.ece
94. Suresh Sharma, "Merits of Cabotage Law Relaxation on Coastal Shipping in India; How Situation Can Be improved," *The Financial Express*, October 9, 2019, https://www.financialexpress.com/industry/merits-of-cabotage-law-relaxation-on-coastal-shipping-in-india-how-situation-can-be-improved/1730728/
95. Akhil Bery, "Sri Lanka's Crisis Likely Won't Be Resolved Soon," *CFR*, July 19, 2022, https://www.cfr.org/blog/sri-lankas-crisis-likely-wont-be-resolved-soon
96. "India airlifts nano nitrogen to help Sri Lanka's fertilizer crisis," *The Economic Times*, November 4, 2021, https://economictimes.indiatimes.com/news/india/india-airlifts-nano-nitrogen-to-help-sri-lankas-fertiliser-crisis/articleshow/87527372.cms?from=mdr
97. Suranjana Tewari, "Sri Lanka crisis is a warning to other Asian nations," *BBC*, July 18, 2022, https://www.bbc.com/news/business-61976928
98. "Sri Lanka to shut 3 foreign missions as dollar crisis worsens," *East Mojo*, December 29, 2021, https://www.eastmojo.com/world/2021/12/29/sri-lanka-to-shut-3-foreign-missions-as-dollar-crisis-worsens/

99. "China's 'opaque' loan deals behind Lanka crisis, says USAID, hails India," *TNN, The Times of India*, Jul 28, 2022, https://timesofindia.indiatimes.com/world/south-asia/chinas-opaque-loan-deals-behind-lanka-crisis-says-usaid-hails-india/articleshow/93171551.cms
100. "Foreign Ministry Spokesperson Zhao Lijian's Regular Press Conference on July 28, 2022," *Ministry of Foreign Affairs, The People's Republic of China*, July 28, 2022, https://www.fmprc.gov.cn/mfa_eng/xwfw_665399/s2510_665401/2511_665403/202207/t20220728_10729508.html
101. "China's debt trap diplomacy responsible for economic calamity in Sri Lanka," *Business Standard*, July 21, 2022, https://www.business-standard.com/article/international/china-s-debt-trap-diplomacy-responsible-for-economic-calamity-in-sri-lanka-122072001498_1.html; also see : Meera Srinivasan, "Dragging debt talks in Sri Lanka put spotlight on Chinese loans," *The Hindu,* December 1, 2022, https://www.thehindu.com/news/international/dragging-debt-talks-in-sri-lanka-put-spotlight-on-chinese-loans/article66210618.ece
102. Arai Etsuyo, "Sri Lanka's Economic Crisis: A Chinese Debt Trap?" *Nippon*, October 11, 2022, https://www.nippon.com/en/in-depth/d00840/
103. Waruna Karunatilake and Alasdair Pal, "China approves $1.5 billion currency swap with Sri Lanka," *Reuters*, March 10, 2021, https://www.reuters.com/article/us-sri-lanka-economy-china-idUSKBN2B21UL
104. "$968 in Four Months, India Pips China to be Top Lanka Lender," *Times of India,* September 19, 2022, https://timesofindia.indiatimes.com/india/968m-in-4-months-india-pips-china-to-be-top-lanka lender/articleshow/94288688.cms
105. Uditha Jayasinghe, "Sri Lanka inks debt deal with creditor nations, including China," *Reuters*, June 26, 2024, https://www.reuters.com/markets/asia/sri-lanka-signs-debt-deal-with-creditor-nations-paris-2024-06-26/
106. Shantanu Roy-Chaudhury, "India-China-Sri Lanka Triangle: The Defense Dimension," *The Diplomat*, July 12, 2019, https://thediplomat.com/2019/07/india-china-sri-lanka-triangle-the-defense-dimension/
107. "SIPRI Arms Transfers Database," SIPRI, https://armstrade.sipri.org/armstrade/page/trade_register.php
108. Shihar Aneez and Ranga Sirilal, "Chinese Submarine Docks in Sri Lanka Despite Indian Concerns," *Reuters*, November 2, 2020, https://in.reuters.com/article/sri-lanka-china-submarine/chinese-submarine-docks-in-sri-lanka-despite-indian-concerns-idINKBN0IM0LU20141102
109. Atul Aneja, "China says its submarine docked in Sri Lanka 'for replenishment'," *The Hindu*, November 28, 2014, https://www.thehindu.com/news/international/world/china-says-its-submarine-docked-in-sri-lanka-for-replenishment/article 6643129.ece
110. Sutirtho Patranobis, "China Dismisses India's Concerns Over its Submarine Docking in Colombo," *The Hindustan Times*, November 3, 2014, https://www.hindustantimes.com/india/china-dismisses-india-s-concerns-over-its-submarine-docking-in-colombo/story-UJjxKzOm5k1BaenjSVSyUP.html
111. "Sri Lanka refuses port call for Chinese submarine after Indian leader Modi's visit," *South China Morning Post*, May 12, 2017, https://www.scmp.com/news/asia/

diplomacy/article/2094093/sri-lanka-refuses-port-call-chinese-submarine-after-indian

112. "Sri Lanka Rejects US Claims, Says No Chinese Military Base at Port," *The Economic Times*, October 11, 2018, https://economictimes.indiatimes.com/news/defence/sri-lanka-rejects-us-claims-says-no-chinese-military-base-at-port/articleshow/66163389.cms.
113. "Sri Lanka to Base Navy's Southern Command at Chinese-run Port," *South China Morning Post*, June 30, 2018, https://www.scmp.com/news/china/diplomacy-defence/article/2153246/sri-lanka-base-navys-southern-command-chinese-run
114. "Chinese 'Spy' Ship Yuan Wang 5 Reaches Sri Lanka's Hambantota Port: Report," *Business Today*, August 16, 2022, https://www.businesstoday.in/latest/world/story/chinese-spy-ship-yuan-wang-5-reaches-sri-lankas-hambantota-port-report-344740-2022-08-16
115. "Another Chinese spy ship stalks the Indian Ocean," *Live Mint*, November 12, 2022, https://www.livemint.com/opinion/online-views/mint-explainer-another-chinese-spy-ship-stalks-the-indian-ocean-11668223948151.html
116. Shaurya Karanbir Gurung, "Alarm over Chinese Research Ships in Indian Ocean Region," *The Economic Times*, January 30, 2020, https://economictimes.indiatimes.com/news/defence/alarm-over-chinese-research-ships-in-indian-ocean-region/articleshow/73755293.cms?from=mdr
117 "Chinese Spy Ship Spotted Close to Indian Coast," *Times Now*, March 30, 2023, https://www.timesnownews.com/india/chinese-spy-ship-spotted-close-to-indian-coast-article-99115159
118. Krishan Francis, "Sri Lanka declares moratorium on research ships for a year amid Indian concerns over Chinese vessels," *Associated Press*, January 5, 2024, https://apnews.com/article/sri-lanka-india-china-research-ships-42ddb725105eb32b3b43fee8fff3838c
119. "Sri Lanka to soon formulate national policy on visits by foreign research vessels: Sri Lanka's Foreign Minister," *The Hindu*, December 21, 2024, https://www.thehindu.com/news/international/sri-lanka-to-soon-formulate-national-policy-on-visits-by-foreign-research-vessels-foreign-minister/article69010399.ece
120. "Sea cucumbers feed China's influence in Sri Lanka," *Financial Times*, February 22, 2022, https://www.ft.com/content/d67e1f47-754e-4c0f-a35f-f28c706cf0bc
121. Sonia Sarkar, "As Indian trawlers steal Sri Lankan fish, Chinese sea cucumber firm offers a lifeline," *South China Morning Post*, September 4, 2022, https://www.scmp.com/week-asia/economics/article/3191231/indian-trawlers-steal-sri-lankan-fish-chinese-sea-cucumber-firm
122. "Chinese company destroying Sri Lankan fishing community," *The Print*, January 25, 2023, https://theprint.in/world/chinese-company-destroying-sri-lankan-fishing-community/1335433/
123. "Chinese firm wins contract for Sri Lanka wind and solar energy projects near Tamil Nadu coast," *The Indian Express*, February 8, 2021, https://indianexpress.com/article/india/chinese-firm-wins-contract-for-lanka-project-near-tamil-nadu-coast-7179109/

124. "Tamil Nadu worried over increased presence of Chinese Army in Sri Lanka," *The Hindu*, October 16, 2022, https://www.thehindu.com/news/national/tamil-nadu-worried-over-the-increased-presence-of-the-chinese-army-in-sri-lanka/article66018297.ece
125. Meera Srinivasan, "Chinese Ambassador's visit to Jaffna sparks concern, commentary in Sri Lanka," *The Hindu*, December 26, 2021, https://www.thehindu.com/news/international/chinese-ambassadors-visit-to-jaffna-sparks-concern-commentary-in-sri-lanka/article38040843.ece
126. Zulfick Farzan, ""This is just the beginning", says Chinese Ambassador as Jaffna visit ends," *News first*, December 17, 2021, https://www.newsfirst.lk/2021/12/17/this-is-just-the-beginning-says-chinese-ambassador-as-jaffna-visit-ends/
127. Amy Yang, "Seeing the world through Sri Lankan eyes," *Sunday Observer*, February 20, 2022, https://www.sundayobserver.lk/2022/02/20/youth-observer/seeing-world-through-sri-lankan-eyes
128. Ross Velton, "The Country that Supplies Eyes," *BBC*, February 1, 2016, https://www.bbc.com/news/magazine-35410148
129. Yasiru Ranaraja and Maya Majueran, "Is the 'Health Silk Road' a 'debt-trap' of China's BRI for Sri Lanka?" *CGTN*, April 25, 2020, https://news.cgtn.com/news/2020-04-25/Is-the-Health-Silk-Road-a-debt-trap-of-China-s-BRI-for-Sri-Lanka--PXqPCPd7Ta/index.html
130. "China defends Sinovac's Non-Disclosure Agreement with Sri Lanka," *Colombo Gazette*, June 27, 2021, https://colombogazette.com/2021/06/27/china-defends-sinovacs-non-disclosure-agreement-with-sri-lanka/
131 Chinese Embassy in Sri Lanka. Twitter, https://twitter.com/ChinaEmbSL?ref_src=twsrc%5Etfw%7Ctwcamp%5Etweetembed%7Ctwterm%5E1409050760327798784%7Ctwgr%5E197b6ee4098b70053d9ebf696d25ade65033fb17%7Ctwcon%5Es1_&ref_url=https%3A%2F%2Fwww.newswire.lk%2F2021%2F06%2F28%2Fchinese-embassy-defends-sinovac-vaccine-price-non-disclosure-agreement-with-sri-lanka%2F
132. "Chinese firm pushing for sanctions against Sri Lanka over disputed organic fertiliser stocks: Report," *The Times of India*, December 30, 2021, https://timesofindia.indiatimes.com/chinese-firm-pushing-for-sanctions-against-sri-lanka-over-disputed-organic-fertiliser-stocks-report/articleshow/88587730.cms
133. "Sri Lankan court extends order to block payment to Chinese company amid contaminated fertilizer row," *The Hindu*, November 6, 2021, https://www.thehindu.com/news/international/sri-lankan-court-extends-order-to-block-payment-to-chinese-company-amid-contaminated-fertilizer-row/article37351132.ece
134. "Fertiliser shipment row: Chinese embassy blacklists People's Bank of Sri Lanka," *Wion News*, October 29, 2021, https://www.wionews.com/south-asia/fertiliser-shipment-row-chinese-embassy-blacklists-peoples-bank-of-sri-lanka-424943
135. "China takes the quality of its exports seriously: FM spokesperson," *Global Times*, November 2, 2021, https://www.globaltimes.cn/page/202111/1237967.shtml
136. "Sri Lanka settles $6.9m fertilizer bill with Chinese supplier," *Nikkei Asia*, January 8, 2022, https://asia.nikkei.com/Politics/International-relations/Sri-Lanka-settles-6.9m-fertilizer-bill-with-Chinese-supplier2

137. Meera Srinivasan, "Sri Lanka Cabinet clears China's role in terminal project," *The Hindu*, November 24, 2021, https://www.thehindu.com/news/international/sri-lanka-cabinet-clears-chinas-role-in-terminal-project/article37670153.ece#:~:text=Sri%20Lanka%20has%20decided%20to,on%20a%202019%20trilateral%20agreement.
138. "Explained: Why Sri Lanka pushed India out of Colombo terminal project, what's being offered as compensation," *The Indian Express*, February 4, 2021, https://indianexpress.com/article/explained/explained-why-sri-lanka-has-pushed-india-out-of-colombo-terminal-project-and-whats-being-offered-as-compensation-7171502/
139. Meera Srinivasan, "Explained: The Adani Group's recent port deal in Sri Lanka," *The Hindu*, October 4, 2021, https://www.thehindu.com/news/national/explained-the-adani-groups-recent-port-deal-in-sri-lanka/article36825539.ece
140. "Colombo Port: Adani Begins Construction Of $700 Million Container Terminal Project," *Swarajyamag*, November 10, 2022, https://swarajyamag.com/news-brief/colombo-port-adani-begins-construction-of-700-million-container-terminal-project
141. "US Commits Over 500 Million Financing for Adani Terminal Venture at Colombo Port Curated," *News18.com*, November 8, 2023, https://www.news18.com/world/us-commits-over-500-million-financing-for-adani-terminal-venture-at-colombo-port-8653375.html
142. "To counter China's influence, US invests $553 million in Gautam Adani-led Colombo Port," *The Telegraph*, November 9, 2023, https://www.telegraphindia.com/business/to-counter-chinas-influence-us-invests-553-million-in-gautam-adani-led-colombo-port/cid/1978604
143. "Sri Lanka nods to Trincomalee oil tank deal with India," *The Telegraph*, January 1, 2022, https://www.telegraphindia.com/world/sri-lanka-nods-to-trincomalee-oil-tank-deal-with-india/cid/1846233
144. Nirupama Subramanian, "Developing Trincomalee oil tank farm: What the deal means for India, Lanka," *Indian Express*, January 3, 2022, https://indianexpress.com/article/explained/trincomalee-oil-tank-what-deal-means-india-lanka-7702794/
145. Zulfick Farzan, "Indian FM commissions Oil Tanks in Trinco," *News First*, November 3, 2023, https://www.newsfirst.lk/2023/11/3/indian-fm-commissions-oil-tanks-in-trinco
146. "$968 in Four Months, India Pips China to be Top Lanka Lender," *Times of India*, September 19, 2022, https://timesofindia.indiatimes.com/india/968m-in-4-months-india-pips-china-to-be-top-lanka-lender/articleshow/94288688.cms
147. "Press Statement by External Affairs Minister, Dr. S. Jaishankar in Sri Lanka," Ministry of External Affairs, January 20, 2023, https://www.mea.gov.in/Speeches-Statements.htm?dtl/36136#:~:text=As%20you%20all%20know%2C%20last,3; Also see "India provided assistance worth 3.8 billion dollars to Sri Lanka to tide over unprecedented economic crisis, says EAM S Jaishankar," *AIR*, July 20,2022, https://newsonair.gov.in/News?title=India-provided-assistance-worth-3.8-billion-dollars-to-Sri-Lanka-to-tide-over-unprecedented-economic-crisis%2C-says-EAM-S-Jaishankar&id=444529

148. "India, Japan to provide relief supplies worth millions to Sri Lanka," *Business Standard*, May 21, 2022, https://www.business-standard.com/article/international/india-japan-to-provide-relief-supplies-worth-millions-to-sri-lanka-122052100383_1.html
149. "Japan extends additional US$ 6.6 million support to Sri Lanka for emergency food and nutrition assistance," *World Food Programme*, March 9, 2023, https://www.wfp.org/news/japan-extends-additional-us-66-million-support-sri-lanka-emergency-food-and-nutrition
150. "IMF Resumes Sri Lanka Bailout After China's Debt Deal," *The Economic Times*, December 13, 2023, https://economictimes.indiatimes.com/news/international/world-news/imf-resumes-sri-lanka-bailout-after-chinas-debt-deal/articleshow/105955355.cms?from=mdr
151. Uditha Jayasinghe, Jorgelina Do Rosario and Leika Kihara, "Sri Lanka says China debt deal covers $4.2 billion as other talks drag on," *Reuters*, October 12, 2023, https://www.reuters.com/markets/asia/sri-lanka-says-it-has-deal-with-china-exim-bank-cover-42-bln-debt-2023-10-12/
152. "Chinese state-owned firm to increase Sri Lanka investment to $2 billion by building new port complex," *Deccan Herald*, May 1, 2023, https://www.deccanherald.com/international/world-news-politics/chinese-state-owned-firm-to-increase-sri-lanka-investment-to-2-billion-by-building-new-port-complex-1214650.html
153. "China's Sinopec signs deal to enter retail fuel market in crisis-plagued Sri Lanka," *MarketWatch*, May 22, 2023, https://www.marketwatch.com/story/chinas-sinopec-signs-deal-to-enter-retail-fuel-market-in-crisis-plagued-sri-lanka-c465b773
154. "Xi Jinping Meets with Sri Lankan President Ranil Wickremesinghe," *Belt and Road Forum*, October 23, 2023, http://www.beltandroadforum.org/english/n101/2023/1023/c124-1311.html
155. "Sinopec proposes to fully finance Sri Lanka refinery," *Argus Media Group*, March 14, 2023, https://www.argusmedia.com/en/news/2428984-sinopec-proposes-to-fully-finance-sri-lanka-refinery; also see Cissy Zhou, "Sri Lanka's China 'debt trap' fears grow as Beijing keeps investing," *Nikkei Asia*, January 2, 2024, https://asia.nikkei.com/Spotlight/Asia-Insight/Sri-Lanka-s-China-debt-trap-fears-grow-as-Beijing-keeps-investing
156. Office of the President, Government of Sri Lanka. "Statement to the Media by the President of Sri Lanka during the State Visit to India, 16 December 2024." *President's Office*, December 16, 2024, https://www.presidentsoffice.gov.lk/statement-to-the-media/.
157. Ministry of External Affairs, Government of India. "Transcript of Special Briefing by Foreign Secretary on the State Visit of President of Sri Lanka to India, December 16, 2024." *Media Briefings*, December 16, 2024, https://www.mea.gov.in/media-briefings.htm?dtl/38800/.

6

The Disquiet in the Archipelago

Introduction

"China has grabbed more land than the East India Company … they have not given development assistance to us … it was a debt trap … we must now get the contracts done … we can't stop that. We have to pay the bill … but the Chinese government must restructure the debt," said former Maldives President Mohamed Nasheed at the Indian Ocean Conference in Malé in December 2019.[1] Perhaps there is considerable exaggeration in Nasheed's comparison of the East India Company's land grab with the Chinese presence in the Indian Ocean. However, the former president's statement was probably the first time a former head of state had compared the Belt and Road Initiative (BRI) to the colonial policies of the East India Company, which indicated an acute anxiety regarding the growing debt burden. Mr Nasheed was also the speaker of the Maldives Parliament when he made such comparisons.

A small archipelagic state attracting considerable international attention because of Chinese engagement indicates a fast-changing geopolitical dynamic in the Indian Ocean. The Maldives, with a population of over 515,696 (in 2022), is not a big market.[2] The Maldives' GDP was USD 3.7 billion in 2014, increased to USD 5.6 billion in 2019, declined to USD 3.7 billion in 2020, and reached USD 6.59 billion in 2023.[3] There would be many Chinese companies with valuations bigger than the Maldives' GDP. Further, the Maldives is not a financial or transit hub, and its economy depends on tourism. On the other hand, the Maldives is strategically located right in the middle of the Indian Ocean. While Diego Garcia Island, with a US base, is to the south, Sri Lanka and peninsular India are to the north. Important shipping routes in the Indian Ocean Region (IOR) traverse the maritime space between the Maldives and Sri Lanka. A sustained presence in the Maldives will give China significant geopolitical advantages. If not a naval/military base, China can increase its maritime domain awareness and signalling capabilities in the IOR.

Historically, the Maldives had a close relationship with India. The ancestry of the population of the Maldives is often traced to the "Tamil and Sinhalese peoples from southern India and Sri Lanka."[4] Buddhism had a strong presence on the islands, and Islam was introduced sometime in the 12th century. After attaining independence from the United Kingdom (UK) in 1965, the Maldives maintained close relations with India. India's development assistance played an important role in developing various projects, such as the Indira Gandhi Memorial Hospital, Maldives Polytechnic, National Police Academy (ISLES), and others.[5] India has been a leading partner in providing aid during humanitarian crises. For example, after the December 2004 tsunami, the Indian government provided relief material and financial assistance to the Maldives.[6] Similarly, in 2014, India airlifted 375 tonnes of drinking water to the Maldives to overcome acute scarcity.[7]

Troubled Political Transition and Chinese Bridges

The Maldives was under the prolonged rule of Maumoon Abdul Gayoom from 1978 to 2008. Abdul Gayoom was the of the longest-serving rulers, and as with many such rulers, anti-government protests rocked the country in 2008.[8] During the same year, multiparty elections were held under a new constitution. While the opposition leader, Mohamed Nasheed, became president after defeating President Gayoom in the elections, his tenure was brief as he was ousted in a coup in 2012, and Vice President Mohamed Waheed took over the reins.[9] Subsequently, Abdulla Yameen, half-brother of former President Gayoom, assumed power in 2013 through an election process deemed unfair by many.[10]

With many opposition party members, including President Nasheed, under arrest, there were concerns regarding the declining space for political freedoms. The stalling of the political reform process in the Maldives prompted many, including India and the UK, to sharply criticise the Abdulla Yameen regime. The Commonwealth threatened to suspend the Maldives from the organisation for failing to revive the movement towards a genuine democracy.

Prior to any punitive measures being taken, Abdulla Yameen announced that his country was leaving the Commonwealth.[11] It was broadly in the context of the troubled transition that the Maldives, under the leadership of Mohamed Waheed and Abdulla Yameen, saw a significant shift in its foreign policy. With Mohamed Waheed in power, China extended a USD 500 million loan to the Maldives in 2012.[12] Simultaneously, the Waheed government started to scale down economic engagement with Indian firms. India's GMR group had entered into an agreement with the Maldives Airports Company Limited (MACL) to modernise and expand the Ibrahim Nasir International Airport.[13] However, the Waheed government demanded that the GMR "return the project to the government and leave the island immediately", as the company's decision to charge Airport Development Charges (ADC) was not as per the contract.[14] The case subsequently went to international arbitration, where it was decided in favour of the government. Subsequently, the GMR demanded cancellation charges, which were upheld in the international arbitration.[15] The GMR airport episode was not just a business dispute but also a political message of the Waheed government's preference to disengage with India.

With the advent of Abdulla Yameen of the Progressive Party of Maldives (PPM) as President, the tilt towards China became even more pronounced. Given the geostrategic location of the Maldives, Chinese leadership quickly seized the opportunity. A year after formally announcing the BRI, President Xi Jinping visited the Maldives in 2014 and reiterated the strategic importance of the island state.[16] Since the diplomatic relations between the two were established in 1972, Xi Jinping was the first President to visit the country.[17] The fact that President Xi Jinping visited a small archipelagic state with no big market, nestled in the middle of the Indian Ocean, indicated that China attached significant geopolitical importance to the Maldives. The visit consolidated economic and political relations between the two countries. During President Xi's visit, Beijing Urban Construction Group Company Limited received the contract to expand the Malé Airport,[18] a project previously awarded to and rescinded from an Indian company.

The upswing in the bilateral relationship between Malé and Beijing was rapid. In 2015, a Chinese company started a resort development project on Kunaavashi Island, which was leased to the company for 50 years.[19] A year later, in 2016, the Maldives leased the uninhabited Feydhoo Finolhu island to China for 50 years, which was reportedly converted into a beach resort by

Chinese developers.[20] In the subsequent years, the island's size has reportedly registered a significant increase as per the satellite images.[21] Since the Feydhoo Finolhu island is located about "75 nautical miles from India's Exclusive Economic Zone", there were concerns that the development activities may create conditions for Chinese monitoring maritime activity around the western coast of India.[22] On the other hand, some news reports from the Maldives hinted that there was nothing unusual about leasing islands to China, as "uninhabited islands have been leased to local and foreign resort developers" to promote tourism in the country.[23] Nonetheless, the activities of Chinese firms on islands in the IOR generated concerns among countries such as India.

In December 2017, President Abdulla Yameen visited China and signed agreements pertaining to the BRI which included cooperation in the fields of free trade, economy, technology, health, meteorology, and finance.[24] After two years of negotiations, both countries signed a Free Trade Agreement (FTA) during Maldivian President Yameen's visit to Beijing. The Maldives was the "second country in South Asia to sign a free trade agreement with China."[25] As per the agreement, 96 per cent of the products of both countries will be subjected to zero tariff, which would benefit Chinese industrial and consumer products, and the Maldives' aquatic products were also supposed to benefit.[26] During the same year, both countries also signed the "Protocol on Establishment of Joint Ocean Observation Station", which raised concerns that the project site, Makunudhoo, was uncomfortably close to Indian waters and would be used for maritime surveillance.[27] There was also increased cooperation between the defence forces of the two countries. In 2017, three Chinese naval ships visited the Maldives, and the Maldives National Defence Force (MNDF) received training on these vessels.[28]

A year later, in 2018, one of the biggest infrastructure projects, the China-Maldives Friendship Bridge between the capital city, Malé, and the neighbouring island, Hulhule, was inaugurated.[29] Prior to the construction of the bridge, people used a ferry to travel between the islands. The new bridge has reduced travel time between the two islands, making the commute easier for four-wheelers and other vehicles. As per the *Global Times* report, the project was built at an estimated cost of USD 184.44 million by the Second Harbor Engineering Company, a China Communications Construction Company unit.[30] In addition, Chinese firms were also involved in social housing projects. In 2018, the China State Construction Engineering Corporation (CSCEC), as well as the China Machinery Engineering Corp, started implementing a housing project that sought to construct 8,500 units.[31] The projects were completed two years later with the capacity to provide accommodation to 30,000 people.[32]

The relentless progress of Chinese construction projects received a jolt in 2018 with the victory of Ibrahim Mohamed Solih of the Maldivian Democratic Party (MDP) over Abdulla Yameen.[33] The election outcome halted the Maldives' drift towards China. The fact that President Abdulla Yameen lost the elections despite the quick implementation of mega infrastructure projects suggests that economic engagement with China became a highly contentious issue. In some segments of the Maldivian society, there was a deep disappointment that engagement with China had pushed them into a deep debt crisis. There was no clarity on the scale of the Maldives' debt to China, with some, such as former President Nasheed, suggesting debt "exposure as high as USD 3 billion."[34] On the other hand, former Maldivian officials and Chinese representatives put the figure around USD 1.1 billion and USD 1.4 billion, respectively.[35] Either way, the debt exposure is undoubtedly very high for a country with over 500,000 people and a gross domestic product of USD 3.74 billion in 2020.[36] The external debt of the Maldives was a source of concern for many international actors. In 2020, the World Bank included the Maldives "among nine countries ranked to be in debt distress or at high risk as a result of loans from China."[37] Moreover, there was no transparency on the commitments made by the previous government. Numerous reports hint that project costs were inflated beyond the actual costs to benefit the Yameen administration.[38] The absence of transparency on the Chinese projects was evident when Finance Minister Ibrahim Ameer stated that his first week in office was spent trying to "reconcile loans that the previous government took for these projects and the sovereign guarantees that it gave for them."[39] In an interesting development, in August 2020, China's Exim Bank asked the Maldives to pay the unpaid instalment (USD 10 million) of a USD 127 million loan extended to a close ally of the former president, Yameen.[40] The previous Maldives government reportedly extended a sovereign guarantee to the loan from China's Exim Bank. As Sathiya Moorthy pointed out, a 'sovereign guarantee' is issued to governments and state sector enterprises.[41] However, in this instance, the sovereign guarantee was extended to a private entity, which points to the complexity of calculating the total debt of the Maldives.[42]

The regime change also brought a critical re-evaluation of economic engagement with China, including the FTA. Dipanjan Roy Chaudhury reported that there was an opinion in the Maldives that the local fisherman community would not benefit from the FTA, and there are calls not to implement it.[43] Further, Maldivian Minister of Economic Development, Fayyaz Ismail, in 2020, opined that operationalising the FTA will negatively impact trade relations with others, such as Singapore, Dubai, and India.[44] Earlier, former President Mohamed Nasheed lamented that "the trade imbalance between China and the Maldives is so huge that nobody would think of an FTA between such parties ... China is not buying anything from us. It is a one-way treaty."[45]

President Solih reduced the pronounced tilt towards China in foreign policy. However, his government maintained sustained engagement with China. For instance, during Chinese Foreign Minister Wang Yi's visit to the Maldives in January 2022, both sides signed five agreements pertaining to "mutual visa exemption, cooperation on grant aid, maintenance of the China-Maldives Friendship Bridge, sea-water desalination project and hospital assistance and cooperation programme."[46] The Chinese foreign minister's visit was also part of the efforts to commemorate 50 years of the China-Maldives bilateral relationship. The visit was also symbolically significant as China sought to demonstrate its commitment to the Maldives and African countries. A few months later, both countries signed an agreement that would enable the Maldives Ministry of Foreign Affairs to receive training and capacity-building assistance from China.[47]

Chinese firms also completed a few important projects even during President Solih's administration. For instance, the CSCEC completed the construction of four bridges.[48] In the third quarter of 2022, Chinese enterprises handed over a housing project, which would reportedly benefit around 10,000 residents, to the Maldives government.[49] The Tripartite Coordinating Mechanism Meetings, attended by official representatives from the two countries and Chinese enterprises, continued without interruptions. Such a meeting in September 2022 sought to facilitate greater cooperation in the domains of fisheries, marine resources, and agriculture.[50] Both countries celebrated 50 years of bilateral ties in October, and President Ibrahim Mohamed Solih and President Xi Jinping exchanged congratulatory messages.[51] Various other activities, such as the Maldives-China parliamentary friendship group meetings and business forums on the 'Belt and Road' between China and the Maldives, also proceeded as per schedule.[52] In December 2022, a Chinese renewable energy firm, Sino Soar Hybrid (Beijing) Technology Co Ltd, won the contract for the implementation of the ADB-supported hybrid solar-diesel power mini-grid project in the 12 islands of Thaa Atoll.[53] Reportedly, the Chinese Embassy in Colombo tweeted that Sino Soar Hybrid Technology's project, which was suspended in Sri Lanka 'due to security concerns from a third party, has inked a contract with the Maldivian government.'[54] The tweet conveyed an impression that Chinese officials were approaching developmental projects in South Asia with an intent to contain or at least compete with Indian presence. It should be noted that over the years, Chinese firms were also involved in projects such as the Thinadhoo Solar Energy Power Station, a solar power station in Hulhumalé, and implemented energy projects in Haa Alifu as well as Haa Dhaalu Atolls.[55] In early 2023, Chinese firms started the construction of the Thilafushi Phase 2 artificial island project, which will host a few warehouses and industries.[56] The China-Maldives Ophthalmology Centre Assistance and Cooperation Program was also inaugurated in February 2023.[57] In March 2023, both countries also held the Joint Meeting Mechanism to deal with the safety of Chinese tourists visiting the Maldives.[58] In April 2023, the Maldives and the China International Development Cooperation Agency (CIDCA) signed several agreements of cooperation in various domains, such as agriculture, climate change, healthcare, infrastructure, and people-to-people exchanges.[59]

'India Out' and China

While President Ibrahim Mohamed Solih maintained relations on an even keel with China, his administration's strategy was to diversify international engagement to prevent over-dependence on one country. Countries such as India were more than willing to work with the Solih government. In 2018, Indian Prime Minister Narendra Modi attended the swearing-in ceremony of President Ibrahim Mohamed Solih's administration and assured the new government of extending all possible assistance to address development challenges in the Maldives.[60] After taking over the reins of government, President Solih reaffirmed his government's commitment to 'India First' policy.[61] Nayanima Basu reported that there was considerable relief in New Delhi with the election of President Solih.[62] Subsequently, Prime Minister Narendra Modi made his first bilateral visit of his second term to the Maldives in June 2019 and promised Indian grant assistance of USD 5.5 million. The Indian government had extended a USD 800 million line of credit towards economic and social development activities.[63] The Indian government increased economic engagement, built a cancer hospital, expanded Hanimaadhoo Airport, and launched the Greater Malé Connectivity Project.[64]

Under President Solih's government, India became critical for the Maldives to address its financial requirements. The Maldives finance minister, Ibrahim Ameer, noted that Malé was able to secure "funding for up to USD 1.4 billion—about USD 400 million as part of a currency swap agreement between the two central banks, another USD 200 million as a cash grant from the Indian government, and the remaining USD 800 million in the form of a credit line from India's Export-Import Bank.[65]" During the pandemic, the Maldives received considerable aid from India in terms of food supplies and essential medicines. In the midst of the pandemic, when most of the countries closed their borders and restricted internal travel, India allowed "over 150 Maldivian patients and their medical attendants ... to travel to India for urgent medical treatment."[66]

The regime change also enabled India to scale up its connectivity projects in the Maldives. In August 2020, India's External Affairs Minister and his Maldivian counterpart signed a series of agreements, which included the Greater Malé Connectivity project (GMCP) and soft loan arrangements for various other projects.[67] The GMCP, which would involve the construction of a 6.74-km-long bridge connecting Malé with the nearby islands of Gulhifalhu, Thilafushi, and Villingli, is regarded as one of the largest projects in the country.[68] Referring to various projects, Parliament Speaker and former Maldivian President Mohamed Nasheed noted that India's development assistance tends to be 'super low cost' and helps in building critical infrastructure compared to the Chinese "eye-wateringly expensive commercial loans that leave the nation mired in debt."[69] India was also involved in various other projects, such as fish processing plants, storage units, jetty renovation, direct cargo services, ensuring a steady supply of essential commodities, construction of a police training centre, improved sporting facilities, and other High Impact Community Development Projects.[70]

While India-Maldives relations were getting consolidated, a few elements in the Maldives' opposition parties started an 'India Out' campaign. These opposition groups contended that there was a permanent Indian military presence in the country, and there was a need to restore the sovereignty of the country. While India has no naval base in the Maldives, the opposition argued that the MOU between the two countries to upgrade the Uthuru Thila Falhu harbour suggests a possible emergence of a naval base.[71] The campaign picked up momentum towards the last two quarters of 2020. Criticising the 'India Out' campaign, Mohamed Nasheed, Parliament Speaker and former president of Maldives, argued that a balanced relationship with India and China is critical for the prosperity of the Maldives.[72] The Maldives Vice President Faisal Naseem referred to India as a "leading development partner, our first responder."[73] The Maldivian Foreign Minister Abdulla Shahid also criticised the campaign as a 'major attempt to stir up enmity' and referred to many benefits that Maldivians avail in India, such as healthcare facilities.[74] Foreign Minister Abdulla Shahid added that not even "a single grain of sand from Maldivian land being relinquished to a foreigner."[75] The Maldives government also tried to address the unfounded speculation that many Indian defence personnel were present in the archipelago. In November 2021, the Maldives National Defense Force (MNDF) informed the Parliament Committee on Security Services that about 75 Indian military personnel work in the Maldives.[76] According to the MNDF, these personnel operate the Dornier Aircraft and two helicopters, which are used for regular surveys of the exclusive economic zone "for anti-terrorist activities and foil drug trafficking operations."[77]

Towards the end of 2021, the former president, Abdulla Yameen, was acquitted on charges of corruption and money laundering due to lack of sufficient evidence. President Abdulla Yameen, known for his pro-China policies, actively participated in domestic politics. The release of the former president, Yameen, gave greater impetus to the India Out campaign. Addressing a political rally organised by the opposition, Yameen declared that he would not "want single Indian military personnel, not even boot, to remain in the country."[78] Subsequently, Yameen participated in political rallies wearing an "India Out" t-shirt.[79] After two years of political imprisonment, the India Out campaign became a launch pad for Yameen's attempts to resurrect his political career. To contain the protests, in April 2022, the Maldives government banned the India Out campaign for undermining national security and inciting hatred towards India, which was criticised by the opposition as an unconstitutional measure.[80] During the same month, India's Chief of Naval Staff, Admiral R. Hari Kumar, visited the Maldives.[81] In his interactions with the Indian naval chief, President Solih referred to increased defence ties and called for continued cooperation in the defence sector.[82]

In June 2022, the protests took an ugly turn, with a few protesters attacking the International Yoga Day celebrations in the capital city, Malé. The protestors reportedly argued that yoga violated the tenets of Islam.[83] The usage of religion to justify anti-India actions did not surprise observers of the Maldives. For instance, N. Manoharan noted that the rise of Islamic radical elements in the Maldives, with trans-national connections 'to the ISIS and Pakistan-based madrasas and jihadist groups', could be involved in the anti-India activities in the archipelago.[84] The growing propensity for violence was a source of concern. A few months later, in December, Yameen was sentenced to 11 years imprisonment in a corruption and money laundering case, which effectively barred him from contesting the presidential elections later in 2023.[85]

Despite the India Out campaign, New Delhi and Malé continued to scale up engagement. In January 2023, India's External Affairs Minister conducted the groundbreaking ceremony for the Hanimaadhoo International Airport project, which would be India's second-largest infrastructure project in the Maldives.[86] The project, with an estimated cost of USD 136.6 million, is being executed by an Indian firm, with India's Exim Bank providing the line of credit.[87] Defence Cooperation Dialogues between India's Defence Secretary and his Maldivian counterpart also continued without disruptions.[88] During his visit to the Maldives in May 2023, the Indian defence minister laid the foundation stone for the Maldives National Defence Force Coast Guard 'Ekatha Harbour' and gifted military ships to the Maldives.[89] Both countries also conducted the 'Ekuverin' joint military exercise.[90] The Indian engagement with the Maldives persisted amid a persistent India Out campaign. The constraints placed by the Maldivian government and the arrest of the former president, Yameen, did not dent the India Out campaign, and it continued to feature significantly in various opposition campaigns.[91] The Maldives' foreign policy became an important agenda item in the run-up to the Maldives' elections.

The 2023 Elections: A Referendum on India and China?

While the elections in 2023 were about selecting the next president of the Maldives, there was considerable discussion as to whether the election was a referendum on the Maldives' foreign policies towards India and China. The prevalence of such discussions indicated the polarisation in domestic policies and the prevalence of a strong perception that external players have a far more significant role in domestic politics. In the run-up to the 2023 elections, after the arrest of Yameen, his protege, Mohamed Muizzu, emerged as a principal opposition candidate of the Progressive Party of Maldives (PPM) and People's National Congress (PNC) coalition.[92] Mohamed Muizzu, the mayor of Male city, was a housing minister in President Yameen's administration and played an important role in operationalising the China-Maldives Friendship Bridge. With a reputation as the implementer of projects and the momentum provided by the India Out campaign, Mohamed Muizzu emerged as a formidable candidate for President Solih.

In the run-up to the elections, President Solih acquired a reputation as a competent administrator. As John Kachtik, writing for *Nikkei Asia*, noted, "the Solih administration has halted the flow of Maldivian fighters going abroad to join terrorist organisations, encouraged the growth of civil society and shown impressive transparency in its response to the COVID-19 pandemic."[93] President Solih implemented progressive policies, such as the minimum wage policy, six-month paid maternity leave, and one-month paid paternity leave.[94] Solih's administration was also examining the possibility of free university education. However, there was considerable disarray in the ruling MDP party. During the primary elections, there was an intense and bitter campaign for the party's leadership between President Solih and Parliament Speaker Nasheed.[95] There were concerns that Parliament Speaker Nasheed's supporters may not fully support President Solih, who won the primary elections. Further, Nasheed said that "former President Yameen is an intellectual", and the only difference of opinion he had with Yameen was the 'India Out' approach. The former speaker also stated that President Solih's government became all about power, not principles, and such statements added to speculation that the ruling MDP vote may get fractured in the presidential elections.[96] In fact, Parliament Speaker Nasheed left the MDP and joined the Democrats.

On September 9, 2023, the first round of presidential elections was held with approximately eight candidates. The principal opposition candidate, Mohamed Muizzu, received about 46.06 per cent of the vote share, while the sitting president, Solih, received about 39.09 per cent.[97] Since none of the presidential candidates were able to get over 50 per cent of the vote share, a run-off election was organised subsequently. The smaller parties, such as the Democrats, and leaders, such as Nasheed, became critical in terms of tilting the voters who did not vote for Solih and Muizzu. President Solih's MDP reportedly tried to build a coalition for the presidential run-off election, which did not materialise.[98] Most of the smaller parties adopted a neutral stance in the presidential run-off elections.

In the presidential run-off elections, the opposition leader, Mohamed Muizzu, registered an emphatic electoral victory. With a 54 per cent vote share, Muizzu defeated the sitting president, Solih, who received a 46 per cent vote share.[99] President Solih graciously conceded the election. He congratulated President-elect Muizzu and the people of the Maldives for reposing faith in the peaceful and democratic process.[100] Further, President Solih announced that the former president, Yameen, would be shifted to house arrest from Maafushi prison.[101] In his initial remarks after the electoral victory, Mohamed Muizzu stated that "every Maldivian citizen is equal in my eyes" and declared his intent to build harmony in accordance with the wishes of the people.[102] The shift to the parliamentary system through a referendum requires constitutional changes approved by the parliament. Prior to the presidential elections, the parliament could not respond to the Election Commission's request on the question needed to organise the referendum due to a lack of quorum in the parliament.[103] It appears that the former president, Solih, and many members of his MDP prefer to continue with the existing presidential system. However, the Democrats and Parliamentary Speaker Nasheed opine that a parliamentary system would be more appropriate for the country.[104] The discussion on the need for a parliamentary system will persist in the near future.[105]

Muizzu's victory was interpreted as a victory for China in the international media. Many international news agencies have defined President-elect Muizzu as a pro-China candidate. Earlier, in his interactions with the representatives of China's Communist Party, Muizzu reportedly noted that if his PPM-PNC coalition returns to power, it would "script a further chapter of strong ties between our two countries."[106] After the election results were declared, Muizzu stated that his foreign policy would be "pro-Maldives".[107] Given the history of the India Out campaign, Muizzu's statements, such as the alleged presence of Indian defence personnel in the archipelago, and policies of the new government were closely scrutinised by New Delhi. Muizzu reportedly stated, "the people have told us that they don't want foreign military here...therefore, what I have to say to the [Indian] ambassador who will come to meet me is [that] close relations can be maintained based on this condition.[108]" The Indian prime minister was quick to congratulate Muizzu and reiterated the commitment to strengthen the bilateral relationship and enhance overall cooperation in the Indian Ocean Region.[109] Former President Solih reportedly requested Muizzu to continue to implement the ongoing projects, including the Thilamale bridge.[110] India would also have had similar expectations that contracts and promises made to Indian firms would be honoured. Continued proactive economic engagement with India will be in tune with a pro-Maldives policy. Most importantly, many in India wanted the Muizzu government to adopt prudent fiscal and international economic engagement policies. An economically healthy Maldives will not be susceptible to unhealthy international influences, which is also in its people's interest.

Muizzu and the India-China Dynamic

Sadly, the cautious optimism that the new president may adopt a pragmatic policy did not materialise. The Muizzu government adopted a two-pronged approach to consolidating its partnership with China and downgrading its relationship with India. Muizzu chose Turkey, followed by China, for his first and second official visits, reinforcing the perception that the Maldivian president was not keen on prioritising a relationship with India. During his visit to China in January 2024, both countries signed about 20 MoUs and declared the intent to build a 'China-Maldives Comprehensive Strategic Cooperative Partnership'.[111] The Maldivian president hinted that his government may implement the FTA, which the previous administrations were reluctant to operationalise.[112] Both countries also agreed "to explore ways towards implementing the Global Security Initiative (GSI) in the efforts to deepen cooperation in law enforcement."[113]

While Indian Prime Minister Modi and President Muizzu did interact on the sidelines of COP28 in the UAE and constituted a core group to deepen the partnership,[114] the bilateral relationship experienced turbulence. The Muizzu government decided not to renew the 2019 MoU with India for joint hydrographic surveys.[115] President Muizzu's persistent demand that New Delhi remove all its defence personnel from the Maldives—about 80 stationed for humanitarian assistance—was seen as an attempt to dilute India's presence in the country. The Maldives did not participate in the Colombo Security Conclave, which is a trilateral maritime security platform comprising India, Sri Lanka, and the Maldives. At the same time, Maldives Vice President

Hussain Mohamed Latheef participated in a meeting on the "China-Indian Ocean Region Forum on Development Cooperation" organised by the China International Development Cooperation Agency (CIDCA).[116] In the midst of growing tensions, a few rash comments by the ministers in the Maldivian government ensured that the bilateral relationship nosedived. In response to the Indian premier's attempt to promote tourism in the Lakshadweep islands in India, a senior member of the ruling Progressive Party of Maldives (PPM) referred to a "permanent smell in the rooms" in India.[117] Maldives Deputy Minister of Youth Empowerment referred to Prime Minister Modi as a "clown and a puppet of Israel".[118] While many leaders across the political spectrum in the Maldives condemned the comments, the image of the Maldives as a friendly tourist destination was severely dented in India. The comments created an uproar, and the hashtag 'Boycott Maldives' trended in Indian social media. With many cancelling their travel plans, there was a significant drop in Indian tourists visiting the Maldives during January 2024.[119]

As the crisis deepened, the opposition party members in the Maldives expressed serious reservations about Muizzu's foreign policy strategy. The Maldivian Democratic Party and the Democrats, in a joint statement issued on January 24, 2024, criticised the government for "making a stark pivot towards an anti-India stance" and for "alienating any development partner, especially the country's most long-standing ally."[120] With the parliament becoming the site of physical confrontation between the members, the relationship between the ruling and opposition parties deteriorated considerably.

Towards the end of January 2024, amid growing tensions in its relationship with India, the Maldives government permitted the Chinese research vessel, Xiang Yang Hong 03, equipped with civilian and military technologies to conduct sea-bed mapping, to enter its exclusive economic zone.[121] The Ministry of Foreign Affairs in Malé justified the arrival of the Chinese ship by stating that "the Maldives has always been a welcoming destination for vessels of friendly countries and continues to host both civilian and military vessels making port calls for peaceful purposes."[122] However, the challenge, as many experts noted, is that the Maldives defence forces do not have the capabilities to ascertain whether the Chinese research vessel is indulging in military surveillance activities.[123]

In May 2024, the International Monetary Fund (IMF) noted that "the Maldives remains at high risk of external and overall debt distress" and went on to add that "uncertainty surrounding the outlook is high and risks are tilted to the downside, including from delayed fiscal consolidation and weaker growth in key sources markets for tourism."[124] As the debt crisis loomed large, the Maldives needed its major economic partners to step in with assistance. In May 2024, despite the stress in the bilateral relationship, India was willing to provide a loan repayment extension to the Maldives.[125] Perhaps there was also a recognition in the Maldives' leadership that because of geography, close people-to-people interactions, and robust economic relationship, relations with India needed special attention. President Muizzu visited India in June to attend the swearing-in ceremony of Indian Prime Minister Narendra Modi for the third term. The visit provided an opportunity for the leadership on both sides to repair the relationship. In the same month, the Maldives' credit rating was downgraded because of "worsening external financing and liquidity metrics."[126] A month later, India and the Maldives resolved their differences regarding the operation of the aircraft and helicopters allegedly by Indian military personnel for medical evacuations. According to news reports, India sent in a fresh batch of civilian personnel to operate the aircraft and helicopters, and the medical evacuations were resumed.[127]

Even as India-Maldives relations started to improve, China continued with its robust engagement with the Maldives. Beijing dispatched large consignments of mineral water to the Maldives to meet drinking water shortages.[128] Maldives' Economic Development Minister, Mohamed Saeed, stated that the Maldives and China "have agreed to cooperate in efforts to pay for imports in their respective countries' currency instead of the US dollar."[129] The Maldives president also thanked India and China for adjusting the loan repayment schedules.[130] India's External Affairs Minister, S. Jaishankar, visited the Maldives and promised capacity building for 1000 Maldivian civil servants and grant assistance to six High Impact Community Development Projects (HICDPs).[131] During the visit, S. Jaishankar also inaugurated reclamation projects, bridges, and other development projects.[132]

In September 2024, amidst growing concerns that Malé may fail to pay USD 25 million on Islamic sovereign debt, the Maldives announced that it had reached an agreement with the People's Bank of China for "promoting the settlement of current account transactions and direct investments in local currencies."[133] While the details of the agreement were not available, the Chinese foreign ministry spokesperson stated that "China will ... provide support and assistance to the economic and social development of the Maldives within its capability."[134] While the assistance from China was a welcome development, the Maldives leadership quickly recognised the importance of reaching out to India to address the immediate financial challenges and long-term development goals.

In October 2024, the president of the Maldives arrived in India on his first bilateral visit. The visit witnessed a significant upswing in the bilateral relationship. India promised to extend "support in the form of USD 400 million and INR 30 billion as a bilateral currency swap agreement", and both sides agreed to cooperate in the domain of Digital Public Infrastructure , establish an Agriculture Economic Zone, and initiate conversations on a Bilateral Free Trade Agreement.[135] President Muizzu, who was sometimes dubbed as a pro-China leader, noted that Indian assistance is "instrumental in addressing foreign exchange issues" and went on to add that "India is fully cognisant of our fiscal situation ... and ... will always be ready to ease our burden, find *better alternatives* [emphasis added] and solutions to the challenges we face."[136]

While the India-Maldives rapprochement proceeded apace, China's economic engagement with the Maldives received a significant fillip. Towards the end of December 2024, China's Ministry of Commerce announced that the China-Maldives Free Trade Agreement (FTA) would be operationalised from January 1, 2025.[137] As noted, there was an anticipation that seafood and handicrafts from the Maldives may find preferential access in the Chinese market.[138] As the FTA got operationalised in the first week of January 2025, Chinese Foreign Minister Wang Yi made a quick visit to the Maldives to further bolster the bilateral relationship.[139]

Conclusion: A Personality-Centred Approach

The troubled political transition in the Maldives gave Beijing opportunities to scale up engagement. Unlike in Pakistan and Myanmar, where institutions such as the military played an important role in developing a robust bilateral relationship with China, Beijing's economic engagement with Malé was centred more on the political personalities of the former president, Abdulla Yameen, and the later president, Muizzu. The emergence of other political personalities, such as President Solih, slowed, albeit temporarily, economic interactions between the Maldives and China. During President Solih's tenure, the Maldives sought to ensure balanced external engagement and refrained from participating in forums that sought to exclude a few major powers in the Indo-Pacific. For instance, Solih's government did not attend

China's multilateral dialogue with South Asian countries to facilitate greater cooperation in the fields of epidemic prevention and poverty reduction.[140] Similarly, the Maldives government did not send any official representative to the Indian Ocean Region Forum convened by the China International Development Cooperation Agency (CIDCA) in November 2022.[141]

As a part of its diversified external engagement strategy, the Maldives scaled up its engagement with the US, Japan, and other international developmental agencies during Solih's tenure. Towards the end of 2020, the Maldives' diplomatic relations with the US and Japan registered positive developments. In September 2020, the Maldives and the US signed the "Framework for US Department of Defense-Maldives Ministry of Defence and Security Relationship" to promote peace and security in the Indian Ocean Region (IOR).[142] A month later, Secretary of State Mike Pompeo, during his visit to Malé (Maldives), announced that the US would open an embassy and appoint a resident Ambassador and reminded his audience about the Chinese Communist Party's "lawless and threatening behaviour."[143] In November 2020, Japan pledged to strengthen the Maldives National Defence Force's (MNDF) Coast Guard with communications equipment, specialised training, and search and rescue professional dive gear at an estimated expense of USD 7.6 million.[144] The Japanese government trained and provided equipment to strengthen marine pollution response in the Maldives.[145] In January 2021, the US and the Maldives held their first dialogue under the security and defence relationship framework rubric. Both countries reiterated their commitment to a free and open Indo-Pacific region.[146] In June 2021, with the approval of its parliament (People's Majlis), the Maldives government decided to join the Islamic Corporation for the Insurance of Investment and Export Credit (ICIEC).[147] Towards the end of 2021, the Abu Dhabi Fund for Development (ADFD) agreed to provide a US $14 million concessionary loan to develop a new waste-to-energy plant in the Maldives.[148] In 2023, the Maldives also scaled up its engagement with international financial institutions, such as the Asian Development Bank and others.[149] These security, defence, and economic interactions suggest that President Solih's administration proactively worked to diversify external engagement.

Despite persistent efforts to diversify international economic interactions, tourism is the most dominant industry in the archipelagic nation and is vulnerable to external shocks. In 2019, approximately 1.7 million tourists visited the country, of which 300,000 were from China.[150] The Maldives tourism industry is increasingly becoming dependent on visitors from China. There was an opinion that China wielded tourist flows to increase its influence in the Maldives. In December 2002, China and the Maldives signed an Approved Destination Status agreement.[151] There was a steady increase in the number of Chinese tourists visiting the Maldives. The tourist outflow picked up momentum before President Xi Jinping's visit. In 2019, China was the top source market of tourists for the Maldives, with 284,029 arrivals.[152] However, the influx of Chinese tourists into the Maldives drastically reduced during the pandemic, with a mere 34,245 arrivals in 2020.[153] After the pandemic restrictions were lifted in China, the visa waiver agreement between Beijing and Malé was operationalised in January 2023. Subsequently, there was increased interest among Chinese tourists in travelling to the Maldives. The Chinese news reports suggested that the data from travel portals, travel bureaus, and related platforms showed an increase in tourists travelling to the Maldives.[154] It is more than a coincidence that the spike in tourists from China came in a year when the Maldives held presidential elections. Increased tourist flows meant opposition groups could point out the tangible benefits of enhanced engagement with China. As noted, Muizzu, who advocated for closer ties with China, won the presidential elections. On assuming office, Muizzu engineered a dramatic shift in foreign policy and the implementation of the China-Maldives 'Comprehensive Strategic Cooperative Partnership' gained momentum. However, the Muizzu government also understood that there are limits to having adversarial relations with India. As the debt-related financial crisis deepened, the Maldives needed diverse partners, and neighbouring India provided significant assistance. Malé's experience demonstrates that relations between the Maldives and India cannot be easily undermined. While there may be episodes of downturn in the bilateral relationship, the close economic engagement and people-to-people interactions can be leveraged by the leadership in both countries to repair the relationship quickly. Further, with India registering significant economic progress and its willingness to generously reach out to most of its neighbours in their hour of crisis, it would always be prudent for the Maldives to maintain a stable relationship with India.

Amidst the changing fortune of China in the Maldives, Chinese scholars called for sustained engagement of the country. For instance, during President Solih's term, Professor Dai Yonghong called for doubling down on engagement with the Maldives despite temporary setbacks and noted that "as a responsible big country, the most important thing at such times is to maintain strategic determination."[155] There was also a perception that the Maldives would inevitably reach out to Beijing, as "China is a rapidly rising and developing country, and the development of these countries [Maldives] is largely inseparable from China."[156] The strategic determination to stay engaged seems to have paid off for China. Similarly, in Nepal, Beijing increased its influence through persistent engagement.

Notes

1. Nayanima Basu, "China Grabbed More Land Than East India Company, Says Ex-Maldives President Mohamed Nasheed," *The Print*, 13 December, 2019, https://theprint.in/diplomacy/china-grabbed-more-land-than-east-india-company-says-ex-maldives-president-mohamed-nasheed/334905/
2. "Maldives," World Bank, January 10, 2025, https://wits.worldbank.org/CountrySnapshot/en/MDV/textview
3. Gross domestic product 2018, World Development Indicators database, *World Bank*, 2024, https://data.worldbank.org/indicator/NY.GDP.MKTP.CD?locations=MV
4. Britannica, The Editors of Encyclopaedia. "Maldives," *Encyclopedia Britannica*, January 10, 2024, https://www.britannica.com/place/Maldives.
5. "India-Maldives Bilateral Relations," *Ministry of External Affairs, Government of India*, August 18, 2019, https://www.mea.gov.in/Portal/ForeignRelation/India_Maldives_Bilateral_Relations.pdf
6. C Uday Bhaskar, "Tsunami Reveals Indian Military's Humanitarian Response Capability," *IDSA Comment,* January 8, 2005, https://www.idsa.in/idsastrategiccomments/TsunamiRevealsIndianMilitarysHumanitarianResponseCapability_CUBhaskar_080105
7. "Operation Neer: Indian Assistance to the Maldives During Malé Water Crisis," *High Commission of India Malé, Maldives,* December 6, 2014, https://hci.gov.in/male/?3840?00#:~:text=High%20Commission%20of%20India,Male%2C%20Maldives&text=Indian%20aircrafts%20flew%20multiple%20sorties,to%20the%20people%20in%20Male.
8. Winston Woo, "The World's Longest-Ruling Dictators," *CNBC,* March 18, 2016, https://www.cnbc.com/2011/03/18/The-Worlds-Longest-Ruling-Dictators.html
9. "Maldives Country Profile," *BBC,* September 24, 2018, https://www.bbc.com/news/world-south-asia-12651486.
10. "Maldives Profile – Timeline," *BBC*, September 24, 2018, https://www.bbc.com/news/world-south-asia-12653969
11. JustinRowlatt, "The Maldives: Political Turmoil Threatens the 'island Paradise'," *BBC News*, August 10, 2017, https://www.bbc.com/news/world-south-asia-40827633.
12. "Maldivian President Mohamed Waheed lauds China's 'non-interference'," *The Indian Express,* September 2, 2012, https://indianexpress.com/article/news-archive/print/maldivian-president-mohamed-waheed-lauds-chinas-noninterference/

13. "Maldives decides not to press GMR for taxes over airport compensation," *Business Standard*, May 26, 2019, https://www.business-standard.com/article/pti-stories/no-taxes-payable-by-gmr-on-male-airport-contract-compensation-119052600267_1.html
14. Ashwini Phadnis & K. Giriprakash, "Why GMR Had to Bail out of Maldives," *Business Line*, December 30, 2012, https://www.thehindubusinessline.com/companies/why-gmr-had-to-bail-out-of-maldives/article23097540.ece
15. "GMR Male Airport wins $270 mn in international tribunal against Maldives," *The Economic Times*, October 28, 2016, https://economictimes.indiatimes.com/industry/transportation/airlines-/-aviation/gmr-wins-international-arbitration-against-maldives-gets-270-million-payout/articleshow/55097067.cms?from=mdr
16. "驻马尔代夫大使张利忠：中国—马尔代夫：面向未来的合作伙伴," *The Embassy of the People's Republic of China in the Republic of Maldives*, October 14, 2018, http://mv.china-embassy.org/chn/sgsd/t1604033.htm
17. "马尔代夫与中国的关系," Institute of International Trade and Economic Cooperation, *Ministry of Commerce of the People's Republic of China*, http://history.mofcom.gov.cn/?bandr=medfyzgdgx
18. Daniel Bosley, "Maldives Gives Airport Contract to Chinese Firm During Xi's Visit," *Reuters*, September 15, 2014, https://in.reuters.com/article/china-maldives/maldives-gives-airport-contract-to-chinese-firm-during-xis-visit-idINKBN0HA1TS20140915
19. "Chinese investors chase Chinese visitors to the Maldives," *TTG Asia*, June 17, 2015, https://www.ttgasia.com/2015/06/17/chinese-investors-chase-chinese-visitors-to-the-maldives/
20. Saikiran Kannan, "How China has expanded its influence in the Arabian Sea," *India Today*, May 15, 2020, https://www.indiatoday.in/world/story/how-china-has-expanded-its-influence-in-the-arabian-sea-1678167-2020-05-15
21. "India Worries China may be Constructing South China Sea-Like Artificial Island in Maldives," *Defense News India*, May 13, 2020, https://www.defencenews.in/article/India-Worries-China-may-be-Constructing-South-China-Sea-Like-Artificial-Island-in-Maldives-830589
22. "China's territorial revisionism of IOR islands," *News 21*, June 8, 2020, https://thenews21.com/chinas-territorial-revisionism-of-ior-islands
23. "Chinese Firm Kicks Off Resort Development on Feydhoo Finolhu Island," *Maldives Insider*, December 27, 2017, https://maldives.net.mv/23874/chinese-firm-kicks-off-resort-development-on-feydhoo-finolhu-island/
24. "Joint Press Communiqué of the People's Republic of China and the Republic of Maldives," *Ministry of Foreign Affairs of the People's Republic of China*, December 8, 2017, http://www.chinacommercialoffice.org/web/zyxw/t1517887.shtml
25. "从天堂变成危地，马尔代夫最近怎么回事？跟中国又有何关系," *Sohu.com*, February 22, 2018, sohu.com/a/223466298_599186
26. "China and Maldives Sign the Free Trade Agreement," *China FTA Network, Ministry Of Commerce, PRC*, December 12, 2008, http://fta.mofcom.gov.cn/enarticle/chinamedfen/chinamedfennews/201712/36458_1.html

27. Sachin Parashar, "In relief to India, Maldives may scrap ocean deal with China," *Times of India*, June 17, 2020, https://timesofindia.indiatimes.com/india/in-relief-to-india-maldives-may-scrap-ocean-deal-with-china/articleshowprint/69818016.cms
28. Shan Anees, "Three Chinese naval ships arrive in Maldives," *Raajjee Television*, August 27, 2017, https://raajje.mv/16679
29. R.K. Radhakrishnan, "Sinamale Bridge: A Symbol of Transformation in the Maldives," *Frontline Magazine*, September 6, 2023, https://frontline.thehindu.com/world-affairs/sinamale-bridge-a-symbol-of-transformation-in-the-maldives/article67278197.ece
30. "China-Maldives Friendship Bridge refreshes Maldivian life," *Xinhua*, September 4, 2019, https://www.globaltimes.cn/content/1163627.shtml
31. Xu Wei, "Two Chinese Firms Kick Off Social Housing Project in Maldives," *Yicai*, https://www.yicaiglobal.com/news/two-chinese-firms-kick-off-social-housing-project-in-maldives
32. "CSEC Delivers Largest Housing Project Ahead of Schedule," *CSEC International Operation*, April 6, 2020, http://csci.cscec.com/en/xwzx/xw/202005/3105247.html"
33. "Maldives Election: Opposition Defeats China-Backed Abdulla Yameen," *BBC*, September 24, 2018, https://www.bbc.com/news/world-asia-45623126
34. Simon Mundy and Kathrin Hille, "The Maldives Counts the Cost of its Debts to China," *Financial Times*, February 11, 2019, https://www.ft.com/content/c8da1c8a-2a19-11e9-88a4-c32129756dd8
35. "China Debt Dogs Maldives' 'Bridge to Prosperity'," *BBC*, September 17, 2020, https://www.bbc.com/news/world-asia-52743072
36. "Maldives Datasets," IMF, https://www.imf.org/external/datamapper/profile/MDV
37. Mariyam Malsa, "Maldives at high risk of debt distress from China: World Bank," *The Edition*, June 27, 2020, https://edition.mv/news/17487
38. Simon Mundy and Kathrin Hille, "The Maldives Counts the Cost of its Debts to China," *Financial Times*, February 11, 2019, https://www.ft.com/content/c8da1c8a-2a19-11e9-88a4-c32129756dd8; also see Sanjay Kapoor, "India's Dilemma in Maldives," *ORF Special Report # 59*, February, 2018.
39. Sanjeev Miglani, "Maldives says China is building projects at inflated prices," *Reuters*, November 26, 2018, https://www.reuters.com/article/maldives-politics-china-idINKCN1NV1YF
40. Palki Sharma, "Chinese banks asks Maldives to repay $10 million loan," *WION*, August 3, 2020, https://www.wionews.com/world/chinese-banks-asks-maldives-to-repay-10-million-loan-317935
41. Sathiya Moorthy, "China asks Maldives to pay up 'private loan', an eye-opener for all debtor-nations?" *Raisina Debates*, July 30, 2020, https://www.orfonline.org/expert-speak/china-asks-maldives-pay-up-private-loan-eye-opener-all-debtor-nations/
42. Ibid.
43. Dipanjan Roy Chaudhury, "Maldives considers scrapping Free Trade Agreement (FTA) with China," *The Economic Times*, October 12, 2020, https://economictimes.indiatimes.com/news/international/business/maldives-considers-scrapping-free-trade-agreement-fta-with-china/articleshow/78612972.cms

44. Mariyam Malsa, "State to Review FTA with China Before Implementation: Minister Fayyaz," *The Edition*, October 11, 2020, https://edition.mv/news/19684
45. Sanjeev Miglani and Mohamed Junayd. "Exclusive: Maldives Set to Pull out of China Free Trade Deal, Says Senior Lawmaker," *Reuters*, November 19, 2018, https://www.reuters.com/article/us-maldives-politics-china-exclusive-idUSKCN1NO0ZC.
46. "Embarking on a New Journey and Embracing a Bright Future," *Chinese Embassy in Maldives,* January 13, 2022, https://www.fmprc.gov.cn/mfa_eng/wjb_663304/zwjg_665342/zwbd_665378/202201/t20220113_10485102.html
47. "Maldives and China Sign Certificate of Assistance for Ministry of Foreign Affairs," *Ministry of Foreign Affairs, Government of the Maldives,* April 27, 2022, https://www.gov.mv/en/news-and-communications/maldives-and-china-sign-certificate-of-assistance-for-ministry-of-foreign-affairs
48. "Feature: "New connections"—China bridges gap in Maldives' hottest growth spot," *People's Daily Online,* April 12, 2022, http://en.people.cn/n3/2022/0412/c90000-10082831.html
49. "Chinese-built third-phase housing project in Maldives handed over," *National Development and Reform Commission (NDRC),People's Republic of China,* July 27, 2022, https://en.ndrc.gov.cn/netcoo/achievements/202207/t20220727_1332760.html
50. "Maldives and China hold the Second Joint Meeting of the Tripartite Coordinating Mechanism," *Ministry of Foreign Affairs, Government of the Maldives,* September 1, 2022, https://www.gov.mv/en/news-and-communications/maldives-and-china-hold-the-second-joint-meeting-of-the-tripartite-coordinating-mechanism
51. Mohamed Rehan, "China-Maldives celebrates Golden Jubilee of Bilateral Relationship," *The Edition,* October 14, 2022, https://edition.mv/news/26007
52. "People's Majlis," Twitter, https://twitter.com/mvpeoplesmajlis/status/1575099712352681984; also see "Remarks by Chinese Ambassador to the Maldives Wang Lixin at the Business Forum on Joint Construction of the "Belt and Road"between China and Maldives," *Ministry of Foreign Affairs, the People's Republic of China,* December 15, 2022, https://www.fmprc.gov.cn/mfa_eng/wjb_663304/zwjg_665342/zwbd_665378/202212/t20221215_10990952.html
53. Nirupama Subramanian, "Chinese firm inks deal with Maldives," *The Indian Express,* December 3, 2021, https://indianexpress.com/article/cities/mumbai/chinese-firm-inks-deal-with-maldives-7653423/
54. Ibid.
55. "China's Solar Energy Power Cooperation Projects in Maldives," *Embassy of the People's Republic of China in the Republic of Maldives,* September 1, 2022, http://mv.china-embassy.gov.cn/eng/zmgx/hfjl/202209/t20220901_10759123.htm
56. David Rogers, "China Harbour begins work on 150ha artificial island in the Maldives," *Global Construction Review,* March 23, 2023, https://www.globalconstructionreview.com/china-harbour-begins-work-on-150ha-artificial-island-in-the-maldives/
57. "China-Maldives ophthalmology center assistance, cooperation program inaugurated," *People's Daily Online,* February 13, 2023, http://en.people.cn/n3/2023/0213/c90000-10206816.html

58. "Fourth Joint Meeting Mechanism to Deal with the Issue of Safety of Chinese Tourists in Maldives," *Ministry of Foreign Affairs,* March 16, 2023, https://www.gov.mv/en/news-and-communications/fourth-joint-meeting-mechanism-to-deal-with-the-issue-of-safety-of-chinese-tourists-in-maldives
59. "Maldives and China sign agreements on infrastructure, health," *PSM News,* April 2, 2023, https://psmnews.mv/en/119035
60 Shubhajit Roy, "With hug, promises, PM Modi reaches out to Maldives President," *The Indian Express,* November 18, 2018, https://indianexpress.com/article/india/with-hug-promises-pm-modi-reaches-out-to-maldives-president-5451832/
61. Nayanima Basu, "India relieved as President Solih's party wins Maldives polls, but shadow of China remains," *The Print,* April 8, 2019, https://theprint.in/diplomacy/india-relieved-as-president-solihs-party-wins-maldives-polls-but-shadow-of-china-remains/218762/
62. Ibid.
63. "India-Maldives Joint Statement During the State Visit of Prime Minister to Maldives," *Ministry of External Affairs, Government of India,* June 8, 2019, https://mea.gov.in/bilateral-documents.htm?dtl/31418/IndiaMaldives+Joint+Statement+during+the+State+Visit+of+Prime+Minister+to+Maldives#:~:text=Prime%20Minister%20of%20India%20H.E.,term%2C%20on%2030%20May%202019.
64. Dipanjan Roy Chaudhury, "India signs Line of Credit pact with Maldives for financing major connectivity project," *The Economic Times,* October 12, 2020, https://economictimes.indiatimes.com/news/economy/finance/india-signs-line-of-credit-pact-with-maldives-for-financing-major-connectivity-project/articleshow/78617443.cms
65. Jacopo Dettoni, "Maldives finance minister looks to lessen Chinese influence," *The Banker,* July 2, 2019, https://www.thebanker.com/Maldives-finance-minister-looks-to-lessen-Chinese-influence-1562054416
66. "India in Maldives," Twitter, August 4, 2020, https://twitter.com/HCIMaldives/status/1290583760375750657
67. Rezaul H Laskar, "India Unveils Economic Aid package for Maldives, Including $500 mn Connectivity Project and Cargo Service," *The Hindustan Times,* August 13, 2020, https://www.hindustantimes.com/india-news/india-unveils-economic-aid-package-for-maldives-including-500-mn-connectivity-project-and-cargo-service/story-akbiRnuSd4hSzdsRHFZt9H.html
68. "India, Maldives to sign pact on Greater Malé Connectivity Project," *The Indian Express,* August 26, 2021, https://indianexpress.com/article/india/india-maldives-greater-male-connectivity-project-7471603/
69. Fathimath Aruma Hussain, "Nasheed: India's assistance genuine, different from loans that leave nation mired in debt," *Sun Siyam,* August 13, 2020, https://en.sun.mv/62345
70. "India–Maldives High Impact Community Development Projects," *High Commission of India, Male, Maldives,* November 2023, https://hci.gov.in/male/?pdf17749
71. "Different narratives: On India-Maldives ties," *The Hindu,* April 23, 2022, https://www.thehindu.com/opinion/editorial/different-narratives-the-hindu-editorial-on-india-maldives-ties/article65345414.ece

72. "Nasheed attributes prosperity, independence to India-Maldives relations," *Dhivehi*, September 3, 2020, https://avas.mv/en/88305
73. "Maldives very fortunate to have India as a neighbour, closest bilateral partner," *Raajje Television*, August 16, 2021, https://raajje.mv/104916
74. "Shahid: #IndiaOut isn't patriotic, its hatemongering," *Sun Siyam*, October 26, 2020, https://en.sun.mv/63652
75. Ibid.
76. "75 Indian military personnel stationed in Maldives to operate aircraft," *Avas Online*, November 14, 2021, https://avas.mv/en/109920
77. Ibid.
78. President Abdulla Yameen officially calls for the removal of Indian military personnel in the Maldives," *Maldives News Network*, December 4, 2021, https://maldivesnewsnetwork.com/2021/12/04/president-abdulla-yameen-officially-calls-for-the-removal-of-indian-military-personnel-in-the-maldives/
79. Ibrahim Adam, "Fmr Pres Yameen Proud of Wearing India Out T-Shirt," *The Maldives Journal*, December 23, 2021, https://themaldivesjournal.com/32788
80. Meera Srinivasan, "Maldives President Solih bans 'India Out' campaign," *The Hindu*, April 21, 2022, https://www.thehindu.com/news/international/maldives-president-solih-bans-india-out-campaign/article65341970.ece
81. "CNS Visit to Maldives," Indian Navy, April 2022, https://www.indiannavy.nic.in/content/cns-visit-maldives#:~:text=In%20his%20first%20overseas%20visit,18%20to%2020%20April%202022.
82. "The Chief of the Naval Staff of India pays a courtesy call on the President," *The President's Office, Republic of Maldives*, April 19, 2022, https://presidency.gov.mv/Press/Article/26524
83. "Protesters Attack Yoga Day Event in Maldives," *Reuters*, June 21, 2022, https://www.reuters.com/world/asia-pacific/protesters-attack-yoga-day-event-maldives-2022-06-21/
84. N Manoharan, "India's Challenges in Maldives," *Deccan Herald*, August 5, 2022, https://www.deccanherald.com/opinion/india-s-challenges-in-maldives-1133187.html
85. "Maldives former president Yameen gets 11-year jail term," *Reuters*, December 25, 2022, https://www.reuters.com/world/asia-pacific/maldives-court-finds-former-president-yameen-guilty-corruption-2022-12-25/
86. "China Outmaneuvered in the Maldives as Construction of India-Funded Airport Begins on Strategic Island," *Swarajya Staff*, January 20, 2023, https://swarajyamag.com/news-brief/china-outmaneuvered-in-the-maldives-as-construction-of-india-funded-airport-begins-on-strategic-island
87. Ibid.
88. Ujjwal Shrotryia, "Maldives: India Takes Another Step To Boot Out Chinese Influence From Neighbourhood With New Defence Agreement," *Swarajya*, March 20, 2023, https://swarajyamag.com/defence/maldives-india-takes-another-step-to-boot-out-chinese-influence-from-neighbourhood-with-new-defence-agreement
89. Sanjib Kr Baruah, "Eye on China, India gifts two homemade military ships to Maldives," *The Week*, May 3, 2023, https://www.theweek.in/news/world/

2023/05/03/eye-on-china-india-gifts-two-homemade-military-ships-to-maldives.html

90. Ujjwal Shrotryia , "A Message To China In IOR Via The Himalayas: Maldives Joins India For A Military Exercise Near LAC In Uttarakhand ," *Swarajya,* June 13, 2023, https://swarajyamag.com/defence/india-kicks-off-two-week-long-joint-military-exercise-ekuverin-with-madives-in-uttarakhands-chaubatia
91. Naizak Mohamed, "Govt. denies opposition accusations on 'India Out' banner," *Sun Siyam*, June 4, 2023, https://en.sun.mv/82898
92. Naizak Mohamed, "Muizzu officially endorsed by Yameen, whole PPM-PNC leadership," *Sun Siyam*, August 8, 2023, https://en.sun.mv/84020
93. John Kachtik, "The Maldives Risks Following in Sri Lanka's Footsteps," *Nikkei Asia,* July 26, 2022, https://asia.nikkei.com/Opinion/The-Maldives-risks-following-in-Sri-Lanka-s-footsteps
94. "The President calls on employers to ensure worker equality and human rights," *The President's Office, Republic of Maldives*, May 1, 2023, https://presidency.gov.mv/Press/Article/28235
95. Mohamed Junayd and Zaheena Rasheed, "Maldives ruling party holds high-stakes presidential primary," *Al Jazeera*, January 28, 2023, https://www.aljazeera.com/news/2023/1/28/maldives-ruling-party-holds-high-stakes-presidential-primary
96. Naizak Mohamed, "Nasheed: Calling 'India Out' is the only issue with Yameen," *Sun Siyam*, January 17, 2023, https://en.sun.mv/80381
97. Mahesh, "Maldives Election 2023 Result – Who will become the President?" *RajNeet PG*, September 29, 2023, https://rajneetpg2022.com/maldives-election-result/
98. "President: 99% of MDP opposed to allowing Nasheed to re-join," *Sun Siyam*, October 2, 2023, https://en.sun.mv/85046
99. Mohamed Junayd, "Maldives opposition candidate Muizzu wins presidential votc", *Reuters*, October 1, 2023, https://www.reuters.com/world/asia-pacific/maldives-opposition-candidate-muizzu-wins-presidential-vote-2023-10-01/
100. Mohamed Afrah, "Who is Mohamed Muizzu, Maldives's pro-China president-elect?" *Al Jazeera*, October 1, 2023, https://www.aljazeera.com/news/2023/10/1/who-is-mohamed-muizzu-maldivess-pro-china-president-elect
101. "Yameen transferred home at Muizzu's request, to protect 'national interest'," *Sun Siyam*, October 1, 2023, https://en.sun.mv/85036
102. "Every Maldivian citizen is equal in my eyes: Dr. Muizzu," *The Edition*, October 2, 2023, https://edition.mv/news/29421
103. Malika Shahid, "Parliament sitting ends due to lack of quorum," *The Edition*, October 2, 2023, https://edition.mv/news/29437
104. "Nasheed: MDP agreed to back system vote if Democrats don't join PPM," *Sun Siyam*, October 3, 2023, https://en.sun.mv/85072
105. Mohamed Rehan, "President Solih endorses presidential system," October 2, 2023, *The Edition*, https://edition.mv/news/29442#:~:text=President%20Ibrahim%20Mohamed%20Solih%20has,Maldivian%20Democratic%20Party%20(MDP).

106. "Maldives frontrunner eyes closer ties with China," *The Hindu*, September 14, 2023, https://www.thehindu.com/news/international/maldives-frontrunner-eyes-closer-ties-with-china/article67307482.ece
107. "Muizzu's response to his label: I'm pro-Maldives," *Sun Siyam*, October 3, 2023, https://en.sun.mv/85075
108. C Krishnasai, "Maldives President-elect Muizzu vows to remove Indian military presence," *WION*, October 3, 2023, https://www.wionews.com/india-news/maldives-president-elect-muizzu-vows-to-remove-indian-military-presence-on-first-day-in-office-642083
109. "PM congratulates Dr Mohamed Muizzu on being elected as the President of Maldives," *PM India*, October 1, 2023, https://www.pmindia.gov.in/en/news_updates/pm-congratulates-dr-mohamed-muizzu-on-being-elected-as-the-president-of-maldives/?comment=disable#:~:text=The%20Prime%20Minister%2C%20Shri%20Narendra,as%20President%20of%20the%20Maldives
110. "Pres Solih's heartfelt requests to Dr. Muizzu: Good governance and project continuation," *Avas*, October 2, 2023, https://avas.mv/en/136131
111. "Key Agreements Exchanged between the Maldives and China," *The President's Office, Republic of the Maldives*, January 10, 2024, https://presidency.gov.mv/Press/Article/29600
112. "Maldives, China Sign 20 Agreements Amid Diplomatic Row with India," *Business Standard*, January 10, 2024, https://www.business-standard.com/world-news/maldives-china-sign-20-agreements-amid-diplomatic-row-with-india-124011000830_1.html
113. "Xi Jinping Holds Talks with President of the Maldives Mohamed Muizzu," *Embassy of the People's Republic of China*, January 10, 2024, http://in.china-embassy.gov.cn/eng/zgxw/202401/t20240127_11234563.htm#:~:text=On%20the%20afternoon%20of%20January,a%20comprehensive%20strategic%20cooperative%20partnership.
114. "PM Modi, President Muizzu Agree to set up Core Group to Further Deepen India-Maldives Ties," *The Hindu*, December 2, 2023, https://www.thehindu.com/news/national/india-maldives-to-set-up-core-group-to-further-deepen-ties-as-pm-modi-meets-new-maldivian-president-muizzu/article67598378.ece
115. "Maldives to not Renew 2019 Water Survey Pact with India: What are Hydrographic Surveys?" *The Indian Express*, December 16, 2023, https://indianexpress.com/article/explained/everyday-explainers/maldives-survey-pact-india-hydrographic-explained-9069657/
116. Sidhant Sibal, "Maldives Skips Key Colombo Security Dialogue in Mauritius," *WION*, December 8, 2023, https://www.wionews.com/south-asia/maldives-skips-key-colombo-security-dialogue-in-mauritius-667338
117. "Permanent smell in the rooms," Maldives politician's remarks on Modi's Lakshadweep visit sparks #BoycottMaldives trend," *The Economic Times*, January 7, 2024, https://economictimes.indiatimes.com/news/india/permanent-smell-in-the-rooms-maldives-politicians-remarks-on-modis-lakshadweep-visit-sparks-boycottmaldives-trend/articleshow/106610952.cms?utm_source=contentofinterest&utm_medium=text&utm_campaign=cppst

118. Sayantani Biswas, "Maldives Govt Clarifies after Minister Shiuna's 'Derogatory' Remarks on PM Modi: 'Will not hesitate to take Action'," *Livemint,* January 10, 2024, https://www.livemint.com/news/world/maldives-government-distances-from-minister-shiunas-derogatory-remarks-on-pm-modis-lakshadweep-visit-11704620526097.html
119. "Amid Diplomatic row, Maldives Sees Massive Drop in Indian Tourists in First 3 Weeks of January," *Business Today,* January 30, 2024, https://www.businesstoday.in/india/story/amid-diplomatic-row-maldives-sees-massive-drop-in-indian-tourists-in-first-3-weeks-of-january-415450-2024-01-30#
120. "Joint Press Statement by the Maldivian Democratic Party and The Democrats," *The Democrats,* January 24, 2024, https://thedemocrats.mv/en/updates/65b0fe356ddac2f354a90a82
121. Yeshi Seli, "Chinese Ship Poses 'Alarming' Threat, Must Leave at Once: Ex-Maldives Envoy," *The New Indian Express,* January 31, 2024, https://www.newindianexpress.com/world/2024/Jan/31/chinese-ship-poses-alarming-threat-must-leave-at-once-ex-maldives-envoy
122. "Statement by the Government of Maldives," *Ministry of Foreign Affairs,* January 23, 2024, https://foreign.gov.mv/index.php/en/media-center/news/statement-by-the-government-of-maldives-2024-pr-14
123. Pradip R Sagar, "Why another Chinese 'research' ship in India's backyard, courtesy Maldives, is cause for alarm," *India Today,* January 24, 2024, https://www.indiatoday.in/india-today-insight/story/why-another-chinese-research-ship-in-indias-backyard-courtesy-maldives-is-cause-for-alarm-2493142-2024-01-24
124. International Monetary Fund. "IMF Executive Board Concludes 2024 Article IV Consultation with the Maldives," *IMF,* May 10, 2024. https://www.imf.org/en/News/Articles/2024/05/10/pr-24152-maldives-imf-executive-board-concludes-2024-art-iv-consultation
125. "Amid Tense Ties, India Gives Maldives an Extension on $200 Million Loan," *Business Today,* May 12, 2024. https://www.businesstoday.in/india/story/amid-tense-ties-india-gives-maldives-an-extension-on-200-million-loan-429272-2024-05-12
126. Fitch Ratings. "Fitch Downgrades Maldives' Long-Term IDR to CCC." *Fitch Ratings,* June 26, 2024. https://www.fitchratings.com/research/sovereigns/fitch-downgrades-maldives-long-term-idr-to-ccc-26-06-2024#:~:text=Fitch%20Ratings%20%2D%20Hong%20Kong%20%2D%2026,of%20'CCC%2B'%20or%20below
127. Press Trust of India. "Maldives Resume Medical Evacuations with India-Gifted Dornier Helicopters; Prez Muizzu Thanks Delhi," *PTI News,* December 2024. https://www.ptinews.com/story/national/maldives-resume-medical-evacuations-with-india-gifted-dornier-helicopters-prez-muizzu-thanks-delhi/1689108
128. "Xizang Autonomous Region Donates Mineral Water," Ministry of Foreign Affairs of the Republic of Maldives, May 23, 2024, https://foreign.gov.mv/index.php/en/media-center/news/xizang-autnomous-region-donates-mineral-water-2024-pr-113.
129. "India, China Have Agreed to Cooperate in Paying in Local Currency for Imports: Maldives," *The Economic Times,* May 30, 2024, https://economictimes.indiatimes.

com/news/economy/foreign-trade/india-china-have-agreed-to-cooperate-in-paying-in-local-currency-for-imports-maldives/articleshow/110329147.cms?from=mdr.

130. "Maldives President Muizzu Thanks India, China for Support to Strengthen His Country's Fragile Economy," *The Hindu*, July 28, 2024, https://www.thehindu.com/news/international/maldives-president-muizzu-thanks-india-china-for-support-to-strengthen-his-countrys-fragile-economy/article68458079.ece
131. Ministry of External Affairs, Government of India. "Visit of External Affairs Minister to Maldives (August 9–11, 2024)," *Ministry of External Affairs, Government of India,* August 11, 2024, https://www.mea.gov.in/press-releases.htm?dtl/38149/Visit_of_External_Affairs_Minister_to_Maldives_August_0911_2024#:~:text=Maldives%20remains%20an%20important%20partner,people%2Dto%2Dpeople%20ties.
132. Ibid.
133. "China, Maldives Sign Financial Cooperation Agreement," *Reuters*, September 13, 2024, https://www.reuters.com/world/asia-pacific/china-maldives-sign-financial-cooperation-agreement-2024-09-13/
134. "As Maldives Faces Debt Default, China Inks New Finance Pact: Details Here," *NDTV*, September 13, 2024, https://www.ndtv.com/world-news/as-maldives-faces-debt-default-china-inks-new-finance-pact-details-here-6559338
135. "India and Maldives: A Vision for Comprehensive Economic and Maritime Security Partnership," *Ministry of External Affairs, Government of India,* October 7, 2024, https://www.mea.gov.in/bilateral-documents.htm?dtl/38384/India_and_Maldives_A_Vision_for_Comprehensive_Economic_and_Maritime_Security_Partnership#:~:text=The%20two%20countries%20agreed%20that,Defence%20Force%20(MNDF)%20'Ekatha
136. Neyaz Farooquee, "Indian financial aid opens 'new chapter' with Maldives," *BBC News*, October 7, 2024, https://www.bbc.com/news/articles/cly4eq78k5qo
137. "Maldives and China to Enhance Bilateral Economic Cooperation," *China Daily*, December 31, 2024, https://www.chinadaily.com.cn/a/202412/31/WS6773644ea310f1265a1d84ab.html
138. "China has signed 23 FTAs with partners on five continents: MOFCOM," *Global Times*, January 9, 2025. https://www.globaltimes.cn/page/202501/1326585.shtml
139. "Chinese FM Wang Yi Visits Maldives, Meets President Muizzu," *Indian Express*, January 11, 2025, https://indianexpress.com/article/news-today/chinese-fm-wang-yi-visit-maldives-president-muizzu-9773625/
140. Ananth Krishnan, "China holds third South Asia multilateral meet in new push," *The Hindu*, January 8, 2021, https://www.thehindu.com/news/international/china-holds-third-south-asia-multilateral-meet-in-new-push/article33531473.ece
141. Ananth Krishnan, "Australia, Maldives officials did not attend China's Indian Ocean meet," *The Hindu*, November 27, 2022, https://www.thehindu.com/news/international/australia-maldives-officials-did-not-attend-chinas-indian-ocean-meet/article66192987.ece

142. "The Maldives and U.S. Sign Defense Agreement," *U.S. Department of Defense*, September 11, 2020, https://www.defense.gov/Newsroom/Releases/Release/Article/2344512/the-maldives-and-us-sign-defense-agreement/
143. "Secretary Michael R. Pompeo and Maldives Foreign Minister Abdulla Shahid at a Press Availability," *United States Department of State*, October 28, 2020, https://www.state.gov/secretary-michael-r-pompeo-and-maldives-foreign-minister-abdulla-shahid-at-a-press-availability/.
144. Fathmath Shaahunaz, "Japan to grant USD 7.6 million to Maldives' Coast Guard," *The Edition*, November 22, 2020, https://edition.mv/news/20514
145. "The Government of Japan provides equipment worth USD 2.8 million to strengthen marine pollution response in the Maldives," *Embassy of Japan in Maldives*, August 17, 2020, https://www.mv.emb-japan.go.jp/itpr_ja/11_000001_00088.html
146. "US, Maldives hold inaugural defence dialogue; reaffirm commitment to free and open Indo-Pacific," *Deccan Herald*, January 6, 2021, https://www.deccanherald.com/world/us-maldives-hold-inaugural-defence-dialogue-reaffirm-commitment-to-free-and-open-indo-pacific-935978.html
147. Aishath Shaany, "Majlis approves for Maldives to join ICIEC," *raajje.mv*, June 21, 2021, https://raajje.mv/102131
148. "ADFD Supports Development of Waste-to-Energy Plant in Maldives," Abu Dhabi Fund for Development (ADFD), December 13, 2021, https://www.adfd.ae/english/NewsandEvents/News/NewsandEvents/Pages/NewsDetailsHome.aspx?Name=539
149. "ADB, BML Sign $41 Million Financing Package to Support SMEs and Blue Economy Tourism in Maldives," *Asian Development Bank*, March 28,2023, https://www.adb.org/news/adb-bml-sign-41-million-financing-package-support-smes-and-blue-economy-tourism-maldives
150. Bertil Lintner, "Quarantined Maldives Needs China to Survive," *Asia Times*, March 31, 2020, https://asiatimes.com/2020/03/quarantined-maldives-needs-china-to-survive/
151. "Tourism Highlights 2002," Ministry of Tourism Maldives, https://archive.tourism.gov.mv/pubs/statistics2002/section_1_5.htm
152. "China Ranks 2nd in Top Source Markets for Tourist Arrivals," *Sun Siyam*, October 16, 2023, https://en.sun.mv/85340
153. "Maldives welcomes Chinese tourists with vibrant ceremony," *Global Times*, January 19, 2023, https://www.globaltimes.cn/page/202301/1284106.shtml
154. Li Xuanmin, "Searches for Maldives trips double on Chinese travel platforms after visa-waiver agreement takes effect," *The Global Times*, February 17, 2023, https://www.globaltimes.cn/page/202302/1285666.shtml
155. 刘栋，"释新闻｜亲印度领导人上台后，马尔代夫会疏远中国吗？," *The Paper*, November 23, 2018, https://www.thepaper.cn/newsDetail_forward_2662636
156. 邱林，"马尔代夫"变天"，新政府是否疏远中国," *Zhihu.com*, October 16, 2018, https://zhuanlan.zhihu.com/p/46855425

7

The Himalayan Ambitions

Introduction

Mao reportedly stated that Tibet is the palm of the hand, with Nepal, Bhutan, and the Indian provinces of Ladakh, Sikkim, and Arunachal Pradesh being its five fingers.[1] Implicit in such a metaphor is the message that controlling Tibet mandates control over the five fingers. It is not certain if Mao actually deployed such a metaphor.[2] In the 1950s and subsequent decades, Tibet was one of the dominant concerns that informed China's policy towards the Himalayan region, including Nepal. China's Nepal policy is a consequence of the latter's geostrategic location and its long cultural and economic relations with Tibet. Buddhabhadra, a Buddhist monk travelled to China in the fifth century and is believed to have translated important scriptures that significantly impacted the evolution of Buddhism there.[3] Nepal and Tibet's religious and cultural interactions grew in the 6th century.[4] Princess Bhrikuti Devi of Nepal married the Tibetan king, Songtsan Gampo, in the seventh century. The marriage and subsequent interactions increased the influence of Nepalese Buddhist texts, art, and architecture on Tibetan society.[5] Given that the Buddha was born in Lumbini, now in modern-day Nepal, and the spread of Buddhism in the Indian subcontinent, Buddhist philosophy also permeated into Tibet through Nepal. Importantly, Buddhist guru Padmasambhava visited Kathmandu valley and travelled extensively in northern Nepal before proceeding to Tibet.[6]

Tibet imported many agricultural commodities from its southern neighbours, and there were instances when currency coins from Nepal were circulated in Tibet.[7] The British forays into the region also impacted Nepal's trade relations with Tibet. The British interest in Tibet resulted from growing concern that Russia may expand its regional influence. Consequent to Colonel Francis Younghusband's military intervention, the British-Tibetan Treaty of 1904 severely restricted Tibet's interactions with foreign powers.[8] The 1904 treaty created conditions for enhanced economic interactions between British India and Tibet through increased trade points and the abolition of trade duties.[9] However, as Alex Mckay argued, the British interventions created a power vacuum in Lhasa that enabled China, over time, to consolidate its control over Tibet.[10] The consolidation of Chinese control negatively impacted the Tibet-Nepal economic interactions.

Border, Delineation, and Differences

After the British withdrew from the Indian subcontinent and decolonisation started gaining momentum worldwide, many new developing countries scaled up their external interaction. Nepal also saw an opportunity in the changing global landscape, and its diplomatic interactions increased in intensity. In Bandung in 1955, the First Asian-African Conference became the platform for Chinese leadership to prod many nations to establish diplomatic relations.[11] Nepal established diplomatic relations with China during the same year. A year later, both countries signed an economic aid agreement, which resulted in a grant of USD 12,600,000 to Nepal.[12] Nepal was onc of the early non-communist countries to receive grant assistance from China. Nonetheless, there was an undercurrent of concern in Nepal regarding the Chinese consolidation in Tibet. An Indian military mission, which arrived in Nepal in 1952, maintained its considerable presence till 1958 and assisted Nepal in reorganising and modernising its army.[13] Scaling up diplomatic recognition and implementation of bilateral aid agreements did little to address the concerns in Nepal regarding the border delineation between the two countries.

A few incidents on the China-Nepal border in 1960 increased Kathmandu's anxiety regarding Chinese intentions. In June 1960, Chinese forces captured 10 Nepali villagers near the Mustang area, and they were subjected to harsh treatment.[14] With an intent to contain the negative fallout of the incident, the Chinese leadership responded quickly. In a letter to the Prime Minister of Nepal, Zhou Enlai stated that "looking at the facts, this incident was an unfortunate incident that occurred entirely due to misunderstanding" and, with an apology, returned the prisoners and paid financial compensation to Nepal.[15]

However, as Tibet's situation remained volatile for a considerable period, the security situation on the China-Nepal border was a concern for both Beijing and Kathmandu. In a volatile political context, the porous borders and easy movement of people increased anxieties. The Tibetan Khampa fighters, Claude Arpi notes, "from their bases in Mustang attacked the Chinese convoys in Tibet in the 1960s ... [and] ... the Tibetan freedom-fighters were financed by the Central Intelligence Agency."[16] Reportedly, the Chinese toyed with the idea of claiming the Mustang region to address the security challenges. A United States assessment brief noted that since "Mustang itself was once a semi-independent feudal holding with only rather loose ties to Nepal ... the Chinese are believed to think that they have some claim to the area, perhaps not unlike their similar claims upon India in Kashmir and Northeast frontier areas."[17]

The political shifts in Tibet also incurred economic costs for Nepal. In addition to enhanced defence expenditure, Prime Minister B.P. Koirala, in 1959, noted that Nepal's relationship with Tibet got altered as "historically, [Nepal] had in a sense a suzerainty over Tibet... Tibet used to pay Nepal annual tributes in cash and kind."[18] With the Chinese controlling Tibet, the flow of tributes was discontinued, and Nepal's economic engagement with territories to its north was disrupted, as traders from neighbouring regions could not continue with their usual economic activities. The establishment of formal diplomatic relations in 1955 placed new restrictions that made it difficult for persons from Nepal to do business in Tibet. While earlier, traders from Nepal could operate all across Tibet, post-1955, the individual traders were permitted to conduct their activity only in Lhasa, Shigatse, Gyangtse, and Yatung.[19] There was increased friction between Chinese authorities and Nepalese in Tibet on taxes to be paid. The Nepalese living in Lhasa lost the privilege of not being subjected to taxation.[20] Further, in 1960, the traders from Tibet "were not able to return to their homes in Lhasa and other Tibetan towns after journeying to Nepal with the stocks of wool, salt, musk, herbs, gold and silver."[21] The consolidation of the Chinese presence in Tibet resulted in new barriers to interactions with Nepal.

As Nepal adjusted to the new geopolitical realities, the India-China border dispute further complicated matters for Kathmandu. Some Nepal leaders attempted to facilitate dialogue between India and China. In his conversations with Chairman Mao Zedong, Prime Minister Koirala referred to his efforts to host a meeting between the leaders of China and India in Kathmandu, which did not materialise.[22] Prime Minister Koirala's attempts to facilitate a rapprochement between India and China predate Sri Lankan leader Bandaranaike's similar efforts. In a way, the India-China conflict increased the utility of India's neighbours for Beijing. The attempts by countries such as Nepal to facilitate conversations between the leading Asian powers were not frowned upon by the Chinese leaders. On the other hand, China and Nepal had disagreements on the border demarcation. On the border dispute regarding Mt. Everest, Nepal Prime Minister Koirala was also quite frank in his interactions with the Chinese leadership and told Mao: "we call it a Sagarmatha, the west calls it Everest, and you call it Qomolangma ... this place has always been within our boundary, but Premier Zhou En Lai said it was within yours."[23] Referring to the territorial dispute of Mount Everest, the premier of Nepal not only contested Chinese claims but also stressed that ownership of the highest mountain in the world is a matter of great national sentiment.[24] Prime Minister Koirala pointedly asked Chairman Mao his views regarding ownership of the mountaintop, and Mao responded that even the mountaintop could be demarcated "half for each side".[25] Mao suggested that Mt. Everest could be renamed the "China-Nepal Friendship Peak".[26] However, the suggestion did not find traction with the leadership in Nepal.

In 1960, during the visit of the Chinese premier, Zhou En Lai, to Nepal, both countries signed the Treaty of Peace and Friendship, reiterated their "commitment to five principles of peaceful coexistence, and exchanged a ratification agreement on the question of the boundary between the two countries."[27] During his visit to Kathmandu, Zhou En Lai pointed to the need for enhanced economic cooperation between the two countries and added that the small amount of aid from China "will be helpful to the cause of Nepal's construction."[28] The progress on the boundary created conditions for operationalising plans to develop a road network between Nepal and Tibet. In 1962, China agreed to provide USD 10 million to construct the road between Kathmandu and Kodari, which would be extended to Lhasa.[29] In the subsequent years, approximately "12,000 Nepalese farmhands directed by 50 Chinese engineers [worked in] the hills of eastern Nepal to build a road to China."[30] Despite the improved bilateral relationships, the trade relations between the two countries were not substantive. While it is difficult to estimate the exact trade volume between Nepal and Tibet, Y. P. Pant concluded that in

1962, "Nepal's trade with Tibet … does not constitute more than one per cent of the country's total trade."[31]

As Nepal-China relations started to stabilise, there were concerns in the US that the Chinese would have greater influence in Nepal. A US government report of the 1960s expressed apprehensions about the growing Chinese influence in Nepalese society. The report noted that Beijing has successfully penetrated student organisations, cultivated individuals, grassroots leaders, and media personnel, and added that the Chinese have beaten out "India by infiltrating important segments of Nepal society."[32] Referring to the Araniko Highway, the report went on to note that "with the new road to Tibet open, the Chinese are using it as a pretext for destroying India's favoured treatment in Nepal."[33] The connectivity projects between China and Nepal continued to elicit similar concerns in the subsequent decades.

Trade and the Search for Viable Routes

In addition to attempts at improving road networks between the two countries, China and Nepal signed the Trade and Payments Agreement in 1974, which was updated in 1981. The 1981 Agreement had the following important elements: 'both countries granted each other the most favoured nation status; China's export items to Nepal and Nepal's export items to China were listed; three trade points for cross-border trade were clearly specified [Kodari/Nyalam; Rasuwa/Kyerong; Yari (Humla)/Purang]; and 30 Kilometers zone for traditional trade on barter basis was accepted.'[34] The export basket from China to Nepal was limited, with items such as textiles, garments, and foodstuff. Similarly, Nepal's exports to China comprised agricultural items, such as jute, sugar, tea, and other commodities. An interesting aspect of the 1981 Agreement is that export/import items for China and the Tibet Autonomous Region in China were listed separately. Overall, the total tradeable items were limited, which may have to do with the nature of the Chinese economy in the late 1970s and 1980s. Deng Xiaoping's reform process was still in its nascent stages. Yet, the fact that both countries reworked the trade agreement in 1981 points to the Chinese recognition that they needed to scale up their economic game in the neighbourhood. Recognising the need for an institutional framework to promote economic relations, in 1982, both countries agreed to establish an Inter-Governmental Economic and Trade Committee (IGETC).[35] Specifically, "the IGETC meetings focused on economic and technical assistance, bilateral trade and tourism."[36] The two countries signed a bilateral Road Transportation Agreement in 1994 to give a fillip to trade.

In 2002, both countries worked out a detailed protocol to regulate and facilitate the movement of people (such as diplomatic personnel, civil servants, border inhabitants, porters, muleteers, drivers of motor vehicles, and artisans) for trade, pilgrimage, and related matters between Nepal and the Tibet Autonomous Region (TAR) of China.[37] The protocol's emphasis on trade indicated growing confidence in the possibilities of enhanced continental trade between the two countries. Simultaneously, there were concerns in the border regions in Nepal that cross-border trade was increasingly becoming a one-way street. Referring to border trade at the Mustang, *Nepali Times*, in 2003, quoted a member of a local royal family as stating: "In the old times, trade took place by barter ... Nepal traded food for salt and other materials.... Now, we are only consumers.... We do not sell anything back to the Chinese."[38] In the subsequent years, the number of border trade points registered an increase, and there was a steady increase in the flow of Chinese goods.

To spur the trade between the two countries, the Chinese government, in 2010, implemented zero tariffs on 60 per cent of imported products from approximately 32 Least Developed Countries (LDCs), including Nepal.[39] In subsequent years, China increased the tariff lines that would attract zero tariffs to 98 per cent of goods from Nepal.[40] In 2016, both countries agreed on a Transit and Transport Agreement, and three years later, a protocol to operationalise the transit understanding was initiated. As per the protocol, Nepal can access "Chinese ports of Tianjin, Shenzhen, Lianyungang and Zhanjiang [and] three land ports in Lanzhou, Lhasa and Shigatse for third-country import."[41] Nepal can use six customs points – Rasuwa, Kodari, Kimathanka, Nechung, Yari, and Olangchungola—on the Nepal-China border for trade and transit.[42] Accessing these Chinese ports means that Nepalese exports will have to travel thousands of kilometres, which would increase the cost of commodities. Further, Nihar R. Nayak points out that "Nepal's northern trading routes are not viable for carrying bulk goods like raw minerals and oil due to the mountainous terrain."[43] Nepal did not import a single consignment from a third country under the Trade and Transit Agreement for about seven years. It was only in September 2023 that the first consignment of turmeric from Vietnam was imported into Nepal via Tianjin port in China.[44]

The China-Nepal trade encountered challenges such as the pandemic. China closed the border trade points between the two countries during the pandemic. As a consequence, traders, especially from Nepal, incurred losses as they could not export their commodities and goods to China. The overall trade between the two countries also declined considerably. China's exports declined from USD 2.38 billion in 2021 to USD 1.84 billion in 2022, and exports from Nepal to China also declined from USD 8.37 million to USD 5.39 million during the same period.[45] As the pandemic waned, in 2022, a limited number of border trade points were opened, and a year later, both sides agreed to resume two-way trade at the Rasuwagadhi/Kerung border point.[46] There were growing concerns in Nepal about the increasing deficit in trade with China, as the Chinese provision of zero tariffs on 98 per cent of goods did not increase exports to China. In March 2023, Nepal's Prime Minister, Pushpa Kamal Dahal, stated that his government had requested China to include more items in "the list of DFQF facilities on a preferential basis" and also address the "gaps in commitment and actual investment of FDI" from China.[47] In addition to difficulties in accessing the Chinese market, Nepal is dealing with problems in accountability and transparency in its engagement with China.

Accountability and Transparency

As in other countries in the Indian subcontinent, the growing Chinese engagement is defined by the diversity of projects and a multi-sector presence. There is a growing presence of Chinese firms in Nepal's information and communication technology domain. In 2018, the Nepal-China cross-border optical fibre link was operationalised, which ended the dominant presence of Indian telecommunications firms in the country.[48] A year later, the Chinese firms were contracted to expand the 4G network in the country.[49] The Chinese fintech platforms had an interesting journey in Nepal. In 2019, the Nepal Rastra Bank banned the Chinese digital payment apps—WeChat Pay and AliPay—for illegal operations in the country. The Nepal Rastra Bank spokesperson contended that using these digital payments resulted in loss of income and added that "any digital transaction made with unregistered foreign payment system like WeChat Pay and AliPay is illegal...anyone using such platforms can be punished."[50] A few years later, in June 2023, the Nepal Rastra Bank permitted the NMB Bank and WeChat Pay, a subsidiary of Tencent, to provide digital financial services in Nepal.[51] Initially, the services were extended to Chinese nationals visiting Nepal.[52] In the realm of social media, in 2023, the Nepal government banned TikTok as the platform allegedly "was disrupting social harmony, goodwill and … [encouraging] … flow of indecent materials."[53] There was an opinion among some in China that the Nepal government needs to provide a more detailed explanation of its position. For instance, a Chinese columnist pointed out that since "all social media applications contain harmful or indecent content that threatens social harmony, the logic of not implementing a ban on other social media platforms [such as] X (the original Twitter), Facebook, and YouTube" need to be communicated clearly.[54] While imposing the ban, the Nepal government called on the social media platforms "to register and open a liaison office in Nepal, pay taxes and abide by the country's laws and regulations."[55] These efforts were reportedly aimed at making the social media platforms more accountable.

There were also concerns about accountability and transparency in healthcare cooperation. In 2021, Nepal reportedly signed a Non-Disclosure Agreement (NDA) to procure four million doses of Vero Cell vaccines from China.[56] This procurement process raised concerns about whether the government can sign NDAs for procurement in non-defence-related areas.[57] Further, the news reports regarding the vaccine's price generated considerable debate. While a non-disclosure agreement mandates not releasing information pertaining to the price, there was considerable speculation in Nepal about whether there is a need for greater discussion on the quantity and mode of payment.[58]

Some of the projects were subjected to regulatory scrutiny. In 2021, the Nepal Army shortlisted a Chinese company to construct bridges and tunnels on the Kathmandu-Terai Expressway. The Public Accounts Committee of Parliament expressed reservations and called for scrapping of the bidding process, and yet, the Nepal Army reportedly awarded the contracts to Chinese firms.[59] A year later, in 2022, a component of the Kathmandu-Terai Fast Track Road project was awarded to a Chinese company, which was earlier rejected on technical grounds.[60] Subsequently, the Nepal Supreme Court issued a stay on awarding the contract to the Chinese company.[61] On the other hand, some projects, such as the Damak Clean Industrial Park, are yet to make significant progress. The industrial park, which was to be built in collaboration with Chinese firms, encountered protests from locals complaining that they did not receive adequate compensation for being displaced from their land.[62] Despite many such concerns, massive infrastructure and connectivity projects between China and Nepal were conceptualised and implemented.

Railways, Feasibility, and Demographic Changes

The idea of the China-Nepal Railway cutting through the Himalayas is often attributed to Mao Zedong. During the visit of Nepal's King Birendra to Beijing in December 1973, Mao Zedong reportedly said, "China will build the Qinghai-Tibet Railway to Lhasa and eventually to Kathmandu."[63] The renewed thinking on the railway connectivity between the two countries partly stemmed from the 2015 earthquake experience. The Arniko Highway and the Kodari town on the highway were severely damaged due to the earthquake and landslides.[64] Consequently, the need to establish more routes to connect Nepal and China to ensure uninterrupted trade and business activities acquired greater urgency.

The railway infrastructure in Tibet has witnessed remarkable improvement over the past one and a half decades. By the mid-2000s, Chinese authorities constructed a 1,956-kilometre railway line from Xining in Qinghai Province to Lhasa in Tibet.[65] The project was operationalised a few years ahead of the scheduled completion date. The completion of the project facilitated greater movement of people, which raised concerns about the impact of the railway project on the socio-cultural landscape of Tibet. Further, in 2014, the existing Xining-Lhasa railway line was extended to Shigatse, which is relatively closer to Nepal.[66] *The Guardian* quoted the Dalai Lama as stating that "some kind of cultural genocide is taking place.... in general, a railway link is very useful in order to develop, but not when politically motivated to bring about demographic change."[67] Despite such severe criticism of the existing railway line in Tibet, the Chinese leadership decided to implement the Sichuan-Tibet Railway project to connect Chengdu with Lhasa.[68] The construction of the Sichuan (Chengdu)-Tibet (Lhasa) Railway was initiated in 2020 and is estimated to be completed by 2030. The Sichuan-Tibet railway line added additional rail connectivity into Tibet. In 2021, a bullet train linking Lhasa (Tibet) to Nyingchi, located near the border, with Arunachal Pradesh, was also operationalised.[69] There are plans to increase the total railway network in Tibet Autonomous Region to 4,000 kilometres in the coming years.[70] According to some reports, the planned railway network between Tibet and Xinjiang may traverse the disputed Aksai Chin region.[71] With the increased density of railway lines in Tibet and the presence of a railway network in Shigatse, located close to the Nepal border, there is anticipation that the China-Nepal railway line can be operationalised.

The proposed China-Nepal railway line will connect Shigatse, Kerung and move into Nepal at Rasuwagadhi. The plan to operationalise the railway line between the two countries may not seem convincing to many. However, both countries have declared an intent to build the railway line through various official declarations. The Joint Statement of the People's Republic of China and Nepal in 2018 termed railway connectivity as "the most significant initiative in the history of bilateral cooperation and ... would herald a new era of cross-border connectivity between the two countries."[72] The Joint Communiqué of the 2nd Belt and Road Forum held in Beijing in 2019 also listed the "Nepal-China Trans-Himalayan Multi-dimensional Connectivity Network, including Nepal-China cross-border railway" in its list of projects.[73]

The proposed railway line will have to navigate hostile weather, high-altitude mountainous terrain, and steep mountain slopes, which will mandate the construction of numerous tunnels and bridges. The Chinese construction companies have demonstrated competence in building a railway network through tough terrain, such as the Kunlun mountain ranges in Tibet. The more significant challenge will be to arrange for the project's funding. The project could cost somewhere between USD 3 billion and USD 5 billion.[74] These estimates are not exact, and the project's total cost may increase with time. Both countries have not articulated the precise modalities of funding the railway project. If the Nepal component of the project is financed as a loan, then the government of Nepal will have to be careful about possible debt burden and will have to evaluate the profitability of the project carefully.

In the first week of June 2020, a Chinese freight train carried COVID-19 medical equipment to Shigatse, which was then transported to Nepal by road.[75] The shipment, though small in quantity, suggested future possibilities of transporting goods from China to Nepal by freight train. The profitability of the freight train from China to Nepal will also be contingent on various factors, such as the relative costs of exporting commodities via India. Of course, traders will factor in various other issues, such as ease of navigating through customs in India and the waiting time at the Indian ports. If there is a further improvement in the ease of transit for Nepali traders at Indian ports, then the relative costs of exporting through China will also increase exponentially. In August 2022, China and Nepal agreed on building a Trans-Himalayan network, consisting of railways and communication lines. As a part of the efforts to build this network, China would finance and send experts to conduct the feasibility study of China-Nepal cross-border railways.[76] By the end of

2023, it was reported that the Chinese technical teams were conducting aerial surveys as a part of the detailed feasibility study for the Kerung-Kathmandu Cross-Border Railway.[77] In July 2024, Prime Minister Pushpa Kamal Dahal's cabinet approved the construction of the Trans-Himalayan Multi-Dimensional Connectivity Network (THMDCN).[78] In September 2024, Ding Xuexiang, Vice Premier of the People's Republic of China, and Nepal's Deputy Prime Minister and Minister for Finance, Bishnu Prasad Paudel, reiterated their intention to quickly complete the projects under THMDCN.[79]

Domestic Politics and External Influence

Given Nepal's growing economic and political engagement with China, Kathmandu had to factor in Chinese interest in its interactions with other countries. For instance, immediately after the 2015 earthquake, Taiwan offered to dispatch a disaster relief team. It is well-known that Taiwan has significant experience in earthquake disaster relief, and yet, Nepal reportedly refused the offer of disaster assistance. Taiwan's foreign minister was quoted as saying: "The Nepalese told us that they would first accept such aid from neighbouring countries..."[80] A *Washington Post* article notes that it is possible that "Beijing probably did not mandate the decision to refuse aid", and Nepal's decision may have been a consequence of "self-censorship".[81] It is pertinent to note that, in 2008, Taiwan dispatched relief materials after the Sichuan earthquake in China.[82] Overall, the episode demonstrates that Nepal's leadership was acutely aware of Chinese sensitivities even amid a massive natural disaster.

Quite often, China claims that it does not interfere with the internal affairs of other countries. However, an examination of China's engagement with Nepal proves otherwise. There have been at least two glaring incidents where China sought to define the trajectory of political developments and the contours of Nepal's external relations. For example, Nepal plunged into a political crisis in December 2020 after Prime Minister KP Sharma Oli dissolved the parliament and called for fresh elections, which the Supreme Court subsequently termed as an unconstitutional move.[83] There was a split in the Nepal Communist Party (NCP), with Prime Minister Oli leading one of the factions and Pushpa Kumar Dahal (Prachanda) and Madhav Kumar Nepal leading the other. To patch up the rival factions, a high-level delegation from the Communist Party of China , headed by the Vice Minister of the International Department, visited Kathmandu and interacted with the rival factions, Prime Minister KP Sharma Oli and President Bidya Devi Bhandari.[84]

Reuters, in its report, noted that the Chinese emissary had "held days of talks to try to stop the Himalayan country's ruling communist party from tearing itself apart."[85] Subsequently, China's Ambassador to Nepal reportedly consulted with Madhav Kumar Nepal and Pushpa Kumar Dahal at their residences to ensure the left forces stayed together.[86] Even before the dissolution of the parliament, the Chinese Ambassador was reportedly playing an active role in the internal politics of the Nepal Communist Party.[87]

Similarly, there was a perception that China also sought to influence Nepal's foreign policy. In late February 2022, the Nepalese parliament ratified the 500-million-dollar agreement between the Millennium Challenge Corporation (MCC) and the Government of Nepal.[88] The ratification of the MCC agreement happened five years after Nepal and the US signed it. However, there was considerable resistance among some Nepalese political parties that the agreement would constitute a step towards a formal alliance with the US. The parliamentary ratification came only after a 12-point explanatory note, which stated that there would be no US security presence in Nepal because of the MCC agreement.[89] In the run-up to the ratification, there was a perception that China had carried out a sustained disinformation campaign against the MCC.[90] There were also reports that China was aggressively lobbying against the parliamentary ratification of the MCC grant.[91] Referring to the MCC grant, China's Ambassador to Nepal stated that "Nepal should become a "demonstration garden" for friendly cooperation among countries, not a "fighting ring" for geopolitical games."[92] In a related development in June 2022, Nepal refrained from joining the State Partnership Programme (SPP) with the United States, which is aimed at building the capacities of personnel dealing with disaster and related matters.[93] There were reports that Nepal was dragging its feet on joining the SPP because of its apprehension of antagonising China.[94] For instance, Chinese state media referred to the SPP as another component of the US' Indo-Pacific Strategy.[95]

While the above example constitutes a probable external involvement in Nepal's domestic politics, there are other mechanisms, such as aid agencies, through which China could increase its influence. For instance, the China International Development Cooperation Agency (CIDCA) was permitted in 2019 to extend developmental aid to 15 northern districts that border Tibet.[96] As per the project proposal, the local governments in these districts will pass on the developmental requirements to the Nepalese consulate in Lhasa, which will transmit the information to Chinese authorities, including the CIDCA.[97]

These developmental programmes will be in addition to various big ticket infrastructure projects. Multiple small-scale developmental projects, such as libraries and schools, will be operationalised under this scheme. The CIDCA's interactions in Nepal have registered a steady increase. At the virtual meeting between the Ministry of Finance and the CIDCA in August 2020, the Nepal government reportedly sought developmental assistance for the construction of "Bir-Hospital Extension Project, Coordinated Border Management at Korala Customs Point, Madan Bhandari Science and Technology University Project [and] Livelihood Improvement Projects in the Northern Region of Nepal."[98] In November 2022, the Nepal government and the CIDCA signed an agreement for the utilisation of assistance of Rs 15 billion (800 million RMB) towards various development projects.[99] The CIDCA was also involved in earthquake-related humanitarian assistance to Nepal in 2023.[100] The aid programme's structure will give Chinese authorities an opportunity to interact more regularly and with greater intensity with local leaders, local government institutions, and other organisations in the border districts.

The Border Issues

While the border demarcation was agreed on decades ago, there were sporadic reports about unfriendly actions by China along the border. In September 2020, reports indicated that the Chinese moved into the Humla district in Nepal and constructed a few illegal structures.[101] Nepal's Ministry of Foreign Affairs, refuting the news reports, stated that the alleged illegal structures were "not located within the Nepali territory."[102] In January 2021, responding to the reports of Chinese activity on the border, Nepal's Prime Minister KP Sharma Oli stated: "In the northern border, there are no Chinese check posts, and we don't allow any side [to put check posts] ... we will not allow them [Chinese] to put their military check posts inside our territory."[103] Subsequently, in September 2021, Nepal's Ministry of Home Affairs dispatched a panel of senior officers to verify the border-related problems with China in the Humla district.[104] While the panel's report was not made public, a *Kathmandu Post* article quoted a senior officer stating that they could "not ascertain who fenced the boundary pillars with wire and who repaired them...to address those issues, we have suggested the formation of a joint inspection team comprising experts from both countries - Nepal and China."[105] In July 2022, both countries agreed to jointly inspect the Nepal-China boundary.[106] However, in subsequent months, there were reports about Chinese incursions into the border districts of Nepal.[107] In August 2023, Beijing released a new standard map of China, which included large parts of territories of various other countries. As with many other Chinese neighbours, even Nepal expressed displeasure with the new Chinese map. Nepal's foreign ministry spokesperson stated, "Nepal remains committed to resolving the boundary matters through dialogues and diplomacy."[108] However, in October 2024, Hannah Beech and Bhadra Sharma, writing for *The New York Times*, observed that "in Nepal's Humla District, residents contend that along several points of this distant frontier, China is encroaching on Nepali territory."[109] The persistent boundary disputes indicate deeper geopolitical rifts in the region.

Connectivity and the India Dimension

There have been instances when the international media erroneously referred to Nepal as a mouse trapped between elephants.[110] Such characterisation fails to capture Nepal's foreign policy. Nepal is a sovereign and independent country and has dealt with big-power politics deftly. Given Nepal's location, Chinese connectivity initiatives, such as the proposed China-Nepal Railway project, often have geopolitical implications. The timing of the Chinese survey in Tibet for the railway project coincided with fast-paced geopolitical developments, such as the India-China standoff at Ladakh and the intensification of a boundary dispute with Nepal. For Indians, the photographs of Chinese officials conducting feasibility studies in Tibet constituted a clear political signal of Beijing's intent to develop connectivity infrastructure close to Indian borders without resolving the boundary dispute with India.

Further, there were reports that China plans to extend the proposed China-Nepal Railway to Lumbini in Nepal, which is close to Indian territory.[111] There is an opinion that Nepal, emerging as a hub of connectivity networks between India and China, will result in greater economic prosperity. For instance, Purushottam Ojha argued that "enabling trans-Himalayan road and rail connectivity could be a game changer in [not only] facilitating trade between the populous states of India and the western provinces of China ... [and] will have a profound spill-over effect on Nepali economy."[112] Simultaneously, there are apprehensions that the project's cost may push Nepal into a debt trap. However, as Sri Lanka has demonstrated, if China can convince Nepal to give large tracts of land on lease, then the railway project will not create enormous financial stress on Nepal. Getting large tracts of land for building a Special Economic Zone (SEZ) or other projects close to India's heartland will give

China an added geopolitical advantage. Given the porosity of the India-Nepal border, Chinese goods transiting via Nepal or goods manufactured by Chinese companies in SEZs in Nepal located close to the Indian border will find it easy to access the Indian market. However, Nepal may not be interested in such a proposal. Currently, Nepal is not staring at a catastrophic debt burden. Therefore, unlike Sri Lanka, Nepal may not transfer large tracts of land on lease to China. From Kathmandu's perspective, it is crucial to ensure that goods transported from China to India have some value addition in Nepal. Otherwise, Nepal would remain as a transit point without substantive benefits.

On the other hand, China will have to surmount a few political challenges in operationalising the railway project. As SD Muni queried: "rail connectivity from Nepal to China will be used by the non-Chinese to travel to China through Tibet. Will China open up Tibet to facilitate connectivity for Nepal?"[113] If China erects barriers to the movement of people, Nepali traders will lose out on economic opportunities in Tibet, while their Chinese counterparts will not face such obstacles. Therefore, it is always difficult to define the possible trajectory of the consequences of the various connectivity projects that are being articulated. However, it should be noted that some of the mega Chinese connectivity projects that are being conceptualised will become financially viable only if they connect with India.

There are China-Nepal projects that mandate coordination with India for their successful completion. Take, for instance, a few projects in the aviation sector. China was involved in constructing the Pokhara International Airport and the Gautam Buddha International Airport in Bhairahawa. The Pokhara International Airport was built with a soft loan of USD 215 million from the Export-Import Bank of China.[114] The Gautam Buddha International Airport was built by a Chinese firm but was funded by the Asian Development Bank and OPEC Fund for International Development.[115] However, there was a concern that both these airports failed to attract business due to high operating costs. The business of these two airports is also contingent on accessing the Indian airspace.[116] The Indian government has hesitated to open additional air routes closer to its border with China. To make airports more commercially viable, Nepal is encouraging more Chinese flights to use its airports. In June 2023, for the first time since its inauguration, the Pokhara International Airport received its first international flight from Sichuan province in China.[117] However, it is unlikely that the long-term viability of these airports can be ensured only by depending on flights from China. During his visit to India in April 2023, Prime Minister Pushpa Kamal Dahal 'Prachanda' advocated for additional air routes (including high altitude) for bilateral flights between the two countries.[118] Reportedly, the Indian government has agreed to open up airspace "for aircraft flying at an altitude of 15,000 to 24,000 ft."[119] These attempts to find a common ground in the Chinese-built airports may take a little more time. However, Nepal wants to have high-altitude flights to make the airports profitable. Prior consultations would have ensured that Nepal and India were on the same page on the airport's construction. There are similar experiences in the hydropower sector as well.

Chinese firms were involved in constructing the Upper Marsyangdi, Upper Tama-koshi Hydropower, and Upper Trishuli 3A Hydroelectric Projects.[120] In 2016, the Upper Marsyangdi, a hydropower station, was operationalised by a Chinese firm, and the electricity from the project powers major population centres, such as Kathmandu and Pokhara.[121] In 2017, Nepal cancelled the Budhi Gandaki hydropower project "with a Chinese firm over irregularities and lack of transparency."[122] Subsequently, the KP Sharma Oli government sought to involve another Chinese company in the construction of the project, which was later revoked by the Sher Bahadur Deuba administration in 2022.[123] Nepal sought to develop the projects by deploying domestic resources. In addition to transparency issues, the shifts in India's electricity trade policy impacted Chinese energy profits in Nepal. The Indian government decided, in 2018, to prohibit the "purchase power produced from the investment of countries with which it does not have a bilateral agreement on power sector cooperation."[124] Such a policy effectively meant that India could not purchase power from hydropower projects in Nepal, which were funded, built, or operated by China.[125] The guidelines for Import/Export (Cross Border) of Electricity subsequently issued in 2021 and revised in 2023 state that: "Any Indian power trader, on behalf of any entity of neighbouring country, may trade in Indian Power Exchanges provided, the neighbouring country which has an agreement on cooperation in the power sector with India, and the generating asset from which power is being traded is also owned/controlled by the said country having agreement on Power Cooperation with India."[126] The provision ensures that Indian firms cannot buy power from hydropower projects built or operated by Chinese firms. Since India is the only international buyer at the moment, it would have to go through the Indian grid, even if power were to be exported to Bangladesh.

The change in Indian policy impacted foreign investment in Nepal's hydropower sector by dampening Chinese involvement. Nonetheless, Chinese investment in Nepal's hydropower sector continues, albeit at a relatively lower intensity. For instance, in 2022, the Investment Board Nepal and National Hydro Power Corporation Ltd. signed a Memorandum of Understanding (MoU) with Chinese firms to develop the West Seti Hydropower Project and the Seti River Hydropower Project at an estimated expense of USD 2.4 billion.[127] It is anticipated that Chinese firms may be involved in the construction of the Tamakoshi V hydropower project (99.8 megawatts) in Dolakha, which is being implemented by the Nepal Electricity Authority.[128]

While Nepal has vast hydropower potential, it is not in a position to harness it with domestic resources. Therefore, it becomes imperative to export power to neighbouring countries. Currently, China cannot import energy because of the terrain and the absence of large human settlements and industrial zones near the Nepal border. Therefore, India is the most critical external buyer of Nepal's hydropower. Along with other international firms, Chinese firms have the technology, finances, and expertise to build hydropower projects in Nepal and can reap significant profits. India's reluctance to buy power from projects built by the Chinese stems from two reasons: first, Chinese firms procured contracts for projects that Indian firms were also interested in. Second, and more importantly, there is an opinion that Indian firms find it difficult to access markets in China because of the prevalence of numerous non-tariff barriers. Given the absence of any reciprocity from China, there is an opinion that it would be imprudent for India to purchase power from Chinese projects built or operated by Chinese firms.

It appears China's hydropower diplomacy has achieved some important political objectives. If India refrained from opposing Chinese projects, Chinese firms would have profited by exporting energy to India. The Indian government's reluctance to purchase power from hydro projects in Nepal with Chinese involvement may have generated disappointment in certain quarters in Nepal that New Delhi is not facilitating diversified economic partnerships and is undermining Nepal's sovereignty. In fact, China's Ambassador in Nepal tried to push such a line of argument in September 2023. Arguing that "India's policy towards Nepal … [is] not so friendly," Chinese Ambassador Chen Song stated, "last fiscal year, you exported 10 billion rupee electricity to India … How much [did] you [import] from India? My Nepalese friends, you imported 19 billion Nepalese rupees of electricity from India … you had a deficit in electricity trade, one of the products you are proud of, and you think that will bring you economic independence."[129] The Chinese economic intervention, at least in some instances, is creating a wedge between India and its neighbour, an outcome in which Beijing may not be entirely unhappy.

Conclusion: Geopolitics and Economic Interactions

In September 2023, Nepal's Prime Minister, Pushpa Kamal Dahal (Prachanda), visited Beijing and interacted with President Xi Jinping on the sidelines of the Asian Games in Hangzhou. Subsequently, he interacted with other leaders, such as Chinese Prime Minister Li Qiang.[130] Interestingly, Prachanda visited India and the United States to attend the 78th General Assembly of the United Nations before he visited Beijing. This is in marked contrast to Prachanda's preference to travel to Beijing in 2008 on his first international visit instead of visiting India, which is the long-held tradition of Nepali prime ministers. During the 2023 visit, both countries signed 12 agreements pertaining to the digital economy, green and low-carbon development fisheries, livestock, and agriculture.[131] Importantly, an MoU pertaining to Nepal-China power grid interconnection from Chilime (Nepal) to Keyrung (China) was agreed upon by both sides.[132] The objective of the MoU seems to be to develop a north-south transmission line that could export power generated by Chinese hydropower projects in Nepal.[133] Both sides discussed the possibility of increasing Chinese flights to Bhairahawa International Airport and Pokhara Regional International Airport in Nepal.[134] Some former Nepali diplomats have put forth proposals to import petroleum products via pipeline from Kazakhstan via China, which indicates growing diversity in the bilateral relationship between Nepal and China.[135]

Despite Nepal-China relations becoming multi-dimensional, there is no denying that securing Tibet continues to be an important objective of the Chinese engagement with Nepal. As economic interactions between the two countries increased in density, Kathmandu became more sensitive to Beijing's security concerns, particularly about Tibet. A United Nations High Commissioner for Refugees (UNHCR) document highlights the shifts in Nepal's Tibetan refugee policy thus: "Pursuant to an oral 'Gentlemen's Agreement', since 1990 Nepal had been allowing Tibetan "new arrivals" safe passage through its territory to India and issuing them exit permits.... However, Nepal ceased the practice of issuing exit visas in 2018."[136] There is a growing opinion that the space for Tibetan refugees is getting constrained in

Nepal. News reports suggest that Tibetan refugees are encountering increased detentions, enhanced surveillance, restrictions on political protests, and a lack of appropriate identification cards.[137] The possibility that Nepal may extradite refugees to China has generated anxiety among many Tibetans living abroad. While the 2019 joint statement "expressed hope for an early conclusion of the Treaty on Extradition," the 2023 statement makes no such mention.[138] Such absence indicates that Kathmandu had resisted Beijing's attempts to formalise the extradition process and thereby gain greater control of the Tibetan refugee activities in Nepal.[139] However, the 2023 joint statement reiterated that "Tibet affairs are China's internal affairs, that it will never allow any separatist activities against China on Nepal's soil."[140] It should be noted that China has also made efforts to increase interactions with provincial-level leaders. Wang Junzheng, the Communist Party of China secretary for the Xizang Autonomous Region of China, during his visit to Nepal in late 2023, interacted with the chief minister of Gandaki province, which borders Tibet, and termed it as an area of their priority.[141] As noted earlier, the Chinese aid agency, CIDCA, also scaled up its operations in Nepal's 15 northern-border districts.

Simultaneously, the Chinese engagement in Nepal is now defined by broader geopolitical objectives as well. Both countries signed an MoU on cooperation under the rubric of the Belt and Road Initiative (BRI) in 2017, and during President Xi Jinping's visit to Nepal in 2019, the bilateral relationship was elevated to a Strategic Partnership of Cooperation Featuring Ever-lasting Friendship for Development and Prosperity.[142] China's President, Xi Jinping, in a signed article published ahead of his state visit, noted that increased bilateral relations benefit not only the "two countries but also the region as a whole."[143] Xi Jinping's visit to Nepal was also an attempt to shore up support for the BRI projects, which would increase economic activity between China and South Asia. It should be noted that there has been very little progress on the BRI between the countries. In fact, the 2023 joint statement calls for accelerated "consultations to finalise the text of the BRI implementation plan at an early date."[144] However, it should be noted that China is involved in various projects, such as constructing airports, upgrading highways, operationalising border ports, and building power plants. Much of this cooperation has happened outside the rubric of the BRI.

The return of KP Sharma Oli as prime minister of Nepal for the third time in July 2024 increased the prospect of implementing the projects under the rubric of the BRI. As is well known, Oli's tenures have often witnessed significant foreign policy shifts aimed at reducing the historically close social, economic, and political interactions with India in favour of China. A few months after his return, the Nepal government removed the ban on the Chinese social media platform, TikTok, and prioritised a visit to Beijing as his first foreign visit after becoming the prime minister. During his state visit to China in the first week of December 2024, Prime Minister Oli interacted with President Xi Jinping, Premier Li Qiang, and other senior leaders. The joint statement issued during Oli's visit had the usual reiterations of the one-China principle. The joint statement also noted that "the Nepali side reiterated that Xizang affairs are internal affairs of China and that it will never allow any separatist activities against China on Nepal's soil."[145] Both sides agreed to expedite a host of connectivity and energy projects.

Referring to the need to deepen the Belt and Road cooperation, Prime Minister Oli announced that Nepal and China agreed on the Framework for Belt and Road Cooperation, which would further strengthen the economic interactions between the two countries.[146] The framework agreement was signed for a period of three years and will be extended for an additional three years unless terminated by one of the parties.[147] As noted earlier, Nepal signed the Belt and Road Initiative (BRI) Memorandum of Understanding in 2017. Since then, Nepal has refrained from moving forward with the framework agreement that would have paved the way for faster implementation of various projects under the BRI. Nevertheless, despite the lack of a framework agreement, China has operationalised numerous infrastructure projects, such as airports and hydropower projects, in Nepal.

In the run-up to Oli's visit to China, there was considerable discussion in Nepal regarding the advisability of building massive infrastructure projects with Chinese loans. Recently, Nepal Foreign Affairs Minister Arzu Rana Deuba stated, "I have told Minister Wang Yi that Nepal is not in a position to take loans... Our discussions in China revolved around progressing with BRI projects through grants."[148] It is not certain if China would be interested in pursuing such projects only through grants. A report in the *South China Morning Post* noted that Nepal wanted to include references to "grants" in the framework agreement, and after much discussion, both sides agreed on the "aid help financing" terminology.[149]

There is an underlying geopolitical context in Nepal's willingness to proceed with the framework agreement. Nepal is one of the core pillars of China's trans-Himalayan connectivity network that extends from Iran to Myanmar.

For China, the BRI framework agreement provides a pathway for greater and faster implementation of infrastructure projects in a strategically important South Asian country. At the moment, transporting goods to Nepal through the high Himalayas is a costly proposition. The Chinese objective would be to create the necessary infrastructure to reduce such costs. Implementing the BRI projects, specifically the connectivity projects in Nepal, will also enable China to access Indian markets through a third country. Not surprisingly, China has also proposed a China-Nepal-India Economic Corridor.[150] If Chinese economic corridors and connectivity projects in Nepal are successful, then the probability of accessing the Indian market will increase significantly. Given that India and Nepal have porous borders, Chinese goods can flow into India without restrictions. At a time when the developed economies are imposing considerable trade barriers on China, accessing the Indian market via Nepal will be a lucrative proposition for Beijing. Such access to the Indian market without resolving the boundary dispute would be a substantive geopolitical gain for China. However, Beijing will have to puncture through New Delhi's frameworks that discourage India-China economic interactions. One of the nodes through which such an endeavour could be achieved would be to argue that Nepal should have unfettered access to Bangladesh. For instance, if there are no limits to Kathmandu's hydroelectricity exports to Bangladesh via India, then Chinese investments in Nepal's energy sector will become a little more financially viable. Over time, a wide range of increased economic interactions between Nepal and Bangladesh could be nudged to ensure that Chinese goods and commodities will spill into India with greater intensity.

Notes

1. Brahma Chellaney, "China's Five-Finger Punch," *Project Syndicate,* July 21, 2020, https://www.project-syndicate.org/commentary/china-xi-resurrects-mao-five-fingers-strategy-by-brahma-chellaney-2020-07
2. See Prashant Kumar Singh, "The Fallacy of Chinese 'Strategy' of Five Fingers of Tibet," *India Review* 23, no. 5 (2024), pp. 409-423
3. "Bhattarai hands over bronze statue of Buddhabhadra to Dongling Monastery," myRepublica, July 23, 2018, https://myrepublica.nagariknetwork.com/news/bhattarai-hands-over-bronze-statue-of-buddhabhadra-to-dongling-monastery/
4. Acharya Kirti Tulku, Lobsang Tenzin, and K. Dhondup, "Early Relations between Tibet and Nepal (7th to 8th Centuries)," *The Tibet Journal* 7, no. 1/2 (1982), pp. 83-86.
5. Min Bahadur Shakya, *The Life and Contribution of the Nepalese Princess Bhrikuti Devi in Tibetan History* (Kathmandu: Pilgrims Book House, 1997).

6. Min Bahadur Shakya, "Buddhism in the Himalaya, its Expansion and the Present Day Aspects." Paper Presented On the Occasion of UNESCO's Integral Study of the Silk Roads: Roads of Dialogue Lumbini Development Trust/Nepal National Commission for UNESCO Buddhist Route Expedition, Nepal, September 21-30, 1995, https://en.unesco.org/silkroad/sites/default/files/knowledge-bank-article/buddhism_in_the_himalaya_1.pdf
7. Leonard R Chapela, "Economic Institutions of Buddhist Tibet," *The Tibet Journal*, Vol. 17, no. 3 (1992), pp. 2-40. http://www.jstor.org/stable/43300440
8. Alexandrowicz-Alexander and Charles Henry, "The Legal Position of Tibet," *The American Journal of International Law, Vol.* 48, no. 2 (1954), pp. 265–74.
9. Y.P. Pant, "Nepal-China Trade Relations," *The Economic Weekly*, April 14, 1962, p. 621.
10. Mckay, Alex, "The British Invasion of Tibet, 1903–04," *Inner Asia 14*, no. 1 (2012), pp. 5-25.
11. "1955·周恩来万隆之行," chinaqw.com, September 7, 2005, https://www.chinaqw.com/node2/node2796/node3436/node3630/node3634/userobject6ai260913.html
12. "Central Intelligence Bulletin - October 9, 1956," *General CIA Records*, CIA-RDP79T00975A002700520001-4; also see "万隆会议以后中国的对外援助," Ministry of Commerce of the People's Republic of China, Beijing, http://history.mofcom.gov.cn/?newchina=%E4%B8%87%E9%9A%86%E4%BC%9A%E8%AE%AE%E4%BB%A5%E5%90%8E%E4%B8%AD%E5%9B%BD%E7%9A%84%E5%AF%B9%E5%A4%96%E6%8F%B4%E5%8A%A9
13. Shokin Chauhan, "Growing Chinese Presence in Himalayan Terrai: India Must Counter China in Nepal Now," *The Financial Express*, June 11, 2021, https://www.financialexpress.com/business/defence-growing-chinese-presence-in-himalayan-terrai-india-must-counter-china-in-nepal-now-2269600/
14. "Central Intelligence Bulletin, August 4, 1960," *General CIA Records, CIA-RDP79T00975A005200300001-0*, https://www.cia.gov/library/readingroom/document/cia-rdp79t00975a005200300001-0
15. "公开道歉：错了就要承认," *Sina.com*, May 30, 2006, http://news.sina.com.cn/c/2006-05-30/101710014202.shtml
16. Claude Arpi, "A Chinese Train to Lumbini?" September 16, 2013, http://claudearpi.blogspot.com/2013/09/a-chinese-train-to-lumbini.html
17. "Bi-Weekly Propaganda Guidance - July 18, 1960," *General CIA Records*, CIA-RDP78-03061A000100020005-5, Document Release Date: August 7, 2000, https://www.cia.gov/readingroom/document/cia-rdp78-03061a000100020005-5
18. "Nepal Leader sees Danger from Tibet," *The New York Times*, August 12, 1959, p. 3.
19. "Nepal Surrenders Concessions in Tibet," *The New York Times*, September 25, 1956, p. 5.
20. Ibid.
21. "Red China Hinders Nepal-Tibet Trade," *The New York Times*, October 2, 1960, p.3
22. The Ministry of Foreign Affairs of the People's Republic of China and the Party Literature Research Center under the Central Committee of the Communist Party of China, *Mao Zedong on Diplomacy*, (Beijing: Foreign Language Press, 1998), p.303
23. Ibid., p. 306.
24. "BP and Mao," *Nepali Times*, May 25-31, 2001, http://himalaya.socanth.cam.ac.uk/collections/journals/nepalitimes/pdf/Nepali_Times_044.pdf

25. Ibid.
26. 韩毓海：此次中印对峙，让我想起了半个世纪前尼泊尔的选择, *Guancha,* July 19, 2017, https://www.guancha.cn/HanZuoHai/2017_07_19_418914_2.shtml
27. "Sino-Nepalese Joint Communique, April 29, 1960," *Peking Review*, May 3, 1960, p. 6.
28. "Speech at the Nepalese Banquet," *Peking Review*, May 3, 1960, p. 9.
29. "Nepal Picks Route of Road to Tibet," *The New York Times*, May 28, 1962, p. 6.
30. "Nepal Road Aims At Link To Tibet; Chinese, Gaining a Supply Line, Aid Construction," *New York Times*, February 9, 1964, https://www.nytimes.com/1964/02/09/archives/nepal-road-aims-at-link-to-tibet-chinese-gaining-a-supply-line-aid.html
31. Y.P. Pant, "Nepal-China Trade Relations," *The Economic Weekly*, April 14, 1962, p. 621.
32. "Red China Escalate Infiltration of Nepal," *General CIA Records*, CIA-RDP69B00369R000100200003-0, February 6, 2004, https://www.cia.gov/library/readingroom/docs/CIA-RDP69B00369R000100200003-0.pdf
33. Ibid.
34. "Treaty of Trade, Treaty of Transit and Trade Related Agreements Between Government of Nepal and Neighbouring Countries (India, People's Republic of China & Bangladesh) (Amended and updated up to July 2010)," Nepal Transit and Warehousing Company Limited, July 2010, http://www.tepc.gov.np/tradeagreement/Treaty%20of%20Trade%20and%20Transit%20Final.pdf
35. "Sixty Years of Nepal Rastra Bank", Nepal Rastra Bank Kathmandu, April 2018, https://www.nrb.org.np/contents/uploads/2019/12/Special_Publications-Sixty_Years_Of_Nepal_Rastra_Bank-new.pdf
36. Consulate General of Nepal, Guangzhou, "Bilateral Relations," *Ministry of Foreign Affairs, Government of Nepal,* https://can.nepalconsulate.gov.np/bilateral-relations/
37. Ministry of Industry, Commerce and Supplies, *A Book on Nepal-China Agreements*, (Kathmandu: Nepal-India Regional Trade and Transport Project, 2021), p. 72.
38. Abhisek Basnyat, "The Road to Lo," *Nepali Times*, August 22–28, 2003, https://archive.nepalitimes.com/news.php?id=3802#.X5R814gzaUk
39. "China Offers Zero Tariff Treatments to 4762 Products from Bangladesh and Other 32 Least Developed Countries," *Embassy of the People's Republic of China in the People's Republic of Bangladesh,* July 1, 2017, https://bd.china-embassy.org/eng/xwdt/t713211.htm
40. Krishana Prasain, "Experts doubt implementation of latest trade deal with China," *The Kathmandu Post,* April 1, 2022, https://kathmandupost.com/money/2022/04/01/experts-doubt-implementation-of-latest-trade-deal-with-china; also see "Press Release on Bilateral Talks between the Foreign Ministers of Nepal and China," Government of Nepal - Ministry Of Foreign Affairs, March 26, 2022, https://mofa.gov.np/press-release-on-bilateral-talks-between-the-foreign-ministers-of-nepal-and-china/
41. "China, Nepal Sign Protocol to Operationalise Key Transit Treaty to Access Chinese Ports," *The Times of India*, April 30, 2019, https://timesofindia.indiatimes.com/business/international-business/china-nepal-sign-protocol-to-operationalise-key-transit-treaty-to-access-chinese-ports/articleshowprint/69117349.cms.

42. Mahendra Subedi, "Nepal, China Come Closer with Protocols on Transit and Transport," *CGTN*, April 30, 2019, https://news.cgtn.com/news/3d3d674d79677a4d34457a6333566d54/index.html
43. Nihar R Nayak, "Nepal-China Transit Agreement: An Evaluation," *IDSA Issue Brief*, September 27, 2018, https://idsa.in/issuebrief/nepal-china-transit-agreement-nnayak-270918
44. "Nepal Imports Goods from Third Country Through Chinese Ports After Seven Years of Transit Agreement," *myRepublica,* September 9, 2023, https://myrepublica.nagariknetwork.com/news/nepal-imports-goods-from-third-country-through-chinese-ports-after-seven-years-of-transit-agreement/
45. Gopal Sharma, "Nepal seeks easier trade access to Chinese markets," *Reuters*, March 14, 2023, https://www.reuters.com/world/asia-pacific/nepal-seeks-easier-trade-access-chinese-markets-2023-03-14/
46. "Nepal, China to resume two-way trade via key border points from today," *Business Standard*, April 1, 2023, https://www.business-standard.com/world-news/nepal-china-to-resume-two-way-trade-via-key-border-points-from-today-123040100289_1.html
47. "PM bats for minimising trade deficit with China," *The Himalayan Times,* October 5, 2023, https://thehimalayantimes.com/business/pm-bats-for-minimising-trade-deficit-with-china
48. "China Builds Cross-Border Optical Fibre Link to Kathmandu," *The New Indian Express,* January 14, 2018, https://www.newindianexpress.com/world/2018/jan/14/china-builds-cross-border-optical-fibre-link-to-kathmandu-1753184.html
49. "Two Chinese Firms Roped in for 4G LTE Expansion Project," *The Kathmandu Post*, February 4, 2019, https://kathmandupost.com/money/2019/02/04/two-chinese-firms-roped-in-for-4g-lte-expansion-project
50. Gopal Sharma, "Nepal says bans WeChat Pay, Alipay," *Reuters*, May 22, 2019, https://www.reuters.com/article/idUSKCN1SS19Z/
51. "NMB Bank Launches WeChat Pay in Nepal," *NMB*, June 22, 2023, https://www.nmb.com.np/news/nmb-bank-launches-wechat-pay-in-nepal
52. "Chinese tourists can now use mobile pay in Nepal," *The Kathmandu Post*, June 26, 2023, https://kathmandupost.com/money/2023/06/26/chinese-tourists-can-now-use-mobile-pay-in-nepal
53. "Nepal Bans TikTok Citing Disruption to Social Harmony," *BBC,* November 14, 2023, https://www.bbc.com/news/business-67411535
54. "突然禁用TikTok，调查中企机场项目，尼泊尔怎么了？", *Sina.cn,* November 17, 2023, https://news-sina-cn.translate.goog/2023-11-17/detail-imzuwqhw5982514.d.html?_x_tr_sl=zh-CN&_x_tr_tl=en&_x_tr_hl=en&_x_tr_pto=sc
55. "Nepal's Government Bans TikTok, Saying it Disrupts Social Harmony," *NPR*, November 14, 2023, https://www.npr.org/2023/11/14/1212838525/nepals-government-bans-tiktok-saying-it-disrupts-social-harmony
56. "Nepal to procure anti-Covid vaccine from China, signs non-disclosure agreement," *The Times of India*, July 3, 2021, https://timesofindia.indiatimes.com/world/south-asia/nepal-to-procure-anti-covid-vaccine-from-china-signs-non-disclosure-agreement/articleshow/84077821.cms

57. "Nepal signs non-disclosure agreement to buy Chinese Covid-19 vaccines but legal questions remain," *The Kathmandu Post,* June 6, 2021, https://kathmandupost.com/national/2021/06/06/nepal-signs-non-disclosure-agreement-to-buy-chinese-covid-19-vaccines-but-legal-questions-remain
58. "China unhappy with Nepal over disclosure of Sinopharm COVID vaccine price," *Livemint*, June 20, 2021, https://www.livemint.com/news/world/china-unhappy-with-nepal-over-disclosure-of-sinopharm-covid-vaccine-price-11624146501724.html
59. "Nepalese Army ignores parliament and awards Kathmandu road deals to Chinese contractors," *GCR*, May 17, 2021, https://www.globalconstructionreview.com/nepalese-army-ignores-parliament-and-awards-kathma/
60. "Nepal awards key expressway project near Indian border to Chinese company," *Business Standard*, November 15, 2022, https://www.business-standard.com/article/international/nepal-awards-key-expressway-project-near-indian-border-to-chinese-company-122111500776_1.html
61. "Nepal Court Bans China from Crucial Project After Protest by Indian Company," *Firstpost*, December 22, 2022, https://www.firstpost.com/world/nepal-court-bans-china-from-crucial-project-after-protest-by-indian-company-11856451.html
62. "Locals Protest China-Sponsored Project in Damak," *The Himalayan,* January 1, 2021, https://thehimalayantimes.com/nepal/locals-protest-china-sponsored-project-in-damak ; also see "Nepal's Damak Industrial Park under China's BRI Now Centre for Local Agitation," *The Print,* February 11, 2023, https://theprint.in/world/nepals-damak-industrial-park-under-chinas-bri-now-centre-for-local-agitation/1367099/
63. 毛主席当年提到的这件事尼泊尔人盼得心急, *China Tibet Net,* September 27, 2016, http://m.tibet.cn/wap//news/focus/1474969351610.shtml
64. Jane Qiu, "Killer Landslides: The Lasting Legacy of Nepal's Quake," *Nature*, Volume: 532, April 28, 2016, pp. 428-431
65. "Top 10 Tibet Railway Facts and Records," China Tibet Train Travel & Tours, Qinghai Tibet Railway Tours, October 17, 2020, https://www.chinatibettrain.com/tibet-train-facts.htm
66. "Journey on the Fast Track: Story of the First Female Tibetan Chief Conductor on the Qinghai-Tibet Railway Line," *CGTN,* October 6, 2020, https://news.cgtn.com/news/33517a4e33514464776c6d636a4e6e62684a4856/index
67. Jonathan Watts, "The Railway Across the Roof of the World," *The Guardian*, September 20, 2005, https://www.theguardian.com/world/2005/sep/20/china.jonathanwatts
68. "President Xi Pushes for Speedy Completion of Sichuan-Tibet Railway," *Tibetan Review*, October 12, 2018,
69. "Lhasa-Nyingchi Railway Benefits Local People, Economy," *Xinhua*, July 31, 2021, http://www.xinhuanet.com/english/2021-07/31/c_1310097982.htm
70. "Tibet Unveils Plan to Upgrade Regional Rail Network," *China Daily,* February 10, 2023, https://www.chinadaily.com.cn/a/202302/10/WS63e59410a31057c47ebadfc5.html

71. Chandan Prakash, "China Plans Railway Line to Connect Tibet, Xinjiang," *Firstpost,* February 13, 2023, https://www.firstpost.com/world/china-plans-railway-line-to-connect-tibet-xinjiang-12145572.html
72. "Joint Statement Between the People's Republic of China and Nepal," *Ministry of Foreign Affairs, the People's Republic of China,* June 22, 2018, https://www.fmprc.gov.cn/mfa_eng/wjdt_665385/2649_665393/t1570977.shtml
73. "Full text of Joint Communiqué of Leaders' Roundtable of 2nd BRF," *The State Council Information Office,* April 27, 2019, http://english.scio.gov.cn/BRF2019/2019-04/28/content_74730528.htm
74. Ed Peters, "China-Nepal Railway: Debt Trap, Threat to India or Pie in the Sky?" *South China Morning Post,* December 1, 2019, https://www.scmp.com/week-asia/politics/article/3039995/china-nepal-railway-debt-trap-godsend-threat-india-or-just-pie; also see Ramesh Bhushal, "The China-Nepal Railway: High Cost and Hidden," *China Dialogue,* June 28, 2019, https://chinadialogue.net/en/business/11336-the-china-nepal-railway-high-cost-and-hidden/#:~:text=Preliminary%20estimates%20put%20the%20costs,the%20extreme%20geology%20and%20climate
75. Ramesh Kumar, "New China-Nepal Rail Corridor," *Nepali Times,* June 5, 2020, https://www.nepalitimes.com/latest/new-china-nepal-rail-corridor/
76. "China, Nepal agree on building a trans-Himalayan network," *Reuters,* August 11, 2022, https://www.reuters.com/world/china/china-nepal-agree-building-trans-himalayan-network-2022-08-11/
77. Prithvi Man Shrestha, "Feasibility Study of Nepal-China Railway 'on Track'," *The Wire,* December 14, 2023, https://thewire.in/south-asia/feasibility-study-of-nepal-china-railway-on-track
78. "Outgoing Nepal PM Approved China Rail Deal Ahead Of Trust Vote: Report," *NDTV,* July 12, 2024, https://www.ndtv.com/india-news/prachanda-belt-and-road-initiative-outgoing-nepal-pm-approved-china-rail-deal-ahead-of-trust vote-report-6093132
79. Ibid.
80. "Nepal Earthquake: No Politics Behind Rejection of Our Rescue Team Offer, Says Taiwan Minister," *NDTV,* April 27, 2015, https://www.ndtv.com/world-news/nepal-earthquake-no-politics-behind-rejection-of-our-rescue-team-offer-says-taiwan-minister-758618
81. Simon Denyer, "The aftermath of Nepal's Earthquake Exposes Asia's Geopolitical Fault Lines," *The Washington Post,* April 28, 2015, https://www.washingtonpost.com/news/worldviews/wp/2015/04/28/the-aftermath-of-nepals-earthquake-exposes-asias-geopolitical-fault-lines/
82. Ibid.
83. Hari Bansh Jha, "Nepal: Supreme Court's verdict on dissolution of Parliament and the emerging situation," *ORF,* February 26, 2021, https://www.orfonline.org/expert-speak/nepal-supreme-court-verdict-dissolution-parliament-emerging-situation/
84. "Visiting CPC delegation meets leaders of rival faction of NCP," *My República,* December 28, 2020, https://myrepublica.nagariknetwork.com/news/visiting-cpc-delegation-meets-leaders-of-rival-faction-of-ncp/
85. Gopal Sharma and Rupam Jain, "China holds sway in Nepal as rival communist factions create crisis," *Reuters,* December 31, 2020, https://www.reuters.com/article/

us-nepal-china-politics/china-holds-sway-in-nepal-as-rival-communist-factions-create-crisis-idUSKBN2950O4/

86. Yubaraj Ghimire, "As Nepal PM moves against party rebels, Chinese envoy meets top leaders," *The Indian Express*, March 23, 2021, https://indianexpress.com/article/world/as-nepal-pm-moves-against-party-rebels-chinese-envoy-meets-top-leaders-7240605/
87. "China Rushes Top-ranking CPC Leader to Kathmandu to Prevent Split in Nepal Communist Party," *Hindustan Times*, December 27, 2020, https://www.hindustantimes.com/world-news/china-rushes-top-ranking-cpc-leader-to-kathmandu-to-prevent-split-in-nepal-communist-party/story-jBGCvXs8rZsWQ78iy4dmYM.html
88. "MCC Statement on Nepal Compact Ratification," *Millennium Challenge Corporation,* March 1, 2022, https://www.mcc.gov/news-and-events/release/stmt-030122-nepal-compact-ratification
89. Yubaraj Ghimire, "Explained: China-US arm-wrestling in Nepal, played out over $500 million grant Written," *The Indian Express*, March 3, 2022, https://indianexpress.com/article/explained/china-us-arm-wrestling-in-nepal-played-out-over-dollar-500-million-grant-7796652/
90. "China's disinformation campaign over Nepal's MCC ratification failed: US envoy nominee," *ANI*, July 16, 2022, https://www.aninews.in/news/world/asia/chinas-disinformation-campaign-over-nepals-mcc-ratification-failed-us-envoy-nominee20220716230115/
91. Ramesh Kumar, "China lobbying against MCC," *Nepali Times*, December 23, 2021, https://www.nepalitimes.com/here-now/china-lobbying-against-mcc/ /
92. Yin Yeping, "Nepal a 'Demonstration Garden' for Friendly Cooperation among Countries, Not a 'Fighting Ring' for Geopolitical Games: Envoy," *Global Times,* April 14, 2022, https://www.globaltimes.cn/page/202204/1259363.shtml
93. "State Partnership Program Factsheet," *US Embassy Kathmandu,* June 17, 2022, https://np.usembassy.gov/state-partnership-program-factsheet/
94. P.K. Balachandran, "Nepal Backs Away from US State Partnership Program," *The Diplomat,* June 22, 2022, https://thediplomat.com/2022/06/nepal-backs-away-from-us-state-partnership-program/
95. Hu Yuwei, "US pushes military pact with Nepal, puts Himalayan peace at stake for geopolitical ambition," *Global Times*, June 20, 2022, https://www.globaltimes.cn/page/202206/1268512.shtml
96. Anil Giri, "Chinese Development Agency to Aid 15 Northern Nepali Districts," *The Kathmandu Post,* March 30, 2019, https://kathmandupost.com/national/2019/03/30/chinese-development-agency-to-aid-15-northern-nepali-districts
97. Ibid.
98. Video Conference Meeting Held Between Ministry of Finance and China International Development Cooperation Agency (CIDCA), *Ministry of Finance, Government of Nepal,* August 27, 2020, https://www.mof.gov.np/uploads/news/file/press%20release%20-Meeting%20with%20CIDCA%20(1)_20200827120607.pdf
99. Anil Giri, "Nepal, China seal a deal for utilisation of Rs15 billion in Chinese grant," *The Kathmandu Post,* November 16, 2022, https://kathmandupost.com/

national/2022/11/16/nepal-china-seal-a-deal-for-utilisation-of-rs15-billion-in-chinese-grant

100. "CIDCA spokesperson: China working on providing quake relief assistance to Nepal," *CIDCA*, November 17, 2023, http://en.cidca.gov.cn/2023-11/07/c_936898.htm
101. "North of the Border," *Nepali Times*, September 24, 2020, https://nepalitimes.com/news/north-of-the-border
102. "Press Statement," Ministry of Foreign Affairs, Government of Nepal, September 23, 2020, https://mofa.gov.np/press-statement-on-news-report-on-nepal-china-border/
103. "Will never allow China to put checkposts on border: Nepal PM Oli to WION," *Wion*, January 11, 2021, https://www.wionews.com/south-asia/will-never-allow-china-to-put-checkposts-on-border-nepal-pm-oli-to-wion-356115
104. "Nepal government forms committee to study border issues with China," *The Hindu*, September 2, 2021, https://www.thehindu.com/news/international/nepal-government-forms-committee-to-study-border-issues-with-china/article36243836.ece
105. Anil Giri, "Panel on Nepal-China Border Issues Calls for Bilateral Intervention," *The Kathmandu Post*, September 29, 2021, https://kathmandupost.com/national/2021/09/29/panel-on-nepal-china-border-issues-calls-for-bilateral-intervention
106. "Press Release," Ministry of Foreign Affairs, July 14, 2022, https://mofa.gov.np/press-release-on-consultation-meeting-on-border-affairs-between-nepal-and-the-peoples-republic-of-china/
107. Saloni Murarka, "Civic group in Nepal Submits Memo to Government against Chinese Encroachment," *Wion*, July 19, 2022, https://www.wionews.com/south-asia/civic-group-in-nepal-submits-memo-to-government-against-chinese-encroachment-498869
108. "Nepal Asks China to 'Respect' Its 2020 Map, Kathmandu Mayor Cancels China Visit," *The Wire*, September 1, 2023, https://thewire.in/world/nepal-asks-china-to-respect-its-2020-map
109. Hannah Beech and Bhadra Sharma, "China's 'New Great Wall' Casts a Shadow on Nepal," *The New York Times*, October 12, 2024, https://nytimes.com/interactive/2024/10/12/world/asia/china-nepal-borders.html.
110. Jim Yardley, "China Intensifies Tug of War With India on Nepal," *The New York Times*, February 18, 2010, https://www.nytimes.com/2010/02/18/world/asia/18nepal.html
111. "Nepal wants China to Build Rail Link to Lumbini," *The Economic Times*, March 22, 2016, https://economictimes.indiatimes.com/news/international/world-news/nepal-wants-china-to-build-rail-link-to-lumbini/articleshow/51514918.cms
112. Purushottam Ojha, "Tap into Connectivity Prospects," *myRepublica*, January 11, 2020, https://myrepublica.nagariknetwork.com/news/tap-into-connectivity-prospects/
113. Suhasini Haidar and Kallol Bhattacherjee, "Nepal Seals Agreement on Transit Rights Through China," *The Hindu*, March 21, 2016, https://www.thehindu.com/

news/international/nepal-inks-transit-treaty-with-china-to-have-first-rail-link/article8381195.ece

114. Anirban Bhaumik,"Nepal seeks India's help to save its new airports built by China", *Deccan Herald*, June 1, 2023, https://www.deccanherald.com/world/nepal-seeks-india-s-help-to-save-its-new-airports-built-by-china-1223773.html
115. Nepal PM Inaugurates $76 Million International Airport Built By China," *NDTV*, May 16, 2022, https://www.ndtv.com/world-news/nepal-pm-inaugurates-76-million-international-airport-built-by-china-2981185
116. "Huge investment in Gautam Buddha International Airport in peril as airline companies struggle to sustain business," *My Republica*, December 29, 2022, https://myrepublica.nagariknetwork.com/news/huge-investment-in-gautam-buddha-international-airport-at-peril-as-airline-companies-struggle-to-sustain-business/
117. Yubaraj Ghimire,"Chinese-built Nepal airport gets first foreign flight 6 months after launch," *The Indian Express*, https://indianexpress.com/article/world/chinese-built-nepal-airport-gets-first-foreign-flight-6-months-after-launch-8678495/
118. Statement by Rt. Hon. Prime Minister Mr. Pushpa Kamal Dahal 'Prachanda' At the Joint Press Meet between the Prime Ministers of Nepal and India, *Ministry of Foreign Affairs, Nepal*, June 1, 2023, https://mofa.gov.np/statement-by-the-rt-hon-prime-minister-at-the-joint-press-meet/
119. Sangam Prasain, "Air route pledge old wine in new bottle, experts say," *The Kathmandu Post*, June 2, 2023, https://kathmandupost.com/money/2023/06/02/air-route-pledge-old-wine-in-new-bottle-experts-say#:~:text=India%20has%20agreed%20to%20allow,is%20too%20low%20for%20jets
120. Chen Song, "China, Nepal and the neighbourhood," *The Kathmandu Post*, December 6, 2023, https://kathmandupost.com/columns/2023/12/06/china-nepal-and-the-neighbourhood
121. "Can India's attempts to squeeze Chinese investment in Nepal's energy sector succeed?" *Global Times*, June 10, 2023, https://www.globaltimes.cn/page/202306/1292320.shtml
122. "Nepal cancels Budhi Gandaki hydropower project with China," *New Indian Express*, November 13, 2017, https://www.newindianexpress.com/world/2017/nov/13/nepal-cancels-budhi-gandaki-hydropower-project-with-china-1700057.html
123. Prithvi Man Shrestha,"Company unable to start Budhi Gandaki hydel project work," *The Kathmandu Post*, November 5, 2022, https://kathmandupost.com/money/2022/11/05/company-unable-to-start-budhi-gandaki-hydel-project-work
124. Ashima Sharma, "How Hydropower is Shaping the Geopolitics of South Asia," *Power Technology*, December 7, 2023, https://www.power-technology.com/features/how-hydropower-is-shaping-the-geopolitics-of-south-asia/#?cf-view
125. Mukesh Pokhrel,"Analysis-Nepal hydropower drive puts India over China, but what's the risk?" *Reuters*, May 24, 2023, https://www.reuters.com/article/nepal-hydro-india-china-idUSL8N36K1Z3
126. The Procedure for approval and facilitating Import/Export(Cross Border) of Electricity, *Ministry of Power, GOI*, February 26, 2021, https://cea.nic.in/wp-content/uploads/2021/03/Amendment_1_Designated_Authority_Procedure_2023.pdf

127. "Indian to develop two hydropower plants in Nepal as China abandons projects," *Business Standard*, August 21, 2022, https://www.business-standard.com/article/current-affairs/indian-to-develop-two-hydropower-plants-in-nepal-earlier-quit-by-china-122082100114_1.html
128. Kedar Shiwakoti, "China's Sinohydro likely to be awarded $165 million Tamakoshi V hydro project," *The Kathmandu Post,* February 28, 2023, https://kathmandupost.com/money/2023/02/28/china-s-sinohydro-likely-to-be-awarded-165-million-tamakoshi-v-hydro-project
129. Manas Joshi, "Chinese Ambassador to Nepal Attempts to Downplay India-Nepal Ties," *Wion*, September 5, 2023, https://www.wionews.com/south-asia/chinese-ambassador-to-nepal-attempts-to-downplay-indo-nepal-ties-632623
130. "Xi Jinping Meets Prachanda, Assures China Will Boost Border Infrastructure," *Business Standard,* January 13, 2024, https://www.business-standard.com/world-news/xi-jinping-meets-prachanda-assures-china-will-boost-border-infrastructure-123092301003_1.html
131. "Nepal, China Sign 12 Agreements During PM Prachanda's Visit to Beijing," *Indian Express*, September 25, 2023, https://indianexpress.com/article/world/nepal-china-sign-12-agreements-during-pm-prachandas-visit-to-beijing-8955838/
132. "Joint Statement Between the People's Republic of China and Nepal," *China.org.cn,* September 26, 2023, http://www.china.org.cn/china/Off_the_Wire/2023-09/26/content_116710098.htm
133. "Nepal-China Deals," *The Himalayan Times*, September 27, 2023, https://thehimalayantimes.com/opinion/editorial-nepal-china-deals
134. "China Visit Highly Successful, PM Dahal Asserts," *Nepal News*, September 30, 2023, https://nepalnews.com/s/nation/china-visit-highly-successful-pm-dahal-asserts
135. Anil Giri, "7 years since transit deal with China, no shipment has moved," *The Kathmandu Post*, April 22, 2023, https://kathmandupost.com/national/2023/04/22/7-years-since-transit-deal-with-china-no-shipment-has-moved
136. United Nations High Commissioner for Refugees, "*Country Strategy Evaluation: Nepal*" (Geneva: UNHCR, 2023), p. vii, https://www.unhcr.org/sites/default/files/2023-05/unhcr-nepal-country-strategy-evaluation-report.pdf
137. Edward Wong, "Nepal Is Said to Detain 41 Tibetans Traveling to India," *Times of India,* November 17, 2016, https://www.nytimes.com/2016/11/18/world/asia/nepal-detains-tibetans-traveling-to-india.html; also see "Tibetan Refugees Caught Between China, Nepal: Report," *Times of India*, January 29, 2023, https://timesofindia.indiatimes.com/world/rest-of-world/tibetan-refugees-caught-between-china-nepal-report/articleshow/97412180.cms?from=mdr
138 "Joint Statement Between the People's Republic of China and Nepal," *Ministry of Foreign Affairs, People's Republic of China,* October 13, 2019, HTTPS://WWW.FMPRC.GOV.CN/MFA_ENG/GJHDQ_665435/2675_665437/2752_663508/275_663510/202406/T20240607_11411413.HTML; "Joint Statement between the People's Republic of China and Nepal," *Ministry of Foreign Affairs, People's Republic of China*, September 26, 2023, https://www.mfa.gov.cn/eng/zy/gb/202405/t20240531_11367499.html#:~:text=The%20two%20sides%20recalled%20President,high%2Dlevel%20exchanges%20to%20the

139. "Joint Statement Between the People's Republic of China and Nepal," *Ministry of Foreign Affairs, the People's Republic of China,* October 13, 2019, https://www.fmprc.gov.cn/mfa_eng/wjdt_665385/2649_665393/201910/t20191013_679597.html ; also see "Joint Statement between the People's Republic of China and Nepal," *Ministry of Foreign Affairs, the People's Republic of China,* September 26, 2023, https://www.fmprc.gov.cn/eng/wjdt_665385/2649_665393/202309/t20230926_11150168.html
140. "Joint Statement between the People's Republic of China and Nepal," *Ministry of Foreign Affairs, the People's Republic of China,* September 26, 2023, https://www.fmprc.gov.cn/eng/wjdt_665385/2649_665393/202309/t20230926_11150168.html
141. "Chinese 'Regional Approach' Apparent in Tibet Delegation's Gandaki Outreach," *The Kathmandu Post,* November 12, 2023, https://kathmandupost.com/national/2023/11/12/chinese-regional-approach-apparent-in-tibet-delegation-s-gandaki-outreach
142. "China, Nepal Upgrade Ties," *Xinhua,* October 13, 2019, http://www.xinhuanet.com/english/2019-10/13/c_138467267.htm
143. "Full Text of Xi's Signed Article on Nepali Newspapers," *Xinhua,* October 11, 2019, http://www.xinhuanet.com/english/2019-10/11/c_138463745.htm
144. "Joint Statement between the People's Republic of China and Nepal," *Government of Nepal - Ministry Of Foreign Affairs,* September 26, 2023, https://mofa.gov.np/joint-statement-between-the-peoples-republic-of-china-and-nepal/#:~:text=The%20Nepali%20side%20reiterated%20its,is%20against%20"Taiwan%20independence."
145. "Joint Statement between the People's Republic of China and Nepal," *CGTN,* December 3, 2024. https://news.cgtn.com/news/files/Joint-Statement-between-the-People%27s-Republic-of-China-and-Nepal.pdf
146. K.P. Sharma Oli. *X.com,* December 4, 2024. https://x.com/kpsharmaoli/status/1864224992017437128?s=61.
147. Giri, Anil, "Nepal and China Sign Framework for BRI Cooperation in Beijing," *Kathmandu Post,* n.d. https://kathmandupost.com/national/2024/12/05/nepal-and-china-sign-framework-for-bri-cooperation-in-beijing.
148. Ghimire, Yubaraj, "Nepal Rules out Loans for BRI Projects: Foreign Minister," *The Indian Express,* November 30, 2024. https://indianexpress.com/article/india/nepal-rules-out-loans-for-bri-projects-foreign-minister-9699396/
149. Sood, Amy, "Nepal's PM Oli Strengthens Ties with China, Bypassing India," *South China Morning Post,* December 5, 2024. https://www.scmp.com/week-asia/politics/article/3289559/nepals-oli-signs-belt-and-road-deal-china-amid-debt-fears-and-india-tensions.
150. Anshuman Behera & M. Mayilvaganan (2021), "The China–Nepal–India Economic Corridor: wishful thinking or regional aspiration beyond rhetoric?" *The Round Table,* 110:2, pp. 250-263.

8

From Inauspicious Beginnings to a Calibrated Engagement

Introduction

During the discussions on Bangladesh's membership to the United Nations (UN) in August 1972, the Chinese representative forcibly argued against the admission: "Before the true implementation of the relevant United Nations resolutions, and pending a reasonable settlement of the issues between India and Pakistan and between Pakistan and Bangladesh, Bangladesh is not at all qualified to be admitted into the United Nations, and the Security Council's consideration of Bangladesh's application for membership in the United Nations is entirely out of the question..."[1] In fact, throughout the liberation struggle in East Bengal and the 1971 India-Pakistan war, China was not favourably inclined towards the formation of Bangladesh. During that phase, China viewed the Bangladesh liberation struggle as a Soviet stratagem. At the December 1971 emergency session of the United Nations (UN), the Chinese representative criticised the Soviet Union for using Bangladesh's liberation struggle "to gain control over the subcontinent, encircle China and strengthen its position in contending with other superpowers for world hegemony."[2]

Subsequently, when Bangladesh applied for UN membership, the Chinese representative used 'the decisive and well-publicised veto' to deny membership, which was also the first veto exercised by China since its admission to the United Nations.[3] Before joining the UN, China often criticised the international body for failing to act in a non-partisan manner.[4] Within a few months after taking the seat at the United Nations Security Council (UNSC), China deployed the veto to protect the interest of a strategic partner and demonstrated its utility to Pakistan. During the deliberations, China's intervention suggested that there were a few critical reasons for vetoing the proposal to grant UN membership to Bangladesh. First, the trial of 90,000 Pakistani prisoners of war (PoW) for violation of human rights would severely dent the image of Pakistan in the eyes of the international community. Second, China was not comfortable with the prospect of India using the PoW as a bargaining chip during the negotiations on the Jammu and Kashmir dispute. If India were to gain a geopolitically advantageous position in Jammu and Kashmir, it would have a long-term impact on the Chinese interests in the region. Third, China harboured deep suspicion over Soviet intentions in the subcontinent.[5] As the Chinese representative noted, "Soviet imperialism is playing the most insidious role in the development of the situation on the South Asian subcontinent ...[and is seeking to] ... to further control India and Bangladesh and infiltrate into regions of the Indian Ocean and the South Asian subcontinent so as to expand its spheres of influence and hegemony."[6] The Chinese veto had less to do with the merits of Bangladesh's candidature and more with its perceptions of the security dynamic on its western border and in the Indian Ocean Region (IOR).

By releasing the prisoners of war without significant concessions from Pakistan on Kashmir, it appears that Indian leadership prioritised ensuring a 'normal-state' status with UN membership for Bangladesh. Such prioritisation may have stemmed from a calculation that the delay in the UN membership could have prevented Bangladesh from accessing support from international institutions, and the general uncertainty would have had a deleterious impact on its economy. However, it should be noted that India lost the leverage to use the surrendered soldiers to extract concessions on Kashmir from Pakistan. Bangladesh also refrained from pressing the issue of placing the surrendered Pakistani soldiers on trial for committing gruesome violent acts on the people of Bangladesh before and during the liberation struggle. It must have been painful for many leaders of Bangladesh to see Pakistani soldiers walking free without even a trial for the crimes committed in Bangladesh. However, it appears that they may have prioritised Bangladesh becoming a regular member of the United Nations. Bangladesh became a member of the United Nations in 1974, only after India released the Pakistan POWs, and the prospect of prosecuting Pakistani military members for genocide also faded away. The need to prosecute the perpetrators of genocide continues to animate political discussions in Bangladesh.

Despite such inauspicious beginnings, the Bangladesh-China bilateral relationship quickly improved. The diplomatic relations between Bangladesh and China were established in 1976, a year after Sheikh Mujibur Rahman, the leader of the liberation struggle, was assassinated. In 1977, his successor, General Zia Ur Rehman, visited China, making him the first head of state from Bangladesh to do so. The establishment of diplomatic relations and the visit to Beijing indicated a shift in the foreign policy away from India and towards Pakistan and China. For China, which opposed the formation of Bangladesh, the uptick in relations with Bangladesh was rather quick. The defence cooperation between China and Bangladesh commenced immediately after establishing the bilateral relationship. China supplied Bangladesh with second-hand fighter aircraft, trainer aircraft, and, in early 1980-1981, with Type-59 battle tanks. The defence partnership was subsequently scaled up with the sale of the Type-05/Jianghu-1 Frigate in 1988-1989.[7]

Geography and Asymmetries

Having played an important role in the formation of Bangladesh, India had to contend with the growing presence of China in India's immediate neighbourhood. India's relations with Bangladesh were impacted by power asymmetries.[8] Despite cultural affinities, there were areas of discord in the India-Bangladesh relationship that emanated from the latter's unique geographic location. While Bangladesh figures in the top 10 countries in terms of population, it has a relatively smaller population compared to India, and to compound anxieties, except for a small land border with Myanmar, India surrounds Bangladesh on all three sides. India also has a dominant presence in the Bay of Bengal region. In addition, the boundary settlement between India and Bangladesh was hindered by the fact that there were large enclaves on both sides of the border. Therefore, the boundary settlement mandated the exchange of territory and generated concerns about the exchange of populations. Given that India had coalition governments with wafer-thin majorities in Parliament, resolving the boundary dispute in the larger interest of the bilateral relationship against the wishes of provincial leaders proved to be a difficult enterprise. The boundary demarcation was settled after India had a government with a majority in Parliament.

The porous border between India and Bangladesh meant there was a constant movement of people and other resources, such as cattle, sometimes outside the legal framework. A punitive response to such movements meant India had to contend with widespread outrage in Bangladesh. So, the conditions—open border and movement of people—which facilitated cooperation between Bangladesh and Indian leaders during the liberation struggle also became the cause of friction between the two countries. Other areas of disagreement stemmed from the fact that the two countries had to share essential resources, such as water. In the subcontinental context, where rivers overflow during certain months and dry up during other seasons, water-sharing tends to be highly contentious. Even within India, the relationship between state (provincial) governments tends to nosedive during lean seasons when water from rivers needs to be shared. Unsurprisingly, India-Bangladesh relations were negatively impacted by disagreements about water-sharing agreements.

Despite such challenges, both countries constructed a strategic partnership, which is reflected in their official documents, such as the bilateral joint statements. Similarly, China and Bangladesh also refer to their relationship as a strategic partnership. While some may argue that strategic partnership is mainly economic, Joyeeta Bhattacharjee notes that there is a sizeable section in "Bangladesh that supports stronger ties with China to counterbalance India.[9]" As noted, such perceptions seem to be emanating from Bangladesh's geographic location and power asymmetries. Consequently, there was always an element of concern among some sections that the asymmetry in power with India would work to the disadvantage of Bangladesh. Therefore, for many in Bangladesh, the relationship with China is also an attempt to address power asymmetry in the Indian subcontinent. In addition to some convergence in strategic outlook, China and Bangladesh are working towards developing a robust economic partnership. In the Chinese vision, Bangladesh is a critical hub in the regional economic corridor. China has made persistent efforts to operationalise the Bangladesh, China, India, and Myanmar Economic Corridor (BCIM). China's 2015 Vision and Actions on Jointly Building Silk Road Economic Belt referred to the BCIM as a corridor closely related to the Belt and Road Initiative (BRI).[10]

While China-Bangladesh economic relations developed over the decades, they witnessed an uptick after Chinese President Xi Jinping visited Dhaka in 2016.[11] Approximately 26 Memorandum of Understandings (MoUs) were signed between the two countries, which promised investment of USD 24 billion.[12] During the visit, both countries decided to "elevate the bilateral relations to the Strategic Partnership of Cooperation", and the bilateral engagement under the rubric of the BRI picked up momentum.[13] In terms of investment, even before participating in the BRI, Bangladesh did attract the attention of Chinese investors. However, the attention did not translate into massive investments in Bangladesh's manufacturing sector. Of course, there were a few instances when Bangladesh figured in the expansion/relocation of various firms from East Asian countries, including China. For example, a 2010 *New York Times* report cited that Li & Fung, a Hong Kong-based textile company that supplied to Walmart and Liz Claiborne, scaled up its production in Bangladesh by as much as 20 per cent in one year.[14]

Textile Industry: The Engine of Economic Growth

Over the years, the Ready-Made-Garment (RMG) has emerged as an engine of economic growth in Bangladesh. The RMG industry in Bangladesh is cotton-dependent, and domestic production does not meet the demand. The domestic shortfall was addressed by imported raw materials. According to the USDA Foreign Agricultural Service Report in 2021-22, India accounted for 35 per cent, Brazil accounted for 13 per cent, and the US accounted for 7 per cent of cotton imports from Bangladesh.[15]

Despite the dependence on large-scale import of cotton, Bangladesh has certain advantages in terms of RMG manufacturing. Saon Ray notes that Bangladesh's RMG manufacturing model is different from that of India.[16] While Indian manufacturers of garments are involved from design to distribution, Bangladesh "followed the Original Equipment Manufacturing OEM model [which implies that manufacturing is done] according to customer specifications and design, and in many cases use raw materials specified by the customer."[17] In addition to the OEM model of garment manufacturing, lower wages also contribute to the low cost of apparel. Pankaj Vashisht and Nisha Rani, in their 2019 working paper, calculated that the "labour cost of producing a cotton shirt in the USA is around 7 dollar while the unit labour cost of producing the same shirt in India is around 50 cent, while in Bangladesh it is only 22 cents."[18] On the other hand, there is criticism that the low cost of Bangladeshi apparel comes at human costs in terms of meagre wages and the absence of safety and social security in the workplace.[19]

The RMG manufacturing firms in Bangladesh have also leveraged the Least Developed Country (LDC) status under the World Trade Organisation (WTO) provisions, which enable Duty-Free-Quota-Free (DFQF) market access in developed countries. Incidentally, India was the 'first developing country to extend the DFQF facility to all LDCs', including Bangladesh.[20] As a consequence, the apparel exports from Bangladesh made steady gains in the Indian market. It is estimated that garment exports from Bangladesh to India witnessed a 69.58 per cent increase in 2021-2022. Reportedly, Bangladeshi apparel tends to be cheaper than Indian products by almost 30 per cent.[21]

The apparel exports from Bangladesh dominate the world market. As per the WTO Statistical Review 2023, Bangladesh was the world's third-largest clothing exporter. In 2022, the top three exporters of clothing in the world were China (USD 182 billion), the EU (USD 156 billion), and Bangladesh (USD 45 billion).[22] In 2023, compared to China, Bangladesh exported more to the EU in terms of volumes of garments.[23] The total merchandise exports of Bangladesh in 2022 was around USD 54.69 billion,[24] which implies that clothing exports accounted for over 82 per cent of the total merchandise exports. Such dominance of one commodity in the overall export suggests that Bangladesh's economy would be vulnerable to shocks (such as rapid technological changes) in the textiles/clothing sector, which will negatively impact the overall economy during a crisis.

Further, Bangladesh's clothing exports are directed more towards the US and European markets. Bangladesh has a preferential tariff structure in its trade with China through the WTO's LDC scheme and under the Asia-Pacific Trade Agreement (APTA).[25] However, the Bangladesh's RMG industry has challenges in accessing Chinese markets. First, China is a textile and clothing manufacturing powerhouse, and its domestic companies control considerable market space. Second, with growing income levels, Chinese consumers seem more interested in high-end designer clothing products. Third, while China imports some RMG, Bangladesh must contend with other competitors, such as Vietnam. Fourth, as the footprint of Bangladesh's textile industry in the international market increases, there will be increased demands to ensure that workers get fair wages and better working conditions, which may increase the cost of production.[26] Such an increase in the cost of production, in turn, may make it difficult to access the Chinese market. The Chinese government in 2020 announced zero tariffs on 97 per cent of items imported from Bangladesh, which was subsequently increased to 98 per cent in 2022.[27] However, these tariff concessions did not substantially increase RMG exports from Bangladesh to China. Many of Bangladesh's ready-made garment product lines are already availing concessional tariffs under WTO LDC and APTA provisions. There was an anticipation that firms from other countries may invest in Bangladesh to leverage concessionary tariffs to access China's RMG market. However, such expectations have yet to be translated into reality.

At the moment, Bangladesh's RMG industry is not China-dependent. The raw materials, such as cotton, are imported from India and other countries. The RMG export market predominantly comprises the US, Europe, and other developed countries. There is anticipation that some Chinese firms may move production units to Bangladesh to take advantage of labour costs. Reports in 2023 indicated that a Chinese textile firm—SSH (BD) Sustainable Fashion Co—signed an agreement to invest USD 24.05 million in the Uttara Export Processing Zone in Bangladesh.[28] In the same year, another Chinese textile firm signed an agreement with the Bangladesh Export Processing Zones Authority to invest USD 60.85 million.[29] Many such investments will enable Chinese firms to export to developed countries by circumventing tariff and non-tariff barriers that Western countries and the United States impose on China. It is still uncertain whether China would prompt its industries to relocate specifically to Bangladesh to mitigate the negative consequences of ongoing trade friction with the West. Such relocation would require that the Chinese firms in Bangladesh have easy access to energy and other transport infrastructure.

Energy: Diversified Collaborations

Given that Bangladesh is a fast-growing economy, it would require an uninterrupted supply of energy resources to power its economy. Further, in democracies in the subcontinent, regular electricity supply is also an electoral issue. Quite often, many governments lose their legitimacy and consequently pay heavy electoral prices if they fail to quickly improve the electricity supply for domestic and agricultural purposes. In Bangladesh, resolving the energy crisis is critical to power the economy and for governments to gain electoral legitimacy. Domestic resources such as natural gas are insufficient to meet the electricity requirements.[30] Bangladesh has experienced a prolonged energy crisis, and therefore, the quick operationalisation of power plants under the BRI assumed considerable importance.

Some of the established Chinese firms, such as China North Industries Group Corporation Limited (NORINCO Group), have invested in the energy sector in Bangladesh. NORINCO International Cooperation Ltd formed a joint venture in collaboration with Rural Power Company Limited in 2017.[31] A year later, the joint venture concluded a deal to establish a 1320 MW (2×660) thermal power plant in Patuakhali district. Because of the pandemic and related challenges, the plant's operationalisation was delayed. The power plant, with 2x660 MW, may go on stream sometime in 2025. Once operationalised, the Patuakhali power plant "will be ultra-critical, meaning it will have higher boiler pressures and burn at higher temperatures."[32] According to officials associated with the project, the power plant will cost around USD 2 billion, about 30 per cent of which will be equity investment, and "70 per cent will be a loan from the Chinese EXIM Bank with a 4 per cent interest rate and a repayment period of 15 years with a five-year grace period."[33]

The 1320 MW Payra Power Plant was constructed by Bangladesh-China Power Company Limited (BCPCL), a joint-venture company comprising North-West Power Generation Company Limited and the China National Machinery Import & Export Corporation (CMC).[34] The Payra project is categorised as 'ultra-supercritical technology', functions on imported coal, and has a supply agreement with Indonesia's PT Bayan.[35] With a 660 MW power plant starting commercial operations, the Payra power plant was partially operationalised in May 2020.[36] The Payra plant was completely operational in 2022, and it supplied electricity to the regions in the southern part of the country. While the BCPCL operated the plant, the CMC paid for the coal and was reimbursed by the Bangladeshi government within six months.[37] Initially, transporting coal to the power plant was costly due to the absence of a deep-sea port with adequate logistics.[38] In mid-2023, the Payra power plant was completely shut down for a few weeks because the government could not pay the coal dues to the CMC.[39] Due to the shutdown, large parts of the country experienced blackouts during peak summer.

In addition to logistics and high input costs, some of the energy projects with Chinese investment encountered a few other challenges. In 2013, the Bangladesh Power Development Board (BPDB) issued a letter of intent for constructing a coal-fired power plant to a joint-venture company, which included S. Alam Group and SEPCO III Electric Power Construction Corporation (subsidiary of Power China Resources) and HTG Group, China.[40] The power plant was to come up near Banshkhali near Chittagong.

Because of its location, it became known as the Banshkhali power plant, and the project involved two coal-fired power plants (2× 660 MW). In 2016, a Power Purchase Agreement was signed between BPDB and the joint venture.[41] However, contrary to the envisaged implementation roadmap, the project faced many challenges. Like in other parts of the world, Chinese investment activity encountered resistance from local communities in Bangladesh. In 2016, the construction of the power plant ran into trouble with clashes between the supporters and opponents of the project, resulting in four deaths, and the protest continued the next year.[42] An important contributor to the protests was the land acquisition process, with allegations of lack of adequate compensation and forcible property eviction.[43] These challenges resulted in considerable delays, and the government threatened to scrap the project. In July 2020, the news reports indicated that the joint venture paid Tk 2 billion (an amount equal to a one-year default) as a penalty for failing to supply electricity, and consequently, the project received an extension till 2022.[44] The power plant started commercial operations in 2023.[45]

There is no denying that China is a major investor in Bangladesh's power sector. However, Dhaka has made efforts to ensure that there are diverse players in its energy sector. Russia's Rosatom is involved in the construction of two civilian nuclear power plants (2×1200 MW) in Rooppur, located about 160 kms from Dhaka.[46] In her interactions with Rosatom officials, Bangladeshi Prime Minister Sheikh Hasina referred to the civilian nuclear cooperation as an extension of "material and moral support during our fight for independence in 1971" and commended Russia for "rebuilding Bangladesh destroyed by the war after we gained independence."[47] A year later, Russia, Bangladesh, and India signed an agreement that enabled Nuclear Power Corporation of India Limited to participate in the construction of nuclear reactors.[48] By mid-2020, Russia-Bangladesh nuclear cooperation matured with agreements for long-term support to "operate, maintain, and repair the units", as well as support the plants with "nuclear fuel for their entire life cycle."[49] A year later, in October 2021, during the installation programme of the reactor pressure vessel of the Rooppur Nuclear Power Plant (RNPP) project, Prime Minister Hasina stated that "if the government can build another nuclear power plant in the country, there'll be no problem in power supply."[50] In the last quarter of 2023, the RNPP received the first shipment of nuclear fuel from Russia for its operations.[51] In a video message, Russian President Putin promised to assist "throughout the entire life cycle of the nuclear project."[52] The project implementation is taking place under the guidance of the International Atomic Energy Agency (IAEA), and its Director General noted that "Bangladesh stands as a success story for newcomer countries in nuclear power development, advancing its program under IAEA's guidance."[53] In mid-2024, there were reports that Dhaka requested Russian assistance to build two more units at the RNPP.[54] The cooperation between Bangladesh and Russia resulted from the former seeking to diversify its energy sources and the latter's attempt to scale up its civil nuclear engagements across the world. Instead of approaching China, Bangladesh chose Russia for civil nuclear cooperation. Russia's track record of building nuclear power plants in the neighbourhood and the fact that it is a strategic partner of India may have influenced Bangladesh's decision.

With Japan, the Bangladesh government has developed a robust economic and developmental partnership. In 2017, a Japanese consortium and the Coal Power Generation Company Bangladesh Ltd signed an agreement to construct the 1200 MW (600MW x 2) Matarbari Ultra Super Critical Coal-Fired Power Project.[55] Two years later, Japan International Cooperation Agency (JICA) agreed to provide a soft loan (¥ 143.127 billion) for the Matarbari project, with an annual interest of 0.90 per cent and a repayment period of 30 years with a 10-year grace period.[56] The project is part of an integrated approach for the overall development of the region, and it has other components, such as a port and river dredging to facilitate the easy flow of vessels.[57] In 2024, there were concerns the coal import ban may impact the operations of the Matarbari Power Project.[58] In September 2024, the Power and Energy Adviser, Muhammad Fouzul Kabir, reportedly criticised the Matarbari power plant as a luxury project without significant benefit to common people.[59]

American multinational conglomerates have also been active in Bangladesh. In 2019, it was announced that the Summit Group and General Electric will co-develop the Meghnaghat II gas power plant (583 MW) at Meghnaghat near Dhaka.[60] American and Indian firms are also collaborating in the Bangladesh power sector. In July 2020, General Electric worked with Reliance Bangladesh LNG and Power to install "its Advanced Gas Path technology for the upcoming 718 MW plant in Meghnaghat near Dhaka."[61] India's National Thermal Power Corporation and BPDB formed a joint venture for the construction of the Maitree Super Thermal Power Project (1,320 mw) at Rampal in Bangladesh.[62] Siemens AG also signed a MOU in

2019 for the construction of a 3,600 MW Liquefied Natural Gas (LNG)-based power plant.[63]

It is important that the Bangladesh government carefully evaluates the contracts pertaining to energy-related projects. According to reports, some contracts mandate that the Bangladesh government would pay according to the power plants' installed generation capacity and not based on actual supply.[64] In other words, if the plants face closure or if there is less than optimal utilisation due to a lack of demand, the government will pay for the full plant capacity.[65] In fact, during the 2023 Payra power plant shutdown, reports suggested that the "government may have to pay Tk 7.66 crore in capacity payments per day."[66] Given the number of power plants that are getting operationalised, there are also concerns that the cost of coal imports may increase steadily in the near future. There are also concerns about ensuring a steady supply of gas for gas-fired power plants as well.[67]

China and Bangladesh also cooperate in other energy-related initiatives, such as the Power Grid Network Strengthening project.[68] Further, Bangladesh does not have a deep sea port and therefore, depends on smaller tankers to offload crude oil from bigger tankers that are parked in the deep seas.[69] A Chinese firm was involved in constructing a single-point mooring (SPM) system at Chattogram Port, which allows oil unloading through pipelines from large oil tankers parked offshore.[70]

The Digital Silk Road and Financial Corridors

Over the past decade, Bangladesh has started scaling up its digital infrastructure. Under the rubric of Digital Bangladesh, the government sought to use Information and Communication Technologies (ICT) to advance human resource development, connect citizens, improve pro-poor service delivery, and enhance overall business operations.[71] The Digital Bangladesh vision proposed to mainstream "ICT as a pro-poor tool to eradicate poverty, establish good governance, ensure social equity through quality education, healthcare and law-enforcement for all and prepare people for climate change."[72] The digital initiative was mainly in consonance with other digital governance initiatives in various countries of the Indian subcontinent. With the growth of ICT, many governments across Asia proactively deployed new digital technologies to facilitate pro-poor governance and strengthen the services sector of the economy. The deployment of digital technology for better governance has also become a much-discussed issue in election campaigns across various countries.

Even in Bangladesh, the Awami League's election manifestos promised digital technologies to improve governance in the country.[73]

The Digital Bangladesh programme made significant progress in terms of connecting government offices with an integrated network, increasing the density of optical fibre cables, mobile phones, and internet subscribers.[74] Chinese firms have become important players in working with the Bangladesh government to operationalise its digital vision. The China Railway International Group (CRIG) was involved in building the Info-Sarker Phase III Project in terms of construction, equipment installation, and personnel training.[75] The Info-Sarker project created an ICT network infrastructure to connect all government agencies/departments to the grassroots.[76] The CRIG signed an agreement with the Department of Information and Communication Technology to "expand broadband internet across the country, including far-flung areas."[77] Further, the ZTE Corporation constructed the Tier IV National Data Center (NDC). With its data processing infrastructure, the centre is designed to ensure safety/reliability and "will be at the heart of building Digital Bangladesh."[78] However, in 2023, there were reports that the functioning of the NDC faced a few challenges due to a few software and hardware issues.[79]

Bangladeshi state-run cellphone operator, Teletalk, enlisted Huawei to upgrade its network infrastructure, particularly in rural areas.[80] The government agencies (Bangladeshi Government's Posts & Telecommunications Division) participated in 5G trials conducted by a consortium of companies led by Huawei.[81] In late 2023, Huawei's bid was the lowest in the Bangladesh Telecommunication Company Ltd (BTCL) tender for developing a nationwide 5G infrastructure.[82] *The Daily Star*, referring to the BTCL's 5G project, reported that "from notifying the financial opening date to awarding the tender, everything proceeded at an unprecedented pace ... and series of rule violations have raised concerns about transparency and fairness in the awarding of the work."[83]

In the financial sector, Huawei worked with bKash, a subsidiary of BRAC Bank, to facilitate monetary transactions using mobile wallets in rural areas.[84] During the pandemic crisis, the bKash was used for international remittances by expatriate Bangladeshis and "remittance disbursement through bKash shot up by 111% year-on-year in 2021."[85] In 2023, bKash and Huawei signed a MoU to deepen their fintech cooperation.[86] In 2024, Huawei also initiated the 'China-Bangladesh Fintech Exchange Program', which was aimed at improving the skillset of experts working in the financial sector of Bangladesh.[87] Overall, Chinese fintech firms are working with partners in the private sector and the government to consolidate their presence in digital and financial infrastructures.

In Pakistan and Bangladesh, Chinese financial firms acquired a stake in the Dhaka Stock Exchange (DSE) in early 2018. However, unlike in the case of Pakistan, Indian officials made strenuous efforts to outbid the Chinese firms for acquiring a 25 per cent stake in the DSE Index. However, the bid by the Chinese firms (Shenzhen Stock Exchange and Shanghai Stock Exchange) was reportedly much higher than the bid by the Indian consortium and was, therefore, shortlisted.[88] The Chinese media reported that the acquisition of the stake in the DSE was aimed at strengthening the Bangladesh-China-India-Myanmar Economic (BCIM) Corridor.[89] It was also noted that the acquisition was aimed at promoting "the joint construction of the China-Bangladesh 'financial corridor'."[90] A year later, the DSE and Shenzhen Stock Exchange launched new online platforms to facilitate Chinese investment in prospective Bangladeshi firms, especially small and medium-sized firms.[91] By acquiring a stake in the DSE, the Chinese stock exchanges sought to create platforms that could facilitate financial flows and investments between the two countries.[92] However, there is an opinion that the DSE partnership with the Chinese firms did not result in 'any significant technology transfer' due to challenges, such as lack of familiarity with the Chinese language-based technologies.'[93] The DSE partnership with the Chinese firms reportedly encountered challenges due to "the COVID-19 pandemic, the instability of the stock market in Bangladesh, and the lack of interest of the DSE members."[94] In 2024, because of political instability, the performance of the DSE was less than satisfactory.[95]

Transport Corridors

In addition to building digital networks, China emerged as a big player in building hard infrastructure, such as transport networks. After the completion of the bridge in Pirojpur, approximately eight Bangladesh-China friendship bridges were constructed by 2022.[96] Joint venture companies comprising Chinese and Bangladeshi firms were awarded the expansion of the Dhaka-Sylhet Highway contract.[97] The Dhaka Bypass Highway is being constructed by the Sichuan Road and Bridge (Group) Company Limited.[98] The bypass highway would connect 'industrial belts around Dhaka with seaport at Chattogram' and would decongest Dhaka as it would bypass the capital city.[99]

The Dhaka-Ashulia Elevated Expressway was conceptualised in 2015, and after much delay, Bangladesh Prime Minister Sheikh Hasina inaugurated the construction work for a 24 km Dhaka-Ashulia Expressway in November 2022, which would be funded by Chinese loans.[100] In 2023, while Phase one of the expressway was inaugurated, the expressway encountered numerous challenges associated with land acquisition and removal of pre-existing structures, including high-voltage power lines.[101] In mid-2023, the Asian Infrastructure Investment Bank (AIIB) approved a loan of USD 75 million for the construction of the Rampura-Amulia-Demra Expressway, which is being implemented by a Chinese consortium under public-private-partnership (PPP) mode.[102] After some delays, in 2024, the work on the Dhaka-Ashulia Expressway gained momentum, and there is anticipation that the Rampura-Amulia-Demra Expressway will be completed by 2026.[103]

There were instances when attempts were made to credit China for transport infrastructure that it did not finance. For instance, in June 2022, the Padma multi-purpose road and rail bridge was inaugurated. The Padma Bridge was constructed at an estimated cost of USD 3.6 billion and is estimated to benefit nearly 30 million people living in the southwestern part of Bangladesh.[104] The Bangladesh-China Silk Road Forum and the Chinese Embassy reportedly organised an event, which termed the Padma Bridge as an "example of Bangladesh and China cooperation under the Belt and Road Initiative".[105] As a consequence, there were sporadic reports, much to the dismay of Bangladeshi authorities, that the Chinese financed the bridge construction.[106] While a Chinese firm constructed the bridge, Bangladesh did not receive any external assistance under the BRI initiative, and it was a self-financed project.[107] In fact, many multilateral agencies refused to fund the project. Prime Minister Sheikh Hasina, at the inauguration of the bridge, stated, "I have no complaints against anyone, but I reckon those who opposed the Padma Bridge construction plan and called it a 'pipe dream' lack self-confidence … I hope this bridge will boost their confidence."[108] Hasina's statement was also a response to the World Bank's reported apprehensions regarding the project's feasibility. It was indeed a herculean task that the Bangladesh government pulled off by arranging for finances and completing the project.

Re-evaluations: Debt Trap or a Treasure Trove?

China is also involved in numerous other projects, such as the Bangabandhu Sheikh Mujib Rahman Tunnel, built under the Karnaphuli River.[109] Similarly,

Chengdu Engineering Corporation Limited constructed a wind farm in the Khurushkul area of Cox's Bazar.[110] These diverse projects demonstrate the growing profile of Chinese engagement in Bangladesh. With an increase in the number of projects and financial commitments, the Bangladesh government has often sought to renegotiate and revise the costs of various projects. Reportedly, such projects include the Joydebpur-Ishwardi dual-gauge double-line rail and the Akhaura-Sylhet dual-gauge rail, with which the Chinese government subsequently expressed reluctance to move forward.[111]

There were also instances when the Bangladesh government cancelled a few projects. In July 2021, Bangladesh cancelled the Sonadia deep-sea port project, in which the Chinese firms were very eager to invest. The project's cancellation undermined the Chinese attempts to gain a foothold in a strategically important port. The cancellation addressed concerns in the neighbourhood that the project could be used to bolster the Chinese naval presence in the Bay of Bengal.[112] The experiences from the neighbourhood have informed the decision as well. As Sahidul Hasan Khokon noted, "While Sri Lanka had to lease out Hambantota to the Chinese once they failed to pay up [the debt], Prime Minister Sheik Hasina was courageous enough to scrap the China-proposed Sonadia deep sea port."[113] According to reports, the Bangladesh government also negotiated hard on a tied loan from China for the Rajshahi Water Supply and Sewerage Authority (WASA) Surface Water Treatment Plant.[114] These developments suggest a growing caution in Bangladesh's approach to accessing Chinese loans for the BRI and other projects. In fact, Bangladesh Foreign Minister Mustafa Kamal, in an interview with *The Financial Times*, had remarked, "Whichever projects are essential and are in process and will pay off as fast as possible, we're only taking care of those ... to other projects, we're saying, no thank you."[115]

This cautious approach could be witnessed in the operationalisation of a few other projects as well. For example, the Bangladesh Power Development Board (BPDB) and China Huadian Hongkong Company Limited (CHDHK) agreed in 2018 to set up a power plant (1,320 megawatts) at Moheshkhali Island near Cox's Bazar.[116] The project would cost over USD 2 billion, and CHDHK and BPDB would each hold a 50 per cent stake.[117] The project did not make much headway. In 2023, there were reports that the government was planning to operationalise LNG and solar-based power plants instead of coal-based power plants.[118] The projects with Chinese involvement encountered a few other challenges, such as protests at the construction sites. In April 2021, five people died, and numerous others were injured at the construction site of a power plant being built by a Chinese firm near Chittagong.[119] The clashes erupted over a dispute about delayed payment of wages and long working hours.[120] Subsequently, there were reports that the power plant was not adhering to prescribed environmental standards.[121]

During the pandemic, Bangladesh procured vaccines from various companies, such as AstraZeneca, Johnson & Johnson, Moderna, Pfizer, and Sinopharm.[122] Reportedly, a large number of Sinopharm vaccines were administered to Bangladeshi nationals. However, there were concerns about a lack of transparency in determining the pricing of the Sinopharm vaccines, and there was an opinion that Chinese firms may be charging higher prices.[123] There were news reports that Dhaka has signed a non-disclosure agreement with Sinopharm, which further raised questions regarding transparency in the procurement and administration of the vaccine.[124] However, a senior government official disclosed that Bangladesh is 'purchasing the vaccine at USD 10 per dose'.[125] The disclosure generated considerable discussion on the prices at which other South Asian governments purchased vaccines from China. With China reportedly getting upset with the pricing disclosure, Bangladesh Foreign Minister AK Abdul Momen expressed "sorrow to the Chinese ambassador for the incident."[126]

In addition to transparency issues, the question of whether Bangladesh's economic engagement with China is resulting in equitable outcomes needs to be evaluated. In the recent past, there has been a significant improvement in Bangladesh's total exports. In 2017-2018, the total exports amounted to USD 41.25 billion, which increased to USD 63.05 billion in 2022-2023.[127] Such an upward trend in total exports happened despite the pandemic and disruption to global supply chains. While China has emerged as Bangladesh's largest trade partner, a disaggregated analysis shows that China benefitted substantially more than Bangladesh. Despite the provision of zero tariffs on 98 per cent of products, there was no uptick in Bangladesh's exports to China. Bangladesh's imports from China, which were USD 9.6 billion in 2015-2016, increased to USD 22.90 billion in 2022-2023.[128] On the other hand, Bangladesh's exports to China, which were USD 808 million in 2015-2016, declined to USD 715.37 million in 2023-2024.[129] These numbers show that Bangladesh has a considerable imbalance in bilateral trade with China. In the coming years, Bangladesh may find it difficult to sustain such high levels of trade deficit with China, and both countries will have to work together to ensure that the trade relationship results in equitable outcomes. On the other hand, the top five export partners of Bangladesh in 2022 were the United States of America, Germany, the United Kingdom, Spain, and France.[130]

It is possible to contend that the Chinese investments are enabling Bangladesh to export more to other countries. However, in terms of the cumulative amount of FDI equity inflow between July 2006 and June 2023, the top five leading investors in Bangladesh are the US, Singapore, China, the Netherlands, and the United Kingdom (UK).[131] The 2023-204 data also indicates that the United Kingdom, China, the Republic of Korea, India, Norway, and Singapore were the leading investors in the country.[132]

As with other South Asian countries, debt-related anxieties also figure prominently in the conversation on BRI-related projects in Bangladesh. According to the Statistics Department of Bangladesh Bank, the "total external debt at end June 2024 was USD 103.79 billion", with loans from the multilateral agencies accounting for 40.80 per cent and loans from bilateral partners accounting for about 27.20 per cent[133] For Bangladesh, in Financial Year 2022, after the World Bank, the Asian Development Bank (ADB), and Japan, China has emerged as the fourth- largest source of foreign loans.[134] However, Ahsan H Mansur points out that the loans from multilateral agencies and Japan have an "extended repayment period, while the timeframe is quite shorter for the Chinese loans ... [which] is creating pressure for repayment."[135] It appears that Bangladesh's debt to China, at the moment, does not appear to be as serious a challenge as it was in the case of Sri Lanka. Nonetheless, many observers would continue to monitor the debts to China, given the reported higher interest rates and short repayment timeframes. Responding to the growing discussion on debt to China, an official of the Embassy of China in Bangladesh commented that "the China-Bangladesh economic and trade cooperation is a "treasure trove" with many touching stories, exemplary projects and remarkable achievements to be explored."[136]

Conclusion: Navigating External and Domestic Faultlines

The birth of Bangladesh was preceded by unprecedented violence against innocent civilians, and some of the big powers questioned its very existence. The economic prospects of the infant nation looked very bleak. In the early 1970s, there was a perception that Bangladesh would remain an "international basket case".[137] There was no denying the fact that the economy of Bangladesh was in tatters, and the country struggled to find its feet on the international platforms. However, a few years later, in 1981, referring to the USD 10 billion in foreign aid that was pledged, a news report noted that "unlike some foreign-aid sinkholes, Bangladesh is generally credited with doing a good job of ploughing its aid into worthwhile economic development projects – most notably, improved agricultural production."[138] In fact, the economic performance of Bangladesh in the first two decades of the new millennium was better than some of its fellow travellers in the subcontinent. According to World Bank estimates, Bangladesh's GDP achieved an annual growth rate of 7 per cent during 2010-2020, and it reduced poverty "from 44.2 per cent in 1991 to 14.8 per cent in 2016/17."[139] In 2018, Bangladesh clocked a 7.86 per cent GDP growth rate, and in 2019, it increased to 8.15 per cent.[140] Subsequently, while many economies experienced negative economic growth during the pandemic, Bangladesh registered a 3.4 per cent growth rate.[141] From approximately USD 138 billion in 2010, the GDP increased to USD 481.86 billion in 2024.[142] However, in 2023, Bangladesh had to encounter an energy crisis because of an increase in crude oil prices, and the volatility in the global economy also had a negative impact on its economy. In 2024, Bangladesh encountered significant political turmoil, resulting in the collapse of Sheikh Hasina's government and the installation of an interim government led by Chief Adviser Muhammad Yunus. The political instability had a negative impact on Bangladesh's economic performance.

While the Chinese economic presence has significantly increased in South and Southeast Asia, India is also scaling up its economic interactions in the immediate neighbourhood. There is growing friction between India and China, which is evident in the border skirmishes between the two countries. Bangladesh has a defining presence abutting the narrow Siliguri corridor that provides access to northeastern parts of India. In such a context, India closely monitored Dhaka's increasing engagement with Beijing, particularly in initiatives such as the Teesta River project. In October 2022, the Chinese ambassador to Bangladesh visited the Teesta Barrage area and suggested that both countries work on the management of the Teesta River Comprehensive Management and Restoration Project, which would involve "dredging, land reclamation, erosion control and river bank protection".[143] The project's objective is to "force the flow of the river into a narrow main channel", and there are apprehensions that such an endeavour may not be viable given that the river is more than five kilometres wide in many places.[144] It is well known that India and Bangladesh are yet to conclude the Teesta River water-sharing agreement. The Chinese involvement in the river project may create a wedge between the two South Asian neighbours. If the project does materialise, as the Chinese ambassador envisaged, it will result in the presence of Chinese technical personnel very close to the strategically important Siliguri corridor in India. Therefore, it is not surprising that the statement by the Chinese ambassador elicited considerable attention in India.

Further, the defence partnership over the decades matured with the supply of a wide array of military equipment from China to Bangladesh. According to SPIRI's data, between 2015 and 2023, Bangladesh was the second major recipient of China's arms transfers.[145] In addition to procuring two submarines, the Bangladesh government, with assistance from the Chinese government, constructed its first submarine base in Cox's Bazar.[146] The construction of the submarine base with Chinese assistance right at the mouth of the Bay of Bengal raised concerns in the region. If the Chinese submarines use the base, then it would fundamentally alter the maritime security dynamic not only in the Bay of Bengal but also in the wider Indian Ocean Region (IOR). To assuage such apprehension, the Bangladeshi leaders sought to ease the concerns of the regional players by noting that the Chinese submarines would not be given access to the base.[147] In July 2024, Sheikh Hasina visited China, and both countries upgraded their bilateral relationships to "a comprehensive strategic cooperative partnership."[148] During the visit, both sides agreed on 21 MOUs and decided to work on seven more projects, including digital technologies, sanitation, and infrastructure projects.[149] However, Sheikh Hasina cut short her visit and returned to Dhaka, which gave rise to considerable speculation that she was unhappy with the scale of Chinese assistance and inadequate interactions with Chinese President Xi Jinping.[150]

Economic engagement with China has enabled Bangladesh to circumvent US sanctions on Russia. The Bangladesh Central Bank permitted the authorised dealer banks to settle cross-border transactions in the Chinese Yuan Renminbi (CNY).[151] According to some estimates, Bangladesh could settle approximately 10 per cent of its import bill using the Chinese currency.[152] Bangladesh also agreed to the Chinese proposal of preferential buyer credit loans in CNY. There was an opinion in Bangladesh that taking Chinese loans in CNY would reduce the transactional costs associated with dollar payments.[153] Overall, the density of Bangladesh's transactions in CNY has increased, and it is using it as leverage in its relationship with Russia. As noted, because of the sanctions, Bangladesh found it challenging to pay Russia in USD for its assistance in building the nuclear power plant. To overcome such challenges, Bangladesh paid about USD 300 million in CNY to Russia through China's Cross-border Interbank Payment Scheme.[154]

While bilateral economic interactions have increased, China has had to contend with Bangladesh's calibrated foreign policy that sought to consolidate diversified economic partnerships. India-Bangladesh relations are deep-rooted and multi-dimensional. Sheikh Hasina was considered as a friend of India. During her tenure, the activities of various Indian insurgent groups operating out of Bangladesh were curtailed. There was an opinion that she was able to prevent, if not eliminate, the radical religious organisations from capturing state power in the country. India-Bangladesh's trade and economic engagement witnessed steady improvement, and both are collaborating on various connectivity projects. Bangladesh has scaled up its cross-border railway interchanges with India. Further, new shipping ways and inland waterway networks between the two countries are being implemented. Today, India accesses its Northeastern states through Bangladesh with relatively greater ease. Towards the end of June 2024, the Prime Minister of Bangladesh, Sheikh Hasina, was on a state visit to India. During the visit, both sides agreed to initiate negotiations on a comprehensive economic partnership agreement , enhance cross-border rail links, foster greater maritime cooperation, further improve physical, digital, and energy connectivity networks, and expand cross-border trade and transit infrastructure.[155] The progress made on the conservation and management of the Teesta River was a significant positive outcome of the visit.[156] Reportedly, India made a better offer in terms of soft loans and the absence of stringent conditionalities for the Teesta River Comprehensive Management and Restoration project.[157] Bangladesh's preference to have India on board rather than, during Hasina's tenure, must have reduced the anxieties of Indian policymakers, given the project's geostrategic location.

Similarly, Japan is also consolidating its engagement with Bangladesh. Japan is providing assistance to a host of projects, such as Chattogram-Cox's Bazar Highway Improvement, Dhaka Mass Rapid Transit Development, strengthening of power grid and transmission lines, Jamuna Railway Bridge Construction, Matarbari Port Development and Matarbari Ultra Super Critical Coal-Fired Power Project.[158] The diversified economic engagement constituted an attempt by Bangladesh to maintain a balance in its external partnerships.

Despite attempts at diversified external partnerships, the growing economic interactions and the power asymmetry between Dhaka and Beijing often prompted conversations about China's possible influence on policymaking in Bangladesh. It appears that China did not view Bangladesh's attempts to build a robust relationship with diverse partners favourably. Beijing was apprehensive that Bangladesh might join the Quad framework. In May 2021, the Chinese ambassador in Dhaka, Li Jiming, cautioned the Bangladesh government against joining the Quad framework.[159] Li Jiming added that Bangladesh joining the Quad initiative would "substantially damage" the bilateral relationship with China.[160] In response, Bangladesh's foreign minister noted that as a sovereign country, Bangladesh is free to pursue policies in its interest. He added that Bangladesh always followed a non-aligned and balanced foreign policy.[161] However, there was considerable friction in the relationship between Bangladesh and the US during Sheikh Hasina's tenure.

The Dhaka-Washington bilateral relationship soured on issues related to democracy and human rights. In 2021, the US Department of the Treasury imposed sanctions on Bangladesh's Rapid Action Battalion for undermining the rule of law and human rights for their alleged extrajudicial killings and torture.[162] In 2023, the US State Department announced that it "has imposed or threatened to impose visa-related sanctions on individuals and institutions working to undermine democracy and human rights in Bangladesh."[163] In addition, Dhaka's policy towards Russia constitutes an additional dimension to the US-Bangladesh discord. Because of the Ukraine war, the US has imposed sanctions on Russia and urged other countries to do the same. However, Dhaka's relationship with Moscow has witnessed steady improvement. In November 2023, Russian naval ships visited Chittagong port, presumably the first such visit in over 50 years.[164] Amidst these developments, the US stated that the 2024 Bangladesh elections were 'not free and fair'.[165] For the Bangladeshi government, such a statement from the US amounted to interference in their country's internal matters.

Meanwhile, tensions were simmering between the students and the government in Bangladesh. In July and August, there were large-scale student protests against the reservation policy in government jobs that gave preference to the children of the martyrs of the 1971 liberation war. The student protests morphed into large-scale protests against Sheikh Hasina's government. The clashes between the police and the protesters resulted in hundreds of fatalities.

In the first week of August, with protesters threatening to take over the residence of Prime Minister Sheikh Hasina, she had to flee the country. The fall of Sheikh Hasina's government had a significant impact on the regional power dynamics.

There was considerable speculation that foreign powers were behind the collapse of Sheikh Hasina's government. Numerous reports speculated that the United States played an instrumental role in bringing down Sheikh Hasina's government. Sheikh Hasina's statement that she could have remained in power if she agreed to a United States base on St Martin's Island in the Bay of Bengal fueled further speculation on the role of external actors in the regime change.[166] Many in Bangladesh would say that such speculation had no basis as there was genuine domestic discontent with her governance. Given that China had reasonably good relations with opposition parties, such as the Bangladesh National Party, there was perhaps a little less anxiety in China about losing influence in Bangladesh. Some analysts pointed out that Pakistan and China stood to gain from the fall of Sheikh Hasina's government. The official statements from China demonstrated that Beijing had adopted a very cautious approach to the political turmoil in Bangladesh. At the same time, Sana Hashmi notes, many "commentators have subtly criticised Hasina's leadership...portrayed the military as the true defender of the people" and opined that the military's intervention was "a potentially positive development for Dhaka's future."[167]

As new political forces sought to acquire a dominant role in Bangladesh's politics, China had to consolidate old friendships and engage diverse political actors. China and Pakistan have always had friendly relations with the BNP. In December 2024, the Chinese ambassador in Dhaka, after interacting with the BNP Secretary General and other party members, expressed hope that Bangladesh would achieve stability under the leadership of the interim government and declared full support to the interim government.[168] In the same month, a delegation of Jamaat-e-Islami travelled to China at Beijing's invitation.[169] While the interim government welcomed the expression of support and greater engagement from the Chinese representatives, it will have to confront issues, such as interest rates and repayment of loans taken from China. In January 2025, the interim government's foreign adviser, Touhid Hossain, stated that he would discuss lower interest rates on loans and steps to encourage Bangladeshi exports with his Chinese counterpart.[170]

In addition to navigating US-China competition and India-China contestations, Bangladesh's external engagement navigated other faultlines, such as the sectarian violence in neighbouring Myanmar. In 2017, to escape the sectarian violence in the Rakhine state in Myanmar, the Rohingya Muslims fled in large numbers to Bangladesh. The Rohingya crisis generated significant deterioration in the bilateral relationship between the two countries. China actively engaged with Bangladesh and Myanmar on the Rohingya crisis. In 2023, the Chinese ambassador to Bangladesh highlighted Beijing's efforts at 'facilitating Bangladesh and Myanmar to repatriate the displaced people from Rakhine State'.[171] The same year, the Chinese foreign minister also reiterated that "China supports Myanmar in improving relations with Bangladesh, with related issues to be resolved through consultation ... [and] is ready to work with the two countries to expand practical cooperation among China, Myanmar and Bangladesh."[172] It should be noted that China has a significant influence in Myanmar because of years of economic and political engagement.

Notes

1. "Chapter VII: Practice Relative to Recommendations to the General Assembly Regarding the Membership in the United Nations," *United Nations*, https://www.un.org/en/sc/repertoire/72-74/72-74_07.pdf
2. William R Feeney, "Sino-Soviet Competition in the United Nations," *Asian Survey* 17, no. 9 (1977), pp. 811-812.
3. Samuel S Kim, "The People's Republic of China in the United Nations: A Preliminary Analysis," *World Politics* 26, no. 3 (1974), p.310. doi:10.2307/2009932.
4. Evan Luard, "China and the United Nations," *International Affairs* (Royal Institute of International Affairs 1944-) 47, no. 4 (1971), pp. 729-44. doi:10.2307/2625680.
5. "Security Council official records, 27th year, 1660th meeting," United Nations, August 25, 1972, New York, pp. 8-9.
6. Ibid.
7. "Transfers of major weapons: Deals with deliveries or orders made for 1976 to 1990 (China to Bangladesh)," *SIPRI Trade Registers*, http://armstrade.sipri.org/armstrade/page/trade_register.php
8. "Bangladesh: Ershad's Visit to the United States," *General CIA Records*, October 7, 1983, https://www.cia.gov/library/readingroom/document/cia-rdp85t00287r000800990001-7

9 Joyeeta Bhattacharjee, "Decoding China-Bangladesh Relationship," *Raisina Dialogue, ORF*, June 27, 2018, https://www.orfonline.org/expert-speak/41935-decoding-china-bangladesh-relationship/

10 "Vision and Actions on Jointly Building Silk Road Economic Belt and 21st-Century Maritime Silk Road," *National Development and Reform Commission,*

March 28, 2015, https://www.fmprc.gov.cn/eng/topics_665678/2015zt/xjpcxbayzlt2015nnh/201503/t20150328_705553.html

11. "Bangladesh, China Sign 26 Deals, MoUs," *The Daily Star*, October 14, 2016, https://www.thedailystar.net/country/bangladesh-china-sign-26-deals-mous-1298677.
12. Ruma Paul, "China Signs Deals Worth Billions with Bangladesh As Xi Visits," *Reuters*, October 13, 2016, https://www.reuters.com/article/us-bangladesh-china-idUSKCN12D34M.
13 "Bangladesh-China Joint Statement," *Press Release, Ministry of Foreign Affairs*, October 14, 2016, https://www.thedailystar.net/frontpage/bangladesh-china-joint-statement-1299403
14. Vikas Bajaj, "Bangladesh, With Low Pay, Moves In on China," *The New York Times*, July 16, 2020, https://www.nytimes.com/2010/07/17/business/global/17textile.html?searchResultPosition=3
15 Tanvir Mahmud, "Bangladesh: Cotton and Products Annual," April 5, 2023, Attaché Report (GAIN)-BG2023-0009, *USDA Foreign Agricultural Service*, https://fas.usda.gov/data/bangladesh-cotton-and-products-annual-7
16. Saon Ray, "What Explains India's Poor Performance in Garments Exports: Evidence from Five Clusters?" *ICRIER Working Paper 376*, May 2019, p.4, https://icrier.org/pdf/Working_Paper_376.pdf
17. Ibid.
18. Pankaj Vashisht and Nisha Rani, "Automation and Future of Garment Sector Jobs: A Case Study of India," *ICRIER Working Paper 385*, September 2019, p.12, https://icrier.org/pdf/Working_Paper_385.pdf
19. Sarah Butler, "Why are wages so low for garment workers in Bangladesh?" *The Guardian*, January 21, 2020, https://www.theguardian.com/business/2019/jan/21/low-wages-garment-workers-bangladesh-analysis
20. Asit Ranjan Mishra, "WTO Flags Poor Utilisation of India Scheme for Least Developed Countries," *Business Standard*, June 2, 2023, https://www.business-standard.com/economy/news/wto-highlights-poor-utilisation-of-india-s-preferential-scheme-for-ldcs-123060200896_1.html
21. "Cheaper Chinese Imports Via Bangladesh Harming Indian Textiles Industry," *Eurasian Times*, February 19, 2019, https://eurasiantimes.com/cheaper-chinese-imports-via-bangladesh-harming-indian-textiles-industry/
22. "World Trade Statistical Review 2023," *World Trade Organization*, (Geneva: WTO, 2023), p. 80.
23. "Bangladesh Overtakes China in RMG Export Volume to EU market," *Prothomalo*, August 7, 2023, https://en.prothomalo.com/business/local/sezxbykxua
24. "World Trade Statistical Review 2019," *World Trade Organization*, (Geneva: WTO, 2019).
25. Md Shahidullah Azim, "Could China be an alternative destination for Bangladesh's apparel?" *The Business Standard*, July 8, 2020, https://tbsnews.net/economy/rmg/could-china-be-alternative-destination-bangladeshs-apparel-103336
26. Pallab Bhattacherja and Md. Sajib Hossain, "Modernising RMG industry: Preparing for post-China era," *The Financial Express*, February 19, 2018, https://www.thefinancialexpress.com.bd/views/views/modernising-rmg-industry-preparing-for-post-china-era-1514304849

27. "Duty-free Treatment of 98% Tariff Lines Goods Originating from Bangladesh Exported to China Will Take Into Effect on September 1st, 2022," *Embassy of the People's Republic of China in the People's Republic of Bangladesh*, August 11, 2022, http://bd.china-embassy.gov.cn/eng/sghd/202208/t20220811_10741180.htm
28. "Chinese Firm to Invest $23.15 mn in Bangladesh's Textile Sector," *Fibre2Fashion*, September 23, 2023, https://www.fibre2fashion.com/news/textile-news/chinese-firm-to-invest-23-15-mn-in-bangladesh-s-textile-sector-290326-newsdetails.htm
29. "Chinese Firm Kaixi to Invest $61 Million in Bepza Economic Zone," *The Daily Star*, November 8, 2022, https://www.thedailystar.net/business/news/chinese-firm-kaixi-invest-61-million-bepza-economic-zone-3163681
30. "Why Bangladesh Probably Has a Lot of Unexplored Natural Gas Reserves," *The Business Standard*, September 19, 2023, https://www.tbsnews.net/thoughts/why-bangladesh-probably-has-lot-unexplored-natural-gas-reserves-702850
31. RPCL-NORINCO INTL Power Limited, 2018, http://www.rnpl.com.bd/about-us/company-profile/
32. Tang Shihua, "China's Norinco to Build 1,320 Megawatt Coal Power Plant in Bangladesh," *YiCai*, September 14, 2018, https://www.yicaiglobal.com/news/china-norinco-to-build-1320-megawatt-coal-power-plant-in-bangladesh
33. Asif Showkat Kallol and Asif Showkat Kallol, "Bangladesh-China plan 1,320-MW coal-based power plant in Patuakhali," *Dhaka Tribune*, November 5, 2017, https://www.dhakatribune.com/bangladesh/power-energy/2017/11/05/bangladesh-china-plan-1320-mw-coal-based-power-plant-patuakhali
34. "PAYRA 1320 MW Thermal Power Plant Project (1st & 2nd Phase)," *Bangladesh-China Power Company (Pvt) Limited*, https://www.bcpcl.org.bd/
35. "Bangladesh's imported coal burn continues to rise," *Argusmedia*, July 16, 2020, https://www.argusmedia.com/en/news/2123891-bangladcshs-imported-coal-burn-continues-to-rise
36. "Payra Power Plant Unit 1 Starts Commercial Operation," *Dhaka Tribune*, May 15th, 2020, Ohttps://www.dhakatribune.com/bangladesh/2020/05/15/payra-power-plant-unit-1-starts-commercial-operation
37. "Starved of Coal: Payra Power Plant May Shut for Weeks," *The Daily Star*, May 28, 2023, https://www.thedailystar.net/news/bangladesh/news/starved-coal-payra-power-plant-may-shut-weeks-3331081
38. Eyamin Sajid, "Unprepared Port Propels Payra Power's Imported Coal Price," *The Business Standard*, September 18, 2019, https://www.tbsnews.net/bangladesh/infrastructure/unprepared-port-propels-payra-powers-imported-coal-price
39. "Payra Coal Power Plant Resumes Production After 20 days," *The Business Standard*, June 25, 2023, https://www.tbsnews.net/bangladesh/energy/payra-coal-power-plant-resumes-production-after-20-days-656142
40. S.Alam Group, http://www.s.alamgroupbd.com/sag_Compa_PnE_d.php
41. "PDB, S Alam Group sign power purchase deal," *Daily Asian Age*, February 18, 2016, https://dailyasianage.com/news/11260/pdb-s-alam-group-sign-power-purchase-deal
42. Serajul Quadir, "Bangladesh Suspends Work on Power Plant after Demonstrators Killed," *Reuters*, April 7, 2016, https://www.reuters.com/article/us-bangladesh-

power-protest/bangladesh-suspends-work-on-power-plant-after-demonstrators-killed-idUSKCN0X40YW

43. Mowdud Rahman, "Coal Aggression and Civil Disobedience," *New Age*, December 17, 2017, http://www.newagebd.net/article/30622/coal-aggression-and-civil-disobedience
44. "S Alam Group pays Tk 2.0b as penalty for power plant delay," *The Finance Today*, July 13, 2020, https://www.thefinancetoday.net/article/business/12748/S-Alam-Group-pays-Tk-20b-as-penalty-for-power-plant-delay
45. "S Alam Group's 1,320 MW Banshkhali coal-fired power plant starts operation," *The Daily Star,* September 18, 2023, https://www.thedailystar.net/environment/natural-resources/energy/news/s-alam-groups-1320-mw-banshkhali-coal-fired-power-plant-starts-operation-3422091
46. "ROSATOM develops cooperation with the Republic of Bangladesh," *Communications Department of ROSATOM*, March 18, 2020, https://www.rosatom.ru/en/press-centre/news/rosatom-develops-cooperation-with-the-republic-of-bangladesh/
47. "Bangladesh hails Russia's Assistance in Building its First Nuclear Power Plant," *TASS*, November 30, 2017, https://tass.com/economy/978224
48. Dipanjan Roy Chaudhury, "India, Russia, Bangladesh sign tripartite pact for civil nuclear cooperation," *Economic Times*, March 1, 2018, https://economictimes.indiatimes.com/news/defence/india-russia-bangladesh-sign-tripartite-pact-for-civil-nuclear-cooperation/articleshow/63127669.cms?from=mdr
49. "Russia and Bangladesh Expand Nuclear Cooperation," *World Nuclear News*, March 18, 2020, https://world-nuclear-news.org/Articles/Russia-and-Bangladesh-expand-nuclear-cooperation
50. "Government considering 2nd nuclear plant in Bangladesh: PM", *The Daily Star*, October 10, 2021, https://www.thedailystar.net/news/bangladesh/governance/news/rooppur-plant-pm-launches-installation-reactor-vessel-2194946
51. "The first batch of nuclear fuel has been delivered to Rooppur NPP," *Rosatom*, October 5, 2023, https://www.rosatom.ru/en/press-centre/news/the-first-batch-of-nuclear-fuel-has-been-delivered-to-rooppur-npp/
52. Rezaul H Laskar, "Russia Supplies First Batch of Fuel for Bangladesh Nuclear Power Plant," *The Hindustan Times*, October 6, 2023, https://www.hindustantimes.com/world-news/russia-supplies-first-batch-of-fuel-for-bangladesh-nuclear-power-plant-101696595919141.html
53. Joanne Liou,"Behind the Scenes of an IAEA Mission: Integrated Regulatory Review Service (IRRS) in Bangladesh," *IAEA*, October 12, 2023, https://www.iaea.org/newscenter/news/behind-the-scenes-of-an-iaea-mission-integrated-regulatory-review-service-irrs-in-bangladesh
54 "Bangladesh considering two more nuclear units at Rooppur," *World Nuclear News,* April 3, 2024, https://www.world-nuclear-news.org/Articles/Bangladesh-considering-two-more-nuclear-units
55. Shahnaj Begum, "Matarbari Power: Plant Deal Signed with Sumitomo-led Consortium, *Energy Bangla*, June 28, 2017, https://energybangla.com/matarbari-power-plant-deal-signed-with-sumitomo-led-consortium/

56. "Signing of Japanese ODA Loan Agreement with Bangladesh: Contributing to Economic Revitalization by Responding to Rapidly Increasing Electricity Demand," *JICA,* July 1, 2019, https://www.jica.go.jp/english/news/press/2019/20190701_31_en.html
57. "Preparatory Survey on the Matarbari Port Development in People's Republic of Bangladesh – Final Report," *Japan International Cooperation Agency (JICA),* December 2018, https://www.jica.go.jp/english/our_work/social_environmental/id/asia/south/bangladesh/c8h0vm0000bikdzb-att/c8h0vm0000dqx3kr.pdf
58. Shamima Rita, "Matarbari power plant faces shutdown risk amid coal import ban," *Dhaka Tribune,* September 7, 2024, https://www.dhakatribune.com/bangladesh/power-energy/357632/matarbari-power-plant-faces-shutdown-risk-amid
59. "Matarbari Power Plant a 'luxury project': Energy adviser," *The Business Standard,* September 14, 2024, https://www.tbsnews.net/bangladesh/energy/matarbari-power-plant-luxury-project-energy-adviser-941421
60. "Summit signs 22-year PPA for upcoming 583 MW gas power plant; GE to co-develop plant in Bangladesh," *The General Electric,* March 18, 2019, https://www.ge.com/news/press-releases/summit-signs-22-year-ppa-upcoming-583-mw-gas-power-plant-ge-co-develop-plant
61. "GE to provide advanced gas turbine technology for Reliance Bangladesh LNG & Power Ltd.'s upcoming 718-MW gas power plant in Bangladesh," *General Electric,* July 31, 2020
62. "NTPC Arm Ties Up USD 1.6 Billion for Maitree Plant in Bangladesh," *The Economic Times,* April 11, 2017, https://economictimes.indiatimes.com/industry/energy/power/ntpc-arm-ties-up-usd-1-6-billion-for-maitree-plant-in-bangladesh/articleshow/58129032.cms?from=mdr
63. Reazul Bashar, "Bangladesh signs deal with Siemens for 3,600MW power plant," *BDNews24,* February 16, 2019, https://bdnews24.com/economy/2019/02/16/bangladesh-signs-deal-with-siemens-for-3600mw-power-plant
64. Azizur Rahman, "Country's biggest Payra coal fired power plant remains shut," *The Financial Express,* May 31, 2020, https://www.thefinancialexpress.com.bd/trade/countrys-biggest-payra-coal-fired-power-plant-remains-shut-1590923302
65. Ibid.
66. Hasan Arif, "Govt Likely to lose Tk200cr as Capacity Payment," *The Business Post,* June 6, 2023, https://businesspostbd.com/news/2023-06-06/govt-likely-to-lose-tk200cr-as-capacity-payment-2023-06-06
67. Azizur Rahman, "Bangladesh struggles to arrange gas supply for new gas-fired power plants," *S&P Global,* March 8, 2024, https://www.spglobal.com/commodity-insights/en/news-research/latest-news/lng/030824-bangladesh-struggles-to-arrange-gas-supply-for-new-gas-fired-power-plants
68. Press Release, Economic Relations Division, Ministry of Finance, June 7, 2020, https://erd.portal.gov.bd/sites/default/files/files/erd.portal.gov.bd/press_release/d5611f16_8fe1_4724_bd73_885b83798c5d/press%20notice%202.pdf
69. "Bangladesh Puts to use China-built Crude Oil Offloading Facility - Official," *Reuters,* December 8, 2023, https://www.reuters.com/business/energy/bangladesh-puts-use-china-built-crude-oil-offloading-facility-official-2023-12-08/

70. "Chinese-built SPM System Delivers Oil Successfully at Bangladesh's Chattogram Port," *Xinhua*, December 9, 2023, http://en.people.cn/n3/2023/1209/c90000-20108052.html
71. "Digital Bangladesh for Good Governance," Prime Minister's Office, *The Government of the People's Republic of Bangladesh,* 2010, p. 2.
72. Ibid.
73. M. Sirajul Islam and Åke Grönlund, "Digital Bangladesh – A Change We Can Believe In?" in *Electronic government and the Information Systems Perspective* (Toulouse: Springer, 2011), p. 107.
74. Shariful Islam, "Digital Bangladesh a Reality Now," *Dhaka Tribune*, July 11, 2018, https://www.dhakatribune.com/bangladesh/2018/07/11/digital-bangladesh-a-reality-now
75. "Bangladesh Info-Sarker Phase III Project is well underway," *China Railway International Group*, August 30, 2020, http://www.crecgi.com/en/?newshow/tp/502/id/41.html
76. "China-supported ICT Project Completed in Bangladesh," *Xinhua,* November 23, 2022, https://english.news.cn/20221123/0f739e2e5c0b4814b28ff3e9d902b647/c.html
77. "Govt signs deal with China CRIG to expand digital connectivity," *Bangladesh Sangbad Sangstha (BSS)*, October 28, 2018, http://www.bssnews.net/?p=111183
78. Jannatul Islam, "Exploring Bangladesh Data Centre," *Daily Sun*, September 30, 2019, https://www.daily-sun.com/printversion/details/427588/Exploring-Bangladesh-Data-Centre
79. "Bangladesh: National Data Centre Faces Failure Due to Pirated Chinese Software," *MSN*, June 9, 2023, https://www.msn.com/en-xl/africa/zimbabwe/bangladesh-national-data-centre-faces-failure-due-to-pirated-chinese-software/ar-AA1cM2YV
80. "Chinese Tech Giant Huawei to Upgrade Bangladeshi State-Run Cellphone Operator's Network," *Xinhua*, April 18, 2023, https://english.news.cn/20230418/d943511d0c1649bdaf096015237d046a/c.html
81. The consortium of companies included Bharti Airtel Limited (India), Axiata Group Berhad (Malaysia), and NTT DoCoMo Inc. (Japan); see Zhang Shasha, "Huawei Demonstrates 5G Technology in Bangladesh," *Beijing Review*, July 25, 2018, http://www.bjreview.com/Business/201807/t20180726_800136580.html
82. "Huawei Awarded BTCL's 5G Readiness Project," *The Business Standard*, November 30, 2023, https://www.tbsnews.net/bangladesh/huawei-awarded-btcls-5g-readiness-project-749398
83. Mahmudul Hasan, "BTCL's Tk 463Cr 5G Project: Huawei's Win Marred by Controversy," *The Daily Star*, December 3, 2023, https://www.thedailystar.net/business/news/btcls-tk-463cr-5g-project-huaweis-win-marred-controversy-3484306
84. Wang Hai and Du Juan, "On the Money in Bangladesh with bKash," *Huawei*, March 2018, https://www.huawei.com/en/huaweitech/publication/winwin/30/on-the-money-in-bangladesh-with-bKash
85. "Remittance through bKash surges in April," *The Financial Express*, May 7, 2020, https://thefinancialexpress.com.bd/economy/remittance-through-bkash-surges-

in-april-1588839418 ; also see "Remittance Through bKash Doubles in 2021," *The Business Standard*, October 15, 2022, https://www.tbsnews.net/economy/remittance-through-bkash-doubles-2021-514250

86. "Huawei and bKash Sign MoU to Strengthen Partnership," *New Age*, March 31, 2023, https://www.newagebd.net/article/198215/huawei-and-bkash-sign-mou-to-strengthen-partnership
87. "Huawei Announces Key Initiatives for Bangladesh," *Dhaka Tribune,* December 15, 2024, https://www.dhakatribune.com/business/368199/huawei-announces-key-initiatives-for-bangladesh
88. Arafat Kabir, "Why Are China And India Vying For A Stake In Bangladesh's Stock Market?" *Forbes*, February 15, 2018, https://www.forbes.com/sites/arafatkabir/2018/02/15/china-and-india-are-vying-for-control-of-bangladeshs-stock-market/#7835a701416e
89. 深交所、上交所联合收购孟加拉国达卡证券交易所25%股权, *Xinhuanet*, May 4, 2018, http://www.xinhuanet.com/fortune/2018-05/04/c_1122783392.htm
90. 深沪交易所联合体与孟加拉国达卡交易所签署股权收购协议, *People's Daily*, May 14, 2018, http://world.people.com.cn/n1/2018/0514/c1002-29989946.html
91. "Wooing Chinese investors: SZSE keen to introduce new index at DSE," *Dhaka Tribune*, November 7, 2019, https://www.dhakatribune.com/business/stock/2019/11/07/wooing-chinese-investors-szse-keen-to-introduce-new-index-at-dse
92. Niaz Mahmud, "DSE, SZSE Joint Initiative: V-Next Launched to Facilitate Chinese Investment," *The Dhaka Tribune*, October 8, 2019, https://www.dhakatribune.com/business/stock/2019/10/08/dse-szse-joint-initiartive-v-next-launched-to-facilitate-chinese-investment
93. Ahsan Habib, "3yrs Into Chinese Partnership: DSE yet to see notable tech advancement," *The Daily Star,* February 24, 2021, https://www.thedailystar.net/business/news/dse-yet-see-notable-tech-advancement-2050145
94. Niaz Mahmud, "High Hopes Turn Into Despair," *The Business Post*, October 29, 2023, https://businesspostbd.com/stocks/high-hopes-turn-into-despair
95. Syful Islam, "Bangladesh stocks sink amid economic and political uncertainty," *Nikkei Asia,* November 29, 2024, https://asia.nikkei.com/Business/Markets/Equities/Bangladesh-stocks-sink-amid-economic-and-political-uncertainty
96. Foisal Ahmed, "8th Bangladesh-China Friendship Bridge to Open in Sept," *The Business Standard*, August 20, 2022, https://www.tbsnews.net/bangladesh/infrastructure/8th-bangladesh-china-friendship-bridge-open-sept-480414
97. Abdul Rab Siddiqi, "Bangladesh highway contract awarded," *Worldhighways*, November 15, 2022, https://www.worldhighways.com/wh8/news/bangladesh-highway-contract-awarded#:~:text=A%20major%20Bangladesh%20highway%20contract%20has%20been%20awarded.&text=A%20major%20highway%20contract%20in,of%20Road%20Transport%20and%20Bridges; also see "Dhaka-Sylhet Highway: RHD Hires 2 Sino-Bangla JVs to Expand 35km Portion," *The Daily Star*, February 8, 2023, https://www.thedailystar.net/news/bangladesh/transport/news/dhaka-sylhet-highway-rhd-hires-2-sino-bangla-jvs-expand-35km-portion-3242556

98. "Chinese-built highway enters new construction phase in Bangladesh," *Xinhua*, December 5, 2023, https://english.news.cn/20231205/1b7d3082da4e45b8b10fa6c551ff0053/c.html
99. "China mega-tech drives Bangladesh mega highway," *Global Times*, January 23, 2022, https://www.globaltimes.cn/page/202201/1246628.shtml
100. "Bangladeshi PM inaugurates construction of mega China-funded elevated expressway project," *Xinhua*, November 12, 2022, https://english.news.cn/20221112/0affc60c073c43a7925a0cef26da7dac/c.html#:~:text=DHAKA%2C%20Nov.%2012%20(Xinhua,km%20Dhaka%2DAshulia%20Elevated%20Expressway; also see Rejaul Karim Byron, Tuhin Shubhra Adhikary, "Dhaka-Ashulia Elevated Expressway: Time, Cost gallop even before Work Starts," *The Daily Star*, https://www.thedailystar.net/news/bangladesh/transport/news/dhaka-ashulia-elevated-expressway-time-cost-gallop-even-work-starts-3031881
101. "Dhaka-Ashulia Expressway," *The Financial Express*, October 22, 2023, https://thefinancialexpress.com.bd/editorial/dhaka-ashulia-expressway
102. Jahidul Islam, "AIIB approves $75m for Rampura-Demra Expressway, but Design not Finalised yet," *The Business Standard*, July 24, 2023, https://www.tbsnews.net/bangladesh/infrastructure/aiib-approves-75m-rampura-demra-expressway-design-not-finalised-yet-670438
103. "Work on Dhaka-Ashulia expressway slowly gaining momentum," *Somoy News*, June 22, 2024, https://en.somoynews.tv/news/2024-06-22/sxNK76Mz
104. Faika Mahboob, "How the Country Paid for the Dream Project," *The Business Standard*, December 10, 2023, https://www.tbsnews.net/bangladesh/transport/how-country-paid-dream-project-169891
105. "Bangladesh Says Padma Bridge Not Part of China's Belt and Road Initiative," *NDTV*, June 18, 2022, https://www.ndtv.com/world-news/bangladesh-says-padma-bridge-not-part-of-chinas-belt-and-road-initiative-3077945
106. Ibid.
107. Sumeda, "Explained | Bangladesh's Padma Bridge and why Dhaka clarified reports linking it with China," *The Hindu*, June 28, 2022, https://www.thehindu.com/news/international/bangladesh-padma-bridge-dhaka-clarified-reports-linking-china-bri/article65566871.ece
108. "PM Sheikh Hasina Inaugurates Bangladesh's Longest Rail-Road Bridge," *NDTV*, June 25, 2022, https://www.ndtv.com/world-news/prime-minister-sheikh-hasina-inaugurates-bangladeshs-longest-rail-road-padma-bridge-3099246
109. Mohammad Suman, "Bangabandhu Tunnel: A New Era Dawns in Road Communication," *The Daily Star*, October 28, 2023, https://www.thedailystar.net/news/bangladesh/transport/news/bangabandhu-tunnel-new-era-dawns-road-communication-3454496
110. "China-Constructed Wind Power Plant Feeds Bangladesh Grid, Facilitates Green Development," *Global Times*, May 29, 2023, https://www.globaltimes.cn/page/202305/1291550.shtml
111. Syful Islam, "Belt and Road Projects in Limbo as Bangladesh Cuts Budgets," *Nikkei Asia*, June 28, 2021, https://asia.nikkei.com/Spotlight/Belt-and-Road/Belt-and-Road-projects-in-limbo-as-Bangladesh-cuts-budgets#:~:text=DHAKA%20

%2D%2D%20China%20has%20withdrawn,feared%20to%20be%20in%20limbo.

112. Rejaul Karim Byron, "Plans for a deep seaport at Sonadia nixed," *The Daily Star*, September 1, 2020, https://www.thedailystar.net/business/news/plans-deep-seaport-sonadia-nixed-1953857
113. Sahidul Hasan Khokon, "Why Bangladesh is not in crisis like Sri Lanka," *India Today*, August 18, 2022, https://www.indiatoday.in/news-analysis/story/why-bangladesh-is-not-in-any-crisis-like-sri-lanka-1989682-2022-08-18
114. Syful Islam, "Bangladesh Urges China Loan Tweaks Amid Scrutiny of BRI Bailouts," *Nikkei Asia*, April 1, 2023, https://asia.nikkei.com/Politics/International-relations/Bangladesh-urges-China-loan-tweaks-amid-scrutiny-of-BRI-bailouts2
115. Benjamin Parkin, "Bangladesh's Finance Minister Warns on Belt and Road Loans from China," *The Financial Times*, August 9, 2022, https://www.ft.com/content/65632129-dd75-4f23-b9c4-9c0496840a54
116. "Bangladesh Signs Deal with China to Set up Coal-Based Power Plant," *Reuters*, May 7, 2018, https://www.reuters.com/article/us-china-bangladesh-power/bangladesh-signs-deal-with-china-to-set-up-coal-based-power-plant-idUSKBN1I80XR
117. "Joint venture agreement signed for Chittagram project," *China Daily*, December 27, 2018, http://www.chinadaily.com.cn/m/powerchina/2018-12/27/content_37420141.htm
118. Saifuddin Saif, "Maheshkhali Now Hopes to be a Green Power Hub," *The Business Standard*, June 27, 2023, https://www.tbsnews.net/bangladesh/energy/maheshkhali-now-hopes-be-green-power-hub-657410
119. "5 Killed During Protest at China-backed Bangladesh Power Plant," *VOA news*, April 19, 2021, https://www.voanews.com/a/south-central-asia_5-killed-during-protest-china-backed-bangladesh-power-plant/6204762.html
120. "Five people killed as police fire at protesting workers in Bangladesh," *Reuters*, April 17, 2021, https://www.reuters.com/world/asia-pacific/police-kill-4-clashes-with-bangladesh-workers-chinese-backed-power-plant-2021-04-17/
121. "China-backed coal plant in Bangladesh is accused of omitting critical pollution data," *The Print*, June 15, 2021, https://theprint.in/world/china-backed-coal-plant-in-bangladesh-is-accused-of-omitting-critical-pollution-data/678585/
122. "9 mln people to get COVID-19 vaccine doses in week-long campaign in Bangladesh," *News.CN*, November 30, 2022, https://english.news.cn/asiapacific/20221130/ec5a9f37a6254b6cbf1dd198a0974d81/c.html
123. "Purchase of Sinopharm Vaccine: Price disclosure sparks confusion," *The Daily Star*, May 28, 2021, https://www.thedailystar.net/frontpage/news/purchase-sinopharm-vaccine-price-disclosure-sparks-confusion-2100137; also see "Expensive Chinese vaccines stir hornet's nest in Bangladesh, Sri Lanka," *Times of India*, June 1, 2021, https://timesofindia.indiatimes.com/world/south-asia/expensive-chinese-vaccines-stir-hornets-nest-in-bangladesh-sri-lanka/articleshow/83138927.cms; also see "Chinese vaccine to cost Bangladesh double of India's Oxford-AstraZeneca," *Business Standard*, May 29, 2021, https://www.business-standard.com/article/current-affairs/chinese-vaccine-to-cost-bangladesh-double-of-india-s-oxford-astrazeneca-121052900820_1.html

124. "Dhaka signs non-disclosure vaccine deal with Beijing," *The Daily Star*, May 18, 2021, https://www.thedailystar.net/frontpage/news/dhaka-signs-non-disclosure-vaccine-deal-beijing-2093977
125. "Purchase of Sinopharm Vaccine: Price Disclosure Sparks Confusion," *The Daily Star*, May 28, 2021, https://www.thedailystar.net/frontpage/news/purchase-sinopharm-vaccine-price-disclosure-sparks-confusion-2100137
126. "China Annoyed that Price of Sinopharm was Publicised by Bangladesh: Foreign Minister," *The Daily Star*, June 5, 2021, https://www.thedailystar.net/coronavirus-deadly-new-threat/news/china-annoyed-price-sinopharm-was-publicised-bangladesh-foreign-minister-2105065?fbclid=IwAR1EpGwCDjSCKDgq6DNvfu7AFjfwnKqKug5hUdnul_fS9vIXKbNz9ldAP4Y
127. "Pocket Export Statistics FY 2022-2023," *Export Promotion Bureau Bangladesh*, September 14, 2023, https://epb.portal.gov.bd/sites/default/files/files/epb.portal.gov.bd/miscellaneous_info/8405d990_9311_41c8_88df_19b340500b6c/2023-09-24-06-29-863f5241834f4be6246cb372783329cc.pdf
128. "Trade Scenario Between Bangladesh and China," *Bangladesh Trade Portal, Ministry of Commerce, Government of the People's Republic of Bangladesh*, https://www.bangladeshtradeportal.gov.bd/index.php?r=site/display&id=1690; also see "FTA with China may cost Bangladesh Tk 15,000cr a year: study," *The Daily Star*, March 29, 2024, https://www.thedailystar.net/business/economy/news/fta-china-may-cost-bangladesh-tk-15000cr-year-study-3577116
129. "Trade Scenario Between Bangladesh and China," *Bangladesh Trade Portal, Ministry of Commerce, Government of the People's Republic of Bangladesh*, https://www.bangladeshtradeportal.gov.bd/index.php?r=site/display&id=1690
130. UNCTAD Stat, "General Profile: Bangladesh," United Nations Conference on Trade and Development, September 21, 2023, https://unctadstat.unctad.org/CountryProfile/GeneralProfile/en-GB/050/index.html
131. "Foreign Direct Investment and External Debt," *Statistics Department Bangladesh Bank*, January-June, 2023, https://www.bb.org.bd//pub/halfyearly/fdisurvey/foreign%20direct%20investment%20and%20external%20debt.pdf
132. "Foreign Direct Investment and External Debt," *Statistics Department Bangladesh Bank*, January-June, 2024, https://www.bb.org.bd//pub/halfyearly/fdisurvey/foreign%20direct%20investment%20and%20external%20debt-final.pdf
133. Ibid.
134. "World Bank, top foreign lender to Bangladesh in FY22," *Dhaka Tribune*, July 14, 2022, https://www.dhakatribune.com/business/274271/world-bank-top-foreign-lender-to-bangladesh-in
135. Jahangir Shah, "China Now 4th Largest Source of Foreign Loans in Bangladesh," *Prothom Alo*, December 20, 2023, https://en.prothomalo.com/business/local/gpgs2q1tgm#:~:text=Loan%20disbursement%20doubles%20in%20four%20years&text=But%20the%20disbursal%20bounced%20back,following%20year%20to%20%241.126%20billion.
136. Song Yang, "A Treasure Trove, not a 'Debt Trap'," *Dhaka Tribune*, May 5, 2023, https://www.dhakatribune.com/opinion/op-ed/310423/a-treasure-trove-not-a-%E2%80%98debt-trap%E2%80%99

137. Mohammad Rezaul Bari, "The Basket Case," *Forum,* March 2008, Volume 3, Issue 3, https://archive.thedailystar.net/forum/2008/march/basket.htm
138. Carol Honsa, "Since 1971 Famine, 'Basket Case' Bangladesh Tries Self-Help Agriculture," *The Christian Science Monitor*, April 28, 1981, https://www.csmonitor.com/1981/0428/042846.html
139. "The World Bank In Bangladesh," *The World Bank*, April 13, 2020, https://www.worldbank.org/en/country/bangladesh/overview
140. "GDP growth (annual%) - Bangladesh," *The World Bank*, 2020, https://data.worldbank.org/indicator/NY.GDP.MKTP.KD.ZG?end=2019&locations=BD&start=1995
141. "Bangladesh," *Asian Development Bank Outlook*, April 2023, https://www.adb.org/sites/default/files/publication/863591/ban-ado-april-2023.pdf.
142. "GDP, current prices," *International Monetary Fund,* https://www.imf.org/external/datamapper/NGDPD@WEO/BGD?zoom=BGD&highlight=BGD
143. "China-backed revival of Teesta River, shared by Bangladesh and India, moves forward amid geopolitical concerns," *SCMP*, November 5, 2022, https://www.scmp.com/economy/china-economy/article/3198483/china-backed-revival-teesta-river-shared-bangladesh-and-india-moves-forward-amid-geopolitical
144. "China Forcing Bangladesh into Unviable Project of Managing River Teesta," *The Sentinel,* March 24, 2023, https://www.sentinelassam.com/international/china-forcing-bangladesh-into-unviable-project-of-managing-river-teesta-642288
145. Pieter D. Wezeman, Aude Fleurant (et al.), "Trends in International Arms Transfers, 2019," *SIPRI Fact Sheet,* March 2020. p.2 , https://www.sipri.org/sites/default/files/2020-03/fs_2003_at_2019_0.pdf; also see Pieter D. Wezeman, Katarina Djokic, Dr Mathew George, Zain Hussain and Siemon T. Wezeman, "Trends In International Arms Transfers, 2023", *SIPRI Fact Sheet,* March 2023, https://www.sipri.org/publications/2024/sipri-fact-sheets/trends-international-arms-transfers-2023
146. Ali Asif Shawon, "Bangladesh's first submarine base starts operation Monday," *The Dhaka Tribune,* March 20, 2023, https://www.dhakatribune.com/bangladesh/307145/bangladesh%E2%80%99s-first-submarine-base-starts-operation
147. Kamran Reza Chowdhury, "China To Help Bangladesh Build Submarine Base, Senior Official Says," *Benar News*, September 12, 2019, https://www.benarnews.org/english/news/bengali/submarine-base-09122019155029.html
148. "Joint Statement between the People's Republic of China and The People's Republic of Bangladesh on the Establishment of Comprehensive Strategic Cooperative Partnership," *Bangladesh Ministry of Foreign Affairs,* July 10, 2024, https://mofa.gov.bd/site/news/495fa5ae-a161-448a-8d96-90e9607e90b6/Joint-Statement-between-the-People's-Republic-of-China-and-The-People's-Republic-of-bd-on-the-Establishment-of-Comprehensive-Strategic-Cooperative-Partnership
149. Ibid., also see "Bangladesh, China Sign 21 Agreements, MoU as PM Hasina Meets President Xi," *The Hindu,* July 10, 2024, https://www.thehindu.com/news/international/bangladesh-china-sign-21-agreements-mou-as-pm-hasina-meets-president-xi/article68390283.ece
150 Nisha Anand, "'Upset' Bangladesh PM Sheikh Hasina cuts short her China visit: Report," *Business Standard,* July 13, 2024, https://www.business-standard.com/

world-news/upset-bangladesh-pm-sheikh-hasina-cuts-short-her-china-visit-report-124071300384_1.html

151. "BB Allows Banks to Maintain China's Yuan Account to Settle Cross Border Transactions," *Prothom Alo*, September 16, 2022, https://en.prothomalo.com/business/local/3zuknelp3f#:~:text=%22To%20bring%20wider%20scope%2C%20it,a%20BB%20circular%20on%20Thursday.
152. Syful Islam, "Bangladesh aims for yuan trade as cushion against mighty dollar," *Asia Nikkei*, September 27, 2022, https://asia.nikkei.com/Economy/Bangladesh-aims-for-yuan-trade-as-cushion-against-mighty-dollar
153. Sakhawat Prince, "Bangladesh Opts for Yuan Loans for Cost Savings," *The Business Standard*, October 26, 2023, https://www.tbsnews.net/economy/bangladesh-opts-yuan-loans-cost-savings-726790
154. Mukul Sharma, "Chinese currency replaces dollar in Bangladesh's payments to Russia," *WION*, April 18, 2023, https://www.wionews.com/south-asia/chinese-currency-replaces-dollar-in-bangladeshs-payments-to-russia-583502
155. "India-Bangladesh Shared Vision for Future: Enhancing Connectivity, Commerce and Collaboration for Shared Prosperity," *Ministry of External Affairs, Government of India*, June 22, 2024, https://www.mea.gov.in/bilateral-documents.htm?dtl/37897/IndiaBangladesh+Shared+Vision+for+Future+Enhancing+Connectivity+Commerce+and+Collaboration+for+Shared+Prosperity
156. Ibid.
157. "Defence: Bangladesh Chooses India's Teesta River Project over China's Proposal," The *Financial Express*. January 14, 2025, https://www.financialexpress.com/business/defence-bangladesh-chooses-indias-teesta-river-project-over-chinas-proposal-3535629/
158. "Bangladesh," Japan International Cooperation Agency, https://www.jica.go.jp/english/overseas/bangladesh/index.html
159. "China Warns of 'Substantial Damage' to Ties if Bangladesh Joins US-led Quad Alliance; Dhaka Calls it 'Aggressive'," *The Economic Times*, May 11, 2021, https://economictimes.indiatimes.com/news/defence/china-threatens-bangladesh-says-ties-will-be-hit-if-it-joins-quad/articleshow/82544639.cms?from=mdr
160. "Chinese ambassador's Quad remarks," *The Daily Star*, May 21, 2021, https://www.thedailystar.net/editorial/news/chinese-ambassadors-quad-remarks-2092117
161. "China's comment on Quad an advance one, we decide our foreign policy: Bangladesh Foreign Minister," *India Today*, May 12, 2021, https://www.indiatoday.in/world/story/china-quad-comment-advance-we-decide-our-foreign-policy-bangladesh-foreign-minister-1801530-2021-05-12
162. "Treasury Sanctions Perpetrators of Serious Human Rights Abuse on International Human Rights Day," *US Department of the Treasury*, December 10, 2021, https://home.treasury.gov/news/press-releases/jy0526
163. "Taking Steps to Impose Visa Restrictions on Individuals Involved in Undermining the Democratic Election Process in Bangladesh," *US Embassy in Bangladesh*, September 22, 2023, https://bd.usembassy.gov/30460/#:~:text=SEPTEMBER%2022%2C%202023,party%2C%20and%20the%20political%20opposition.

164. Dhairya Maheshwari, "Russian Navy Squadron Visits Bangladesh Amid Political Tensions With US," *Sputnik*, November 12, 2023, https://sputniknews.in/20231112/russian-navy-squadron-visits-bangladesh-amid-political-tensions-with-us--5366638.html
165. Matthew Miller, "Parliamentary Elections in Bangladesh," *Press Statement, US Department of State,* January 8, 2024, https://www.state.gov/parliamentary-elections-in-bangladesh/
166 Bhaswar Kumar, "Bangladesh: Why is St Martin's island in news and what Sheikh Hasina said," *Business Standard,* August 12, 2024, https://www.business-standard.com/external-affairs-defence-security/news/bangladesh-why-is-st-martin-s-island-in-news-and-what-sheikh-hasina-said-124081201401_1.html
167 Sana Hashmi, "China is keeping a close watch on Bangladesh. It's an opportunity to counterbalance India," *The Print,* August 7, 2024, https://theprint.in/opinion/eye-on-china/china-is-keeping-a-close-watch-on-bangladesh-its-an-opportunity-to-counterbalance-india/2212318/
168 "BNP's tie with China will grow stronger: Fakhrul," *The Daily Star,* August 21, 2024, https://www.thedailystar.net/news/bangladesh/news/bnps-tie-china-will-grow-stronger-fakhrul-3682851
169 "Chinese Embassy in Bangladesh Hosts the Pre-departure Reception for the Bangladesh Islamic Political Parties Friendship Delegation," *Embassy of China in Bangladesh,* November 26, 2024, http://bd.china-embassy.gov.cn/eng/zmjw/202412/t20241219_11506734.htm
170 "Dhaka to seek lower interest rates during foreign adviser's China visit," *The Daily Star,* January 15, 2025, https://www.thedailystar.net/news/bangladesh/diplomacy/news/dhaka-seek-lower-interest-rates-during-foreign-advisers-china-visit-3799931
171. "Chinese Ambassador to Bangladesh Yao Wen Delivers Lecture at Defence Service Command and Staff College of Bangladesh," Ministry of Foreign Affairs of PRC, July 12, 2023, https://www.fmprc.gov.cn/eng/wjb_663304/zwjg_665342/zwbd_665378/202307/t20230717_11114027.html
172. "Myanmar Leader Min Aung Hlaing Meets with Qin Gang," *Consulate-General of the People's Republic of China in Mumbai*, May 3, 2023, http://mumbai.china-consulate.gov.cn/eng/zgyw/202305/t20230504_11070139.htm

9

Cooperation with Suspicion

Introduction

In October 1954, in a conversation with the Indian prime minister, Chairman Mao Zedong stated that the "Burmese government is the most suspicious of us, and that is because there is a revolution in their country...they suspect that we will help the revolutionaries to overthrow the government and that we will deliver weapons to the revolutionaries."[1] Mao Zedong went on to add that Chiang Kai-shek-led Kuomintang (KMT) troops operated from Burma, and they had received support from the United States.[2] Mao Zedong's statement summed up the mutual suspicion and anxieties between the neighbouring countries. For China, Myanmar constitutes both a challenge and an opportunity. Myanmar is a relatively easy route to access the Indian Ocean. The presence of outside powers in Myanmar could potentially increase the vulnerabilities of the relatively backward region of southwest China.

Thant Myint U's analysis sheds light on Myanmar's geopolitical situation as a country between China and India.[3] India and China are ancient civilisations with complex histories, contrasting political systems, and foreign policy orientations. With China, Myanmar shares about 2204 kilometres of border, and with India, it shares about 1643 kilometres of border.[4] Myanmar's leaders were acutely conscious of being between various big powers from the early days after independence. As Prime Minister U Nu noted: "Take a glance at our geographical position—Thailand in the East, China in the North, India in the West, and stretching southward, Malaya, Singapore and so on ... we are hemmed in like a tender gourd among the cactus ... we cannot move in an inch."[5]

Myanmar's interactions with China and India went through many phases. Between the Third Anglo-Burmese War in 1885 and the end of the Second World War, India had a significant impact on Myanmar's social, political, and economic realms. This was because, until Burma's separation from India in 1937, it was governed from Calcutta as a province of British India. The British colonial apparatus in Burma was largely manned by Indians; as a consequence, there was significant movement of people between the two countries. As Lalita Hingkanonta calculated, "by the beginning of the 20th century, Rangoon was a ... [Indian] city ... the Indian population in the entire province exceeded one million for the first time."[6] Given the common colonial apparatus, the economic interactions with the rest of British India were also dense. The Second World War, the emergence of an independent Burmese nation-state, and, most importantly, General Ne Win's policies, which contributed to the exodus of Indians, fundamentally altered the economic engagement between India and Burma.

On the other hand, China's presence in Myanmar increased during and after the Second World War. During the Second World War, the Allied powers supported the Chiang Kai-shek-led Kuomintang (KMT) troops. Myanmar became the transit country through which significant material and military support were extended to the KMT forces. However, in the civil war, Chinese communist forces prevailed over the KMT forces. The withdrawing KMT forces fought the communist forces in Yunnan province from the bases they operationalised in Myanmar's northeastern regions. The establishment of the KMT bases and the support they received from the United States happened without the consent of the Myanmar government.[7] Probably, it is this early experience of becoming a battleground of larger powers that prompted Yangon to adopt a policy of non-alignment rigorously.

Though a welcome development, the evacuation of the KMT troops did not significantly improve the relations between Myanmar and China. Many in Myanmar suspected that China was supporting insurgencies in their country. It is well known that Myanmar, an ethnically diverse country, has experienced multiple insurgencies since its independence. The major ethnic groups living along the border regions have demanded autonomy and a federal democratic structure to protect their identity within the larger union. However, the failure to meet ethnic aspirations and decades of military rule has prevented genuine federalism from taking root in the country. Consequently, Myanmar has experienced sustained conflict, undermining harmony and prosperity. Various Ethnic Armed Organisations (EAOs) and the Communist Party of Burma (CPB) have contested military rule for decades and demanded regional autonomy. Chinese involvement in various insurgencies in Myanmar contributed to less than harmonious relations between the two countries. Mao's Cultural Revolution (1966) had a deleterious impact on domestic politics and contributed to strained relations with neighbours such as Myanmar. With Beijing's attempts to export the revolution to other countries, students of the Chinese community in Myanmar "wore Chairman Mao badges and recited his sayings."[8] Such explicit declaration of affiliation to a political figure and the ruling ideology of a neighbouring country also contributed to the anti-Chinese sentiment in Myanmar. A brawl between Chinese students and teachers in 1967 resulted in widespread anti-Chinese riots.[9] The low point in the relationship was the stabbing of a Chinese diplomat, and over 30 Chinese nationals were killed during the anti-Chinese riots of 1967.[10] Subsequently, China scaled up its assistance to the CPB, and there were reports that Chinese Red Guards of the Cultural Revolution, as well as regular PLA troops, sometimes supported the CPB in its insurgency operations.[11] During the Cultural Revolution phase, the Chinese media often made persistent propaganda efforts in support of the CPB. For instance, in 1967, the Chinese Communist Party's Central Committee, referring to its support to the CPB, stated: "We regard such support as our bounden proletarian international duty.... It is our firm conviction that the CPB headed by Comrade Thakin Than Tun, which persists in the revolutionary line to win the war and seize political power ... will assuredly overthrow the reactionary Ne Win Government."[12] The Chinese support for the CPB complicated matters for the Tatmadaw (Myanmar military) as it simultaneously battled many other armed ethnic groups. The aggressive Chinese support for the communist insurgency prompted some to rally around their government headed by General Ne Win.[13]

China's Outreach

With the death of Mao Zedong in 1976, Deng Xiaoping quickly consolidated power and emerged as the new leader. Deng Xiaoping started to roll back some of the policies, such as promoting the communist revolution in neighbouring countries. Further, he worked on building robust economic relationships with many Southeast Asian countries, including Myanmar. This change in Chinese policy was also informed by a realisation that Southwest China's economic progress is closely tied with continental Southeast Asian countries, such as Myanmar. In 1978, Deng Xiaoping, on one of his first international trips, visited Burma and promised substantial financial assistance—a USD 63 million loan without interest—and both countries signed agreements pertaining to the construction of rice mills and a cotton mill.[14] Through the visit, Deng Xiaoping reiterated that China is committed to reimagining the bilateral relationship and scaling up economic interactions. In the early 1980s, China made efforts to improve relations with Myanmar and, in this direction, refrained from supplying arms to insurgent groups, sought to facilitate dialogue with the CPB and scaled up development assistance.[15] Although limited, the development assistance amounted to approximately 10 per cent of Chinese foreign assistance. The withdrawal of Chinese support to the CPB tilted the balance in favour of the Myanmar military in combating insurgencies. The CPB quickly disintegrated, and the Myanmar army was able to focus on other insurgent groups with greater vigour. Not surprisingly, the shift in Chinese policy facilitated improvement in the bilateral relationship with Myanmar. Further, the end of the Cold War resulted in significant shifts in the external engagement of China and Myanmar. After the harsh clampdown on the student unrest in 1988 and the failure to recognise the election results in 1990 by the Tatmadaw, the international community, led by the United States, imposed sanctions on Myanmar. It is broadly in this context that China extended diplomatic support to Yangon and called on the international community to refrain from intervening in Myanmar's domestic affairs.

The international economic sanctions coincided with Chinese policy preference to engage more with Southeast Asian countries to foster economic development in Southwest China. Further, Myanmar was also important in accessing the Indian Ocean as a part of China's Two Ocean Strategy. However, given the growing economic interactions and close relationship between the two countries, there was always an apprehension that China may eventually get a naval base operationalised somewhere along the Bay of Bengal coast. Such suspicions were further fuelled by news reports that Beijing may secure permission to operate a military listening post in the Coco Islands of the Bay of Bengal.[16] However, the Tatmadaw often stated that the Chinese did not have a military installation in the Coco Islands. Nonetheless, these apprehensions hinted that China's economic engagement was also possibly guided by defence considerations.

In addition to diplomatic support on international fora, China also provided military assistance to Yangon. Since 1989, Myanmar has had relatively easy access to Chinese weapons.[17] The diplomatic support, coupled with defence cooperation, ensured that the most important institution in Myanmar—the Tatmadaw (military)—was favourably disposed towards China in economic interactions. Given the sanctions of the international community, after 1990, Myanmar-China relations expanded significantly. In the economic realm, for China, there was very little international competition. Myanmar had significant resources, such as precious stones, natural gas, and abundant forest resources. Porous borders, lax border control mechanisms, and the growing dependence of the military leadership on Beijing created conditions for China to benefit from Myanmar's natural resources.

In 2008, China National Petroleum Corporation signed a 30-year contract to import natural gas from the Shwe gas fields in the Bay of Bengal.[18] Earlier, the Shwe gas fields were discovered by a consortium consisting of Daewoo, India's Oil and Natural Gas Corp. Ltd , GAIL (India) Ltd, Korea Gas Corp., and the Myanmar Oil and Gas Enterprise.[19] Moreover, there was a proposal to ship the natural gas from the Shwe gas fields to India either through Northeast India or Bangladesh, which did not materialise. Subsequently, the Myanmar government signed an agreement to sell the Shwe gas fields' resources to China. While some criticised the Indian government for not acting with alacrity,[20] it can also be argued that perhaps the Myanmar government was not keen on selling the resource to India. After all, unlike India, China has a permanent seat in the United Nations Security Council (UNSC) with veto power. Myanmar's need for diplomatic support may have also guided its economic and trade decision-making.

The conceptualisation of gas and oil pipelines was defined by a larger geopolitical context. Over 80 per cent of China's energy resources were transiting through the Straits of Malacca, which constituted an important security challenge for Beijing. In order to reduce the dependence on these maritime routes, Beijing started building numerous pipelines into China from Central Asia and from the Bay of Bengal coast of Myanmar to Yunnan province in China. From Myanmar, there were two pipelines of crude oil and natural gas. A 793-kilometre gas pipeline was completed in 2013, and running parallel, a 771-kilometre crude oil pipeline was operationalised in 2017.[21]

There has been a steady increase in the transportation of crude oil and natural gas via pipelines. In 2019, approximately 10.8 million tonnes of crude oil and 3.4 million tonnes of natural gas were imported through the pipelines.[22] These pipelines generated considerable criticism within Myanmar. There was an opinion that given Myanmar's energy crisis, it would be prudent to use the natural gas from the Shwe fields for domestic consumption rather than exporting it to China. The pipelines did provide significant economic benefits to China. However, the Chinese economic engagement had to navigate the changing political dynamics in Myanmar.

Political Shifts and Renegotiations

The 2010 general elections heralded the presidency of Thein Sein, who quickly implemented numerous reform measures. Aung San Suu Kyi was also released from prison. These developments generated anticipation that Myanmar's transition towards participatory frameworks of governance may slow down its economic interactions with China. While many projects that had Chinese involvement were operationalised, there were some that encountered a few challenges. The Letpadaung copper mine project, which had the involvement of a Chinese company—Wanbao Mining Ltd—received considerable international attention, as it became a site of massive protests. The protests started one year after the general elections in 2010. The leading opposition party, the National League of Democracy, did not participate in the elections, and unfair electoral practices resulted in a government headed by a former military general, Thein Sein. President Thein Sein's actions conveyed an impression that his government's approach would differ from that of the previous military regime. The partially open political system and relatively free media meant that anti-mining protests received considerable attention. Moreover, domestic and international audiences closely monitored the developments to see if there was indeed a shift in the attitude of the semi-military government towards open dissent and protest. Sadly, in 2012, the police used smoke grenades to disperse crowds near the mining site, resulting in serious injuries to many, including at least 67 monks who were part of the protestors.[23] In response to the growing protests, President Thein Sein suspended the project's operations and asked leading opposition leader Aung San Suu Kyi to lead the committee to investigate the project. Based on the committee's recommendations, a new agreement was renegotiated wherein the Myanmar government received a larger share of the profits and enhanced compensation for the villagers, and greater allocations to corporate social responsibility activities were made.[24] Four years later, the mining company restarted its operations.

While the Letpadaung copper mine project was renegotiated, the suspension of the Myitsone hydroelectric project was a major setback for China in Myanmar. Both countries signed a memorandum of understanding (in 2006) and subsequently, a memorandum of agreement (in 2009), pertaining to the Myitsone hydroelectric project. It was envisaged that there would be a series of seven dams, including the Myitsone Dam, on the Irrawaddy River and its tributaries. These agreements were signed when the military was in full control, and there was very little space for dissent. The Myitsone project was estimated to cost around USD 3.6 billion.[25] However, after the 2010 elections, there was a qualitative change in public response to these projects. The proposal to construct a massive hydroelectric project generated public disapproval not only in the Kachin State but also across the country. The disapproval was not surprising as the Irrawaddy River is seen as the lifeline of the country. In addition, there were concerns that the construction of a series of dams would result in severe water shortages and hinder navigation along the waterways.

In 2011, with growing public disapproval, President Thein Sein, as in the case of the Letpadaung copper mine project, sought to demonstrate that the governance style of the new regime would be different from that of the earlier regime. President Thein Sein made it a point to note that "being the government elected by the people", it has to uphold the aspirations of the people and "therefore, will suspend the Myitsone dam project during its tenure."[26] A careful reading of the president's statements shows that the project was suspended and not cancelled. More importantly, the suspension can be revoked if all the stakeholders agree to do so. The decision to suspend rather than scrap the project meant that the Chinese authorities had an opportunity to occasionally ramp up pressure on Myanmar to restart the construction of the hydroelectric dam. For instance, in January 2019, the Chinese Embassy in Myanmar stated that "if this issue fails to be resolved after a long day delay, it will seriously hurt the confidence of Chinese entrepreneurs in investing in Myanmar."[27] There were also reports that cancellation of the project would require the Myanmar government to "repay some USD 800 million that the state-owned Chinese developer says it has already spent on the project" on items such as feasibility/technical studies and other preliminary infrastructure.[28] In early 2019, China scaled up its diplomatic pressure on Myanmar to resolve the Myitsone hydroelectric power project issue. Joe Kumbun notes that growing international concerns about the sectarian violence and the defence requirements of the Tatmadaw were probably perceived by the Chinese authorities as constituting a window of opportunity to scale up pressure on Myanmar to resolve the project in their favour.[29] While the findings of the 20-member commission were not released, the commission reportedly considered the possibility of working with China on other projects to mollify Beijing.[30] The developments around the Letpadaung copper mine and the Myitsone dam projects did not completely undermine the bilateral relationship. The China-Myanmar relationship flourished with Myanmar's participation in the Belt and Road Initiative (BRI).

Three Pillars of the CMEC

In May 2017, Myanmar's State Counsellor Aung San Suu Kyi participated in the Belt and Road Forum (BRF) for International Cooperation and endorsed the BRI. She called for "closer exchanges between two governments … [to] … enhance the mutual trust and the '*Paukphaw*' friendship."[31] During the visit, both countries agreed to scale up cooperation under the China-Myanmar Economic Corridor (CMEC) rubric within the BRI framework.[32] Suu Kyi also visited China to participate in the Second BRF in 2019, and both countries signed agreements that focused on developing a decadal vision plan for the CMEC and fostering increased interactions in the domains of economy, technology, and trade.[33]

Chinese President Xi Jinping's visit to Myanmar in January 2020 gave a significant boost to bilateral economic relations. During his visit, President Xi Jinping interacted with all the important power centres, such as Aung San Suu Kyi, the Commander-in-Chief of the Myanmar military, and even the leaders of various ethnic parties. Approximately 33 Memorandum of Understanding (MOUs) were signed during the visit, and the Chinese leadership articulated a more comprehensive vision of the China-Myanmar Economic Corridor (CMEC).[34] The CMEC would consist of two corridors—Yunnan to Mandalay to Kyaukpyu and Yunnan to Mandalay to Yangon. A few days before his visit, President Xi Jinping penned an article in three Myanmar newspapers in which he called for efforts to be made "to promote the three pillars of the China-Myanmar Economic Corridor (CMEC), namely the Kyaukpyu Special Economic Zone, the China-Myanmar Border Economic Cooperation Zone and the New Yangon City."[35] As noted, the Kyauk Phyu port has emerged as an important gateway to the Indian Ocean for China. Not surprisingly, China scaled up its engagement of the strategically located Kyauk Phyu port by clinching a 2015 tender to construct a Special Economic Zone (SEZ) led by the China International Trust and Investment Corporation (CITIC).[36] The SEZ promised to provide a hundred thousand jobs to locals with an estimated tax revenue of USD 15 billion over a few decades.[37] Given that much of the economic activity happened around Mandalay and Yangon, the Kyauk Phyu SEZ promised to kickstart economic activity in the restive province of the Rakhine state. The proposed project was dormant for a while and was revived subsequently during Chinese President Xi Jinping's visit to Myanmar in January 2020. The revised proposal consisted of a deep sea port in addition to the SEZ. While the Myanmar consortium would hold 30 per cent stake in the project, the CITIC will hold approximately 70 per cent stake.[38] Nan Lwin reported that "along with an agreement that the project would be based on demand", the original share of the Chinese developer, which amounted to almost 85 per cent, was brought down by sustained negotiations of the National League for Democracy (NLD) government.[39] While there were reports that over 40 private Myanmar companies were expected to invest in the SEZ, the economic viability was not certain. Therefore, the "project's estimated cost was reduced from USD 9.5 billion to USD 1.3 billion to prevent Myanmar from becoming too indebted to China."[40] To a large extent, the success of the Kyauk Phyu SEZ would be contingent on the success of economic activity in Yangon and Mandalay. Both cities have very high-density populations, educational institutions, and other skilled manpower. As a consequence, operationalising the SEZ in and around Yangon has a greater prospect of success. Japan's Thilawa SEZ near Yangon has taken off successfully and promises to grow even faster.

Border trade and economic cooperation constitute an important pillar of the CMEC. Myanmar-China border regions witness significant trade and movement of people. In order to provide a fillip to economic activity and also reduce informality in trade, both countries signed a memorandum of understanding in 2017 on the border economic cooperation zones (BECZs), and a year later, the Myanmar government constituted a committee to examine the details for operationalising the BECZs.[41] The objective of the BECZs seems to be to create amenities for government institutions, tourist facilities, and robust infrastructure required for trade facilitation. Three sites in Shan and Kachin States were identified to operationalise economic cooperation zones, which included "Kanpiketi town in Kachin State's Special Region 1, Chinshwehaw in Shan State's Laukkai Township and Shan State's Muse Township."[42] Some of these zones fell under the areas controlled by local ethnic armed groups or under Self-Administered Zone. The economic factors played an important role in the shortlisting of Muse for the BECZ. With significant trade and considerable movement of people and vehicles transiting through the border, the Muse (Myanmar) – Ruili (China) border trade point is the most economically vibrant zone on the border.[43] It was anticipated that increased border trade could ensure sustainable peace in restive ethnic regions located on Myanmar's border areas. There was also an opinion, as Toshihiro Kudo observed a decade ago, "without the Myanmar military government's ceasefires with the ethnic insurgencies along Myanmar-China borders, border trade would have never grown since 1988."[44] Having partially stabilised the border regions and promoted border trade, Beijing and Nay Pyi Taw were keen on consolidating their control on their respective border regions. There was an expectation in Myanmar that the operationalisation of the BECZ would also prompt Myanmar's migrant workers in Yunnan to look for employment opportunities within the country along the border.[45] For the Myanmar government, the spurt in economic activity and formalisation of trade would also ensure greater law enforcement in the border regions. Further, there was hope that growing border trade would tie various ethnic organisations on both sides of the border with economic activity in China. Therefore, the BECZ was in consonance with the larger political objectives of both China and Myanmar.

The need to tap into Yangon's economic opportunities prompted the Chinese leadership to focus on urban development projects, which are an important component of the CMEC. Keeping in view the rapid growth of Yangon City, the need for a new city as an adjunct to the existing city has animated policy discussions for more than a decade. Yangon accounts for almost 26 per cent of the country's GDP and, in the coming years, will witness the expansion of economic activity, which requires an expanded urban area in the form of a new city.[46] While Yangon City no longer retains its languid character, it retains many colonial-era buildings. On the other hand, the proposed New Yangon City will be swanky with tall glass buildings. The new city, which would fall on the western side of the Yangon River, proposes to host 1.2 million people, and the estimated expenditure for the first phase amounts to about USD 1.5 billion.[47] The nodal agency for the project is the New Yangon City Development Company (NYCDC), an outfit of the regional government. As per the agreement of 2018, China Communications Construction Co Ltd (CCCC) prepared a detailed infrastructure proposal. It was decided that the company to implement the project would be selected based on the Swiss Challenge "under which other companies will submit counter proposals for the infrastructure work."[48] However, in January 2020, both countries signed a Letter of Intent, which mandated that "the NYCDC and CCCC have committed to cooperate on the implementation of Stage 1 infrastructure projects through a competitive procurement process."[49] While the letter of intent pointed to a "competitive process", given Xi Jinping's reference to the city project as an important pillar of the CMEC, there was an opinion that the project would be awarded to a Chinese firm. Concerns as to whether local stakeholders would receive a legitimate share in the profits and the 'Hambantota experience', wherein Sri Lanka leased land to Chinese firms, seemed to have weighed heavily on the Myanmar government. In response to such growing concerns, the Myanmar government opened up the selection process to firms from other countries. Towards the end of 2020, over nine firms from Myanmar, Singapore, Taiwan, and India expressed interest in the Swiss Challenge. However, due to political instability, the project did not make anticipated progress.

The CMEC indicated an ambitious Chinese vision for rapidly expanding the economic engagement with Myanmar. While Chinese firms have operated in urban commercial centres, such as in Mandalay and Yangon, they have not acquired significant importance in the broader Chinese strategy. The CMEC constituted an attempt to correct the neglect of urban centres in China's BRI vision. The CMEC took a multisectoral approach, emphasising access to the ports of the Bay of Bengal, ensuring border stability through increased economic activity, and focusing on urban infrastructure projects. However, the Chinese attempts to rapidly increase economic engagement in Myanmar encountered severe political turbulence.

The Coup and China's Response

The Suu Kyi-led NLD registered an emphatic electoral victory in November 2020, winning approximately 396 seats out of 476 in the Union Parliament.[50] Along with other international leaders, China's President, Xi Jinping, congratulated Suu Kyi for NLD's 'victory in the general elections' and added that he was willing to work with Myanmar's leadership "to strengthen the two countries' cooperation in building the Belt and Road and the China-Myanmar Economic Corridor."[51] However, the hope that Myanmar would experience sustained political stability was short-lived, as Myanmar's tentative transition to democracy was curtailed on February 1, 2021, because of a military coup. The Tatmadaw ousted the civilian government and arrested the civilian leaders, including State Counsellor Aung San Suu Kyi and President Win Myint. Senior General and Commander-in-Chief of Defence Services Min Aung Hlaing quickly constituted the State Administration Council (SAC) to oversee the governance of the country. The Tatmadaw leadership alleged that the general elections witnessed considerable fraud.[52]

The coup prompted widespread protests across the country. With Suu Kyi back in prison and the military in control of governance, the governance process resembled the pre-election era. However, the people of Myanmar had very little appetite for authoritarian governance. Many parts of Myanmar witnessed spontaneous protests against the military rule. The protestors came from all walks of life, and the opposition to the military morphed into a Civil Disobedience Movement (CDM). Government employees, doctors, healthcare workers, police officers, teachers, labour organisations, and civil society groups participated in the CDM. Over time, the protests evolved into a concerted action to achieve specific political objectives. The ousted parliament members formed the Committee Representing Pyidaungsu Hluttaw (CRPH) and vowed to work towards (1) the establishment of a full-fledged democracy, (2) rescinding the 2008 Constitution, (3) writing a new Constitution based on a federal system, and (4) release of all unlawful detainees.[53] On April 16, 2021, the CRPH also constituted a parallel National Unity Government.[54] Subsequently, the NUG constituted the People's Defense Force (PDF) to carry out armed insurrection against the military. Meanwhile, amid sustained protests and a raging pandemic, the Tatmadaw continued with its attempts to consolidate its rule. In July 2021, alleging widespread fraud, the Tatmadaw formally nullified the November 2020 election results.[55] With formal nullification, the prospect of a negotiated settlement between the military and the democracy movement was further curtailed.

Many leading Western democracies condemned the military coup and demanded a quick restoration of the democratic process. On the other hand, China leaned towards supporting the Tatmadaw. The Chinese state media have refrained from defining the political developments in Myanmar as a significant rearrangement of political power. Instead, they have framed the coup as a part of the ongoing transition in Myanmar. For instance, Xinhua reported the coup as "a major cabinet reshuffle".[56] In many sections of Myanmar's society, there was considerable anger towards China for its support of the military coup. There were protests in front of the Chinese Embassy in Yangon. The protestors carried placards that read, "Myanmar's military dictatorship is made in China" and "if this is an internal affair, why are you helping the junta?"[57] Responding to speculation that Beijing had prior knowledge of the military coup, China's ambassador to Myanmar termed the rumours of Chinese involvement in the coup as "completely nonsense" and stressed that Beijing was "not informed in advance of the political change in Myanmar."[58] The clarification did little to subdue the anti-China sentiment. In March 2021, approximately 32 Chinese firms/factories were vandalised in Yangon, "with property losses amounting to 240 million yuan (USD 36.89 million)."[59] The military authorities claimed that the democracy protestors torched the factories. Subsequently, 28 people were sentenced to 20 years in prison by a military court.[60] On the other hand, the CDM protestors claimed that the military carried out arson to gain greater support from China.

The growing violence did not portend well for the considerable investments that China had made in Myanmar. Protecting and nurturing these investments constituted the top priority of Chinese foreign policy. Further, as noted earlier, Myanmar constitutes a land corridor that provides access to the Indian Ocean for Chinese provinces such as Yunnan. The enhanced economic interactions with Myanmar, as well as oil/gas pipelines, have added to Yunnan's economic growth. Therefore, there was a perception in China that the protests for democracy had the potential to undermine the Chinese economic presence. The attacks on Chinese firms/industries strengthened such anxieties. After the military coup, concerns were expressed in Chinese social media regarding the safety of China-Myanmar pipelines. There was an opinion in Myanmar that the pipelines were transporting national resources to a neighbouring country without significant political benefit to the local communities. From the perspective of China, such criticism against the pipelines was unfair as the pipelines were a bilateral project with economic benefits to Myanmar, and the Chinese companies did not violate any regulatory frameworks of Myanmar.[61] A few months after the military coup, an attack on the station on the China-Myanmar oil/gas pipeline resulted in the death of three personnel.[62] Some in Chinese social media opined that while the military coup constituted an internal affair of Myanmar, the attack on pipelines was not acceptable as the legitimate interests of Chinese companies were involved.[63] There was also an opinion that the attack on the pipelines was the handiwork of the external forces.[64] An opinion article in the *Global Times* noted that "the West has been making use of the situation in Myanmar to attack China" for geopolitical gains and to "force China to interfere in the Myanmar situation, so as to trap China in the spiral [of conflict]."[65] Implicit in the opinion piece was the argument that the protests for democracy were aimed at undermining Chinese economic interests. There were reports that Chinese troops scaled up their presence in the Jiegao border trade zone close to Shan State in Myanmar to protect the oil/gas pipelines in case of large-scale attacks.[66]

China also reportedly bolstered the capacity of the Tatmadaw to deal with the protests. There were news reports that Chinese-made CH-3A tactical unmanned aerial vehicles (UAV) were being used to monitor and "support [Tatmadaw's] operations against protest movements."[67] The Janes Defence News report noted that the UAVs may have been "delivered to Myanmar around the 2013-2015 timeframe."[68] Further, news reports suggested growing apprehension among protestors that the Tatmadaw may be deploying "Chinese facial recognition technology."[69] A *New York Times* report also noted that "the assembly of Myanmar's modern surveillance state has depended partly on patrons like China and Russia that have few qualms about equipping authoritarians."[70] The Irrawaddy reported that China delivered six FTC-2000G fighters, which 'could be used by the Tatmadaw against the resistance forces.'[71] China's supply of military equipment received sharp criticism from some in the international community. For instance, the United Nations (UN) Special Rapporteur on the Situation of Human Rights in Myanmar, in his report, noted that the Russian Federation, China, and Serbia supplied weapons to the Myanmar military "with the full knowledge that they would be used to attack civilians, in probable violation of international law."[72] Overall, available public reports give the impression that China sought to build capacities of the Tatmadaw to control the protests. However, there are inherent limitations to bolstering a regime that lacks public legitimacy and suffers from low morale among personnel manning the various institutions. In addition to the legitimacy crisis, the Tatmadaw suffered from capability attrition. As a consequence, China also modified its policy towards Myanmar.

Modulated Engagement and Border Security

In July 2022, Wang Yi visited Myanmar to attend the seventh Lancang-Mekong Cooperation (LMC) Foreign Ministers' Meeting, which was the first visit by the Chinese foreign minister after the military coup. The visit generated considerable discussion as to whether China has bolstered the legitimacy of the military regime.[73] The Chinese media reiterated that "Wang's visit was to attend the LMC rather than engage in bilateral talks."[74] Chinese academic Xu Liping argued that "Wang's trip, although being the highest-ranking Chinese official visit to Myanmar since its major cabinet reshuffle, does not hint at China 'recognising' the current administration as hyped by some Western media, as the purpose of Wang's visit is to attend the LMC rather than engage in bilateral talks."[75] On the sidelines of the LMC meeting, Wang Yi and Tatmadaw's foreign minister, U Wunna Maung Lwin, agreed to "speed up the construction of the China-Myanmar Economic Corridor (CMEC)", and also "explore the 'CMEC plus' cooperation at a proper time, and elevate the level of bilateral trade and commercial cooperation."[76]

Almost a year later, in May 2023, China's Foreign Minister, Qin Gang, visited the Myanmar border and urged the People's Liberation Army to "strengthen the border defence systems" and maintain "distinct and stable borders, and severely cracking down on cross-border criminal activities."[77] Subsequently, during his interactions with the Tatmadaw's Min Aung Hlaing in Nay Pyi Taw, Qin Gang called on the international community to "respect Myanmar's sovereignty and play a constructive role in helping Myanmar achieve peace and reconciliation."[78] During his Myanmar visit, Qin Gang promised to "accelerate key cooperation projects of the China-Myanmar Economic Corridor."[79] While Qin Gang sounded optimistic about the bilateral relationship, the reference to containing the criminal networks hinted at disappointment with the Tatmadaw for its failure to contain cross-border criminal activities.

Despite high-level visits, China modulated its engagement with the Tatmadaw, as there was a dramatic shift in the political dynamics in Myanmar. Beijing was also reportedly miffed with the Myanmar military's unwillingness to take action against various crime syndicates operating on the China-Myanmar border. For decades, the Northeastern parts of Myanmar were the hubs of a wide array of illegal activities. The northeastern regions of Shan State in Myanmar were part of the infamous Golden Triangle, which produces large quantities of narcotic drugs. With the advent of new technologies, the established criminal networks in the region diversified and scaled up their activities to include online scam networks during the pandemic. The Myanmar military, to raise resources, had either encouraged or looked the other way when the transnational crime syndicates emerged as powerful players operating online scams. In fact, numerous news reports pointed out that the Myanmar military leadership may have protected the online scamming syndicates.[80] The emergence of online scamming centres in Myanmar posed an important challenge for China. The infamous online scamming centres fleeced Chinese citizens and also engaged in human trafficking. According to a BBC report, over "100,000 foreign nationals, many of them Chinese, were estimated to have been lured to these scam centres ... and forced to work long hours running sophisticated online fraud operations targeting victims all over the world."[81] Despite numerous demands from China, the Tatmadaw reportedly dragged its feet in containing the operations of the scamming centres. There were reports that a few Chinese citizens, including a few undercover police officers, were killed when they attempted to escape from the scamming centres.[82] Given the reluctance of the Tatmadaw to act against the criminal syndicates, it was likely that China consented to offensive operations by the Ethnic Armed Organisations (EAOs).

On October 27, 2023, the Three Brotherhood Alliance—comprising the Arakan Army, the Myanmar National Democratic Alliance Army , and the Ta'ang National Liberation Army —launched massive operations against the Tatmadaw. Operation 1027 (based on the date it was launched) inflicted massive losses on the military in the Shan State. Since the constituent organisations of the Three Brotherhood Alliance had a close relationship with China, there was a perception that their military offensive had tacit consent from Beijing. As Jason Tower noted, China leveraged "Operation 1027...to maximize pressure on the military regime to compel it to begin a crackdown on cross-border crime that targets Chinese nationals."[83] After the ethnic organisations made significant territorial gains and dismantled some of the online scamming centres in Shan State, China brokered a ceasefire between the Tatmadaw and the Three Brotherhood Alliance. Because of the Chinese tactics, the Tatmadaw also took action against the crime syndicates. In early 2024, the Tatmadaw reportedly "handed over 10 alleged cyber scam suspects to China."[84] A few months later, hundreds of Chinese nationals, who were trafficked to work in scamming centres in Myanmar, were freed and repatriated to their home country.[85]

The success of Operation 1027 demonstrated the capabilities of the EAOs and the People's Defence Forces (PDFs) to inflict significant damage and losses on the Tatmadaw. The Myanmar military steadily lost ground and lost control of major towns and trade routes in Shan, Kachin, Rakhine, and other provinces. By the end of 2023 and early 2024, the morale of the Tatmadaw soldiers was at an all-time low. There have been many instances when Tatmadaw soldiers surrendered without a fight and fled to a neighbouring country. On the other hand, the success of Operation 1027 was a confidence booster for the EAOs and PDFs. With some external support, these armed organisations demonstrated the capability to inflict significant pain on one of the largest armies in Southeast Asia. Having tasted success, it would require considerable external pressure to prevent these organisations from launching more operations against the Myanmar military. However, it is difficult to determine if China would prefer a complete collapse of the Tatmadaw. It is possible that China may perceive that such a collapse may result in a power vacuum, which could be filled by organisations with stronger affiliations towards Western countries. Given the experience of the KMT conducting operations from Myanmar after the Second World War, China would be keen not to have an increased foreign presence in its neighbourhood, especially in a country that provides access to the Indian Ocean Region.

Myanmar, China, and Regional Frameworks

It is likely that China's objective to remain a dominant external actor with a significant influence in Myanmar also guided its interactions with the Association of Southeast Asian Nations (ASEAN). A few days after the coup, the Chinese foreign minister, Wang Yi, in his discussion with his Indonesian counterpart, noted that the "military of Myanmar and political parties shoulder the important responsibility for the country's stability and development" and emphasised the necessity to "solve the problems peacefully and within its constitutional and legal frameworks."[86] In Wang Yi's analysis, since constitutional issues are involved, it is imperative that other countries should refrain from interfering in the internal affairs of Myanmar.

The military coup elicited sharp criticism from some of the Association of Southeast Asian Nations (ASEAN) countries, such as Singapore. Indonesia took the lead in proactively engaging with some of the stakeholders to resolve the crisis. It is broadly in this context of growing disappointment in some of the Southeast Asian countries with the Tatmadaw's tactics that China made efforts to define the trajectory of the ASEAN's approach to the Myanmar crisis. On April 23, 2021, during a telephonic conversation with the foreign ministers of Thailand and Brunei, Chinese Foreign Minister Wang Yi pointed to the need for "fending off external interference" and called on the ASEAN for a "soft landing of the situation in Myanmar."[87] Wang Yi also noted that efforts to resolve the crisis should be based on "new understanding through political dialogues within the constitutional and legal framework."[88] Wang Yi's approach can be interpreted as supporting the position of the Tatmadaw as many democracy activists and ethnic organisations rejected the constitution since it gave the military primacy in the decision-making process.

On April 24, 2021, the ASEAN issued a five-point consensus (5PC) statement on Myanmar and promised to send an envoy "to meet with all parties concerned."[89] However, the Myanmar military leadership declared that the special envoy would be entertained after the domestic situation becomes stable, foreclosing the possibility of an active role of the regional organisation. The ASEAN's subsequent efforts to resolve the crisis have been sporadic as well as contentious. On June 4, Lim Jock Hoi (ASEAN Secretary-General) and Erywan Yusof (the second minister for foreign affairs for Brunei) met with Myanmar's Senior General Min Aung Hlaing and did not interact with opposition leaders.[90] The visit of the ASEAN leaders generated considerable controversy, as the visit was conducted without prior notification, and after the meeting, there was no briefing to fellow ASEAN foreign ministers, and the press release referred to Senior General Min Aung Hlaing as "Myanmar Leader".[91] After much criticism, the press release was hastily withdrawn from the ASEAN website. Subsequently, during the Special ASEAN-China Foreign Ministers' Meeting on June 7, Wang Yi, referring to the Myanmar crisis, urged "all countries to abide by the principles of the UN Charter and avoid unilateral sanctions and undue interference."[92] These developments indicate China was keen on foreclosing the possibility of the US and other Western countries' influencing political developments in Myanmar through the ASEAN.

There was a growing disappointment among the democracy activists with the ASEAN's role. A spokesperson of Myanmar's parallel National Unity Government (NUG) stated: "we no longer have any faith in ASEAN's efforts, and we have no expectation…ASEAN does not have a solid plan for their credibility."[93] The fact that the ASEAN has formally interacted with Senior General Min Aung Hlaing and refrained from interacting with representatives of NUG or other democratic activists was cited as evidence that suggests the ASEAN wilted under sustained Chinese pressure. While some Southeast Asian countries sharply criticised the Tatmadaw's actions, the ASEAN could not make much headway in resolving the crisis and often expressed its disappointment regarding the growing violence in Myanmar. In 2022, the ASEAN reiterated that the "5PC remains as ASEAN's main reference to address the political crisis in Myanmar" and expressed deep disappointment with "the lack of substantial progress on its implementation by the Authority in Myanmar."[94] In the same year, with the Tatmadaw's leadership failing to demonstrate an accommodative attitude, the ASEAN's foreign ministers decided to bar Myanmar's military leadership from participating in the meetings of the regional framework.[95] Instead, the ASEAN often called on Myanmar to send a non-political representative to attend its meetings, which the Tatmadaw refused to accept. In September 2023, the ASEAN established the Troika framework to address Myanmar-related political developments. The Troika would have three ASEAN Chairs—Indonesia (2023), Laos (2024), and Malaysia (2024)—as members.[96] The Troika framework was reportedly designed to blunt China's influence over Laos, "as it is in Vientiane's rational self-interest to prioritise debt restructuring and bilateral trade over resolving the Myanmar crisis."[97] Other than expressing deep disappointment and exploring new frameworks to scale up pressure on the Tatmadaw, the ASEAN could do little to alter the trajectory of political developments in Myanmar. However, there was no change in the attitude of the Tatmadaw in 2024. With large tracts of territory falling into the hands of the resistance groups, in January 2024, the Tatmadaw leadership relented and accepted the ASEAN's invitation to send a non-political representative by sending a bureaucrat to attend the regional framework's foreign ministers' meeting.[98]

Overall, the ASEAN's Myanmar policy was caught among the Chinese preference, the need to generate consensus among all members, and reluctance to interfere in the domestic matters of the member countries. The concern that China may influence Myanmar's policy, especially when states with relatively limited capacities assume the Chair of the ASEAN, prompted the creation of a Troika framework. The Troika framework would ensure that the ASEAN's policy positions on Myanmar must be vetted by the Chair and two other member countries. Also, the weaker countries could fend off pressure from bigger powers by pointing out that the Troika was an important arbitrator in articulating the ASEAN's Myanmar position.

Conclusion

China's engagement in Myanmar is multisectoral, and it has a significant presence in the country's ethnic, political, and economic landscape. The bilateral trade is tilted in favour of China. Myanmar exports primary products, such as natural gas and precious stones (such as jade), as well as agricultural and forest produce, to China. Myanmar is China's biggest supplier of rare earths, accounting for approximately "40 per cent of its supplies of minerals, including dysprosium, yttrium, and terbium."[99] On the other hand, Chinese exports consist of manufactured goods, such as electrical/electronic machinery and industrial machinery. China is Myanmar's leading trade partner. It should be noted that the economic interactions between the two countries were defined by informality. Due to military rule, sustained civil war, and weak law enforcement, the absence of robust institutional infrastructure meant that much of the economic activity with China went unrecorded. For instance, there was considerable outflow of forest resources to China, and much of the cross-border trade was not documented.

China had to often account for an element of hesitation in Myanmar's engagement with it. The perception that China is disproportionately benefitting from bilateral economic engagement is strongly prevalent among large sections of Myanmar's society. Such hesitation in engagement is evident in the suspension of the Myitsone hydroelectricity project and renegotiation of the Letpadaung copper mine project. However, given China's economic strength and clout in the region, Myanmar's leaders also made efforts to assure China's leadership that BRI projects would get fast-tracked. For instance, the Myanmar government, in 2019, operationalised a steering committee for the implementation of BRI projects, which was chaired by Aung San Suu Kyi.[100] After the coup, the Myanmar military was even more accommodating of Chinese interests. The current military regime reportedly appointed some personnel with longstanding relations/connections with China to senior positions in the administration.[101] The Tatmadaw leadership has appointed new members to the China-Myanmar Economic Corridor (CMEC) Joint Committee and the Central Committee to Myanmar-China Cross-Border Economic Cooperation Zones (CBECZ).[102] Further, news reports suggest that provisions that "encourage the participation of Myanmar people in the establishment of CEMC" have been deleted.[103] Further, the Tatmadaw leadership has reportedly "approved a USD 2.5bn power plant that will run on liquefied natural gas and be built and operated by Chinese companies" in

Ayeyarwady Region."[104] A few months after the coup, Phase 1 of the Kyauk Phyu power plant was completed, and the land acquisition for the New Yangon City was initiated.[105]

There are many reasons for Myanmar's enhanced economic engagement despite many concerns regarding the Chinese projects. Myanmar's vulnerability on international platforms regarding its human rights record mandated a closer relationship with China, which is a permanent member of the United Nations Security Council (UNSC). Myanmar needs China to fend off international pressure on human rights issues on various international platforms. Further, as noted earlier, China shares a close relationship with some of the EAOs in Myanmar and has facilitated negotiations between various armed groups and the Myanmar military. Moreover, there are also apprehensions that Chinese economic engagement may have created constituencies of support within the ruling elite of Myanmar, who are keen on continuing collaboration with China. On the other hand, China also requires a robust relationship with Myanmar. The economic progress and security of Yunnan province are closely tied to the bilateral relationship with Myanmar. Further, as the trade frictions between China and developed economies intensify, Beijing will have to engage with all the Southeast Asian countries, including Myanmar, with greater intensity. Myanmar also provides easy access to China to the Bay of Bengal and the Indian Ocean.

In its engagement with Myanmar after the coup, China has adopted a multi-pronged strategy. On international platforms, China often extended support to the Tatmadaw. After considerable delay, the SAC leader and Tatmadaw's Commander-in-Chief, Min Aung Hlaing, was invited to China, and the Chinese foreign minister visited Myanmar and engaged with the Tatmadaw leaders on advancing the BRI projects. Simultaneously, China is also strengthening its relationship with the EAOs. By simultaneous engagement of the Tatmadaw and the EAOs, China has significant leverage in Myanmar's domestic politics. The success of Operation 1027 by the Three Brotherhood Alliance has demonstrated that China can alter the power dynamic in Myanmar's internal politics. As noted, it will be difficult to predict if China will allow the disintegration of the Tatmadaw, as it may give the Western powers an opportunity to make deep inroads in a neighbouring country. Simultaneously, it is uncertain if China can prevent the complete disintegration of a delegitimised military due to sustained mass uprisings, armed resistance, and internal dissent. Given the multiplicity of actors with varying capabilities, it is difficult to plot the trajectory of Myanmar's politics. Nonetheless, amid all uncertainty, China will be singularly focused on maintaining the substantive influence that it has among the stakeholders in Myanmar to implement the BRI projects and scale up economic engagement.

The apprehensions that Mao Zedong referred to—mutual suspicion that China and Myanmar may host forces inimical to each other's security—continue to impact their bilateral relationship. The protests in front of the Chinese Embassy were indicative of the continued disappointment with China's alleged interference in Myanmar's internal politics. The Chinese statements indicate an apprehension in Beijing that Western powers will exert influence in a continental Southeast Asian country with abundant natural resources, which also provides China access to the Indian Ocean. China's increased economic and political engagement has not contributed to political stability in Myanmar. Despite many twists and turns in Myanmar's politics, China has retained significant influence in Myanmar, which shares a long border with India. The consolidation of Chinese presence on India's eastern borders and growing activity in the Bay of Bengal adds to the complexities of security challenges that New Delhi has to contend with.

Endnotes

1 "Minutes of Chairman Mao Zedong's Third Meeting with Nehru," *The Wilson Center Digital Archive*, October 26, 1954, https://digitalarchive.wilsoncenter.org/document/minutes-chairman-mao-zedongs-third-meeting-nehru

2. Ibid.

3. Myint-U, Thant, *Where China Meets India: Burma and the New Crossroads of Asia*, (New York: Farrar, Straus and Giroux, 2011)

4. "Chinese military to conduct live ammunition drill along Myanmar border amid disputes with India," *Business Today,* April 1, 2024, https://www.businesstoday.in/india/story/chinese-military-to-conduct-live-ammunition-drill-along-myanmar-border-amid-disputes-with-india-423683-2024-04-01#:~:text=China%20shares%20a%202204%2Dkilometer,has%20friendly%20ties%20with%20Myanmar.

5. Hongwei Fan, "China–Burma Geopolitical Relations in the Cold War," *Journal of Current Southeast Asian Affairs* 31 (2012), p. 10.

6 Lalita Hingkanonta (2013), "The police in colonial Burma." PhD Thesis. *SOAS, University of London*, p. 69.

7. See Bertil Lintner, *Burma in Revolution: Opium and Insurgency Since 1948*, (Chiangmai: Silkworm, 2003), pp. 125-157.

8. Fan, Hongwei, "The 1967 Anti-Chinese Riots in Burma and Sino-Burmese Relations," *Journal of Southeast Asian Studies 43*, no. 2 (2012), pp. 234-56.

9. Ibid.

10. Wei Yan Aung, "The Day Anti-Chinese Riots Erupted in Myanmar," *The Irrawaddy*, June 26, 2020, https://www.irrawaddy.com/specials/on-this-day/day-anti-chinese-riots-erupted-myanmar.html
11. See Bertil Lintner and Robert A. Holmes, "China-Burma Relations since the Rift," *Asian Survey*, Vol. 12, No. 8, August 1972, pp. 688-689.
12. Frank N. Trager, "Burma: 1967-A Better Ending than Beginning," *Asian Survey*, Vol. 8, No. 2, February 1968, p. 114.
13. John H Badgley, "Burma's China Crisis: The Choices Ahead," *Asian Survey*, Vol. 7, No.11, November 1967, p. 687.
14. Wei Yan Aung, "The Day Deng Xiaoping Arrived to Bolster Ties With Myanmar," *The Irrawaddy*, January 26, 2020, https://www.irrawaddy.com/specials/on-this-day/day-deng-xiaoping-arrived-bolster-ties-myanmar.html; also see "The first Chinese leader to visit Myanmar," *Lost Footsteps*, https://lostfootsteps.org/en/history/the-first-chinese-leader-to-visit-myanmar
15. "China's Balancing Act in Burma," *Directorate of Intelligence, General CIA Records*, October 29, 1985, CIA-RDP85T01058R000202030001-9, https://www.cia.gov/library/readingroom/document/cia-rdp85t01058r000202030001-9
16. Indrani Bagchi, "China Eyeing Base in Bay of Bengal?", *Times of India*, August 9, 2008, http://timesofindia.indiatimes.com/articleshow/msid-3343799,prtpage-1.cms
17. "Allies in Isolation: Burma and China Move Closer," *Jane's Defence Weekly*, September 15, 1990, p. 475, as cited in by Daniel Byman, Roger Cliff, "China's Arms Sales: Motivations and Implications," *Report of Rand Corporation*, 1999, http://www.rand.org/content/dam/rand/pubs/monograph_reports/MR1119/MR1119.chap3.pdf
18. "Shwe Gas Movement - Chronology of Oil and Gas Events in Burma," *The Shwe Gas Movement*, November 22, 2020, https://www.shwe.org/chronology/
19. "China beats India to 30-year natural gas deal with Myanmar," *Mint*, December 30, 2008, https://www.livemint.com/Companies/G4MMTDIgSs6bVVW06fPVTP/China-beats-India-to-30year-natural-gas-deal-with-Myanmar.html
20. Latha Jishnu, "How MEA torpedoed the Bangladesh-India gas pipeline," *Down to Earth*, December 20, 2013, https://www.downtoearth.org.in/interviews/how-mea-torpedoed-the-bangladeshindia-gas-pipeline-43066
21. "Overview of the Myanmar-China Oil & Gas Pipelines," *CNPC*, https://www.cnpc.com.cn/en/myanmarcsr/201407/f115a1cc6cdb4700b55def91a0d11d03/files/dec09c5452ec4d2ba36ee33a8efd4314.pdf
22. "China-Myanmar pipeline carries 10.8 mln tonnes crude oil in 2019," *Xinhua*, January 14, 2020.
23. Andrew R.C. Marshall, "Special Report: Myanmar's deep mine of old troubles," *Reuters*, December 28, 2012, https://in.reuters.com/article/us-myanmar-reforms/special-report-myanmars-deep-mine-of-old-troubles-idUKBRE8BR02P20121228
24. Zarni Mann, "Govt Denies Failing to Implement Suu Kyi's Letpadaung Report," *The Irrawaddy*, January 9, 2015, https://www.irrawaddy.com/news/burma/govt-denies-failing-implement-suu-kyis-letpadaung-report.html
25. Atul Aneja, "China, Myanmar Jostle over Myitsone Project During Suu Kyi's Visit," *The Hindu*, August 18, 2016, https://www.thehindu.com/news/international/China-

Myanmar-jostle-over-Myitsone-project-during-Suu-Kyi%E2%80%99s-visit/article14576488.ece

26. Thomas Fuller, "Myanmar Backs Down, Suspending Dam Project (Published 2011)," *The New York Times*, October 1, 2011, https://www.nytimes.com/2011/10/01/world/asia/myanmar-suspends-construction-of-controversial-dam.html
27. Li Ruohan, "Delayed Dam Project Awaits Resolution in Myanmar," *Global Times*, February 21, 2019, https://www.globaltimes.cn/content/1139702.shtml
28. Mike Ives, "A Chinese-Backed Dam Project Leaves Myanmar in a Bind," *The New York Times,* March 31, 2017, https://www.nytimes.com/2017/03/31/world/asia/myanmar-china-myitsone-dam-project.html?searchResultPosition=4
29. Joe Kumbun, "Why Is China In a Hurry to Revive the Myitsone Dam Projects?," *The Irrawaddy*, January 16, 2019, https://www.irrawaddy.com/opinion/guest-column/china-hurry-revive-myitsone-dam-projects.html#:~:text=First%2C%20China%20wants%20to%20push,as%20part%20of%20the%20BRI.
30. Nan Lwin, "Popular Kachin Party Calls for Abolition of China-Backed Dam in Election Policy Platform," *The Irrawaddy*, August 31, 2020, https://www.irrawaddy.com/news/burma/popular-kachin-party-calls-abolition-china-backed-dam-election-policy-platform.html
31. "Xi Jinping Meets with State Counselor Aung San Suu Kyi of Myanmar," *Permanent Mission of the People's Republic of China to the UN,* May 16, 2017, http://un.china-mission.gov.cn/eng/zgyw/201705/t20170519_8394303.htm#:~:text=On%20May%2016%2C%202017%2C%20President,for%20International%20Cooperation%20(BRF).
32. Jiang Zhida, "Belt and Road boosting Myanmar development," *China Daily*, January 14, 2020, https://global.chinadaily.com.cn/a/202001/14/WS5e1cf966a310128217270a0b.html
33. Nan Lwin, "Myanmar Signs 3 Agreements at Belt and Road Forum," *The Irrawaddy*, April 26, 2019, https://www.irrawaddy.com/news/burma/myanmar-signs-3-agreements-belt-road-forum.html
34. "Press Release on the State Visit of H.E. Mr. Xi Jinping, President of the People's Republic of China to the Republic of the Union of Myanmar," *The Global New Light of Myanmar,* January 18, 2020, https://www.moi.gov.mm/moi:eng/announcements/317
35. Xi Jinping, "Writing a New Chapter in Our Millennia-Old Pauk-Phaw Friendship," in *Full Text of Xi's Signed Article on Myanmese Newspapers*, January 16, 2020, Ministry of Foreign Affairs, the People's Republic of China, https://www.fmprc.gov.cn/mfa_eng/wjdt_665385/zyjh_665391/t1733312.shtml
36. Wang Yamei, "How the Development of Myanmar's Kyaukpyu Port Won the Hearts of Locals," *Xinhua*, January 20, 2020, https://www.xinhuanet.com/english/2020-01/20/c_138720186.htm.
37. Ibid.
38. Chan Mya Htwe, "Industrial Zone in Kyaukphyu SEZ to Be Built at $30B," *The Myanmar Times*, February 20, 2020, https://www.mmtimes.com/news/industrial-zone-kyaukphyu-sez-be-built-30b.html
39. Nan Lwin, "China's Strategic Port Project Moves Step Closer to Reality as Myanmar OKs Joint Venture," *The Irrawaddy*, August 10, 2020, https://www.irrawaddy.com/

news/burma/chinas-strategic-port-project-moves-step-closer-reality-myanmar-oks-joint-venture.html#:~:text=Burma-,China's%20Strategic%20Port%20Project%20Moves%20Step%20Closer,as%20Myanmar%20OKs%20Joint%20Venture&text=The%20approval%20moves%20the%20long,and%20Road%20Initiative%20(BRI)

40. Nan Lwin, "Gov't Working on Final Decision for Myitsone Dam, Minister Says," *The Irrawaddy*, January 29, 2019, https://www.irrawaddy.com/news/burma/govt-working-final-decision-myitsone-dam-minister-says.html
41. "China-Myanmar Economic Cooperation Zone to Be Developed Along Border Area," *Xinhua*, January 20, 2019, https://www.xinhuanet.com/english/2019-01/20/c_137759156.htm
42. "Myanmar Plans Economic Zones on Chinese Border," *ASEAN Business News*, November 2, 2018, https://www.aseanbriefing.com/news/myanmar-plans-economic-zones-chinese-border/
43. Meng Qingsheng, "Cross-border E-commerce Boosts China-Myanmar Trade," *CGTN*, January 18, 2020, https://news.cgtn.com/news/2020-01-18/Cross-border-e-commerce-boosts-China-Myanmar-trade-NlSvSYiH4I/index.html
44. Toshihiro Kudo, "Myanmar's border trade with China: Situation, Challenge and Prospects," in *Japan and Korea with the Mekong River Basin Countries*, edited by Mitsuhiro Kagami, BRC Research Report No. 3, 2010, Bangkok Research Centre, IDE–JETRO, Bangkok, Thailand, p. 288.
45. Myo Pa Pa San, "Work on Muse-Ruili Economic Cooperation Zone to Begin Soon," *The Irrawaddy*, November 20, 2018, https://www.irrawaddy.com/news/burma/work-muse-ruili-economic-cooperation-zone-begin-soon.html
46. Jiang Yifan, "New Yangon City: A Controversial Blueprint," *China Dialogue*, June 20, 2020. https://chinadialogue.net/en/cities/11687-new-yangon-city-a-controversial-blueprint-2/
47. Jack Board, "Speculative Yangon City Mega-project Draws 'white Elephant' Concerns for Myanmar," *CAN*, November 23, 2019, https://www.channelnewsasia.com/news/asia/yangon-city-mega-project-myanmar-china-state-investment-12051770
48. Sithu Aung Myint, "Yangon's 'new City' Plan Raises a Billion-dollar Question," *Frontier Myanmar*, March 8, 2019, https://www.frontiermyanmar.net/en/yangons-new-city-plan-raises-a-billion-dollar-question/
49. "Progress Updates," *The New Yangon Development Company Limited (NYDC)*, https://www.nydc.com.mm/rh-company-profile/
50. Cape Diamond and Yuichi Nitta, "Suu Kyi's NLD confirms 396 seats, surpassing 2015 landslide victory," *Nikkei Asia*, November 13, 2020, https://asia.nikkei.com/Politics/Myanmar-election/Suu-Kyi-s-NLD-confirms-396-seats-surpassing-2015-landslide-victory
51. "Xi Jinping congratulates Aung San Suu Kyi on election victory," *CGTN*, November 17, 2020, https://news.cgtn.com/news/2020-11-17/Xi-Jinping-sends-congratulatory-letter-to-Aung-San-Suu-Kyi-Vuv98Wwi9G/index.html
52. "Crisis in Myanmar after army alleges election fraud," *Reuters*, February 1, 2021, https://www.reuters.com/article/idUSKBN2A1139/
53. CRPH Myanmar, https://twitter.com/crphmyanmar/status/1367813348297822213?lang=en

54. "CRPH announces lineup of interim 'national unity government'," *Myanmar Now*, April 16, 2021, https://myanmar-now.org/en/news/crph-announces-lineup-of-interim-national-unity-government
55. "Myanmar military-appointed commission officially nullifies Nov. poll," *Kyodo News,* July 27, 2021, https://english.kyodonews.net/news/2021/07/d859812abf20-myanmar-military-appointed-commission-officially-nullifies-nov-poll.html?phrase=emperor%20survey&words=
56. "Major cabinet reshuffle announced in Myanmar," *Xinhua*, February 2, 2021, http://www.xinhuanet.com/english/2021-02/02/c_139713877.htm
57. Zaheena Rasheed, "Myanmar protesters urge China to condemn coup. Will Beijing act?," *Al Jazeera,* February 18, 2021, https://www.aljazeera.com/news/2021/2/18/myanmar-protesters-urge-china-to-condemn-coup-will-beijing-act
58. "China's ambassador to Myanmar says situation 'not what China wants to see'," *Reuters*, February 16, 2021, https://www.reuters.com/article/us-myanmar-politics-china/chinas-ambassador-to-myanmar-says-situation-not-what-china-wants-to-see-idUSKBN2AG1AA/
59. "Myanmar locals urged not to be incited by West as 32 Chinese factories in Yangon suffer from attacks," *Global Times,* March 15, 2021, https://www.globaltimes.cn/page/202103/1218466.shtml
60. "Myanmar sentences 28 rioters to 20 years for setting fire to Chinese-invested companies," *Global Times,* May 26, 2021, https://www.globaltimes.cn/page/202105/1224593.shtml
61. "缅甸军方夺权：那条连接中国的油气管道还好吗？," *Sohu,* February 2, 2021, https://www.sohu.com/a/448078107_117460
62. "Deadly Attack on Pipeline Station Spotlights China's High Stakes in Myanmar," *The Irrawaddy*, May 6, 2021, https://www.irrawaddy.com/news/burma/attack-oil-and-gas-pipelines-china-off-take-station-spotlight-stakes-junta-regime-protect-protesters-arson-attack-strategic-investment-unsc-support.html
63. "缅甸不能继续乱下去！有武装袭击中缅油气管道，事关中国能源安全, "*NetEase,* May 17, 2021, https://www.163.com/dy/article/GA5MPO1I05373IGG.html
64. "缅甸乱局波及中国，中缅油气管道遭不明武装袭击，背后势力不简单," *Sohu,* May 10, 2021, https://www.sohu.com/a/465554024_121074364
65. "West utterly manipulates Myanmar situation as a tool in anti-China campaign," *Global Times*, March 17, 2021, https://www.globaltimes.cn/page/202103/1218717.shtml
66. "Chinese Troops Gather on Myanmar's Border to 'Protect Pipelines'," *The Irrawaddy*, April 1, 2021, https://www.irrawaddy.com/news/burma/chinese-troops-gather-myanmars-border-protect-pipelines.html
67. "Wings over Mandalay: Myanmar's junta deploy Chinese-made CH-3A tactical UAVs to observe protest movements," *Janes*, April 8, 2021, https://www.janes.com/defence-news/news-detail/myanmar-junta-deploy-chinese-made-ch-3a-tactical-uavs-to-observe-protest-movements
68. Ibid.

69. "Fears of 'digital dictatorship' as Myanmar deploys AI," *Reuters,* March 18, 2021, https://www.reuters.com/world/china/fears-digital-dictatorship-myanmar-deploys-ai-2021-03-18/
70. "Myanmar's Military Deploys Digital Arsenal of Repression in Crackdown," *New York Times*, March 12, 2021, https://www.nytimes.com/2021/03/01/world/asia/myanmar-coup-military-surveillance.html
71. "Myanmar Junta Takes Delivery of FTC-2000G Fighter Jets from China," *The Irrawaddy*, December 5, 2022, https://www.irrawaddy.com/news/burma/myanmar-junta-takes-delivery-of-ftc-2000g-fighter-jets-from-china.html
72. "A/HRC/49/CRP.1: Conference Room Paper of the Special Rapporteur, Enabling Atrocities: UN Member States' Arms Transfers to the Myanmar Military," *OHCHR*, February 22, 2022, https://www.ohchr.org/en/documents/thematic-reports/ahrc49crp1-conference-room-paper-special-rapporteur-enabling-atrocities
73. "China's top diplomat visits Myanmar amid opposition protest," *The Hindu,* July 2, 2022, https://www.thehindu.com/news/international/chinas-top-diplomat-visits-myanmar-amid-opposition-protest/article65593101.ece
74. Fan Anqi and Cui Fandi, "China proposes 6 programs with Lancang-Mekong countries despite 'customary' Western provocation of ties," *The Global Times*, July 4, 2022, https://www.globaltimes.cn/page/202207/1269760.shtml
75. Ibid.
76. "China, Myanmar agree to further build community with shared future," *Xinhua,* July 3, 2022, https://english.news.cn/20220703/584ffcd372c44ec786e8d9947a4c4ef0/c.html
77. "China's Foreign Minister Makes Rare Visit to Myanmar Border," *VoA,* May 2, 2023, https://www.voanews.com/a/china-s-foreign-minister-makes-rare-visit-to-myanmar-border/7074832.html
78. "Myanmar Leader Min Aung Hlaing Meets with Qin Gang," *Ministry of Foreign Affairs, the People's Republic of China*, May 3, 2023, https://www.fmprc.gov.cn/eng/zxxx_662805/202305/t20230504_11070139.html
79. Ibid.
80. "Myanmar Military 'Provided Protection For US$ 14 Billion a Year Scam Hub' on China Border," *The Irrawaddy*, January 5, 2024, https://www.irrawaddy.com/news/burma/myanmar-military-provided-protection-for-us-14-billion-a-year-scam-hub-on-china-border.html; also see "Myanmar military 'protected $4bn scam hub'," *Bangkok Post,* January 6, 2024, https://www.bangkokpost.com/world/2719303/myanmar-military-protected-14bn-scam-hub
81. Jonathan Head, "The Chinese mafia's downfall in a lawless casino town," *BBC,* November, 23, 2023, https://www.bbc.com/news/world-asia-67471138
82. "China Offers Bounty for Myanmar Junta's Scam Kingpin in Kokang," *The Irrawaddy,* November 13, 2023, https://www.irrawaddy.com/news/burma/china-offers-bounty-for-myanmar-juntas-scam-kingpin-in-kokang.html
83. Nectar Gan, "How online scam warlords have made China start to lose patience with Myanmar's junta," *CNN,* December 19, 2023, https://edition.cnn.com/2023/12/19/china/myanmar-conflict-china-scam-centers-analysis-intl-hnk/index.html

84. Sylvie Zhuang, "'Extremely heinous': Myanmar Hands Over 10 Leading Cyber Scam Suspects to China," *South China Morning Post*, January 31, 2024, https://www.scmp.com/news/china/diplomacy/article/3250407/extremely-heinous-myanmar-hands-over-10-leading-cyber-scam-suspects-china
85. Jonathan Head & Lulu Luo, "China repatriates hundreds of scam factory workers from Myanmar," *BBC,* March 1, 2024, https://www.bbc.com/news/world-asia-68444058
86. "Wang Yi Speaks with Indonesian Foreign Minister Retno Marsudi on the Phone," *Ministry of the Foreign Affairs of China,* February 20, 2021, https://www.fmprc.gov.cn/mfa_eng/wjb_663304/zzjg_663340/yzs_663350/xwlb_663352/t1855503.shtml
87. "China expects ASEAN leaders' special meeting to be conducive to Myanmar situation: Chinese FM," *ECNS.CN,* April 23, 2021, http://www.ecns.cn/news/2021-04-23/detail-ihakufzf0695966.shtml
88. Ibid.
89. "Chairman's Statement on the ASEAN Leaders' Meeting," *ASEAN.org,* April 24, 2021, https://asean.org/storage/Chairmans-Statement-on-ALM-Five-Point-Consensus-24-April-2021-FINAL-a-1.pdf
90. "ASEAN envoys meet Myanmar junta chief - state TV," *Reuters,* June 4, 2021, https://www.reuters.com/world/asia-pacific/asean-envoys-meet-myanmar-junta-chief-state-tv-2021-06-04/
91. "Brunei's disastrous mission," *The Jakarta Post*, June 10, 2021, https://www.thejakartapost.com/academia/2021/06/09/bruneis-disastrous-mission.html
92. "Wang Yi Talks about the Situation in Myanmar," *Ministry of Foreign Affairs, the People's Republic of China*, June 8, 2021, https://www.fmprc.gov.cn/mfa_eng/zxxx_662805/t1882086.shtml
93. "Myanmar's National Unity Govt 'No Longer Has Faith' in ASEAN," *The Irrawaddy*, June 5, 2021, https://www.irrawaddy.com/news/burma/myanmars-national-unity-govt-no-longer-has-faith-in-asean.html
94. "Chairman's Statement of the 43rd ASEAN Summit Jakarta, Indonesia," *ASEAN*, September 5, 2023, https://asean.org/wp-content/uploads/2023/09/CHAIRMAN-STATEMENT-OF-THE-43RD-ASEAN-SUMMIT-FIN-2.pdf
95. "Myanmar generals banned from ASEAN until peace plan progress," *Al Jazeera,* August 6, 2022, https://www.aljazeera.com/news/2022/8/6/myanmar-generals-banned-from-asean-until-peace-plan-progress
96. Jayanty Nada Shofa, "ASEAN Establishes New Troika to Find Solution on Myanmar Crisis," *Jakarta Globe,* September 8, 2023, https://jakartaglobe.id/news/asean-establishes-new-troika-to-find-solution-on-myanmar-crisis
97. Mark S Cogan, "Low Expectations for ASEAN's Handling of Myanmar Crisis," *National Interest,* April 8, 2024, https://nationalinterest.org/feature/low-expectations-asean's-handling-myanmar-crisis-210447; also see Kiki Siregar, "ASEAN to set up troika mechanism of group's rotating chairs to handle Myanmar crisis," *Channel NewsAsia*, September 5, 2023, https://www.channelnewsasia.com/asia/asean-summit-myanmar-philippines-chairmanship-3747826
98. Ananda Teresia, "ASEAN foreign ministers back 'Myanmar-owned and led' solution to Crisis," *Reuters*, January 29, 2024, https://www.reuters.com/world/

asia-pacific/with-generals-barred-myanmar-junta-sends-bureaucrat-asean-meeting-2024-01-29/

99. "China's rare earth imports from Myanmar surge in first half of 2023," *Reuters*, July 20, 2023, https://www.reuters.com/article/idUSKBN2Z00PR/
100. "Myanmar forms steering committee for implementation of Belt and Road projects," *Xinhua*, December 10, 2018, https://eng.yidaiyilu.gov.cn/p/74085.html
101. "Myanmar Regime's Cabinet Includes Some Old China Hands," *The Irrawaddy*, March 29, 2021, https://www.irrawaddy.com/opinion/analysis/myanmar-regimes-cabinet-includes-old-china-hands.html
102. "Myanmar Regime Reorganizes Committees to Press Ahead With BRI Projects," *The Irrawaddy*, May 18, 2021, https://www.irrawaddy.com/news/burma/myanmar-regime-reorganizes-committees-to-press-ahead-with-bri-projects.html
103. Ibid.
104. "Junta approves $2.5bn power plant project backed by Chinese companies," *Myanmar Now*, May 14, 2021, https://www.myanmar-now.org/en/news/junta-approves-25bn-power-plant-project-backed-by-chinese-companies
105. "Myanmar Junta Implementing China's BRI Projects by Stealth," *The Irrawaddy*, July 23, 2021, https://www.irrawaddy.com/opinion/analysis/myanmar-junta-implementing-chinas-bri-projects-by-stealth.html

10

Reaping Benefits without Friendship

Introduction

Chairman Mao Zedong, in his interactions with Indian Prime Minister (PM) Jawaharlal Nehru on October 19, 1954, candidly stated that "China is not an industrialised country, but an agricultural country…the level of our industrial development is lower than that of India…it will take us another ten to twenty years [of] effort to achieve some tangible results."[1] Given the evolving boundary dispute between the two countries, perhaps Chairman Mao referred to his country's backwardness to give the impression that China is focused on the domestic economy rather than pursuing an aggressive foreign policy. However, a few days later, discussing the rapid changes in military warfare with PM Nehru, Chairman Mao stated: "China so far has no atomic bombs, and I do not know whether India has them … we have begun research in this respect, yet building the atomic bomb requires financial input … we may not have one for some time to come."[2] While Mao did refer to financial constraints, he categorically declared China's intent to acquire nuclear weapons. Implicit in Mao's comments is a policy preference for China to evolve as a major power with significant military prowess, which would include nuclear weapons. A few years later, in 1962, China invaded India and usurped large tracts of territory. There was considerable discussion among academics, policymakers, and others in India and abroad regarding the reasons that prompted China to initiate the 1962 war. Bertil Lintner contends that one of the objectives of the Chinese aggression was to displace India "as a leading voice among the newly independent nations of Asia and Africa" and emerge as the leader of the Third World.[3]

From the Chinese perspective, India's rise in the new millennium constitutes a significant challenge. India seeks to emerge as a leading power and has often unhesitatingly positioned itself as a power that can influence the trajectory of global politics. India pursued an independent foreign policy and often sought to bridge the differences between contesting powers. New Delhi has been demanding the reform of global institutions to make them more inclusive and is championing the causes of the developing world on various international platforms. With one of the world's largest standing armies, which is getting rapidly modernised, India has emerged as a net security provider in its immediate and extended neighbourhood. In addition, Indian defence forces have been at the forefront of addressing numerous maritime challenges, such as piracy, and have an outstanding track record in performing humanitarian assistance and disaster relief activities. Significantly, India has often demonstrated the capacity to push back aggressive territorial assertions by China, as evident during the Galwan clashes in 2020. For China, India constitutes an economic challenge as it can evolve into an alternative investment destination. More importantly, India is demonstrating that a non-western country with a democratic framework not in alliance with any major powers can also register robust economic growth. Simultaneously, India is also an economic opportunity for China. With over 1.4 billion people and a rapidly growing economy, India constitutes a massive market. With China's trade relations with the Western developed countries increasingly becoming acrimonious, a market of India's size appears attractive. However, Beijing needs to ensure that its economic interactions benefit China without contributing to the rise of India as a major power.

Trade Relations

In 2023-2024, China was India's second-largest trade partner, with over USD 118.39 billion in trade.[4] During the same period, the United States (USD 119.71 billion) and the United Arab Emirates (USD 83.65 billion) were India's first and third- largest partners, respectively. Indian exports to China, as a percentage of its total exports, amounted to a mere 3.81 per cent in 2023-2024. On the other hand, imports from China accounted for 15 per cent of total imports of India during the same time period. While imports from

China have steadily increased, Indian exports to China have been struggling. In 2023-2024, while Indian exports to China amounted to USD 16.65 billion, imports accounted for about USD 101.73 billion, resulting in a trade deficit of USD 85.07 billion.[5] The trade imbalance persisted even after both countries agreed in 2019 to constitute a high-level committee, chaired by China's vice-premier and India's finance minister, to reduce the trade deficit.[6]

Indian exports always found it difficult to penetrate the Chinese market due to non-tariff barriers, such as excessive regulation and the preference for domestic firms.[7] The presence of non-tariff barriers is hindering India's pharma exports to China. In 2023-2024, India's pharma exports to the US were about USD 8.73 billion.[8] However, India's pharma exports to China in 2023-2024 were a meagre USD 357 million.[9] Overall, the non-tariff barriers hinder the export of manufactured goods from India to China. While India exports large quantities of rice, cotton, and iron ore to China, the experience of trying to export other items, such as pharma, has been mixed.

With an intent to boost exports, India's Department of Commerce signed three protocols with China in 2018 pertaining to the export of rice, fishmeal/fish oil, and tobacco.[10] Subsequently, there was a significant increase in Indian seafood exports to China. However, in 2020, Chinese authorities suspended shipments from over 100 seafood exporting units, allegedly due to COVID concerns.[11] The suspensions were lifted in 2023, and China emerged as the second-largest importer of seafood from India.[12]

Indian rice exports to China had to navigate numerous challenges. Subsequent to the 2018 protocol, a consignment of 100 tonnes of non-basmati rice was shipped from Nagpur in India to China.[13] Chinese officials identified approximately two dozen rice mills in India, with strict phytosanitary measures, for export.[14] A few months later, in December, Beijing agreed to import rice from the US. Since the US export of rice was not in large quantities, it did not have a long-term impact on the rice exports of countries such as India. Towards the end of 2020, China placed an order to import 100,000 tonnes of rice from India, despite tensions on the border between the two countries.[15] It was speculated that China's food grain crisis has prompted Beijing to import rice from countries such as India.[16] Despite robust domestic production, because of rapid economic growth, there were changes in dietary patterns, promoting the import of agricultural commodities. It is estimated that China's food self-sufficiency ratio, between 2000 and 2020, 'decreased from 93.6 per cent to 65.8 per cent.'[17] In the Financial Year 2021-22, India emerged as a leading supplier of rice for China.[18] However, in 2022 and 2023, India discouraged rice exports, with exceptions being South Asian neighbours and strategic partners, to stabilise the domestic prices.[19] The Indian government lifted the restrictions towards the end of 2024.[20]

Recently, India has emerged as one of the world's largest producers of cotton, with China as a significant export destination.[21] However, due to the economic slowdown, the Chinese import of cotton from India witnessed a drastic reduction in 2014-15.[22] This fall in cotton exports to China was adjusted to a large extent by increased demand from countries such as Bangladesh. However, the trade war between the US and China opened up new opportunities for India. With China imposing additional import duties on US cotton, there were opportunities for greater exports of Indian cotton to China. In fact, in 2018, China signed contracts to import '500,000 bales (85,000 tonnes) of cotton from India.'[23] After the pandemic-induced slowdown, cotton exports from India to China witnessed a significant uptick in 2023.[24] In 2023-2024, China was the third- largest importer of Indian cotton after Bangladesh and Sri Lanka.[25]

Iron ore constitutes an important export item from India to China, and its export prices were impacted by the ebb and flow of the Chinese economic growth. The slowdown in China ensured that prices of iron ore in the international market were low, and there was also increased competition from other international companies operating out of Brazil and Australia.[26] Nonetheless, there was anticipation among some traders that Indian low-grade iron ore would find a market in China.[27] The COVID-19—related challenges in Brazil and supply disruptions from Australia ensured that there was a spike in Indian iron ore exports to China in 2020.[28] In 2023-24, news reports estimated that over 90 per cent of Indian iron ore exports went to China.[29]

China was also the largest market for copper products from India.[30] Indian copper product exports to China, which were at USD 2 billion in 2011-12, fell to approximately USD 1.14 billion in 2015-16. Reduction of export incentives and imports into India from the Association of Southeast Asian Nations (ASEAN) countries [due to the Free Trade Agreement (FTA)] and Japan [Comprehensive Economic Partnership Agreement between India and Japan compounded the misery of the Indian copper industry.[31] Further, domestic troubles associated with the Sterlite Copper plant, the second largest in India, resulted in a drastic reduction in copper exports to China in 2018-2019.[32]

India's rapid economic growth and massive investment in infrastructure ensured a rapid increase in copper imports into the country.[33] In 2023-2024, for over half a decade, India became a net importer of copper.[34] On the other hand, imports from China have registered a significant increase in the recent past. Consumer electronics, auto components, iron and steel products, and solar cells/photovoltaic cells constitute the important items that are being imported from China.[35] In 2019, approximately "a quarter of India's auto part imports came from China."[36] The trend continued in 2023-2024, with China accounting for 30 per cent of auto components imports.[37]

Till about 2020, the import of power equipment manufactured in China has witnessed a steady increase. There were concerns that initial cost advantages tend to fritter away quickly due to high maintenance costs, and there are apprehensions that due to increased automation of the power sector, imported equipment may be more vulnerable to malicious attacks.[38] Therefore, there were demands from the Indian industry that domestic power equipment manufacturers should be protected from artificially low-priced imports from China. Responding to such demands, India's power minister, in 2020, banned the import of Chinese power equipment, stating that the "power system is vulnerable to malware attacks, which can shut down our communications, database and defence systems ... that is why all imports need to be inspected, and a few countries need to be banned."[39] In addition, there is persistent anxiety about the dumping of Chinese goods in India. It appears that vehicle parts, steel, chemicals, and electrical and electronic goods are some of the sectors that are being adversely impacted by the artificially low-priced Chinese products. Chinese iron and steel exports to India witnessed a 177.93 per cent growth in 2014-15. In the subsequent years, there was also a spike in steel imports from China. Steel imports from China accounted for about 26.1 per cent in June 2022 and 37.1 per cent in 2023.[40] Towards the end of 2024, it was estimated that India imported 1.96 million metric tons of steel, which amounted to a 22.8 per cent year-on-year increase.[41] Similarly, organic chemical imports from China witnessed significant growth. Between April 2019 and February 2020, China accounted for 74 per cent of organic chemical imports.[42] While India imported raw materials from China, it emerged as a net exporter of drug formulations and biologicals in 2019-2020.[43] As per the CRISIL report, the chemicals industry in China has been negatively impacted by slow growth, a trade war with the US, and the rising cost of labour.[44] Nonetheless, in 2023, the import of organic chemicals from China increased by nine per cent.[45]

China has made rapid inroads in India's smartphone market. However, the duty protection measures initiated by the Indian government prompted many Chinese companies to increase manufacturing in India.[46] In 2022, Chinese companies, such as Xiaomi, Oppo, Realme and Vivo, accounted for around 70 per cent of the smartphone market share.[47] The Indian market share assumes importance for the Chinese firms, as their share in the US, Europe, and Japan markets is coming under stress.[48] The Indian government has reportedly been encouraging Chinese firms to employ more Indians in managerial positions, localise supply chains, and increase exports from India.[49] While the Chinese firms have a significant market share in India, they contribute just about 4 per cent of India's smartphone exports.[50]

The import of solar power equipment from China often received considerable media attention in India. India has made persistent efforts to scale up its solar power generation capacity. The Indian government has launched numerous initiatives, such as the green energy corridor and solar park schemes, and sought to promote foreign direct investments (FDI) in the sector. Consequently, India's solar power generation capacity witnessed a rapid increase from 2.6 GW (2014) to 30 GW (2019) to 70.1 GW (2023).[51] The increase in capacities was indicative that the Indian government was willing to invest considerable resources in the solar energy segment. However, a significant challenge in this journey was the dependence on Chinese components to power India's solar dreams. During 2018-2019, about 80 per cent of solar panels used in India were imported from China.[52] Chinese companies enjoyed structural advantages over Indian firms. As an Indian solar manufacturer noted: "there is undue competition from China because of the incentives Chinese companies get, the effects of which we cannot deal with because of our limitations. For a domestic company of our stature, the interest cost is in low double digits, while Chinese companies get credit at 2 per cent and sometimes at 1 per cent, which is a very big difference."[53] Not surprisingly, there was a surge in Chinese solar exports to India. Chinese firms enjoyed significant production capacities, and with support from their government, they could cut back on prices and dominate the overseas markets.[54] Like India, many countries have grappled with large-scale import of solar equipment from China. There were instances when the European Council imposed punishing anti-dumping and anti-subsidy duties on Chinese solar panel imports.[55] The Indian government has offered numerous incentives to encourage domestic manufacturing of solar modules and also imposed additional tariffs on Chinese imports. Consequently, in 2023, there was not only a dramatic reduction of approximately 76 per cent in solar module imports from China, but India also exported these components to markets in developed countries.[56] A similar trend continued towards the end of 2024 as well.[57] However, the Indian solar industry continues to import various sub-components, such as cells and wafers, in large quantities from China.[58]

Demands for an Import Ban and Reluctance on Market Economy Status

While the growing trade deficit was a source of concern for the policymakers in India, the large-scale import of commodities, such as firecrackers, festive lamps and even idols of deities, generated backlash from some sections of society. This concern was articulated by various leaders from across the political spectrum. The Government of India's response to these demands was pragmatic. In 2016, Commerce Minister Nirmala Sitharaman, in a parliamentary debate, stated: "Just because I don't like a country, I cannot ban all goods from that country ... a complete ban of import from any country is not possible under World Trade Organisation (WTO) rules just because we have problems, diplomatically, territorially or militarily."[59] Similarly, during the same year, Defence Minister Manohar Parrikar also referred to the difficulties of imposing a ban due to the principles of the WTO but added that individuals can choose not to buy Chinese commodities.[60] It should be noted that the calls for banning Chinese products also resulted from the deteriorating bilateral relationship between the two countries. In 2016, China opposed India's attempts to join the Nuclear Suppliers Group (NSG) and two years earlier, there was a standoff between the security forces of the two countries at Chumar in Ladakh.

Responding to the conversations on the boycott of goods, the spokesperson of the Chinese Embassy in Delhi, in his remarks in 2016, listed a few critical areas that India should consider: (1) the boycott will not just affect Diwali products but may get extended to other products; (2) exports to India account for only 2 per cent of China's total exports, and therefore, China may not experience significant economic pain due to a possible decline in trade relations; (3) Indians should recognise that China is one of the largest importers of cotton, and it brings benefits to 1.2 million cotton growers in the country; (4) the Indian pharmaceutical industry sources its raw materials from China; and (5) the boycott will negatively impact Chinese investments in India.[61] The Chinese media also noted that the boycott was unsuccessful as Chinese products remain top sellers on the major Indian online retailers.[62] In the subsequent years, as India made efforts to reduce unhealthy economic interactions between the two countries, Chinese authorities articulated the above arguments with a few modifications. The calls for banning Chinese consumer products persisted in the subsequent years as well. For instance, when China blocked Indian attempts to get Masood Azhar designated as a global terrorist by the United Nations (in 2019) and during the India-China standoff in Ladakh (in 2020), there were calls for boycotting Chinese goods in India. In 2020, in response to the Indian government's decision to ban Chinese mobile apps, Chinese officials criticised the policies as violating "the market principles and rules of the World Trade Organization."[63]

The calls for the ban from various segments of Indian society indicate that the India-China bilateral trade has resulted only in temporary transactional outcomes, and it did not result in the structural intertwining of the economies of the two countries. There was little fear that the boycott of Chinese commodities would result in massive job losses in India. On the contrary, there is a strong perception that trade with China is resulting in job losses as Indian small and medium-sized enterprises cannot withstand the unfair competition from the big Chinese firms. Constrained trade relations with China may result in temporary setbacks in a few sectors. While the Chinese spokesperson referred to cotton exports, it should be noted that Indian cotton exports were getting diversified to other countries, such as Vietnam and Bangladesh.

While the Indian government did not give in to demands for wholesale banning of imports from China, it has been deploying various strategies permissible under the WTO in response to Chinese imports. It is not surprising that of the "535 cases where anti-dumping duties … imposed by India from 1994-2014, a maximum of 134 has been on goods from China", and the trend continued in the subsequent years as well.[64] In 2017, India extended anti-dumping duties on steel products for five years.[65] In 2023, in response to growing concerns in domestic industry, India imposed an "anti-dumping duty on some Chinese steel for five years."[66] In 2024, the Indian government imposed anti-dumping duties on numerous products for a period of five years.[67] Around the same period, an anti-dumping probe on solar glass imports from China was also initiated by the Indian government.[68]

Thus far, to determine anti-dumping measures, India has been using the pricing data of third countries to assess the normal value of the goods exported from China. This was done according to the 2001 China-WTO agreement that allows the WTO member countries to use third-country data to determine the appropriate export price of a commodity from China for 15 years until December 2016. However, India has refrained from giving China the 'Market-Economy Status' (MES). India's position was more in tune with "the US and European Union that unlike in 'market economies' where prices of items are market determined (based on demand & supply conditions), there is still a significant government influence in the Chinese market."[69] Bestowing the market economy status to China will make it difficult for India to levy anti-dumping duties on China. There is a strong opinion in India that MES cannot be accorded to Beijing, as China indulges in unfair trade practices. For instance, Mohan Kumar, a former Indian negotiator at the WTO, noted, "China has gamed the multilateral trading system for its own benefit."[70] To demonstrate the point that China has gamed the trading system, Dr Mohan Kumar lists a series of concerns, such as the remarkable opacity of the policy regime, sizeable subsidies by the federal government, barriers for foreign companies to operate in digital as well as data economy, dominant role of SOEs in the economy, and forced technology transfer and intellectual property (IP) theft.[71]

The apprehensions that Chinese goods may flood the Indian market also informed the Indian government's decision not to join the Regional Comprehensive Economic Partnership (RCEP). In 2023, Commerce and Industry Minister Piyush Goyal stated that the government is "already concerned that the bilateral trade, even though USD 130 billion, is largely skewed in favour of China" and went on to add that the Indian industry believed that the RCEP would have further increased the trade deficit.[72] In October 2024, Commerce and Industry Minister Piyush Goyal expressed a similar sentiment by arguing that RCEP negotiations were about "getting India to do an FTA with China," which would have proved very costly for India.[73]

Minimal Investments and Exaggerated Expectations

In addition to trade and related matters, geopolitical rifts and territorial conflicts between the two countries also impacted Chinese investments in India. China invested in many developed and emerging economies worldwide, including in India's immediate neighbourhood. In addition to accessing new markets, such investments were geared towards accessing natural resources or designed with geopolitical considerations. However, Chinese investments in India were not commensurate with the latter's market size.

There were instances when there was an anticipation that India would receive significant investments from China. In 2014, after Narendra Modi's election as Prime Minister, there was optimism that India-China relations will witness an upward swing. Phrases such as "an orbital jump" and "handshake across the Himalayas—a lot warmer than usual" were used to describe the possible trajectory of the India-China relationship.[74] The statements from Chinese officials also added to this optimism. For instance, China's consul-general in Mumbai stated: "on a conservative estimate, I can say that we will commit investments of over USD 100 billion.... These will be made in setting up of industrial parks, modernisation of railways, highways, ports, power generation, distribution and transmission, automobiles, manufacturing, food processing and textile industries."[75] Such statements before Xi Jinping visited India resulted in exaggerated expectations regarding possible Chinese investments. The joint statement issued after the visit in 2015 referred to a possible USD 20 billion investment over five years, which did not materialise.[76]

In October 2016, India's NITI Aayog and its Chinese counterpart, the National Development and Reform Commission, agreed to increase Chinese investments in coastal manufacturing zones, high-speed rail networks, clean energy, and urban development and ensure greater access to Indian IT firms in China.[77] While such goals are laudable, there was limited success. There have been instances when Chinese firms invested in Indian technological companies, such as Paytm and Snapdeal. In the limited investments that Chinese firms made in India, sectors such as fintech, tech start-ups, and related domains received priority. The Chinese prioritisation was not in consonance with India's requirements for attracting investments in the infrastructure. Perhaps the Chinese firms were reluctant to invest in the infrastructure in India as it would involve long-term commitment, which was not in tune with Chinese geopolitical objectives. The Chinese investments were also stymied by the fact that India is not abundant in natural resources such as energy and rare earth metals. Between April 2000 and September 2024, Chinese investments in India amounted to a mere USD 2,505.91million, and China was the 22nd largest investor.[78]

Competing Connectivity Networks: India's Response

The ballooning trade deficit and minimal Chinese investments prompted India to be cautious in embracing the Chinese connectivity frameworks. As noted, the Chinese leaders formally announced the Silk Road Economic Belt in September 2013. A month later, the Indian Prime Minister visited Beijing, and his visit was preceded by Chinese incursions in the Depsang plains in the Ladakh region. The Indian news reports pointed out that the Chinese incursions took place up to a depth of 19 kilometres, and over 750 square kilometres were at stake.[79] The then Defence Minister, A K Antony, observed that "there are disputed points where both sides are going there, which sometimes causes some embarrassing situations."[80] The Depsang incident, the subsequent visit of Prime Minister Manmohan Singh to Beijing, and Chinese proposals pertaining to the Southern Silk Road suggest that Beijing was confident that it was possible to insulate the economic relationship from aggressive posture on the borders. For a few years, the Chinese expectations were validated partially as the economic relations continued to blossom in favour of China.

Before PM Manmohan Singh's visit to Beijing, there were news reports, which hinted that the Bangladesh- China- India- Myanmar (BCIM) corridor, the Southern Silk Road to South Asia, could be revived.[81] It is well known that the BCIM corridor would originate from Chengdu, then proceed to Yunnan province, travel through the northern part of Myanmar, traverse through Northeast India, and reach Bangladesh. The joint statement issued during PM Manmohan Singh's visit referred to the Study Group on the BCIM and the need "to study the specific programs on building the BCIM Economic Corridor."[82] While the reference to the BCIM in the joint statement was significant, India did not commit to operationalising the BCIM framework. With the benefit of hindsight, it is now evident that the Chinese were keen on an economic corridor into India, which would subsequently be part of the BRI. However, there was a lack of enthusiasm in India for the idea of the BCIM. There was an apprehension regarding Chinese interest in plugging into a region with significant economic challenges. Further, there was a possibility that Northeast India would become a supplier of natural resources to China under the BCIM rubric. Such a prospect, instead of addressing Northeast India's economic challenges, will further accentuate them.

Despite border incidents, the Indian government did not make efforts to curtail economic interactions with China. In his speech at the Central Party School in Beijing, Indian PM Manmohan Singh referred to the importance of drawing on Chinese expertise for the expansion of infrastructure, quality urbanisation, and promotion of innovation in manufacturing.[83] Prime Minister Manmohan Singh also referred to the need for joint promotion of renewable energy resources, food security and sustaining an open international trade regime. The Prime Minister suggested an expansive economic framework for engagement and, more importantly, sought to assure Beijing that "India welcomes China's emergence ... [and] ... old theories of alliances and containment are no longer relevant."[84] During the visit, both countries agreed on the Border Defence Cooperation Agreement, which highlighted the importance of "exchange information-including information about military exercises ... [and] ... not follow or tail patrols of the other side."[85]

In September 2014, days before Xi Jinping's visit to India, the defence forces of both countries were locked in a standoff in the Chumar sector of eastern Ladakh.[86] The Indian PM, Narendra Modi, did not mince words in expressing displeasure in the presence of the visiting dignitary. Alluding that the standoff may be confined to a small area but may have larger consequences, Prime Minister Modi stated, "even such small incidents can impact the biggest of relationships just as a little toothache can paralyse the entire body."[87] On the economic front, during President Xi's visit, the joint statement referred to the prospect of China establishing "two industrial parks in India ... [and invest] ... USD 20 billion in India ... [over] ... the next 5 years."[88] During President Xi's visit, a Five-Year Trade and Economic Development Plan was signed, which sought to develop a roadmap to reduce trade imbalance and also strengthen investment cooperation.[89] In his press statement, PM Narendra Modi referred to the worsening trade imbalance, called for improved market access and, referring to the BCIM corridor, added that the "efforts to rebuild physical connectivity in the region would also require a peaceful, stable and cooperative environment."[90] This was probably one of the early references by PM Narendra Modi that the compartmentalisation of security issues and economic issues may not continue in the face of aggressive Chinese actions on the border. Subsequently, India's External Affairs Minister, Sushma Swaraj, expressed concerns regarding the Chinese infrastructure projects in Pakistan-Occupied Kashmir and called for an immediate cessation of such activities.[91]

During PM Modi's visit to China in May 2015, both countries agreed to open new consulates in Chengdu and Chennai, enhance railway cooperation, establish a State/Provincial Leaders' Forum to promote economic interactions, and increase trade at border points, such as Nathu La, Lipu-Lekh Pass, and Shipki La.[92] The Indian premier travelled to Shanghai to interact with top Chinese CEOs and after the meeting, addressed the business leaders and suggested that there was significant potential for Chinese investments in the manufacturing sector in India as well as in infrastructure.[93] In 2016, aggressive Chinese border actions continued to raise concerns in India. Chinese troops reportedly moved across the LAC and halted canal construction in the Demchok area in Ladakh (India).[94] Meanwhile, the Chinese connectivity projects in Pakistan and Sri Lanka picked up momentum. As the Chinese economic activities in the Indian subcontinent gained pace, there were deliberations in India on the prudence of joining the Chinese initiatives. Noted Indian journalist Prem Shankar Jha opined that "if India chooses to stay out of One Belt One Road (OBOR), it will only increase its isolation within South Asia and hasten the end of its regional hegemony."[95] Similarly, others argued that India "should use the infrastructure and institutions that are being created to further India's transformation."[96] The Chinese policymakers/academicians also urged India to be "more pragmatic and flexible" and join the CPEC framework.[97] Tsinghua University Professor Li Xiguang called for "'soft borders', one that avoids a 'hard' settlement of disputed boundaries, offers a way forward for regional cooperation." Li Xiguang added, "if Kashmir has a 'soft border', I think CPEC could unlock Kashmir and make it a part of a much grander regional transportation network, with Srinagar as one of its important nodes ... Remember, in earlier times, Kashmir used to be the terminal of the Silk Road—it was part of the route pursued by diplomats, connecting Central Asia, Kashgar, Ladakh and Delhi."[98] However, the Indian government was steadfast in its reluctance to join the BRI. Indian Foreign Secretary S. Jaishankar reiterated India's preference for building connectivity networks through consultative processes rather than participating in connectivity frameworks implemented through unilateral decisions.[99] Jaishankar's statement implied that since the BRI was a plan the Chinese articulated without any prior consultation, participation in such an enterprise would not be possible. Further, Tanvi Madan, referring to the speeches of Indian policymakers, pointed out, "India ... sees China's OBOR as a national Chinese initiative" and not as a genuine multilateral initiative.[100]

The Chinese government held the first Belt and Road Forum on May 14-16, 2017 and extended invitations to many countries, including India. There was anticipation that India would at least send an official-level representation if not a ministerial participation. Contrary to such expectations, India refrained from participating in the forum. A day before the forum, the Indian government made a formal statement on the BRI forum. The statement noted that "Connectivity initiatives must follow principles of financial responsibility to avoid projects that would create unsustainable debt burden for communities ... [and] ... must be pursued in a manner that respects sovereignty and territorial integrity."[101] Referring specifically to the China-Pakistan Economic Corridor (CPEC), the statement said, "no country can accept a project that ignores its core concerns on sovereignty and territorial integrity."[102] The Indian government's statement was not merely a criticism of the CPEC but also questioned the approach and values guiding China's Silk Road initiatives. A month later, Chinese military personnel attempted to move into Doklam Plateau to construct a road at the India-Bhutan-China trijunction. The Chinese actions violated the 2012 agreement, which stated that "the tri-junction boundary points between India, China and third countries will be finalised in consultation with the concerned countries ... any attempt, therefore, to unilaterally determine tri-junction points is in violation of this understanding."[103] The Chinese actions resulted in a tense standoff between India and China. Subsequently, in late August, both countries agreed to expedite disengagement at Doklam.[104] On the sidelines of the Brazil-Russia-India-China-South Africa (BRICS) summit at Xiamen, Indian leadership conveyed to their Chinese counterparts that for the "relationship to go forward, then peace and tranquillity on the border area should be maintained."[105] Given the timeline of Chinese actions, it could be interpreted that the Doklam incursions constituted Beijing's attempts to penalise India for its stance on the BRI. If that was the objective, then Chinese actions may have contributed to further hardening India's stance.

The Wuhan Summit in April 2018, between Indian PM Narendra Modi and Chinese President Xi Jinping, was an attempt to repair and restore the bilateral relationship between the two countries. Both leaders called for improved strategic communication at various levels and sustainable bilateral trade between the two countries.[106] Post-Wuhan, there was anticipation in some quarters that India might modify its position on the BRI and might be more willing to work on some projects in third countries. Contrary to such expectations, in June 2018, India was the only country at the Shanghai Cooperation Organisation meeting that refused to endorse China's BRI.[107] Given the areas of contestation between the two countries, the relationship was characterised more as "Frenemies". At the Chennai summit in 2019, efforts were made to bridge the gap between the two countries, specifically on border security and trade issues.[108] At the 2nd India-China Informal Summit, both countries decided "to establish a High-Level Economic and Trade Dialogue mechanism … [and] … identified sectors through the development of a manufacturing partnership."[109] However, the summit meetings' attempts at mending the relationship did not make much progress. The emergence of the COVID-19 pandemic and the clashes on the border generated considerable stress on the bilateral relationship.

Pandemic, Border Tensions, and Economic Relations

In India, the spread of the coronavirus generated considerable disappointment with the lack of transparency and delay on the part of the Chinese authorities in sharing the information regarding the outbreak. There was an opinion that if China had disclosed the information about COVID-19 in its early stages, it would have been possible to contain the spread of the virus. The rapid spread of the virus resulted in healthcare emergencies and economic crises worldwide, including in India. The economic crisis generated considerable distress for many firms, and their stocks lost value in the market. It is broadly in this context that Chinese corporations started to pick stakes in various companies across the world. Even in India, there were news items that the Chinese had invested in or picked up shares in some of the leading financial sector companies in the country.[110] The disappointment with China for its inability to contain the COVID-19 virus quickly morphed into serious concerns as China initiated steps to financially benefit from the economic distress caused by the pandemic. The Indian government took quick corrective measures to prevent foreign direct investment from China into India. In April 2020, the Indian government mandated that investments from countries sharing land borders with India require prior governmental approvals.[111] On the other hand, the pandemic created economic opportunities for India. There was anticipation that India would benefit from the investments that are moving away from China because of non-transparent decision-making processes. Various multinational corporations (MNCs) that had invested in China during the pandemic recognised that they didn't have a full mapping of the supply chain in that country. The vagueness of the spread of the supply chain was seen as a variable which would impose sudden and unanticipated costs in terms of the operations of various MNCs.

Meanwhile, India-China relations deteriorated significantly in 2020. In April/May, Chinese troops made aggressive manoeuvres across the Line of Actual Control (LAC). India quickly scaled up its presence all along the LAC, specifically in the Ladakh region, and contested the People's Liberation Army (PLA) troops' attempts to move across the LAC. There were understandings that in disputed spaces, both sides would refrain from creating permanent structures and fortified positions or deploying heavy military equipment.[112] However, the Chinese actions were contrary to such agreements.

The border tensions spiked in June 2020, as Indian forces contested the Chinese troops that tried to move across the LAC in the Galwan Valley region. The clashes resulted in the death of 20 Indian soldiers and an unspecified number of casualties/fatalities on the Chinese side. While China admitted it lost four soldiers, there was considerable speculation that the number could be much higher.[113] This was the first time since 1975 that the LAC witnessed fatalities due to skirmishes between the two armies. These developments resulted in a complete collapse of trust in India towards China. Subsequently, in September, both "militaries accused each other of opening fire during a confrontation,"[114] which happened after a gap of 25 years. In a substantive and symbolic gesture, India deployed the Special Frontier Force (SFF) to move into strategically important heights in the Kailash range near Pangong Tso.[115] It should be noted that the SFF troops also had soldiers of Tibetan origin.

Chinese news sources gave multiple reasons for the Chinese belligerence towards India. Some argued that the dilution of Article 370 in the Indian Constitution on August 5, 2019, which accorded special status to Jammu and Kashmir, could have triggered the Chinese response. A Chinese diplomat in Pakistan tweeted: "India's actions of unilaterally changing the status quo of Kashmir and continuing to exacerbate regional tensions have posed a challenge to the sovereignty of China and Pakistan…"[116] However, such a line of argument validates India's concerns that it needs to have better control on Jammu and Kashmir and Ladakh regions and therefore, dilution of autonomous provisions were much needed. Therefore, China's aggressive actions on the border will not prompt the Indian government to roll back the constitutional amendments. More importantly, the operationalisation of the CPEC, which preceded the dilution of Article 370, altered the status quo of the Jammu and Kashmir dispute.

There was speculation that India's infrastructure building in Ladakh at a rapid pace may have caused the Chinese belligerence. The Chinese foreign ministry spokesperson noted that China is "opposed to conducting infrastructure development for military purposes in the border area."[117] However, China already has a significant advantage in terms of terrain (accessing contested points from the Tibet Plateau is relatively easier compared to the steep gradient from the Indian side). China also has much better infrastructure facilities in the Tibet region right up to the Indian border. Moreover, numerous reports showed that China rapidly scaled up its defence infrastructure (such as air bases, air defence positions, and heliports) to be closer to the Indian border after the Doklam incident in 2017.[118]

There was an argument that India's evolving relations with the United States may have triggered a Chinese response. For instance, a *Global Times* op-ed article alleged that "seduced by the current US government's 'Indo-Pacific' plot—which aims to encircle China geographically and stifle China's rise by any means—Indian leaders seem to have taken the bait and followed on the heels of Washington by hamstringing this country."[119] Similar arguments were made in 1962 and many times after that. Compared to India, China has far greater interactions with the United States in the economic realm. According to the United States Trade Representative data, in 2002, the trade in goods and services between the US and China amounted to a whopping USD 758.4 billion.[120] India's economic interactions with the US are nowhere close to China's. Even if India moved closer to the United States, threatening to occupy Indian territory is undoubtedly not a prudent approach to wean India away from the United States.

None of the above arguments explain the reasons for the Chinese aggressive tactics. There was an opinion in India that the Chinese actions constituted a diversionary tactic. Shishir Gupta noted that the "Chinese move is multi-pronged as it not only diverts attention from the domestic economic crisis, [but also from] Hong Kong and Taiwan."[121] It was also possible that the Chinese perceived that they might have a window of opportunity to make quick territorial gains. Chinese leaders may have calculated that the international community was busy with the global pandemic and consequent economic challenges. They may have also calculated that India, which was busy combating the pandemic and its economic consequences, may look the other way on China's incremental territorial advances.

The belligerent actions of the Chinese prompted a fundamental shift in Indian policymakers' attitude toward economic engagement with China. Before the 2020 Ladakh standoff, economic interactions with China were relatively more insulated from aggressive tactics by Beijing on the borders. However, after the Ladakh standoff, the Indian leadership sought to discourage enhanced economic engagement with China. An important step was the amendment to the General Financial Rules of India "to enable the imposition of restrictions on bidders from countries which share a land border with India on the grounds of ... national security."[122] Countries that receive lines of credit or developmental assistance from India were exempted from this regulation, which meant that this rule would apply only to China and Pakistan. Since there is very little FDI from Pakistan, the new rules were aimed at China.

In a series of actions, the Indian government agencies blocked over 200 Chinese apps and their clones or variants.[123] Dipanjan Roy Chaudhury argued that the app ban was operationalised to curb the possibility of Chinese surveillance and data collection tactics.[124] The blocking of these apps was done under Section 69 of India's Information Technology Act 2000, which empowered the government with the "power to issue directions for blocking for public access of any information through any computer resource."[125] The legislation created a proper institutional mechanism, involving a committee of officers from relevant ministries tasked with making appropriate decisions after due diligence. There was sharp criticism that the legislation undermined individual rights, and the provisions of the legislation and its validity were subjected to judicial scrutiny. While the Supreme Court struck down the provisions that undermined free speech, it noted that the government could issue an order for blocking online portals/apps if the reasons for such action were recorded in writing, and such decisions were subject to judicial scrutiny.[126] A closer examination of the government's decision demonstrates that in addition to national security concerns, there were a host of other concerns relating to data security and safeguarding the privacy of individuals, which guided the decision to block the Chinese apps. Further, these decisions were also based on numerous complaints received from the Cyber Crime Coordination Centre and the Computer Emergency Response Team. Moreover, there were instances when Chinese applications, such as TikTok, censored videos of Indian stand-up comedians for criticising Chinese foreign policy.[127]

Chinese firms have also come under the scanner for tax evasion and other financial irregularities in India. In 2022, Indian agencies launched an investigation against Vivo, a Chinese firm, for alleged money laundering.[128] In 2023, India's Ministry of Corporate Affairs ordered a Serious Fraud

Investigation Office investigation against Vivo Mobiles' operations in India.[129] The Indian agencies have claimed that about "USD 12.87 billion was remitted outside India by Vivo to some trading companies controlled by its Chinese parent [through] a "masking layer" intended to escape government notice."[130] In the same year, India's Enforcement Directorate reportedly issued a show cause notice to Xiaomi for alleged illegal remittances.[131] In 2024, China's Xiaomi informed the Indian government that "there are apprehensions among component suppliers regarding establishing operations in India, stemming from the challenges faced by companies in India, particularly from Chinese origin."[132] While Indian authorities opined that some Chinese firms were resorting to financial irregularities, Chinese news reports suggested that India was creating hurdles for Chinese businesses "fueled by purely political motives."[133] However, the Indian government's position was that they "are open to doing business with any company anywhere as long as they are investing and conducting their business lawfully and are in compliance with the Indian laws."[134] In 2024, Chinese digital platforms were under investigation for loan fraud, and there were reports that hackers from China had gathered immigration data from Indian government agencies.[135] The investigations are impacting the Chinese firms' ability to collaborate with Indian firms. Gulveen Aulakh and Shouvik Das reported that Chinese smartphone makers "are talking to Indian groups ... but talks on taking majority equity have not progressed because of the tax cases and investigations by the Enforcement Directorate, which have a direct bearing on the brand."[136]

Along with blocking tech apps, various "Chinese think tanks, business fora, and advocacy groups" were placed under "the requirement of prior screening/ clearance."[137] Further, the Indian government announced that it is "reviewing the presence of China's Confucius Institutes in universities" in India as they are "extensions of the Chinese government that censor certain topics and perspectives in course materials on political grounds, and use hiring practices that take political loyalty into consideration."[138] All these measures suggest that the Indian government decided to push back the Chinese presence in the Indian economy and other sectors.

Conclusion

China has adopted a multi-pronged strategy towards India. Beijing's sustained territorial violations have ensured that India cannot give full attention to other long-standing and emerging security threats. Given the scale of Chinese deployments on the border, India will have to constantly look over its shoulder in case it needs to take punitive action against Pakistan's support of terrorism. China is bolstering the defence capabilities of countries, such as Pakistan, that have adversarial relations with India. Other countries in the subcontinent, such as Bangladesh, have also been recipients of Chinese defence equipment and related cooperation. China is increasing its naval presence in the Indian Ocean Region (IOR) and is constructing advanced maritime infrastructure to project power into the region. Beijing is also making persistent efforts to contain India's presence on various international platforms, such as the Nuclear Supplier Group (NSG), and has been reluctant to support New Delhi's demands for reforming the United Nations Security Council (UNSC). China has deployed its veto power in the UNSC to delay India's request to censure and sanction international terrorists acting against India. For instance, Indian officials often pointed to the fact that China, all through 2017, was blocking the United Nations' terrorist tag to Pakistani terror group Jaish-e-Mohammed Chief Masood Azhar.[139] In 2023, India sharply criticised China for blocking "a proposal to designate Pakistan-based Lashkar-e-Taiba (LeT) leader Sajid Mir as a global terrorist."[140] A year later, in 2024, India's Permanent Representative to the United Nations, Ruchira Kamboj, speaking at the UNSC open debate, stated: "For genuine, evidence-based listing proposals for globally sanctioned terrorists to be blocked, without giving any due justification, is uncalled for and smacks of doublespeak when it comes to the Council's commitment in tackling the challenge of terrorism."[141] While deploying numerous tactics to prevent India's rise, China continues to explore new economic opportunities in India.

Interestingly, China has been articulating multiple connectivity frameworks into India through third countries. The Bangladesh, China, India, Myanmar (BCIM) and China-India-Nepal Economic Corridor are examples of such efforts. It is pertinent to note that China has thus far refrained from proposing a direct economic corridor with India. A direct economic corridor between India and China mandates the delineation of the Line of Actual Control (LAC), at least in some sectors. Therefore, the Chinese objective seems to be to access India's massive market without resolving the boundary dispute.

The Chinese approach prompted India to adopt a more cautious approach to the Chinese economic initiatives. As noted, India refused to participate in the 2017 BRI Forum. Among the major powers, India was the only country that boycotted the forum, and the title of Sadanand Dhume's essay aptly summed up the Indian response as "One Belt, One Road, One Boycott".[142] India's reluctance stemmed from the fact that the CPEC was passing through Indian territory, which was occupied by Pakistan. India's Ministry of External Affairs spokesperson, in May 2017, stated: "Regarding the so-called 'China-Pakistan Economic Corridor', which is being projected as the flagship project of the BRI/OBOR, the international community is well aware of India's position.... no country can accept a project that ignores its core concerns on sovereignty and territorial integrity."[143] On the other hand, Beijing always stated that through the CPEC, China is not taking a position on the Kashmir dispute, which India and Pakistan should resolve.[144] From New Delhi's perspective, growing economic interactions between China and Pakistan directly impacted Kashmir and India's internal security.

Further, the aggressive Chinese military manoeuvres in Ladakh added impetus to the Indian government's rethinking of the bilateral relationship. For instance, Minister of External Affairs S Jaishankar, in April 2021, stated, "The Chinese, without provocation, brought an enormous force to the border ... this is not rocket science; you cannot disrupt peace & tranquillity at the border and carry on with the rest of the relationship."[145] While India was reluctant to embrace Chinese economic initiatives, the Indian policy after the Ladakh standoff abandoned treating the border dispute and economic interactions as two separate tracks. Instead, the Indian government approached economic interactions, the border dispute, and associated political differences as closely intertwined variables.

The Indian government has made persistent efforts to modulate economic engagement with China. Constraints on investments and the banning of tech platforms were initiated, which significantly impacted the operations of the Chinese firms in the Indian economy. The Chinese firms could not make inroads in the 5G telecommunications market and other hi-tech segments in the Indian economy. However, imports from China continued on an upward trajectory. Such a trend has much to do with the fact that India is a rapidly growing economy, and its industries tend to import a fairly large amount of intermediate products from China. Further, given that Indian consumers tend to be price-conscious, the relatively lower-priced Chinese products tend to find the market easily. The imports from China attest that India continues to be a free market economy, and the Indian private sector is free to import raw materials and consumer products from China.

The imports from China have undermined local employment opportunities and industry in India. To promote domestic manufacturing, the Indian government has launched various initiatives and schemes, which include Digital India, Electronics Hardware Technology Park Scheme/ Export Oriented Unit Scheme, Make in India, Software Technology Parks, and Special Economic Zones.[146] The Production Linked Incentive (PLI) Scheme has significantly accelerated domestic manufacturing in various sectors, such as automobiles, auto components, electronics, and IT hardware. According to Indian government data in November 2024, the PLI scheme may have created approximately 950,000 jobs in various sectors.[147] The PLI scheme also resulted in increased FDI inflows into various sectors, such as food processing industries, medical appliances, and drugs and pharmaceuticals. With increased domestic manufacturing, India's imports of critical components may decline in the medium term.

Despite efforts aimed at encouraging domestic manufacturing, the massive imports from China persisted. It was often assumed that enhanced economic interactions between countries would result in improved bilateral relationships. However, in the India-China bilateral dynamic, increased economic interactions and a tense border standoff happened simultaneously. Interestingly, during the skirmishes, the defence forces of both countries did not fire a single shot and instead indulged in hand-to-hand combat with rudimentary weapons, such as sticks and spikes.

Despite the tense standoff on the borders, India and China had multiple negotiations to find common ground. For instance, in July 2024, the foreign ministers of India and China interacted on the sidelines of the Shanghai Cooperation Organization meeting. At the meeting, India's External Affairs Minister, S Jaishankar, reiterated that the standoff could be resolved by adhering to "three mutuals—mutual respect, mutual sensitivity and mutual interests."[148] In the same month, both leaders interacted again on the sidelines of the ASEAN-related Foreign Ministers' Meeting in Vientiane, Lao PDR. In September 2024, India's National Security Adviser Ajit Doval interacted with his Chinese counterpart, Wang Yi, in Saint Petersburg, Russia, to find an early resolution to the standoff on the borders.[149] On October 21, 2024, India and China agreed on the principles governing patrolling and resumption of grazing by civilians in the Depsang and Demchok areas in Ladakh.[150] Two days later, the Indian premier and the Chinese president met on the sidelines of the BRICS Summit in Kazan, which were their first formal talks in over five years.[151] For the past few years, the standoff at Depsang and Demchok proved to be knotty for a quick resolution, and therefore, the October 2024 agreement on disengagement was significant. However, it should be recognised that what was achieved was the disengagement of troops deployed in proximity, and both countries have yet to make progress on the demobilisation of forces.

As the tensions between the two countries showed signs of subsiding, the voices in India that called for calibrated economic engagement with China got amplified. For instance, the Economic Survey, released in 2024, called for increased FDI from China as "it is more effective to have Chinese companies invest in India and then export the products to these markets rather than importing from China, adding minimal value, and then re-exporting them."[152] Responding to the requests from the industry, the Indian government expedited visa approvals for technicians from China engaged by companies operating in 14 strategic sectors under the PLI Scheme.[153] The Indian government also approved investment proposals from Chinese firms in the electronic manufacturing sector.[154] Referring to the Indian government's decision to approve Chinese investments, the *Global Times*, in its report, pointed out that "more efforts and practical actions are needed from the Indian side if it aims to regain the trust."[155]

Perhaps some Indian policymakers want to replicate the Chinese approach to foreign direct investments. Despite territorial contestations, China was able to leverage investments from Japan to achieve higher economic growth rates. Can India achieve faster economic growth rates with Chinese investments amidst occasional border standoffs? It should be noted that not all foreign direct investments are similar as they are defined by the political and economic requirements of the countries that send the capital. The Chinese foreign investments will seek not only profits but also act as platforms to export surpluses stemming from domestic overcapacities in its manufacturing sector. The possibility that Chinese authorities may be hesitant to share hi-tech equipment and other resources needs to be factored into India's China policy. Referring to Beijing's efforts to prevent the movement of Foxconn's technical manpower, who are Chinese citizens, to work in iPhone factories in India and withholding the shipment of specialised equipment needed to manufacture iPhones, Jabin Jacob argues that "China will continue its zero-sum approach towards India in economic affairs, as in other matters."[156] Atul Kumar and Antara Ghosal Singh also point out that some in the Chinese strategic community contend that "since India's great power ambitions and its overall strategic goals of outcompeting China have not changed much, China needs to exercise caution, particularly Chinese companies still need to adopt a cautious attitude when investing in India."[157] So, New Delhi's economic engagement with Beijing will have to factor in the competitive lens through which such interactions are viewed in China.

Even as India tries to figure out beneficial ways of economic engagement, the disengagement on the borders is indeed a welcome development. Both countries must travel considerably different distances before normalcy can be restored. The Chinese government's decision to create new counties in Aksai Chin, a territory that India claims, and its proposal to construct a massive hydropower project on the Brahmaputra River generated considerable dismay and disappointment in India. The Brahmaputra River is the lifeline of Northeast India and Bangladesh. Massive dams that alter river flow will have a significant impact on the livelihoods of millions in India and Bangladesh. Further, the hydropower project is being constructed along Himalayan fault lines, which is a seismically very sensitive region. The announcement of the project, a few weeks after the disengagement agreement on the border, demonstrates that the relationship with China will be very challenging for India.

The developments in the recent past have demonstrated that China may not be interested in the immediate resolution of the border dispute. The border dispute gives an opportunity for China to distract India from addressing other challenges emanating from its west. The persistent border tensions did not fundamentally undermine Chinese economic interests in India. China may continue with its strategy of reaping economic benefits without resolving the border disputes. In the coming years, the India-China relations will be defined by the growth of their respective economies. Despite considerable challenges, such as a slowdown in the major economies following the pandemic, India has emerged as a fast-growing major economy in the world. On the other hand, the Chinese economy, with a GDP of over USD 17 trillion, is slowing down and is facing considerable structural challenges. The changing character of the Chinese economy will define its external economic engagement and the projects it will implement under the BRI.

Notes

1. "Minutes of Chairman Mao Zedong's First Meeting with Nehru," *The Wilson Center Digital Archive*, October 19, 1954, https://digitalarchive.wilsoncenter.org/document/minutes-chairman-mao-zedongs-first-meeting-nehru

2. "Minutes of Chairman Mao Zedong's Second Meeting with Nehru," *The Wilson Center Digital Archive*, October 23, 1954, https://digitalarchive.wilsoncenter.org/document/minutes-chairman-mao-zedongs-second-meeting-nehru
3. Bertil Lintner, *India's China War*, (New Delhi: Oxford University Press, 2018), p: xix
4. Export Import Data Bank (2023-2024), Department of Commerce, Government of India, https://tradestat.commerce.gov.in/eidb/iecnttopn.asp
5. Ibid.
6. Elizabeth Roche, "India-China trade panel to meet soon," *LiveMint*, November 14, 2019, https://www.livemint.com/news/world/india-china-meet-at-brics-new-panel-for-trade-deficit-should-meet-early-11573704227992.html
7. "Regulatory, internal market barriers of China impact India's exports: GTRI," *Business Standard*, January 15, 2023, https://www.business-standard.com/article/economy-policy/regulatory-internal-market-barriers-of-china-impact-india-s-exports-gtri-123011500158_1.html
8. "Pharmaceutical Exports from India," *IBEF*, 2023-2024, https://www.ibef.org/exports/pharmaceutical-exports-from-india
9. "20 Annual Report 2023-2024," Pharmaceuticals Export Promotion Council of India (Pharmexcil), 2023-2024, https://pharmexcil.com/uploads/annualreports/Pharmexcil_20th_Annual_Report_Final_21_12_2024.pdf
10. "Promoting more balanced India-China Trade," *Press Information Bureau*, February 8, 2019, https://pib.gov.in/Pressreleaseshare.aspx?PRID=1563552
11. "China lifts suspension from 99 Indian seafood processing, exporting units," *Business Standard*, February 16 2023, https://www.business-standard.com/article/current-affairs/china-lifts-suspension-from-99-indian-seafood-processing-exporting-units-123021601189_1.html
12. "India's seafood exports touch an all-time high in FY 2022-23; grow 26.73% in quantity terms and 4.31% in value terms over FY 2021-22," *Press Information Bureau*, June 14, 2023, https://pib.gov.in/PressReleasePage.aspx?PRID=1932317
13. "India to Export First Consignment of Non-basmati Rice to China on Friday: Commerce Ministry," *The Times of India*, September 27, 2018, https://timesofindia.indiatimes.com/business/india-business/india-to-export-first-consignment-of-non-basmati-rice-to-china-on-friday-commerce-ministry/articleshow/65978457.cms.
14. "Five More Non-Basmati Rice Mills Cleared for Exports to China," *The Economic Times*, October 25, 2018, https://economictimes.indiatimes.com/news/economy/foreign-trade/five-more-non-basmati-rice-mills-cleared-for-exports-to-china/articleshow/66362509.cms
15. "China imports Indian rice for first time in 30 years amid tightening supplies," *Business Today*, December 2, 2020, https://www.businesstoday.in/current/economy-politics/china-imports-indian-rice-for-first-time-in-30-years-amid-tightening-supplies/story/423648.html
16. Orange Wang, "China Food Security: How's it Going and Why's it Important?" *South China Morning Post*, November 29, 2020, https://www.scmp.com/economy/china-economy/article/3111623/china-food-security-hows-it-going-and-whys-it-important

17. Zongyuan Zoe Liu, "China Increasingly Relies on Imported Food. That's a Problem," *Council for Foreign Relations,* January 25, 2023, https://www.cfr.org/article/china-increasingly-relies-imported-food-thats-problem#:~:text=Between%202000%20and%202020%2C%20the,%2C%20meat%2C%20and%20processed%20foods.

18. Harikishan Sharma, "China takes over as biggest importer of Indian broken rice," *The Indian Express,* June 14, 2022, https://indianexpress.com/article/india/china-takes-over-as-biggest-importer-of-indian-broken-rice-7968116/

19. Dhirendra Kumar, "India feeds strategic partners despite ban on rice exports," *Mint,* January 2 2024, https://www.livemint.com/industry/agriculture/india-feeds-strategic-partners-despite-ban-on-rice-exports-11704211003997.html

20. Joseph Glauber and Abdullah Mamun, "India Lifts Export Restrictions on Rice," *IFPRI,* November 8, 2024. https://www.ifpri.org/blog/india-lifts-export-restrictions-on-rice/

21. "India's Cotton Exports to Rise as Bangladesh Takes China's Place," *Reuters,* November 3, 2015, http://in.reuters.com/article/india-cotton-exports-idINKCN0SS1NX20151103

22. "India's cotton exports to China plunge 56.7% in 2014-15," *The Economic Times,* July 22, 2015, https://economictimes.indiatimes.com/news/economy/foreign-trade/indias-cotton-exports-to-china-plunge-56-7-in-2014-15/articleshow/48173600.cms?from=mdr

23. Rajendra Jadhav and Dominique Patton, "India Ships More Cotton to China As 25 Percent Tax Spoils U.S. Supply," *Reuters,* June 20, 2018 https://www.reuters.com/article/us-usa-trade-india-cotton/india-ships-more-cotton-to-china-as-25-percent-tax-spoils-us-supply-idUSKBN1JG1AC.

24. "India's cotton yarn export to China sees massive upsurge in July'23," *Apparel Resources News-Desk,* October 16, 2023, https://apparelresources.com/business-news/trade/indias-cotton-yarn-export-china-sees-massive-upsurge-july-23/#:~:text=As%20of%202022%2C%20India%27s%20cotton,has%20undergone%20a%20dramatic%20reversal.

25. "Cotton Industry and Exports," *IBEF,* November 2024, https://www.ibef.org/exports/cotton-industry-india#:~:text=In%20terms%20of%20cotton%20yarn,million%20kg%20of%20cotton%20yarn.

26. Kunal Bose, "How India Lost the Plot in Global Iron Ore Trade," *Business Standard,* January 27, 2016, http://www.business-standard.com/article/economy-policy/how-india-lost-the-plot-in-global-iron-ore-trade-116012701128_1.html

27. "Hard-Hit China Steel Mills Offer Hope for India's Iron Ore," *Reuters,* October 30, 2015, http://in.reuters.com/article/india-iron-china-idINKCN0SO0GQ20151030

28. Mahesh Kulkarni, "Iron Ore Exports to China May Double in FY21," *Deccan Herald,* June 2, 2020, https://www.deccanherald.com/business/business-news/iron-ore-exports-to-china-may-double-in-fy21-844880.html.

29. "The Growth of Iron Ore Exports from India: A 2024-25 Perspective," *Export Import Data,* September 5, 2024, https://www.exportimportdata.in/blogs/iron-ore-exports-from-india.aspx#:~:text=With%2018.8%20million%20tons%20(%2B,top%20exporters%20of%20raw%20materials

30. "Copper Producers face Risk of Losing China Market," *The Financial Express*, July 24, 2015, http://www.financialexpress.com/market/commodities/copper-producers-face-risk-of-losing-china-market/106442/
31. Vikas Dhoot, "As Cheaper Imports Increases Copper Industry ends SOS to Government," *The Economic Times*, October 14, 2015, http://economictimes.indiatimes.com/industry/indl-goods/svs/metals-mining/as-cheaper-imports-increases-copper-industry-sends-sos-to-government/printarticle/49344924.cms ;
32. "India's copper exports fell 70 percent in 2018/19 - trade body," *Reuters*, April 24, 2019, https://in.reuters.com/article/india-copper-exports/indias-copper-exports-fell-70-percent-in-2018-19-trade-body-idINKCN1S013O
33. Subhash Narayan, "Copper imports at all time high amid supply disruptions," *Mint*, June 3, 2023, https://www.livemint.com/economy/copper-imports-at-all-time-high-amid-supply-disruptions-11685725493728.html
34. V Narayanan, "India becomes net copper importer for a fifth year in a row bl-premium-article-image," *Businessline*, May 30, 2023, https://www.thehindubusinessline.com/economy/india-becomes-net-copper-importer-for-a-fifth-year-in-a-row/article66906853.ece ; also see Aggam Walia, "As Copper Mining Stalls and Imports Surge, Players Eye Overseas Assets," *Indian Express*, January 17, 2025, https://indianexpress.com/article/business/economy/as-copper-mining-stalls-and-imports-surge-players-eye-overseas-assets-9559097/
35. "Imports from China for at least 25 commodity groups rose in FY22-23," *Business Standard*, August 9, 2023, https://www.business-standard.com/india-news/imports-from-china-for-at-least-25-commodity-groups-rose-in-fy22-23-123080900930_1.html
36. "India's Auto Sector Not Ready to Quit China Habit," *Hindustan Times*, June 26, 2020, https://auto.hindustantimes.com/auto/news/india-s-auto-sector-not-ready-to-quit-china-habit-41593137651083.html
37. "China Remains Largest Import Source for Auto Parts: ACMA," *Business Line*, August 22, 2022, https://www.thehindubusinessline.com/companies/china-remains-largest-import-source-for-auto-parts-acma/article65797566.ece ; also see Rimjhim Singh, "China Participates in India Motor Show 2025," *Business Standard*, January 15, 2025, https://www.business-standard.com/auto-expo/news/china-participates-india-motor-show-2025-125011500229_1.html
38. "Indian Power Equipment Makers Demand Halt to China Imports," *Nikkei Asian Review*, January 26, 2017, http://asia.nikkei.com/magazine/20170126/Business/Indian-power-equipment-makers-demand-halt-to-China-imports?page=2
39. Sarita C Singh, "Ban on power equipment imports from China, Pak; Can't give jobs to country that transgresses into India: R K Singh," *Economic Times*, July 3, 2023, https://energy.economictimes.indiatimes.com/news/power/ban-on-power-equipment-imports-from-china-pak-cant-give-jobs-to-country-that-transgresses-into-india-r-k-singh/76765596#:~:text=New%20Delhi%3A%20India%20will%20not,other%20nations%20will%20need%20permissions.
40. "India's steel imports surge in June 2023, China and Vietnam dominate share," *Livemint*, July 17, 2023, https://www.livemint.com/economy/indias-steel-imports-surge-in-june-2023-china-and-vietnam-dominate-share-11689570446578.html

41. Neha Arora, "India Steel Imports from China Hit Record High, Data Shows," *Reuters*, December 20, 2024, https://www.reuters.com/markets/commodities/india-steel-imports-china-hit-record-high-data-shows-2024-12-20/
42. Vaidik Dalal, "Dolls to Drugs, Trade Links Run Deep," *Mint*, June 26, 2020, https://www.livemint.com/news/india/dolls-to-drugs-trade-links-run-deep-11593133953149.html.
43. Banikinkar Pattanayak, "Silver Lining! India Turned Net Exporter of Chemicals After 10 Years in FY 20," *The Financial Express*, July 21, 2020, https://www.financialexpress.com/economy/silver-lining-india-turned-net-exporter-of-chemicals-after-10-years-in-fy-20/2030122/
44. "Chinese blessing for the chemicals industry," *CRISIL*, https://www.crisil.com/content/dam/crisil/our-analysis/reports/Research/documents/2019/may/chinese-blessing-for-the-chemicals-industry.pdf
45. "India's imports from China across at least 25 major commodity groups rise on year," *Reuters*, August 10, 2023, https://www.reuters.com/world/asia-pacific/indias-imports-china-across-least-25-major-commodity-groups-rise-year-2023-08-09/
46. Subhrojit Mallick, "WTO's recent ruling against India to impact top Chinese handset makers' local manufacturing," *ET Telecom*, April 2023, https://telecom.economictimes.indiatimes.com/news/devices/wtos-recent-ruling-against-india-to-impact-top-chinese-handset-makers-local-manufacturing/99655945
47. Gulveen Aulakh, "Dominance of Chinese smartphones to wane," *Mint*, January 4, 2023, https://www.livemint.com/companies/news/dominance-of-chinese-smartphones-to-wane-11672852635365.html
48. Subhrojit Mallick, "Chinese smartphone makers in the eye of multiple storms," *Economic Times*, December 26, 2023, https://economictimes.indiatimes.com/industry/cons-products/electronics/chinese-smartphone-makers-in-the-eye-of-multiple-storms/articleshow/106280625.cms?from=mdr
49. "Shrinking market share, govt pressure trouble Chinese smartphone makers," *Business Standard*, December 26, 2023, https://www.business-standard.com/industry/news/shrinking-market-share-govt-pressure-trouble-chinese-smartphone-makers-123122600396_1.html
50. Chinmay Dhumal, "Indian Government Not Happy With Low Export Numbers of Chinese Smartphone Brands," *MySmartPrice*, https://www.mysmartprice.com/gear/indian-government-not-happy-with-low-export-numbers-of-chinese-smartphone-brands/
51. The Ministry of New and Renewable Energy (MNRE), Government of India, https://mnre.gov.in/solar/current-status/ also see "Nearly 70.1 GW Solar Power Capacity Installed in the Country: Union Minister for New & Renewable Energy and Power," *PIB*, August 9, 2023, https://pib.gov.in/PressReleaseIframePage.aspx?PRID=1947140
52. Utpal Bhaskar, "With an Eye on China, India to Offer Land Near Ports to Solar Equipment Makers," *Mint*, August 13, 2020, https://www.livemint.com/industry/energy/with-an-eye-on-china-india-to-offer-land-near-major-ports-for-solar-equipment-manufacturing-11597316045422.html.
53. Gireesh Chandra Prasad and Mayank Aggarwal, "For solar panel makers, low tariffs no cause for cheer," *LiveMint*, December 12, 2016, http://www.livemint.com/

Industry/VYrjpmLpqBZ8bLkQP49uNJ/For-solar-panel-makers-low-tariffs-no-cause-for-cheer.html

54. Soumya Sarkar, "India's solar dreams, too, are made in China," *Quartz*, August 17, 2016, https://qz.com/760079/indias-solar-dreams-too-are-made-in-china/
55. Foo Yun Chee, "EU wins court backing on anti-dumping duties on Chinese solar panels," *Reuters*, February 28, 2017, http://in.reuters.com/article/eu-china-court-trade-idINKBN1671AG
56. "India Slashes Solar Imports from China as Domestic Manufacturing Thrives," *Business Today*, September 14, 2023, https://www.businesstoday.in/latest/economy/story/india-slashes-solar-imports-from-china-as-domestic-manufacturing-thrives-398373-2023-09-14
57. "India's Solar Cell and Module Imports Drop Sharply in Q2 2024," *Mercom India*, 2024, https://www.mercomindia.com/indias-solar-cell-and-module-imports-drop-sharply-in-q2-2024.
58. "Indian solar industry still heavily reliant on Chinese imports," *Economic Times*, December 15,2023, https://energy.economictimes.indiatimes.com/news/renewable/indian-solar-industry-still-heavily-reliant-on-chinese-imports/106021347
59. Aditi Nigam, "Blanket ban on import of Chinese products not possible: Nirmala Sitharaman," *The Hindu Business Line*, April 25, 2016, http://www.thehindubusinessline.com/economy/blanket-ban-on-import-of-chinese-products-not-possible-nirmala-sitharaman/article8519587.ece
60. "India can't ban Chinese products but individuals can decide not to buy: Manohar Parrikar," *DNA*, October 12, 2016. http://www.dnaindia.com/india/report-india-can-t-ban-chinese-products-but-individuals-can-decide-not-to-buy-manohar-parrikar-2263621
61. "Chinese Embassy Spokesperson's Remarks on Boycott of Chinese Goods," *Press Release, Embassy of the People's Republic of China in India*, October 27, 2016, http://www.fmprc.gov.cn/ce/cein//eng/xwfb/t1409009.htm
62. Zhen Bo, "India boycott hasn't hurt China goods," *The Global Times*, October 13, 2016, http://www.globaltimes.cn/content/1011219.shtml
63. "China expresses grave concerns after India banned another 43 Chinese apps," *CGTN*, November 25, 2020, https://news.cgtn.com/news/2020-11-25/India-adds-43-mostly-Chinese-apps-to-ban-VHsc7tUTSw/index.html
64. Arun S, "India studying impact of market economy status for China," *The Hindu*, February 21, 2016, http://www.thehindu.com/business/Economy/india-studying-impact-of-market-economy-status-for-china/article8264686.ece
65. "India extends anti-dumping duty on some Chinese steel items by 5 yrs," *Reuters*, Feb 20, 2017, http://in.reuters.com/article/india-steel-antidumping-idINKBN15Z1CK
66. "India Imposes Anti-Dumping Duty on Some Chinese Steel for 5 years," *Reuters*, September 11, 2023, https://www.reuters.com/markets/commodities/india-imposes-anti-dumping-duty-some-chinese-steel-5-years-2023-09-11/
67. "India Imposes Anti-dumping Duty on Three Chinese Products for Five Years," *The Economic Times*, January 10, 2024, https://economictimes.indiatimes.com/news/economy/foreign-trade/india-imposes-anti-dumping-duty-on-3-chinese-products-for-5-years/articleshow/106696998.cms?from=mdr; also see "Govt Imposes Anti-Dumping Duty on Five Chinese Products for 5 Years," *Business*

Standard, October 23, 2024, https://www.business-standard.com/external-affairs-defence-security/news/govt-imposes-anti-dumping-duty-on-five-chinese-products-for-5-years-124102301372_1.html

68. "India Initiates Anti-Dumping Probe into Imports of Solar Glass from China, Vietnam," *The Hindu,* February 26, 2024, https://www.thehindu.com/business/markets/india-initiates-anti-dumping-probe-into-imports-of-solar-glass-from-china-vietnam/article67852609.ece
69. "India is 'non-committal' about market economy tag for China," *The Hindu*, November 18, 2016, http://www.thehindu.com/business/India-is-%E2%80%98non-committal%E2%80%99-about-market-economy-tag-for-China/article16667486.ece
70. Mohan Kumar, "How China Gamed the Multilateral Trading System," *Hindustan Times*, August 9, 2020, https://www.hindustantimes.com/opinion/how-china-gamed-the-multilateral-trading-system-opinion/story-BugAzmhdCWidbZAxnfhlUI.html
71. Ibid.
72. "India's Heart With US: Minister On Staying Out Of China-Led Trade Bloc," *NDTV*, August 25, 2023, https://www.ndtv.com/india-news/india-heart-with-us-minister-on-staying-out-of-china-led-trade-bloc-rcep-4330377
73. Prashant Jha, "Goyal Hits Out at Cong Over Trade Deficit with China," *Hindustan Times*, January 16, 2025. https://www.hindustantimes.com/india-news/goyal-hits-out-at-cong-over-trade-deficit-with-china-101728066912872.html
74. Debasish Roy Chowdhury, "Why Modi's India is warming to China," *The South China Morning Post*, September 17, 2014, http://www.scmp.com/news/china/article/1594227/why-modis-india-warming-china
75. "China to invest $100 billion in India over 5 years," *The Times of India*, September 13, 2014, http://timesofindia.indiatimes.com/business/india-business/China-to-invest-100-billion-in-India-over-5-years/articleshow/42386772.cms
76. Nayanima Basu, "China dashes $100-bn hope, to invest $20 bn over 5 years," *Business Standard*, September 19, 2014, http://www.business-standard.com/article/economy-policy/china-dashes-100-bn-hope-to-invest-20-bn-over-5-years-114091800557_1.html
77. "Agreements signed to increase Chinese investments in India," *The Indian Express*, October 11, 2016, http://indianexpress.com/article/business/economy/agreements-signed-to-increase-chinese-investments-in-india-3076063/
78. "Fact Sheet on Foreign Direct Investment (FDI) Inflow – From April, 2000 To September, 2024," *DPIIT*, September, 2024, https://dpiit.gov.in/sites/default/files/FDI%20Factsheet%20September%202024.pdf
79. Rajat Pandit and Sanjay Dutta, "Chinese Incursion 19km, but 750 sq km at Stake for India," *Times of India*, May 2, 2013, https://timesofindia.indiatimes.com/india/Chinese-incursion-19km-but-750-sq-km-at-stake-for-India/articleshow/19826487.cms
80. "India, China trying to develop mechanism to prevent face-offs: Antony," *The Hindu*, July 26, 2013, https://www.thehindubusinessline.com/news/india-china-trying-to-develop-mechanism-to-prevent-face-offs-antony/article23122431.ece

81. "The Ancient 'Silk Route' Between China and India Might Be Revived," *Firstpost,* June 9, 2013, https://www.firstpost.com/india/the-ancient-silk-route-between-china-and-india-might-be-revived-855589.html.
82. "Joint Statement- A Vision for Future Development of India-China Strategic and Cooperative Partnership," *Ministry of External Affairs, Government of India,* October 23, 2013, https://mea.gov.in/bilateral-documents.htm?dtl/22379
83 "PM's Speech at the Central Party School in Beijing - India and China in the New Era," *Ministry of External Affairs,* October 24, 2013, https://archivepmo.nic.in/drmanmohansingh/speech-details.php?nodeid=1382
84. Ibid.
85. "Agreement between the Government of the Republic of India and the Government of the People's Republic of China on Border Defence Cooperation," *Ministry of External Affairs, Government of India,* October 23, 2013, https://www.mea.gov.in/bilateral-documents.htm?dtl/22366/Agreement+between+the+Government+of+the+Republic+of+India+and+the+Government+of+the+Peoples+Republic+of+China+on+Border+Defence+Cooperation
86. Shishir Gupta, "China, India in border skirmish ahead of Xi visit," The *Hindustan Times,* September 16, 2014, https://www.hindustantimes.com/india/china-india-in-border-skirmish-ahead-of-xi-visit/story-es46bqLyFXY5qgosyMnQAK.html
87. "Chinese Incursion in Ladakh: A Little Toothache Can Paralyze Entire Body, Modi Tells Xi Jinping," *The Times of India,* September 20, 2014, https://timesofindia.indiatimes.com/india/Chinese-incursion-in-Ladakh-A-little-toothache-can-paralyze-entire-body-Modi-tells-Xi-Jinping/articleshow/42940337.cms
88. "Joint Statement between the Republic of India and the People's Republic of China on Building a Closer Developmental Partnership," *Ministry of External Affairs, Government of India,* September 19, 2014, https://mea.gov.in/bilateral-documents.htm?dtl/24022
89. "List of Documents Signed During the State Visit of Chinese President Xi Jinping to India," *Ministry of External Affairs, Government of India,* December 30, 2020, https://www.mea.gov.in/bilateral-documents.htm?dtl/24012/List+of+Documents+signed+during+the+State+Visit+of+Chinese+President+Xi+Jinping+to+India
90. "Press Statement by Prime Minister during the visit of President Xi Jinping of China to India (September 18, 2014)," *Ministry of External Affairs, Government of India,* September 18, 2014, https://www.mea.gov.in/Speeches-Statements.htm?dtl/24014/Press+Statement+by+Prime+Minister+during+the+visit+of+President+Xi+Jinping+of+China+to+India+September+18+2014
91. Q.No.†*260.Projects of China and Pakistan in Neighbouring Countries, Lok Sabha Starred Question No. 260, *Ministry of External Affairs, Government of India,* December 10, 2014, https://www.mea.gov.in/lok-sabha.htm?dtl/24458
92. "Joint Statement between India and China during Prime Minister's visit to China," *Ministry of External Affairs, Government of India,* May 15, 2015, https://www.mea.gov.in/bilateral-documents.htm?dtl/25240/Joint_Statement_between_the_India_and_China_during_Prime_Ministers_visit_toChina
93 "Full Text of Prime Minister Narendra Modi's Speech at the India-China Business Forum in Shanghai," *NDTV,* May 16, 2015, https://www.ndtv.com/india-news/

full-text-of-prime-minister-narendra-modis-speech-at-the-india-china-business-forum-in-shanghai-763508

94. "India-China troops face off in Ladakh over a canal: All you need to know," *Business Standard*, November 4, 2016, https://www.business-standard.com/article/current-affairs/why-demchok-water-canal-is-an-issue-between-india-china-116110400291_1.html

95. Prem Shankar Jha, "Why India Must Embrace China's One Belt One Road Plan," *The Wire*, August 13, 2016, https://thewire.in/diplomacy/india-must-embrace-chinas-one-belt-one-road-plan

96 Shiv Shankar Menon, "We Must Now Choose," *Outlook*, January 23, 2016, https://www.outlookindia.com/website/story/we-must-now-choose/296484

97. "Urging India To Back CPEC Project, Chinese Media Likens PoK With Taiwan," *NDTV*, March 7, 2017, http://www.ndtv.com/india-news/urging-india-to-back-cpec-project-chinese-media-likens-pok-with-taiwan-1666879

98. Atul Aneja, "Soft border approach can bring India into CPEC," *The Hindu*, December 26, 2016, https://www.thehindu.com/news/international/%E2%80%98Soft-border-approach-can-bring-India-into-CPEC%E2%80%99/article16943237.ece

99. Anirban Bhaumik, "India opposed to China's One-Belt-One-Road," *Deccan Herald*, March 3, 2016, deccanherald.com/content/532353/india-opposed-chinas-one-belt.html

100. Tanvi Madan, "What India thinks about China's One Belt, One Road initiative (but doesn't explicitly say)," *Brookings*, March 14, 2016, https://www.brookings.edu/articles/what-india-thinks-about-chinas-one-belt-one-road-initiative-but-doesnt-explicitly-say/

101. "Official Spokesperson's response to a query on participation of India in OBOR/BRI Forum," *Ministry of External Affairs, Government of India*, May 13, 2017, https://mea.gov.in/media-briefings.htm?dtl/28463/Official+Spokespersons+response+to+a+query+on+participation+of+India+in+OBORBRI+Forum

102. Ibid.

103. "Recent Developments in Doklam Area," *Ministry of External Affairs, Government of India*, https://www.mea.gov.in/press-releases.htm?dtl/28572/recent+developments+in+doklam+area

104. "Press Statement on Doklam disengagement understanding," *Ministry of External Affairs, Government of India*, August 28, 2017, https://mea.gov.in/press-releases.htm?dtl/28893/Press_Statement_on_Doklam_disengagement_understanding

105. Elizabeth Roche, "Narendra Modi, Xi Jinping create space to reset India-China ties," *Mint*, September 6, 2017, https://www.livemint.com/Politics/eCI7VWj50rADSrsjPB6EnI/Brics-Summit-2017-Narendra-Modi-Xi-Jinping-to-hold-bilater.html

106. "India-China Informal Summit at Wuhan," *Ministry of External Affairs, Government of India*, April 28, 2018, https://mea.gov.in/press-releases.htm?dtl/29853/IndiaChina_Informal_Summit_at_Wuhan

107. "India refuses to endorse China's Belt and Road Initiative," *The Hindu*, June 10, 2018, https://www.thehindu.com/news/national/india-refuses-to-endorse-chinas-belt-and-road-initiative/article24128902.ece

108. Jeffrey Gettleman, "They Run the World's Biggest Countries. Their Talk Won't Be Easy," *The New York Times,* October 11, 2019, https://www.nytimes.com/2019/10/11/world/asia/narendra-modi-xi-jinping-india-china.html.
109. "2nd India-China Informal Summit," *Ministry of External Affairs, Government of India,* October 12, 2019, https://www.mea.gov.in/press-releases.htm?dtl/31938/2nd_IndiaChina_Informal_Summit
110. Anand Adhikari, "After HDFC and ICICI Bank, People's Bank of China aims for Bajaj Finance," *Business Today*, September 21, 2020, https://www.businesstoday.in/sectors/banks/after-hdfc-and-icici-bank-the-people-bank-of-china-now-invests-in-bajaj-finance/story/416617.html
111. "Government amends the extant FDI policy for curbing opportunistic takeovers/acquisitions of Indian companies due to the current COVID-19 pandemic," Press *Information Bureau,* Government of India, April 18, 2020, https://pib.gov.in/newsite/PrintRelease.aspx?relid=202359
112. Pranab Dhal Samanta, "Chinese action violates 1993, 1996, and 2013 border agreements," *The Economic Times,* June 18, 2020, https://economictimes.indiatimes.com/news/defence/chinese-action-violates-1993-1996-and-2013-border-agreements/articleshow/76405795.cms?utm_source=contentofinterest&utm_medium=text&utm_campaign=cppst
113. "China admits it lost four soldiers in 2020 India border clash," *Al Jazeera,* February 19, 2021, https://www.aljazeera.com/news/2021/2/19/china-admits-it-lost-four-soldiers-in-2020-india-border-clash
114. Ajai Shukla, "India-China Ladakh Standoff: Firing on LAC, a First in 45 Years," *Business Standard,* September 9, 2020, https://www.business-standard.com/article/defence/india-china-ladakh-standoff-firing-on-lac-a-first-in-45-years-120090900057_1.html
115. Sandeep Unnithan, "Pangong Retreat: Detente at the Roof of the World," *India Today,* February 22, 2021, https://www.indiatoday.in/magazine/the-big-story/story/20210301-detente-at-the-roof-of-the-world-1770785-2021-02-20
116. "Article 370 Abrogation Led to Ladakh Standoff? Chinese Report Causes Stir," *The Week*, June 13, 2020, https://www.theweek.in/news/world/2020/06/13/article-370-abrogation-led-to-ladakh-standoff-chinese-report-causes-stir.html
117. "China Says It is Opposed to India's Infrastructure Development at Borders in Ladakh," *The New Indian Express*, September 29, 2020, https://www.newindianexpress.com/world/2020/sep/29/china-says-it-is-opposed-to-indias-infrastructure-development-at-borders-in-ladakh-2203598.html
118. "China Doubles Air Bases, Air Defence Positions and Heliports Near LAC After 2017 Doklam Standoff," *The Times of India*, September 22, 2020, https://timesofindia.indiatimes.com/india/china-doubles-air-bases-air-defence-positions-and-heliports-near-lac-after-2017-doklam-standoff-stratfor/articleshow/78257851.cms.
119. Li Hong, "India Should Not Make a Bad Situation with China Worse," *Global Times*, July 5, 2020, https://www.globaltimes.cn/content/1193568.shtml
120. "The People's Republic of China: China Trade & Investment Summary," *USTR*, https://ustr.gov/countries-regions/china-mongolia-taiwan/peoples-republic-china

121. Shishir Gupta, "China's Tactical Play in Ladakh Isn't Just About the Boundary," *Hindustan Times*, May 24, 2020, https://www.hindustantimes.com/analysis/china-s-tactical-play-in-ladakh-isn-t-just-about-the-boundary-analysis/story-aJy8XQDURYzT6nN70GsxzK.html
122. "Restrictions on Public Procurement from Certain Countries," *Press Information Bureau*, July 23, 2020, https://pib.gov.in/PressReleasePage.aspx?PRID=1640778
123. Vibhuti Agarwal and Eric Bellman, "India Bans More Chinese Apps As Part of Its Digital Campaign to Pressure Beijing," *The Wall Street Journal*, November 24, 2020, https://www.wsj.com/articles/india-bans-more-chinese-apps-as-part-of-its-digital-campaign-to-pressure-beijing-11606235329?mod=searchresults_pos7&page=3; Sankalp Phartiyal, "India Bans 200-Plus Chinese Mobile Apps in Boon for Paytm," *Bloomberg*, February 7, 2023, https://www.bloomberg.com/news/articles/2023-02-07/ant-backed-paytm-soars-after-report-india-banned-chinese-rivals
124. Dipanjan Roy Chaudhury, "Banning of Chinese apps in India to loosen Communist party's espionage work," *The Economic Times*, December 7, 2020, https://economictimes.indiatimes.com/news/defence/banning-of-chinese-apps-in-india-to-loosen-communist-partys-espionage-work/articleshow/79612742.cms
125. Srishti Ojha, "Laws under which government can pass content blocking orders—Explainer," *India Today*, January 24, 2023, https://www.indiatoday.in/law/story/laws-under-which-government-can-pass-content-blocking-orders-explainer-2325969-2023-01-24#
126. Gnanith A, "Shreya Singhal v. Union Of India AIR 2015 SC 1523," *Legal Service India.com*, March 4, 2015, https://www.legalserviceindia.com/legal/article-10124-shreya-singhal-v-union-of-india-air-2015-sc-1523.html
127. Chandrima Banerjee, "Does TikTok Censor Content That's Critical of China?" *Times of India*, June 6, 2020, https://timesofindia.indiatimes.com/india/does-tiktok-censor-content-thats-critical-of-china/articleshow/76228715.cms
128. "After ED arrests Vivo employees, Beijing urges India not to discriminate against Chinese firms," *Scroll*, December 25, 2023, https://scroll.in/latest/1061145/after-ed-arrests-vivo-employees-beijing-urges-india-not-to-discriminate-against-chinese-firms#:~:text=The%20case%20report%20alleged%20that,Lou%20and%20Zhang%20Jie%20with
129. Timsy Jaipuria, "Ministry of Corporate Affairs orders serious fraud probe on Vivo India; regional director to inspect MG Motor India," *CNBC*, December 1, 2023, https://www.cnbctv18.com/business/companies/ministry-of-corporate-affairs-refers-vivo-money-laundering-case-to-serious-fraud-investigation-office-18455391.htm
130. "India accuses China's Vivo of visa violations, siphoning off $13 billion," *The Economic Times*, October 12, 2023, https://economictimes.indiatimes.com/industry/cons-products/electronics/india-accuses-chinas-vivo-of-visa-violations-siphoning-off-13-billion/articleshow/104367963.cms?from=mdr
131. "India's ED issues show-cause notice to Xiaomi over illegal remittances," *Wion*, June 9, 2023, https://www.wionews.com/business-economy/indias-ed-issues-show-cause-notice-to-xiaomi-over-illegal-remittances-602695

132. Aditya Kalra and Munsif Vengattil, "Xiaomi says India's scrutiny of Chinese firms unnerves suppliers," *Reuters*, February 12,2024, https://www.reuters.com/technology/xiaomi-says-indias-scrutiny-chinese-firms-unnerves-suppliers-2024-02-11/
133. "India's Intensified Probe into Chinese Companies Casts A Shadow on its Image: Experts," *Global Times*, January 3, 2024, https://www.globaltimes.cn/page/202401/1304725.shtml
134. "India open to Chinese investments: Centre as Ajit Doval affirms strained strategic trust," *The Mint*, July 26, 2023, https://www.livemint.com/economy/open-to-chinese-investment-despite-clashes-says-rajeev-chandrasekhar-bjp-govt-narendra-modilacgalwantiktok-11690360457868.html
135. "Chinese Firms Under Corporate Affairs Ministry's Scanner for Links Loan Apps," *Times of India*, February 27, 2024, http://timesofindia.indiatimes.com/articleshow/108046193.cms#?utm_source=contentofinterest&utm_medium=text&utm_campaign=cppst ; "Chinese firm hacked Indian immigration data: Post," *The Indian Express*, February 23, 2024, https://indianexpress.com/article/india/post-chinese-firm-hacked-indian-immigration-data-9176301/
136. Gulveen Aulakh and Shouvik Das, "Why China's smartphone tsars want Indians to make their phones," *Mint*, July 4, 2024, https://www.livemint.com/industry/telecom/chinese-smartphone-makers-looking-for-indian-partners-for-manufacturing-11720005880208.html
137. Sushant Singh, "As with Pak, Select China Entities Face Extra Visa Scan," *The Indian Express*, August 22, 2020, https://indianexpress.com/article/india/select-china-entities-face-extra-visa-scan-6564818/
138. "'Cultural Exchange' or Propaganda?: Centre Reviews China's Confucius Institutes Amid Global Concern," *Firstpost*, August 6, 2020, https://www.firstpost.com/india/cultural-exchange-or-propaganda-centre-reviews-chinas-confucius-institutes-amid-global-concern-8676241.html.
139. "China Again Blocks UN Terror Tag For Jaish Chief Masood Azhar," *NDTV*, August 3, 2017, https://www.ndtv.com/india-news/china-again-blocks-un-terror-tag-for-jaish-chief-masood-azhar-1732841.
140. "India slams China at UN for blocking move to designate 26/11 accused Sajid Mir as 'global terrorist'," *The Hindu*, June 21, 2023, https://www.thehindu.com/news/national/india-slams-china-at-un-for-blocking-move-to-designate-2611-accused-sajid-mir-as-global-terrorist/article66993043.ece
141. "UNSC Open Debate on Working Methods: Statement by Ambassador Ruchira Kamboj," *Permanent Mission of India to the UN, New York*, March 11, 2024, https://pminewyork.gov.in/statementsecurity?id=eyJpdiI6ImMxZkhPSytsQ05YT2QyN0FuNFcrcGc9PSIsInZhbHVlIjoiSGJcL3BQZnJvMmJ2UnpsYTI3MFJzdFE9PSIsIm1hYyI6IjI2MDZmYmU5YzZhZjc2MTUzODk1Y2I2ZmRmNzY2OTlkMTM2Y2QzNDAwMDhhNmU0MzE0ZGQ4NDgxYmVjZTRlZDEifQ==
142. Sadanand Dhume, "One Belt, One Road, One Boycott," *The Wall Street Journal*, May 18, 2017, https://www.wsj.com/articles/one-belt-one-road-one-boycott-1495126360

143. "Official Spokesperson's response to a query on participation of India in OBOR/BRI Forum," *Ministry of External Affairs, Government of India,* May 13, 2017, https://www.mea.gov.in/media-briefings.htm?dtl/28463/Official_Spokespersons_response_to_a_query_on_participation_of_India_in_OBORBRI_Forum
144. "China trying to convince India CPEC is for prosperity," *The Express Tribune,* November 16, 2017, https://tribune.com.pk/story/1559666/china-trying-convince-india-cpec-prosperity
145. "China brought enormous force to border without provocation: Jaishankar," *ANI,* April 20, 2021, https://www.aninews.in/news/world/asia/china-brought-enormous-force-to-border-without-provocation-jaishankar20210420003007/
146. "Trade Deficit Between India and China," *Press Information Bureau,* June 26, 2019, https://pib.gov.in/Pressreleaseshare.aspx?PRID=1575818
147. "PLI Schemes: Shaping India's Industrial Growth," *PIB,* November 18, 2024, https://static.pib.gov.in/WriteReadData/specificdocs/documents/2024/nov/doc20241125451701.pdf
148. "External Affairs Minister's Meeting with Member of the Communist Party of China (CPC) Political Bureau and Foreign Minister H.E. Mr. Wang Yi on the Sidelines of SCO Council of Heads of State Meeting," *Ministry of External Affairs, Government of India,* July 4, 2024, https://www.mea.gov.in/press-releases.htm?dtl/37922/External+Affairs+Ministers+meeting+with+Member+of+the+Communist+Party+of+China+CPC+Political+Bureau+and+Foreign+Minister+HE+Mr+Wang+Yi+on+the+sidelines+of+SCO+Council+of+Heads+of+State+Meeting
149. "External Affairs Minister's Meeting with Member of the Communist Party of China (CPC) Political Bureau and Foreign Minister H.E. Mr. Wang Yi on the Sidelines of SCO Council of Heads of State Meeting," *Ministry of External Affairs, Government of India,* September 12, 2024, https://www.mea.gov.in/press-releases.htm?dtl/38287/Meeting+of+National+Security+Adviser+with+his+Chinese+counterpart+on+the+sidelines+of+the+BRICS+NSA+Meeting
150. "Statement by External Affairs Minister Dr. S. Jaishankar in Lok Sabha," *Ministry of External Affairs, Government of India,* December 3, 2024, https://www.mea.gov.in/Speeches-Statements.htm?dtl/38665/Statement+by+External+Affairs+Minister+Dr+S+Jaishankar+in+Lok+Sabha
151. "Meeting of Prime Minister with Mr. Xi Jinping, President of the People's Republic of China, on the Margins of the 16th BRICS Summit," *Ministry of External Affairs, Government of India,* October 23, 2024, https://www.mea.gov.in/outoging-visit-detail.htm?38457/Meeting+of+Prime+Minister+with+Mr+Xi+Jinping+President+of+the+Peoples+Republic+of+China+on+the+margins+of+the+16th+BRICS+Summit
152. "Economic Survey 2023-2024," *Ministry of Finance, Government of India,* https://www.indiabudget.gov.in/economicsurvey/
153. Ravi Dutta Mishra, "Portal for Ease of Entry of Chinese Technicians into India Has Begun Functioning: Official," *The Indian Express,* August 8, 2024, https://indianexpress.com/article/business/portal-ease-entry-chinese-technicians-india-begun-functioning-official-9500630/

154. Kiran Rathee, "Forbidden No More: India Begins Okaying Chinese Proposals," *The Economic Times,* August 22, 2024, https://economictimes.indiatimes.com/news/economy/foreign-trade/forbidden-no-more-india-begins-oking-chinese-proposals/articleshow/112691334.cms?from=mdr
155. "India reportedly approves Chinese investment proposals in electronics manufacturing, as action is needed to win back trust," *Global Times,* August 22, 2024, https://www.globaltimes.cn/page/202408/1318528.shtml
156. Jabin T Jacob, "Vikram Misri's Beijing Visit Underlines India's Limited Options," *Deccan Herald,* February 4, 2025, https://www.deccanherald.com/opinion/vikram-misris-beijing-visit-underlines-indias-limited-options-3388166
157. Atul Kumar and Antara Ghosal, "Depsang to Kazan: Emerging détente between China and India," *Raisina Debates,* November 4, 2024, https://www.orfonline.org/expert-speak/depsang-to-kazan-emerging-d-tente-between-china-and-india

11

Conclusion: Asymmetry and Geopolitics

The customary photograph of Chinese President Xi Jinping with other world leaders at the Third Belt and Road Forum (BRF), 2023, held in Beijing, generated considerable discussion in the international media. Observers pointed out that only 23 world leaders participated in the Third BRF compared to 37 at the second BRF (in 2019) and 27 at the first BRF (in 2017).[1] Unlike the previous editions, the third BRF did not animate international conversations. It is likely that since the BRF became a regular feature in the international political calendar, it may not receive the excitement generated by the inaugural edition. Further, the Israel-Palestine conflict may have grabbed the global headlines and overshadowed the BRF conversations in Beijing. However, the waning interest may also be a consequence of growing scepticism about China's grand connectivity and infrastructure plans. On the other hand, President Xi Jinping sounded confident and noted that "more than 150 countries and over 30 international organisations have signed Belt and Road cooperation documents."[2] Xi's speech also referred to mega projects, such as the China-Europe Railway Express, and the need for 'institutional building for international Belt and Road cooperation.'[3]

Geopolitics and Territorial Disputes

It has been more than a decade since the launch of the Belt and Road Initiative (BRI). Since then, there have been significant changes in geopolitical dynamics in Asia and beyond. The international environment was relatively more conducive to China's external economic engagement in the years before the BRI's launch. Consequently, China was able to project economic and political power across Central Asia and South Asia. Beijing's ability to project power across the regions was also a consequence of robust economic growth and the favourable geopolitical winds that China enjoyed for a few decades. The rapprochement with the United States in the 1970s resulted in a steady flow of Western investments into China. Subsequently, after the end of the Cold War, the pre-eminent power, the United States, was busy with wars in the Middle East, which provided space for China to build its capacities. In addition, there was an opinion in the United States and other Western capitals that the robust economic engagement of China over time would socialise Beijing into playing according to international rules and norms. However, many in the larger East Asian region noted that China had given up its "hide your strength and bide your time" strategy and indulged in aggressive territorial assertions. Instead of getting socialised into playing by international norms, China appeared to be keen on normalising its incremental territorial aggression and grey zone violations. India had significant experience with Chinese tactics of enhanced economic engagement and simultaneous forceful territorial assertions, and it stayed away from participating in the BRI.

While India prudently stayed away from participating in the BRI, many Western-developed countries sent delegations to the BRI Summits. Senior officials in Beijing sought to convince their Western counterparts by stating that for the success of the BRI, "China wants to combine its manufacturing and construction know-how with the advanced technology of Western firms ... [and BRI projects] ... could also benefit from partnerships with United States (US) and European enterprises on professional services."[4] Consequently, there was anticipation that some Western firms would get a significant share of the pie in the BRI implementation. However, such hopes did not materialise, as Chinese firms procured a dominant share of the BRI contracts.[5]

A decade after the launch of the BRI, the US was hesitant to further upgrade its economic relations with China. In September 2023, US President Joe Biden called the BRI a "debt and noose agreement."[6] There are growing geopolitical divergences between the US and China, with speculations of a military confrontation between the two countries in Taiwan. Such concerns were further accentuated when the US released information about Chinese jets often flying dangerously close to US aircraft.[7] The US and China are engaged in technology competition in multiple domains, including quantum technologies, which 'have the potential to disrupt economies and security.'[8] The consolidation of the China-Russian partnership, in the context of the Ukraine War, added impetus to the European powers' re-evaluation of enhanced economic interactions with China. Reflecting on European presence at the Third BRF, a Nikkei Asia report stated that "except for Hungarian Prime Minister Viktor Orban and Serbian President Aleksandar Vucic, leaders from richer European economies were conspicuously absent at the two-day forum."[9] The European re-evaluation was evident from Italy's withdrawal from the BRI initiative towards the end of 2023. Italy was the first G7 country to sign up to the BRI. While Italy's exports to China have risen from 13 billion Euros (in 2019) to 16.4 billion Euros (in 2022), China's exports to Italy have seen a significant increase from 31.7 billion Euros (in 2019) to 57.5 billion Euros (in 2022).[10] Such trade imbalances may have generated a perception in Italy that China benefitted more from the bilateral economic relationship.

However, the advent of the Trump presidency in the US has added new uncertainties for Europe. Trump's trade policy has generated concerns that European firms will find their products too expensive to sell in the US. On the Ukraine conflict, President Trump and European leaders have sharp policy differences. The impact of the tariff and foreign policy differences with the United States on Europe's policy towards China needs careful evaluation.

While Europe is dealing with its territorial questions, there are concerns in East Asia, Southeast Asia, and the continental Asian landmass about China's aggressive territorial assertions, which have prompted many countries to contemplate the prudence of enhanced economic engagement with China. In the subcontinent, China's efforts at improving infrastructure did not create conditions for the peaceful resolution of border disputes with its neighbours. Instead, such efforts have amplified the existing territorial contestations. The connectivity projects were also critical in consolidating China's hold on Tibet. Further, China is also able to project power from Tibet, which is evident along the border regions of India, Nepal, and Bhutan. China has scaled up the physical infrastructure in Tibet by building a robust road and rail network. In fact, China operationalised the high-speed rail to Lhasa from Nyingchi[11] and has completed another high-speed rail connecting Sichuan with Tibet. There were reports that the Lhasa-Nyingchi high-speed rail was also used by a "combined arms brigade affiliated with the PLA Tibet Military Command" to move troops for military exercises.[12] Because of the improved infrastructure networks, China created new human settlements close to the borders of countries that share a boundary with Tibet.

These infrastructure projects were clearly designed to consolidate the Chinese presence in Tibet. In July 2021, President Xi Jinping visited Tibet and "in ... a clear message to domestic audiences and to India and the Dalai Lama" stressed the importance of "stability, development, ecology and border-area consolidation."[13] As a part of his first trip to Tibet, President Xi Jinping visited the national park in eastern Nyingchi and called on the people to "set down roots in the border area, safeguard the Chinese territory and develop their hometown."[14] It should be noted that the Chinese attempts to resettle the population have altered the demographic profile and increased the population in border regions. The senior officials of the Communist Party of China (CPC) in the Tibet Autonomous Region (TAR) were quoted stating that "the population living at the border regions in Tibet has increased 10.5 per cent."[15] There is an opinion that the Chinese attempts to alter the population in the border regions may have spilled over into the neighbouring countries. In May 2021, the *Foreign Policy* magazine reported that China had constructed approximately three villages, "66 miles of new roads, a small hydropower station, two Communist Party administrative centres ... five military or police outposts ... a military base, and up to six security sites" in Bhutan.[16] Further, Beijing has scaled up its territorial claims in Bhutan by claiming Sakteng Wildlife Reserve as part of Chinese territory.[17] Similarly, there were reports regarding Chinese activities in the Humla District in Nepal.[18] While the territorial violations in Ladakh (India) received considerable international recognition and response from the Indian government, a similar pattern was evident with reference to Nepal and Bhutan, which requires closer scrutiny. The growing concerns about Chinese territorial assertions in the Indian subcontinent did not slow down the Chinese infrastructure build-up in India's vicinity. In July 2022, there were reports that China was building a new highway between Mazha County in Xinjiang and Lhunze County in Tibet, which would enable the rapid deployment of Chinese troops close to the Indian border.[19] In the midst of a military standoff with India, China continued with its rapid infrastructure development in Tibet and in regions close to the Line of Actual Control (LAC). In May 2022, there were reports of China building bridges connecting the north and south banks of Pangong Tso. There were also reports that China was building a new airbase in the Tashkurgan district in Xinxiang.[20] Further Claude Arpi points that the Chinese construction of

G216 strategic highway, connecting Xinjiang and Tibet, will increase India's military vulnerabilities on its northern borders.[21] Overall, the infrastructure build-up enhanced the Chinese ability to project military power from Tibet. The infrastructure projects and increased economic engagement altered the bilateral dynamic between China and its South Asian neighbours.

A Quasi Alliance?

Through its economic and political engagements, China attempts to develop alliance-like relationships with some of the countries on the Indian subcontinent. While there is no formal and explicit alliance, there is considerable coordination between China and Pakistan. More specifically, China and Pakistan are coordinating their actions with reference to India. China's military deployment across India's Ladakh border and Pakistan's actions across the LAC in Kashmir have created a two-front threat. *The Global Times*, in a report, cautioned that "if India were to wage massive armed clashes or even war with China and Pakistan simultaneously, no country would likely help India apart from conditionally providing some weaponry."[22] In case of a two-front conflict, both China and Pakistan will be able to mobilise rapidly because of improved infrastructure facilities in Tibet and Pakistan Occupied Kashmir (PoK). There were reports that, amid the Ladakh standoff, China assisted Pakistan with the "installation of a surface-to-air missile (SAM) system near Lasadanna Dhok in PoK."[23] There were also reports of China upgrading its air bases in Xinjiang (Hotan and Shakche) and Tibet (Nyingchi).[24] It is estimated that 15 airports in Xinjiang were upgraded, with seven of them getting equipped with dual-use facilities.[25]

There were also reports that "the Chinese frigate Jiangwei-Il was spotted not very far from Porbandar, around 11 nautical miles inside Pakistani waters."[26] R S Vasan notes that given the growing commonality between the defence equipment and growing Chinese presence in the northern Arabian Sea, the Indian Navy, in case of a conflict, will find it difficult to differentiate between the defence assets of these two countries.[27] Further, the close defence cooperation between Pakistan and China is one of the critical components of their bilateral relationship. Both countries are conducting defence exercises to improve the coordination, co-operability, and capacities of their defence forces. China has emerged as the leading exporter of defence equipment to Pakistan, and both countries are also involved in co-producing weapons systems, such as JF-17 fighter aircraft. For China, Pakistan is important not only for maintaining favourable security dynamics in South Asia and West Asia but also for countering the US influence in global politics. As Yan Xuetong notes, "the more allies China makes, the more balanced and stable the relationship [with the US] will be."[28] In this direction, Yan Xuetong calls on China to "consider having military bases in countries it considers allies" and added that since China emphasises the 'non-alliance principle', it would be "too early to say where China would build military bases since China now has only one real ally, Pakistan."[29]

The BRI and enhanced economic interactions with Pakistan and the Middle Eastern countries have helped China to temper criticism of its policies in Xinjiang province. Numerous international agencies and civil society organisations have expressed concerns regarding the Chinese policies in Xinjiang province. For instance, Amnesty International, in its report, referred to Xinjiang as a 'dystopian hellscape' and went on to add that "Uyghurs, Kazakhs and other Muslim minorities face crimes against humanity" perpetrated by the Chinese authorities.[30] On the other hand, Chinese authorities received steadfast support from Pakistan's leadership. For instance, former Prime Minister, Imran Khan, noted that Pakistan accepts the Chinese 'version of what is happening in Xinjiang.'[31] Towards the end of August 2022, the Office of the High Commissioner for Human Rights, in its report on human rights in Xinjiang, noted that the Chinese policies towards Uyghurs "may constitute international crimes, in particular crimes against humanity."[32] Subsequently, Pakistan's foreign office supported "China's efforts for socio-economic development, harmony and peace and stability in Xinjiang" and called for "non-interference in internal affairs of states."[33] There have been reports of Pakistan deporting many Uyghurs to China.[34] Ayjaz Wani reported that between 2017 and March 2022, 'more than 682 Uyghurs' were detained and sent back to China by various Middle Eastern countries.[35]

Pakistan also played an important role in providing China with an opportunity to voice its views on platforms such as the Organisation of Islamic Cooperation (OIC). In March 2022, the Chinese foreign minister, for the first time, participated in and addressed 'the opening ceremony of the session of the Council of Foreign Ministers of the OIC' in Islamabad, Pakistan. In his remarks, the Chinese foreign minister, Wang Yi, noted that "China has signed BRI cooperation documents with 54 Islamic countries and launched nearly 600 large-scale projects worth USD 400 billion" and went on to add that "China and the Islamic world have found a path of friendship and win-win cooperation among civilisations."[36] The fact that Wang Yi was invited to deliver opening remarks at the OIC, despite the concerns about the condition of Uyghur Muslims in China, indicated an ideological congruence between the two countries. Earlier, Pakistan's Prime Minister, Imran Khan, had noted, "until now, we had been told that the best way for societies to improve was through Western democracy ... but the CPC has achieved much better [outcomes] without democracy."[37] Pakistan's interactions with China were not just aimed at economic gains but also had an ideological purpose of working together to contest 'Western ideas of democracy and liberty'.

Ideology as Interest

The Chinese policymakers contend that the BRI does not seek to achieve ideological objectives. In 2021, China's State Councilor and Foreign Minister Wang Yi, in a keynote speech, noted that "the BRI is a public road open to all, and has no backyard or high walls ... it is open to all kinds of systems and civilisations and is not ideologically biased."[38] Wang Yi's comment raised an important question regarding the role of ideology in the BRI. It is indeed true that Chinese investments under the banner of the BRI were ideologically agnostic. From democracies to authoritarian regimes, China economically engaged with countries with varied ideological persuasions. However, the interaction between ideology and China's external economic engagement requires closer attention. As per the CPC's regulations, "any organisation that has three or more party members has to provide the necessary conditions for cadres to establish a party cell."[39] While these provisions were not strictly implemented earlier, after the advent of Xi Jinping, the party's presence has grown in various business organisations. Party cells reportedly also operate in many foreign firms operating in China.[40] When Chinese public/private companies operate in other countries, they are doing so under the constant surveillance of the CCP, which ensures that the party's ideological and other interests are not compromised.

Further, as Yan Xuetong notes, China has been making efforts to "shape an ideological environment favourable to its rise, pushing back against the notion that Western political values have universal appeal and validity."[41] By engaging with regimes with varied governance frameworks and contentious human rights records, the BRI performs an important ideological function by openly discarding adherence to universal values. Jiang Jing unpacks and maps three essential ideological functions of the initiative: first, the BRI helps various countries to "effectively respond to various challenges of globalisation" by deploying "Chinese wisdom to answer global development problems and jointly improve governance capabilities"; second, the BRI seeks to address the "China Threat Theory" and will act as a platform to "accurately, correctly, and comprehensively know and understand China"; and third, the BRI has enabled "Chinese culture to "go global" and effectively address the challenge of Western culture's penetration in various countries."[42] To sum up, the BRI is the brainchild of the CCP, the Chinese private/public organisations implement the BRI with embedded party units, and it deploys Chinese wisdom, promotes correct understanding of China, and enables Chinese culture to go global. It is in the interest of the CPC to ensure that the BRI and increased global economic engagement do not dilute the party ideology at home. Therefore, perhaps, it would be erroneous to assume that the BRI does not have anything to do with the ideology of the CPC.

Asymmetry and Governance

There is considerable power asymmetry between China and the South Asian countries. The Chinese firms' revenue flows are often more than the GDP of some of the countries in the region. Therefore, interactions between some of these sovereign states and Chinese corporations are often defined by considerable asymmetry in terms of information and other power resources. For instance, Sri Lankan officials reportedly were not fully aware of the obligations pertaining to the Colombo Port City project agreement. Consequently, when Sri Lanka tried to cancel the project, the Chinese firms claimed compensation, which was way beyond the means of Sri Lanka, and Colombo found it difficult to withstand the diplomatic pressure from China.[43] Such examples have demonstrated that it is essential to factor in all the financial, administrative, and political dimensions when evaluating Chinese infrastructure and BRI projects. On the issue of lending, Brad Setser notes that the Export-Import Bank of China and the China Development Bank do not "self-report their existing exposure by their country, and they have at times insisted on limited disclosure by their borrowers as well."[44] The South Asian experience demonstrates, as in the case of the Maldives, that there was a lack of transparency in Chinese loans. Furthermore, Sri Lanka's economic crisis exemplifies that there is no quick fix or silver bullet to surmount developmental challenges, and the principles of transparency, prudence, and economic sobriety are not vague rhetoric but essential foundations in a country's financial management.

Many BRI participant countries preferred not to access funding from the World Bank, IMF, and other international agencies as they demanded rigorous market/financial viability reports, environmental impact assessments, and other relevant studies. Therefore, BRI partner countries took loans from Chinese institutions at relatively higher interest rates and on shorter repayment schedules. Such funding approaches to infrastructure projects created conditions for "debt-traps". Debt traps, therefore, are a consequence of decisions made by political leadership and are not accidental financial outcomes. It is estimated that "China extended 128 bailouts in 22 debtor countries worth a total of USD 240 billion between 2000 and the end of 2021," which indicates the scale of the debt burden of some BRI countries.[45] Given the financial distress in some developing countries, major powers and regional/multilateral institutions must initiate capacity-building training on infrastructure finance and contract negotiation for finance and related ministries in countries participating in BRI projects. There were instances when countries have successfully renegotiated the contracts. The renegotiation of the agreements was contingent on various factors, such as the geopolitical context and the scale of the domestic opposition to the BRI projects. Myanmar was able to renegotiate the Leptadung copper mine project, scale down the Kyaukphyu SEZ, and suspend the Myitsone Dam project. The scale of the domestic unrest, robust opposition parties such as NLD, and the growing presence of other international actors in the economy may have prompted such decisions. However, after the coup in Myanmar in 2021, the military appeared to be eager to renegotiate some of the projects on terms that were favourable to China. So, the negotiating ability of a country is contingent not only on the capacities of its negotiators but also on the overall domestic political and regional geopolitical dynamics.

There were instances when the BRI implementation generated new governance frameworks in South Asia. In Pakistan, a CPEC authority was created and later abrogated. In Sri Lanka, a Colombo Port City Commission was created. In both instances, there were apprehensions that these new agencies were usurping the functions of other institutions and line ministries. The new frameworks did not amount to institutional innovation aimed at creating stakeholder participation and increased transparency. Instead, there were criticisms that these new agencies centralised the decision-making process.

In addition to new institutional frameworks, Chinese involvement in the domestic politics of South Asia has emerged as a topic of discussion. Chinese leaders and officials often proclaimed that they would never interfere in the internal affairs of other countries. However, the massive BRI investments made by Chinese firms often prompted Beijing to be active in the domestic politics of other countries. It is difficult to deny that China is not an interested and active participant in the domestic politics in the South Asian countries, such as the Maldives, Sri Lanka, and Nepal. In Myanmar, China engages with multiple stakeholders, including armed ethnic organisations, across the faultlines. Nepal has experienced prolonged spells of political instability. Numerous reports suggest that Beijing has often leveraged its influence to ensure a China-friendly political coalition retains power in Nepal.[46] While such efforts may not have always met with success, they indicate the growing presence of China in a country that shares long and porous borders with India. In Pakistan, various political and civil society groups often voice concerns regarding the human rights of Muslims in various countries across the world. However, the same groups have maintained sustained silence on issues pertaining to Uyghur Muslims in China, which could be a consequence of Beijing's influence in the country. Chinese personnel were reportedly part of teams that closely monitored the investigations related to attacks on the CPEC projects.[47]

Over the past few years, China has operationalised many projects in hostile environments in Asia and Africa as part of BRI projects. Securing such investments mandates that China engage with multiple stakeholders. Many South Asian countries either share a land boundary with China or are strategically located in the Indian Ocean Region (IOR) and have received considerable investments from Beijing. Given the geostrategic location of these countries, China may find it imperative to invest in political actors who will promote and protect its interests in South Asia and beyond. Such actions also imply that adhering to the principle of 'non-interference in internal affairs' of other countries will be a challenging enterprise for China despite its claims to the contrary on various international platforms, including the United Nations Security Council (UNSC).

China has also deftly used its presence in the UNSC to expand its external economic interaction worldwide, including in South Asia. Beijing often extended diplomatic support to Pakistan on various United Nations (UN) platforms. From the 1971 India-Pakistan war to the most recent UN resolutions related to terrorism, China used its status as a permanent veto-holding member of the UNSC to protect and promote the interests of its friend, viz., Pakistan. In the past decade, China successfully blocked multiple attempts to prevent the UN from branding Masood Azhar, Pakistan-based JeM chief and Pathankot terror attack mastermind, as a terrorist.[48] In early 2020, the Financial Action Task Force Asia Pacific Joint Group, which deals with terror financing and money laundering, with China as the co-chair, noted that Pakistan made visible progress in strengthening its domestic counter-terrorist finance mechanisms.[49] Chinese support ensured that Pakistan was not blacklisted for failing to improve the counter-terror finance mechanisms and remained on the grey list. Simultaneously, China used its permanent membership in the UNSC to promote Pakistan's interests in the region. The most striking example has been China's repeated attempts to ensure that the UNSC discussed the Kashmir dispute. From August 2019 to August 2020, China initiated approximately three discussions on Kashmir at the UNSC.[50] While these discussions were aimed at creating difficulties for India on international platforms, they did not result in any tangible outcomes that were favourable to Pakistan.

Similarly, China provided diplomatic cover to Sri Lanka when Colombo's human rights record was scrutinised on international platforms. The Myanmar military often depended on Chinese support to curtail the possibility of concerted international action against human rights violations within the country. For instance, after the Myanmar military mishandled the Cyclone Nargis relief efforts, China stepped in with diplomatic support and ensured that the international community's anger did not get translated into humanitarian intervention. A few years later, after the International Court of Justice called for the prevention of genocide against the Rohingya Muslims, China curtailed the possibility of a UNSC statement against Myanmar.[51] These are a few examples wherein China used its presence in the UNSC to explicitly support regimes/governments that were accused of failing to uphold norms of international order. Perhaps such support from China often came at a price, which included contracts to Chinese firms under the rubric of the BRI.

The above examples also demonstrate a need to critically evaluate the tactics being deployed to promote democracy and human rights. There can be no contention that human rights should be protected across all countries. All efforts should be made to zealously guard human life under all circumstances. However, the developments in the Indian subcontinent constitute an interesting challenge: How does one promote human rights in the short and long term? The threats of punitive action against political leadership in some countries turned out to be mere rhetoric. Punitive measures, such as the withdrawal of economic concessions or the imposition of economic sanctions, have not worked as there was no consensus among all the countries in the region and major powers. In the absence of such consensus, it became easy for regimes violating human rights to break through economic sanctions. In the absence of credible punitive measures, ineffective sanctions have allowed China to make deep inroads into the polity and the economy of countries that were subjected to international censure. The United States Senate Committee on Foreign Relations, in its report, noted that there is a need for a more holistic approach, and such an "approach should be multidimensional ... [and] ... not driven solely by short-term humanitarian concerns but rather an integrated strategy that leverages political, economic, and security tools for more effective long-term reforms."[52] Perhaps Walter Russel Mead›s contention that "moral foreign policy often requires pragmatism" needs greater reflection.[53] While regimes indulging in human rights violations should not be allowed to go scot-free, alternative approaches to meet the economic needs of the poor and vulnerable in developing countries need to be explored. Quite often, political turmoil is witnessed in countries that are undergoing political transitions. International financial institutions and developed countries should recognise the tremendous hunger for connectivity projects in developing countries, especially those undergoing political transitions. Therefore, it becomes imperative that global financial institutions and big powers develop mechanisms to fast-track the financing of essential connectivity projects, specifically in countries undergoing transition towards democracy.

The BRI Variants and Varying Concerns

A critical component in the governance frameworks is the deployment of digital technologies. Countries such as Bangladesh, Pakistan, and Myanmar have deployed Chinese digital technologies in governmental and financial frameworks. However, the use of Chinese technologies has raised numerous apprehensions regarding data security and related matters. Such concerns stem from the perception that the usual distinctions between a government and private sector company often do not apply to Chinese firms. Chinese companies are socialised into accepting CPC norms and rules. Scott Livingston points out that CCP influence is exerted through formal governmental laws and also through "informal workings of firms' internal Party organisations ... and ... from the overlap of key Party organisation members with corporate management and the board of directors."[54] Given such party-firm dynamics, there will always be anxiety that the Chinese government will use the digital infrastructure operationalised by Chinese firms in other countries for political gains. Furthermore, there are apprehensions that Chinese companies may clamp down on certain digital services at the request of local governments in various countries. It was reported that China is also exporting digital surveillance technologies. According to a *New York Times* report, "18 countries, including Pakistan, are using Chinese-made intelligent monitoring systems and 36 countries have received training in 'public opinion guidance', which is typically a euphemism for censorship."[55] The deployment of these technologies can monitor citizens, undermine dissent and freedom of expression, and thereby enhance the state's power over citizens. In the long run, as Josh Chin notes, with the emergence of the Chinese Digital Silk Road , the global digital map is getting divided into "two parallel universes ... in one, people buy goods on Amazon; in the other, it's Alibaba ... in the West, Alphabet Inc.'s Google is so popular it's a verb, but you can't Google in China – there's Baidu for that ... in London, Apple Pay can get you on the Tube; in Beijing, it's Alipay ... to do all this in one app in China, there's WeChat, which lets a billion people also send texts, hail cabs and do many other tasks."[56] The division of the global digital landscape also implies that users in democratic countries may be subjected to relatively less surveillance than users in autocracies that deploy Chinese technologies. On the other hand, Minxin Pei contends that China's model of surveillance is "not only a technological feat" but also requires a "vast network of millions of informers and spies whose often unpaid work has been critical to the regime's survival," which makes it difficult to export.[57] Nonetheless, the prospect of a security breach prompted some to refrain from using Chinese-manufactured digital equipment. The US government launched a 'rip and replace' programme that sought to "tear out telecom equipment made by the Chinese companies Huawei and ZTE ... [as they] ... could be used by Beijing for espionage and to steal commercial secrets."[58] The United Kingdom, which was inclined towards deployment of the Chinese Huawei 5G network, albeit in a limited manner, decided to ban the Huawei 5G equipment from its high-speed networks.[59] The US opposition to the deployment of the Huawei 5G network within the country and even in the high-speed networks of allies/friends is well known. Due to persistent US prodding, Germany has also decided to "remove Chinese components from the country's 5G mobile networks by the end of 2029."[60] New Delhi also banned a large number of Chinese apps, and the Indian digital market likely will become progressively difficult for Chinese firms to access. With access to developed Western markets increasingly becoming difficult, increasing Chinese firms' presence in other digital markets would assume greater importance. China will seek to scale up its digital presence among other developing economies, including South Asia, Africa, and South America. To have a greater market across the world, China will also increase its digital cooperation in healthcare and related domains.

The COVID-19 crisis disrupted the existing work patterns, and there was greater reliance on digital platforms. Beijing attributed its success in fighting the pandemic to rigorous monitoring and containment measures using various digital platforms.[61] Further, the Chinese government often stated that it provided digital platforms to many African countries to assist them in implementing anti-contagion efforts and hastening the transition to a digital economy to mitigate shocks caused by the pandemic.[62] However, the advent of the pandemic created new challenges for China's external economic engagement.

China was an important hub of global supply chains. The pandemic and related lockdowns disrupted global supply chains. So, the economies of many countries were disrupted by a twin dynamic—pandemic-related lockdowns in their own countries, as well as disruptions caused to global supply chains by persistent lockdowns in China. Further, the trust deficit between China and other countries was accentuated by the perception that Beijing did not fully disclose the scale of COVID-19 infections in the country. To overcome these challenges, China relied on the Health Silk Road, launched vaccine diplomacy, and sought to position itself as a leader in pandemic assistance. For instance, President Xi Jinping, addressing the 73rd session of the World Health Assembly in 2020, stated that "COVID-19 vaccine development and deployment ... will be made a global public good, which will be China's contribution to ensuring vaccine accessibility and affordability in developing countries.[63]" In tune with President Xi's statement, according to an October

2023 *Global Times* report, China provided approximately "10 billion masks and 2.3 billion doses of vaccines to other countries and jointly produced vaccines with over 20 countries" during the pandemic.[64] By supplying vaccines and through production agreements, China acquired a better understanding of local manufacturing capacities, legal frameworks, and business groups associated with the pharmaceutical and healthcare sectors in various countries. China also sought to demonstrate that its governance framework was much superior to others. For instance, Chinese news reports claimed that the COVID-19 vaccination was a success and contended that such success was a consequence of the "strong organising and operating capacity of Chinese government and growing public willingness to get vaccinated."[65] On the other hand, the *Wall Street Journal* reported that some of the Chinese vaccines were not "as effective as the mRNA-based vaccines that were available in the West."[66] While many countries across the world opened their economies and allowed easy movement of people, China experienced prolonged lockdowns, which were attributed to the use of relatively less effective vaccines.[67] In addition, the supply of Chinese vaccines to some South Asian countries was criticised for lack of transparency in procurement agreements and higher prices.

Alternative Regional Frameworks

The pandemic-related assistance and multiple variants of the BRI provided an opportunity for China to explore the possibility of creating an alternative regional framework in South Asia. Regional initiatives, such as the South Asian Association for Regional Cooperation (SAARC) and the Bay of Bengal Initiative for Multi-Sectoral Technical and Economic Cooperation (BIMSTEC), were designed to promote regional interactions in the subcontinent. However, such initiatives were working with varying degrees of efficiency. More importantly, from Beijing's perspective, China was not a full member of either the SAARC or the BIMSTEC. With increased economic interactions, China attempted to create new regional cooperation frameworks.

Since 2020, China has been organising regional dialogues with Pakistan, Nepal, Sri Lanka, and Bangladesh to combat the pandemic and poverty. While these dialogues aimed to create more space for Chinese pharma and medical products, the possibility of these platforms evolving into wider regional frameworks was speculated. For instance, Jagannath Panda alluded to the possibility that China is creating a "Trans-Himalayan Quad"[68] and Maria Siow in the *South China Morning Post* deliberated on the challenges of creating a formal alliance involving some of the South Asian countries.[69] The subsequent meeting of the Chinese foreign minister further added to the speculation. On April 27, 2021, Chinese Foreign Minister Wang Yi interacted with his counterparts from China, Afghanistan, Bangladesh, Nepal, Pakistan, and Sri Lanka through a video conference on pandemic response.[70] The Chinese foreign ministry quickly clarified that Wang Yi's meeting with his South Asian counterparts is more of a follow-up of earlier meetings and does not constitute an attempt at creating an alternative regional framework. A Chinese official denounced the Himalayan Quad as a "military-political alliance dominated by a Cold War mentality."[71] However, the Chinese actions suggest that Beijing is keen on creating its version of South Asian regional frameworks. In July 2021, Beijing launched the China Poverty Alleviation and Cooperation Development Center (CPACDC) with an 'intent to pool strength, integrate resources, and exchange wisdom' to tackle poverty.[72] All South Asian countries, except India, are members of the CPACDC. The fact that new regional platforms were created suggests that China may create alternative regional frameworks that would alter the balance of power in the South Asian region. The Chinese attempts to create new regional frameworks in South Asia are part of a more significant endeavour to develop similar frameworks across Asia and Europe. In addition to the hard infrastructure of the BRI, China also proactively worked to ensure the conclusion of various trade agreements, such as the Regional Comprehensive Economic Partnership (RCEP). These agreements focus on softer aspects of economic engagement, such as tariffs and investment protocols. As Umut Ergunsü notes, the "FTAs would lay the groundwork for improving the rules and regulations of global trade and investment … the BRI would complement these FTAs in a way that would help facilitate trade by improving the physical conditions on the ground."[73]

Further, given the growing trade friction with the US, China has been making persistent efforts to develop free trade routes along the BRI. While many of the countries in the BRI may not trade in hi-tech products like the US, economic engagement of BRI countries, including Russia, will help Beijing address the negative spillover effect of trade friction with Washington DC.[74] China's domestic economic policy is also propelling the need for more significant synergies between the BRI and the RCEP. To scale up benefits from BRI engagement, China has operationalised new free trade zones (FTZ), with the total number of FTZs reaching 21.[75] At a larger level,

Beijing is working towards developing alternative economic architectures/global governance frameworks which align with Chinese economic interests. China's attempt to develop the Green Silk Road is also defined by the need to restructure global economic arrangements.

President Xi Jinping called for the establishment of "open, green and clean cooperation" at the Second Belt and Road Forum in 2019.[76] Lofty ideals such as the need "to protect the Earth which we all call home" may have impacted the conceptualisation of the Green Silk Road. Of course, the Green Silk Road can also be used to fend off criticism that BRI projects are exacerbating climate change and simultaneously, push Chinese companies to factor in local communities' concerns regarding environmental issues.[77] It should also be recognised that the Green Silk Road is also a response to evolving geopolitical/geo-economic dynamics. Despite the significant contribution of emerging and developing economies to global economic growth, Zhou Yamin argues that there are many environmental clauses in trade agreements that tend to disfavour these economies.[78] In this context, the Green Silk Road facilitates policy communication, seeks to influence global green governance frameworks, and, more importantly, creates a new green development model.[79] In the long run, China seems keen on setting the domestic standards of green finance and exporting such standards "to countries along the Silk Road Economic Belt."[80] Further, China seems to be keen on "building a green supply chain for the development of the Silk Road Economic Belt."[81]

Structural Challenges and External Economic Engagement

The scale and the nature of the BRI projects will also be defined by the slowdown of the Chinese economy. China's economic slowdown is eliciting considerable discussion among academics and policymakers. Adam Posen argued that China is experiencing "economic long COVID," which was "caused by CPC's arbitrary interference in everyday commercial life."[82] Posen noted that since the 1980s, there was an unstated compact according to which "the CPC ultimately controlled property rights, but as long as people stayed out of politics, the party would stay out of their economic life."[83] With the advent of Xi Jinping, this compact had broken down with excessive government intervention in the market and consequently, "the public's immune response to extreme intervention produced a less dynamic economy."[84] On the other hand, Michael Pettis argued that "government intrusion is not China's biggest problem...its biggest problem is that it has not substantially adjusted its growth model."[85] Pettis contended that "government intrusion is the consequence of weak private investment, not its driver…it must address the demand side of the economy by strengthening the share of its GDP that Chinese households retain."[86]

While the debate rages on the causes of China's economic crisis, the consequences are becoming evident. The reports suggested that youth unemployment is growing rapidly.[87] The performance of the star of the Chinese economy, the real estate sector, has been the cause of much dismay. Considerable oversupply was a significant cause of the crisis in this sector. A senior official of the National Statistics Bureau reportedly stated that even "China's entire population (1.4 billion) would not be sufficient to fill the empty apartments across the country."[88] With the stock value of one of China's biggest real estate developers nose-diving, the probability of the real estate segment experiencing a crash has become an important node of discussion. Many small entrepreneurs and workers, such as builders, cement makers, painters, and real estate agents, will struggle to sustain their businesses if the real estate sector experiences further collapse.[89] The real estate collapse may inflict considerable pain on first-time buyers and middle/lower middle classes. Further, the real estate crash will undermine people's faith that the government can repair the economy.

The property crisis is also testing the Chinese banking system as nearly "40 per cent of all bank loans are related to property."[90] The banks had taken various measures, such as giving more time to borrowers, which many opined would result in a continuation of unhealthy property speculation.[91] Simultaneously, Chinese authorities have reportedly instructed state-owned banks to roll over "existing local government debt with long-term loans at lower interest rates."[92] According to the International Monetary Fund's Chief Economist: "The challenge has been trying to give the sector enough support to cope with the transition without stimulating another property bubble or a rebound that makes these problems worse."[93] The slowdown of real estate has impacted the revenue generation of many local governments. Consequently, they are looking for new sources of revenue to service the debt. According to some reports, local governments have USD 9 trillion in hidden debt, and in an attempt to address such large debt, the local governments are issuing 'refinancing bonds to service outstanding liabilities.'[94] In early 2024, addressing the National People's Congress , Chinese Premier Li Qiang reflected on the challenges confronting the economy and stated, "we should not lose sight of worst-case scenarios and should be well prepared for all risks and challenges."[95]

These domestic economic challenges have coincided with growing external constraints. China's external environment, especially access to developed economies, is slowly getting restricted. With increased tensions in bilateral relations, the United States imposed controls on the export of sensitive technologies, including semiconductors, chip manufacturing, and related equipment, to China. As is well known, semiconductors play a significant role in developing cutting-edge artificial intelligence tools/products and have considerable use in military technologies. Because of the US restrictions, there was a considerable 'decline in the semiconductor imports year-on-year in the first nine months of 2023.'[96] It should be noted that the initial round of tech restrictions did not target Chinese subsidiary companies in various other countries, which ensured that semiconductor components were easily smuggled into China.[97] Subsequently, the US has updated its policies to prevent such circumvention by placing restrictions on exports to Macao and countries under the US arms embargo, and there was an expansion of the list of manufacturing equipment that can be exported as well.[98] With new restrictions in place, it is likely that the tech war will persist and may impact other technologies. Additionally, Chinese economic engagement with Europe is coming under the scanner. There were persistent demands on the European Union (EU) to conduct "anti-subsidy investigations into steel makers producing in countries such as China."[99] Meanwhile, the EU top diplomat, Josep Borrell, stressed the importance of finding a "common ground, to repress imbalances in economy and trade relations."[100]

China has responded to the growing constraints in accessing the Western markets by scaling up engagement in other markets through free trade agreements, such as the RCEP, and by increasing efforts to internationalise its Renminbi (RMB) currency. The Ukraine war increased the use of the Chinese Renminbi. With Russia under stringent US and European sanctions, Moscow depended more on the yuan as a regional currency reserve.[101] To speed up the internationalisation of the Renminbi, China developed the Cross-Border Interbank Payment System (CIPS) as an alternative to SWIFT. While the CIPS is yet to be adopted by others in a significant way, there is a growing trend of countries such as Brazil and Bangladesh accepting the yuan for investments and trade settlements.[102] Pakistan has agreed to use RMB for bilateral trade, and Myanmar also accepted the Chinese currency for border trade with

China.[103] China has established currency swap agreements with South Asian countries, such as Pakistan, Nepal, and Myanmar. China is attempting to strengthen monetary cooperation with countries in Asia and beyond. All this may not immediately result in the de-dollarisation of the global economy, but it may, as Daniel McDowell noted, "usher in the beginning of a more fractured system that could ultimately blunt the US's ability to use financial sanctions as a weapon."[104] It should also be noted that China's monetary cooperation measures are in tune with its growing trade relationships. China is a dominant trading partner of many South Asian countries. In spite of significant stress in the bilateral relationship and serious political differences, China is one of India's leading trade partners. So, China is deploying a wide range of measures, such as increasing trade and consolidating monetary cooperation with developing countries, to overcome challenges resulting from friction with Western countries. The domestic economic crisis and external challenges mandate that China will continue to emphasise the BRI as an essential platform for its external economic engagement. However, there may be subtle changes in the nature and scale of the BRI projects. In addition to a few big-ticket projects, as President Xi noted, China may implement "small yet smart people-centred programs."[105]

Conclusion: A Game Changer?

The BRI was a response to the domestic challenges in the Chinese economy. As noted in the earlier chapters, many sectors in the Chinese economy, such as cement, steel, and others, had significant excess capacities. The BRI acted as a platform that provided an outlet for excess domestic capacity. The BRI did benefit China immensely. In the first three quarters of 2023, China's trade with the BRI countries amounted to about USD 1.96 trillion.[106] Much of the increased trade is a consequence of increased Chinese exports to BRI countries. For instance, many South Asian countries ended up with massive trade deficits with China. On the other hand, for many South Asian countries, India, Europe, and the US were important export markets. Consolidating the relationship with Beijing under the rubric of the BRI has not increased market access in China for South Asian countries. The BRI investments enabled Chinese firms to access new markets, ensured a steady supply of minerals, and allowed China to gain control of strategically important ports and airports. The BRI enabled China to develop deep networks of influence in many participant countries.

Over the past ten years, China has accrued significant geopolitical benefits because of the BRI and enhanced economic engagement with South Asia. The words "game changer" are often used to describe the growing presence of China in the subcontinent. In geopolitics, a 'game changing' phenomenon implies a fundamental shift in the balance of power in a region. The Chinese economic engagement did alter the power dynamic in the Indian subcontinent. As Constantino Xavier pointed out, "China's penetration of the Indian subcontinent is the biggest game changer in 100 years ... the Russians tried, the Americans tried.... This is the first time since at least World War II that you have a massive power contesting the Indian state."[107]

It is not only in the continental domain but also in the maritime domain, where there is a growing Chinese presence in the seas adjoining India. As Dinakar Peri noted, there was a massive expansion of the Chinese Navy, which coincided with "increasing forays into the Indian Ocean Region, beginning with the deployment of ships for anti-piracy operations in the Gulf of Aden in 2008."[108] To support an increased naval presence in the IOR, China is building various port-related infrastructure projects around the Indian subcontinent. In addition to Djibouti, China now has a presence in Gwadar in Pakistan, Hambantota in Sri Lanka, and Kyauk Phyu in Myanmar. Further, China has unprecedented access to other ports, such as Karachi in Pakistan. In the Maldives, while President Mohamed Muizzu's government refused to renew an agreement with India to conduct hydrographic surveys, it signed a defence cooperation agreement for military assistance with China.[109] The increased military presence prompts an important question: will China intervene militarily to protect its economic interests in various countries of the BRI? To intervene requires the capability to project power beyond the neighbourhood. The fact that Chinese military presence is increasing in the continental and maritime domain indicates that Beijing may be creating the necessary infrastructure to back its economic investments with military presence. Because of such increased military presence, India will have to factor in the growing Chinese activity in the neighbourhood while responding to Chinese grey zone violations on its border.

The geopolitical shifts have not created favourable conditions for the rapid economic growth of relatively smaller countries in the Indian subcontinent, and the BRI was not a Marshall Plan for South Asian countries. It is possible to contend that the BRI is just a decade-old initiative and would require more time to demonstrate positive spin-offs. However, it should be noted that, in the 1960s, collaboration with the US in the domain of agriculture resulted in dramatic improvements in agricultural productivity in India, which is often referred to as the "green revolution". Similarly, India's engagement with the US in the domain of information technology contributed to a substantive growth of India's service sector. However, the BRI engagement has yet to bring about such dramatic results in South Asian economies. In the political realm, the experience demonstrates that smaller countries have limits to playing India and China against each other. Such tactics create dynamics that are beyond the control of some of these countries and will have a serious impact on domestic politics as well. Sometimes, policy initiatives that begin with the objective of balancing India with the Chinese presence quickly morph into a suffocatingly close relationship with Beijing.

Since the power asymmetry between India and China is relatively less acute compared to other countries in South Asia, New Delhi was able to resist the suggestion that it join the BRI. There were multiple reasons for India's firm rejection of the BRI. The China-Pakistan Economic Corridor (CPEC), an important component of the BRI, traverses Pakistan-Occupied Kashmir, which India considers an integral part of India. Alluding to the BRI and the CPEC, the Indian foreign minister stressed that "connectivity projects should respect the sovereignty and territorial integrity of member states and respect international law."[110] There was also a perception in India that the articulation of the CPEC and the BRI did not happen after comprehensive consultations with all the regional stakeholders. Instead, China unilaterally defined the contours of the proposed BRI in the subcontinent. The Indian policymakers often stressed that the "connectivity initiatives must be based on universally recognised international norms, good governance, the rule of law, openness, transparency and equality."[111]

Despite India's reluctance, some Chinese scholars have proposed that Beijing and New Delhi collaborate on various connectivity and infrastructure projects in India's immediate neighbourhood. For instance, Long Xingchun refers to the Chinese government's "2+1 cooperation plan ... wherein ... China and India can use their respective advantages to cooperate in the Maldives and Sri Lanka, and a win-win or multi-win situation can be achieved."[112] Some in India also advocated "that India can assist the Maldives and other littoral states in their quest for economic growth ... China, in its turn, can enhance its aid for infrastructure development."[113] However, such an approach has many challenges to surmount. For instance, the government of the Maldives rescinded an Indian company's contract to build the Male International Airport. Subsequently, the construction of the project was handed over to Chinese firms. The episode demonstrated that economic activity is often viewed through the lens of geopolitical competition. Moreover, there is a difference between Chinese and Indian project implementation methods. In India, there is a perception that Chinese investments need more transparency and often push countries into a debt burden. Therefore, collaboration with the Chinese in building infrastructure projects would expose India to similar criticisms at home and abroad.

With growing Chinese investments in the subcontinent, India has also scaled up overseas development assistance in the immediate neighbourhood and the construction of infrastructure projects. It should be noted that India has a long history of building connectivity projects in the neighbourhood. A few years after Indian independence, India completed the construction of the Tribhuvan Rajpath and, in subsequent decades, was also instrumental in the construction of the Mahendra Rajmarg (East-West) highway in Nepal. Over the years, the Indian government has emerged as an important player in Nepal's hydro-power sector. India has scaled up its cooperation with Nepal in the realms of cross-border petroleum pipelines, new transmission lines, highways, I-ways, and trans-ways.[114] In 2023, the India-Nepal cross-border railway line (Jaynagar-Bijalpura-Bardibas) was also operationalised.[115] In the same year, India's Unified Payments Interface (UPI) and Nepal's National Payments Interface agreed to facilitate cross-border digital payments.[116] With RBI updating its regulations to facilitate cross-border payments to Nepal, the digital payment mechanism between the two countries has become a reality.[117] India, Nepal, and Bangladesh are also working towards a tripartite power trade deal.[118]

India and Bangladesh have made persistent efforts to improve rail connectivity between the two countries, which was impaired by the partition and subsequent geopolitical developments. As Constantino Xavier noted, "India-Bangladesh rail links decreased from around a dozen in the 1960s to just one in the mid-2000s."[119] However, in the subsequent years, rail connectivity between the countries witnessed significant improvement. The Khulna-Mongla Port Rail Line and the Akhaura-Agartala Cross-Border Rail Link were operationalised.[120] While the operationalisation of over half a dozen cross-border rail links constitutes an attempt at restoring the pre-1960s rail connectivity, both countries have scaled up cooperation on other connectivity projects as well.[121] In addition to bus services, there were significant improvements in inland waterway connectivity, and there was an increase in the use of Mongla and Chattogram ports in Bangladesh to transport goods to Northeast India.[122] In the realm of energy infrastructure, the Maitree Super Thermal Power Project was operationalised, which was built with an Indian concessional financing scheme.[123] In the same year, the first energy pipeline between the two countries was also inaugurated, and it would carry high-speed diesel to multiple districts in northern Bangladesh.[124]

Similarly, in Sri Lanka, India is involved in a host of energy projects, such as the Trincomalee tank farms and renewable energy initiatives, and there are proposals to develop a 'power grid interconnection to enable bidirectional electricity trade' between the two countries.[125] India's Adani Ports & SEZ is involved in constructing the West Container Terminal in Colombo and has received investment from the US International Development Finance Corporation. India was also involved in a wide range of projects, such as upgrading railway lines, building hospitals, and providing boats and fishing gear.[126] Approximately 50,000 of the promised 60,000 houses were constructed in Sri Lanka with a grant under the rubric of the Indian Housing Project.[127] In terms of financial interactions, the operationalisation of UPI connectivity in 2024 has improved the digital payment connectivity between India and Sri Lanka.[128] Most importantly, when Sri Lanka experienced a severe economic crisis, the Indian government provided financial assistance of USD 4.5 billion, much bigger than the IMF package of USD 3 billion.[129] Reflecting on the rationale for providing substantive assistance, India's External Affairs Minister, S Jaishankar, stated: "blood is thicker than water.... It was natural for India to see what it could do to stand by Sri Lanka at this very difficult time."[130] As in Sri Lanka, in the Maldives, India has extended assistance to numerous initiatives, including airport redevelopment, construction of ports, providing for social housing, improving water and sanitation, and implementing the High-Impact Community Development Projects (HICDP). India has extended a USD 400 million Line of Credit (LoC) and USD 100 million as a grant for the Greater Male Connectivity Project, which involves the construction of bridges, causeways, and roads connecting various islands in the Maldives.[131]

Even in countries experiencing civil war, such as Myanmar and Afghanistan, India extended considerable development assistance. Despite a hostile security environment, India financed and constructed the Zaranj-

Delaram Road, which constituted a critical link for Afghanistan to connect with the Chabahar Port.[132] Other major Indian projects include the construction of transmission lines, the construction and commissioning of the Salma Dam, and the construction of the Afghan Parliament.[133] India had a large menu of outreach activities, which included educational scholarships, food aid, medical missions, and construction of healthcare facilities, among others.[134] India's development assistance generated considerable goodwill among the various stakeholders in Afghanistan. On its eastern borders, Indian engagement had to navigate complex security challenges in Myanmar. With a troubled political transition and multiple ethnic armed groups controlling large tracts of territory, building infrastructure and connectivity projects was always a challenge. The work on the India-Myanmar-Thailand Trilateral Highway has made slow progress because of the prevalent security situation and related administrative challenges. The construction of the Kaladan Multimodal project is in its final stages. Even in Myanmar, the Indian government has successfully operationalised numerous HICDP initiatives and also capacity-building institutions, such as the Myanmar-India Entrepreneurship Development Centre, Centre for English Language Training, IT Skills Enhancement Centre, and Industrial Training Centres.[135]

India has collaborated with other friendly powers in the subcontinent on building infrastructure and connectivity projects. The scale, pace, and consequences of the BRI have prompted a few important shifts in India's foreign policy. As Raja Mohan pointed out, the BRI "has also encouraged India to shed its traditional "lone-ranger" mentality and consider working with others, especially Japan, Australia and the United States, in promoting regional connectivity in the Indo-Pacific."[136] Japan has launched the Partnership for Quality Infrastructure (PQI) to meet the infrastructure demand in Asia and is actively implementing connectivity projects in the region. For instance, during Shinzo Abe's visit to Bangladesh, the Bay of Bengal Industrial Growth Belt connecting Dhaka, Chittagong, and Cox's Bazar was announced.[137] The Economic Research Institute for ASEAN and East Asia has been advocating for a Mekong-India Economic Corridor.[138] There seems to be a growing convergence between Indian and Japanese connectivity frameworks, as both of them are centred on the Bay of Bengal. In 2022, the Indo-Pacific Economic Framework for Prosperity (IPEF) with 14 partner countries was launched to foster economic cooperation in the domains of trade, supply chains, clean economy, and fair economy.[139] In a related development, the G7 countries are also working to meet the 'global demand for high-quality infrastructure' through the Partnership for Global Infrastructure and Investment (PGII) framework.[140] At the G20 Summit in Delhi in 2023, the European Union (EU), the United States , India, Saudi Arabia, and the United Arab Emirates agreed to launch the India-Middle East-Europe Economic Corridor (IMEC). While these multiple initiatives constitute a welcome development, they must surmount a few challenges. Unlike the BRI led by China, Rajeswari Pillai Rajagopalan points out, the "PGII and such initiatives involve a number of countries as well as private sector participation from the participant countries, which means bringing out a coherent, coordinated approach to make it work is going to be that much more challenging..."[141] Nonetheless, these initiatives suggest that multiple platforms are emerging to meet the increasing demand for infrastructure projects across the world. While the BRI will have to contend with these new initiatives, at least some of these initiatives should explore innovative financing strategies to build connectivity projects.

The BRI had raised considerable hopes that alternative financing frameworks favouring developing countries would emerge. Additionally, the emergence of the Asian Infrastructure Investment Bank (AIIB) and the Brazil, Russia, India, China, and South Africa (BRICS) New Development Bank was viewed positively by many developing countries. However, thus far, the AIIB and BRICS banks have not deployed significant financial resources to meet the infrastructural requirements of the developing countries. Chinese loans largely funded most BRI projects in South Asia and elsewhere. Simultaneously, China has not offered radically new and alternative ways to finance the much-needed infrastructure projects in developing countries. On the contrary, there are concerns that China provided loans at high interest rates that are marked by considerable opaqueness. Within a short period, Chinese funding has created considerable suspicion among many recipient countries. Therefore, it is debatable whether developing countries will see China-led institutions as a genuine alternative to an equitable world order. Therefore, it is imperative that initiatives (such as PQI, IPEF, PGII, and IMEC) and major powers seriously explore innovative infrastructure finance, which instil confidence in developing countries. The future trajectory of the BRI will be defined by various factors, such as the emergence of new connectivity and infrastructure initiatives, China's relations with major economies, and the persistence of its economic slowdown. Further, if Beijing continues with its territorial assertions with various countries, events may spiral out of control in some theatres. In such an eventuality, precious economic and political resources will be diverted, which may negatively impact the BRI.

Overall, there is no denying that China's economic engagement and BRI projects have altered the balance of power in South Asia. However, geopolitical gains tend to be transient, and their longevity will depend on the prudent pursuit of domestic and international policies. The BRI was a product of the Chinese state. Therefore, the governance frameworks of the initiative also exhibited the characteristics of the Chinese state. Right from its inception, the BRI was criticised for its lack of consultative spirit and transparency. While there was considerable discussion on whether the BRI is exporting authoritarianism, there is a need to study the initiative's impact in transmitting new political ideas from the external world back into China. A large number of technicians, policymakers, academics, and others from China have intensely engaged with the external world under the rubric of the BRI. At the moment, it is unclear as to what political and social ideas from other parts of the world have made their way into China. Enhanced Chinese external economic engagement happened in a context when many liberal democracies indulged in persistent, prolonged, and harsh interrogation of their polities. The considerable scepticism and cynicism that the Chinese may have encountered would have comforted them that their political system, with all its challenges, after all, may not be significantly imperfect. It is uncertain if the legitimacy of the Chinese political system gets contested because of attractive political ideas from the West. Instead, such contestation may happen if the CPC fails to address domestic economic challenges. Perhaps, in such moments of rupture, the influence of external political ideas which were internalised may become evident. And it is during such moments that we will know the impact of the BRI, not just on the external world but also on Chinese polity and society.

Notes

1. Shashank Mattoo, "Why the outcome of China's latest BRI Forum should please India," *Mint*, October 19, 2023, https://www.livemint.com/news/india/mint-explainer-why-the-outcome-of-chinas-latest-bri-forum-should-please-india-11697701197062.html
2. Xi Jinping, "Building an Open, Inclusive and Interconnected World For Common Development," *ECNS*, October 18, 2023, https://www.ecns.cn/news/politics/2023-10-18/detail-ihcuappp4691649.shtml
3. Ibid.

4. "China Calls for U.S. and European Companies to Join Belt and Road," *Bloomberg News,* March 14, 2019, https://www.bloomberg.com/news/articles/2019-03-14/china-calls-for-u-s-european-companies-to-join-belt-and-road
5. Denghua Zhang Jianwen Yin, "China's Belt and Road Initiative, from the inside looking out," *The Interpreter*, July 2, 2019, https://www.lowyinstitute.org/the-interpreter/china-s-belt-road-initiative-inside-looking-out
6. Nadeen Ebrahim, "New US-backed India-Middle East trade route to challenge China's ambitions," *CNN*, September 11, 2023, https://edition.cnn.com/2023/09/11/middleeast/us-india-gulf-europe-corridor-mime-intl/index.html
7. Natasha Bertrand and Oren Liebermann, "US accuses China of 'coercive and risky' behavior in the air over the Pacific," *CNN*, October 17, 2023, https://edition.cnn.com/2023/10/17/politics/us-china-risky-behavior-pilots/index.html
8. Brandon Kirk Williams, "The Innovation Race: US-China Science and Technology Competition and the Quantum Revolution," *The Wilson Centre,* 2023, https://www.wilsoncenter.org/sites/default/files/media/uploads/documents/Williams_2022-23%20Wilson%20China%20Fellowship_Understanding%20China%20Amid%20Change%20and%20Competition.pdf
9. CK Tan, "Belt and Road Forum shows China recalibrating after 10 years," *Nikkei Asia,* October 19, 2023, https://asia.nikkei.com/Spotlight/Belt-and-Road/Belt-and-Road-Forum-shows-China-recalibrating-after-10-years
10. Jianli Yang and André Gattolin, "Italy's Decision on China's Belt and Road Initiative and Beyond," *Politico*, July 18, 2023, https://www.politico.eu/article/china-belt-and-road-italy-trade/
11. "Tibet gets first bullet train, links Lhasa to border with India," *The Hindu*, June 25, 2021, https://www.thehindu.com/news/international/china-launches-first-bullet-train-in-tibet-close-to-indian-border/article34959794.ece
12. Liu Xuanzun, "Lhasa-Nyingchi Railway hosts its first military transport mission," *Global Times*, August 4, 2021, https://www.globaltimes.cn/page/202108/1230590.shtml
13. Jun Mai and Mimi Lau, "What message was Xi Jinping trying to send on his visit to Tibet?" *South China Morning Post,* July 28, 2021, https://www.scmp.com/news/china/politics/article/3142911/what-message-was-xi-jinping-trying-send-his-visit-tibet
14. "Xi tells Tibetan herders to protect Chinese territory near Arunachal border," *Hindustan Times*, October 29, 2017, https://www.hindustantimes.com/india-news/guard-chinese-soil-xi-jinping-tells-herdsmen-from-arunachal-border/story-YdGdwV4LfpkYnGjCBcfB3M.html
15. Sutirtho Patranobis, "Over 10% rise in population in border regions of Tibet: China," *Hindustan Times*, Aug 20, 2021, https://www.hindustantimes.com/world-news/over-10-rise-in-population-in-border-regions-of-tibet-china-101629379005894.html
16. Robert Barnett, "China Is Building Entire Villages in Another Country's Territory," *Foreign Policy*, May 7, 2021, https://foreignpolicy.com/2021/05/07/china-bhutan-border-villages-security-forces/#:~:text=Since%202015%2C%20a%20previously%20unnoticed,a%20sacred%20valley%20in%20Bhutan.&text=In%20O-

ctober%202015%2C%20China%20announced,Tibet%20Autonomous%20Region%20(TAR)

17. Geeta Mohan, "Bhutan demarches China on its claim to Sakteng Sanctuary, Beijing reiterates position," *India Today*, July 6, 2020, https://www.indiatoday.in/world/story/china-bhutan-territory-dispute-demarche-chinese-embassy-new-delhi-sakteng-sanctuary-1697392-2020-07-05
18. Michael Bristow, "China Encroaching Along Nepal Border - Report," *BBC*, February 8, 2022, https://www.bbc.com/news/world-asia-60288007
19. "China plans to build new highway along LAC with India, says report," *Press Trust of India, Business Standard,* July 20, 2022, https://www.business-standard.com/article/international/china-plans-to-build-new-highway-along-lac-with-india-says-report-122072001101_1.html
20. G G Dwivedi, "Why is China building bridges over Pangong Tso: the genesis and ramifications," *The Indian Express*, May 27, 2022, https://indianexpress.com/article/cities/chandigarh/china-ladakh-standoff-pangong-tso-bridge-7939190/
21. Claude Arpi, "Beware, India! China's Most Strategic Road", *The Daily Guardian*, January 11, 2021, https://thedailyguardian.com/others/beware-india-chinas-most-strategic-road-is-coming/
22. Liu Zongyi, "India Hurts Itself with Border Belligerence," *Global Times,* September 15, 2020, https://www.globaltimes.cn/content/1200916.shtml
23. "Amid Ladakh stand-off, China helping Pakistan set up surface-to-air missile system in PoK, says report," *Financial Express,* October 9, 2020, https://www.financialexpress.com/business/defence-amid-ladakh-stand-off-china-helping-pakistan-set-up-surface-to-air-missile-system-in-pok-says-report-2101647/
24. "China developing new airbase in Shakche near Ladakh, India watching closely," *India Today*, July 19, 2021, https://www.indiatoday.in/india/story/india-china-eastern-ladakh-lac-standoff-pla-air-base-1830080-2021-07-19
25. "China upgrading military infra along western frontier in Tibet, Xinjiang," *Economic Times*, March 26, 2022, https://economictimes.indiatimes.com/news/defence/china-upgrading-military-infra-along-western-frontier-in-tibet-xinjiang/articleshow/90464733.cms
26. "China is helping Pakistan set up missile systems in PoK: New Intel says," *Indian Express*, October 9, 2020, https://indianexpress.com/article/india/new-intel-says-china-helping-pakistan-set-up-missile-systems-in-pok-6716553/
27. Cmde RS Vasan at the seminar on "CPEC- Challenges Galore," *PRF,* November 26, 2022, Hyderabad.
28. Yufan Huang, "Q and A.: Yan Xuetong Urges China to Adopt a More Assertive Foreign Policy," *The New York Times*, February 9, 2016, https://www.nytimes.com/2016/02/10/world/asia/china-foreign-policy-yan-xuetong.html?_r=0
29. Ibid.
30. "China: Draconian repression of Muslims in Xinjiang amounts to crimes against humanity," *Amnesty International,* June 10, 2021, https://www.amnesty.org/en/latest/news/2021/06/china-draconian-repression-of-muslims-in-xinjiang-amounts-to-crimes-against-humanity/

31. "Pakistan's Khan backs China on Uighurs, praises one-party system", *Al Jazeera*, July 2, 2021, https://www.aljazeera.com/news/2021/7/2/pakistan-imran-khan-china-uighurs
32. "OHCHR Assessment of human rights concerns in the Xinjiang Uyghur Autonomous Region, People's Republic of China," *OHCHR*, August 31, 2022, https://www.ohchr.org/sites/default/files/documents/countries/2022-08-31/22-08-31-final-assesment.pdf
33. "Press Release," *Ministry of Foreign Affairs, Government of Pakistan*, September 6, 2022, https://mofa.gov.pk/press-release-522/
34. "Pakistan Deports Uyghurs," *Radio Free Asia,* August 10, 2011, https://www.rfa.org/english/news/uyghur/pakistan-08102011175506.html; also see Brent E. Huffman, "Pakistan Is Cracking Down on Uyghur Muslims Who Fled China," *Pulitzer Centre,* May 21, 2021, https://pulitzercenter.org/stories/pakistan-cracking-down-uyghur-muslims-who-fled-china
35. Ayjaz Wani, "Wang Yi at OIC shows China's deep inroad into the Muslim world," *The Print,* March 28, 2022, https://theprint.in/opinion/wang-yi-at-oic-shows-chinas-deep-inroad-into-the-muslim-world/891987/; also see Jomana Karadsheh and Gul Tuysuz, "Uyghurs are being deported from Muslim countries, raising concerns about China's growing reach," *CNN,* June 8, 2021, https://edition.cnn.com/2021/06/08/middleeast/uyghur-arab-muslim-china-disappearances-cmd-intl/index.html
36. "Remarks by H.E. Wang Yi at the Opening Ceremony of The Session of the Council of Foreign Ministers of the Organization of Islamic Cooperation," *Ministry of Foreign Affairs, the People's Republic of China*, March 22, 2022, https://www.fmprc.gov.cn/mfa_eng/wjb_663304/wjbz_663308/2461_663310/202203/t20220323_10654638.html
37. "Pakistan accepts China's version on Xinjiang's Uighurs: PM Imran," *Dawn,* July 1, 2021, https://www.dawn.com/news/1632539/pakistan-accepts-chinas-version-on-xinjiangs-uighurs-pm-imran
38. Wang Yi, "Let Us Strengthen Confidence and Solidarity and Jointly Build a Closer Partnership for Belt and Road Cooperation," *Ministry of Foreign Affairs, the People's Republic of China,* June 23, 2021, https://www.fmprc.gov.cn/mfa_eng/wjb_663304/wjbz_663308/2461_663310/t1886403.shtml
39. "China's Communist Party extends reach into foreign companies," *The Straits Times*, January 29, 2018, https://www.straitstimes.com/asia/east-asia/chinas-communist-party-extends-reach-into-foreign-companies
40. Chun Han Wong and Eva Dou, "Foreign Companies in China Get a New Partner: The Communist Party," *The Wall Street Journal*, October 29, 2017, https://www.wsj.com/articles/foreign-companies-in-china-get-a-new-partner-the-communist-party-1509297523
41. Yan Xuetong, "Becoming Strong," *Foreign Affairs*, July/August 2021, https://www.foreignaffairs.com/articles/united-states/2021-06-22/becoming-strong
42. "姜婧："一带一路"倡议与意识形态安全," *National Office for Philosophy and Social Science*, July 28, 2017, http://www.nopss.gov.cn/n1/2017/0728/c373410-29434988.html

43. Sivaram, Karthik, "'Locked-In' to China: The Colombo Port City Project," *Freeman Spogli Institute for International Studies Case Study*, Stanford University, September 25, 2020.
44. Brad W Setser, "Debt Distress: Can Emerging Markets Withstand Rising Costs?" *Council on Foreign Relations*, July 28, 2022, https://www.cfr.org/article/debt-distress-can-emerging-markets-withstand-rising-costs-china-IMF-inflation
45. Syful Islam, "Bangladesh urges China loan tweaks amid scrutiny of BRI bailouts," *Nikkei Asia*, April 1, 2023, https://asia.nikkei.com/Politics/International-relations/Bangladesh-urges-China-loan-tweaks-amid-scrutiny-of-BRI-bailouts2
46. "China had no role in change of ruling coalition, UML chief Oli clarifies," *The Kathmandu Post*, March 13, 2024, https://kathmandupost.com/national/2024/03/13/china-had-no-role-in-change-of-ruling-coalition-uml-chief-oli-clarifies
47. "Chinese investigators join probe into suicide attack in Pakistan," *Times of India*, March 30, 2024, https://timesofindia.indiatimes.com/world/pakistan/chinese-investigators-join-probe-into-suicide-attack-in-pakistan/articleshow/108889948.cms
48. Sriram Lakshman and Suhasini Haidar, "UN Designates JeM chief Masood Azhar as Global Terrorist," *The Hindu*, May 2, 2019, https://www.thehindu.com/news/international/un-designates-jem-chief-masood-azhar-as-global-terrorist/article27002685.ece
49. "FATF meeting: China says Pakistan made 'visible progress' to curb terror financing," *The Economic Times*, January 23, 2020, https://economictimes.indiatimes.com/news/defence/fatf-meeting-china-says-pakistan-made-visible-progress-to-curb-terror-financing/articleshow/73552783.cms?from=mdr
50. "Kashmir: After China's Third Call for UNSC Meeting, India Rejects 'Interference'," *The Wire*, September 19, 2020, https://thewire.in/diplomacy/china-unsc-kashmir-meeting-india-reject-internal-matters-interfernce
51. "UN Fails to Take Action on Order Against Myanmar on Rohingya," *Al Jazeera*, February 5, 2020, https://www.aljazeera.com/news/2020/02/fails-action-order-myanmar-rohingyas-200205020402316.html
52. A Report for The Committee on Foreign Relations United States Senate, "Sri Lanka: Recharting U.S. Strategy After The War," (Washington: U.S. Government Printing Office, December 7, 2009), https://www.foreign.senate.gov/imo/media/doc/SRI.pdf#page=19
53. Walter Russell Mead, "Scolding Isn't a Foreign Policy," *The Wall Street Journal*, April 17, 2023, https://www.wsj.com/articles/scolding-isnt-a-foreign-policy-blinken-philippines-china-vietnam-communism-pragmatism-morality-3028f9c
54. Scott Livingston, "The New Challenge of Communist Corporate Governance," *CSIS*, January 15, 2021, https://www.csis.org/analysis/new-challenge-communist-corporate-governance
55. Paul Mozur, Jonah M. Kessel and Melissa Chan, "Made in China, Exported to the World: The Surveillance State," *The New York Times*, April 24, 2019, https://www.nytimes.com/2019/04/24/technology/ecuador-surveillance-cameras-police-government.html?smid=nytcore-ios-share
56. Josh Chin, "The Internet, Divided Between the U.S. and China, Has Become a Battleground," *The Wall Street Journal*, February 9, 2019, https://www.wsj.

com/articles/the-internet-divided-between-the-u-s-and-china-has-become-a-battleground-11549688420
57. Minxin Pei, "Why China Can't Export Its Model of Surveillance, *Foreign Affairs*, February 6, 2024, https://www.foreignaffairs.com/china/why-china-cant-export-its-model-surveillance#
58. Cecilia Kang, "'Rip and Replace': The Tech Cold War Is Upending Wireless Carriers," *The New York Times*, May 10, 2023, https://www.nytimes.com/2023/05/09/technology/cellular-china-us-zte-huawei.html#:~:text=The%20program%2C%20which%20took%20effect,and%20to%20steal%20commercial%20secrets.
59. Adam Satariano, Stephen Castle and David E. Sanger, "U.K. Bars Huawei for 5G as Tech Battle Between China and the West Escalates," *The New York Times*, July 14, 2020, https://www.nytimes.com/2020/07/14/business/huawei-uk-5g.html
60. Bertrand, Benoit, "Germany to Remove Huawei From Mobile Networks," *The Wall Street Journal,* July 10, 2024, https://www.wsj.com/tech/germany-to-remove-huawei-from-mobile-networks-f96ddf81?mod=article_inline
61. Matteo Giovannini, "The Digital Silk Road's Growing Strategic Role During the Epidemic," *CGTN*, June 10, 2020, https://news.cgtn.com/news/2020-06-10/The-Digital-Silk-Road-s-growing-strategic-role-during-the-epidemic-RbN21gC6xW/index.html
62. "Digital Silk Road Assists Africa in Combating COVID-19," *National Development and Reform Commission (NDRC), People's Republic of China,* https://en.ndrc.gov.cn/newsrelease_8232/202006/t20200601_1229673.html
63. Pan Zhaoyi, "Chinese vaccines will be made global public good, says Xi," *CGTN*, May 19, 2020, https://news.cgtn.com/news/2020-05-19/Chinese-vaccines-will-be-made-global-public-good-says-Xi-QCpFSGlL2g/index.html
64. Hu Yuwei and Bai Yunyi, "China empowers BRI partners in building vaccine production system," *The Global Times*, October 20, 2023, https://www.globaltimes.cn/page/202310/1300259.shtml
65. Leng Shumei, "China completes half-year vaccination goal early, will cover as many people as possible in H2," *Global Times*, June 30, 2021, https://www.globaltimes.cn/page/202106/1227529.shtml
66. Chao Deng, "Get Vaxxed or Stay Home, Some Local Chinese Governments Say," *The Wall Street Journal*, July 15, 2021, https://www.wsj.com/articles/covid-19-vaccines-are-becoming-mandatory-in-parts-of-china-11626259091
67. Devi Sridhar, "China's Covid crisis demands terrible choices. The world will suffer if this goes wrong," *The Guardian,* November 28, 2022, https://www.theguardian.com/commentisfree/2022/nov/28/china-abandon-zero-covid-protests-mass-vaccination; also see "China-manufactured vaccines turn out ineffective amid rising COVID-19 cases," *The Economic Times,* June 25, 2022, https://economictimes.indiatimes.com/news/international/world-news/china-manufactured-vaccines-turn-out-ineffective-amid-rising-covid-19-cases/articleshow/92454999.cms?from=mdr
68. "The Trans-Himalayan 'Quad,' Beijing's Territorialism, and India," *IDSA*, November 21, 2020, https://idsa.in/idsanews/the-trans-himalayan-quad-beijings-territorialism-and-india

69. Maria Siow, "'Himalayan Quad': is China about to start its own security bloc with Nepal, Pakistan and Afghanistan?" *The South China Morning Post*, April 17, 2021, https://www.scmp.com/week-asia/politics/article/3129902/himalayan-quad-china-about-start-its-own-security-bloc-nepal
70. "Wang Yi Hosts Video Conference of Foreign Ministers of China, Afghanistan, Bangladesh, Nepal, Pakistan and Sri Lanka on COVID-19," *Ministry of Foreign Affairs, the People's Republic of China*, April 27, 2021, https://www.fmprc.gov.cn/mfa_eng/gjhdq_665435/2675_665437/2752_663508/2754_663512/202104/t20210428_9168712.html
71. "'Himalayan Quad' hype is Cold War mentality," *Global Times,* April 20, 2021, https://www.globaltimes.cn/page/202104/1221560.shtml
72. "Assistant Foreign Minister Wu Jianghao Attends Launching Ceremony of China-South Asian Countries Poverty Alleviation and Cooperative Development Center," *Ministry of Foreign Affairs, the People's Republic of China*, July 7, 2021, https://www.fmprc.gov.cn/mfa_eng/wjb_663304/zygy_663314/gyhd_663338/202107/t20210709_9168425.html
73. "RCEP, CAI, BRI can boost global trade together," *China Daily,* December 19, 2020, https://www.chinadaily.com.cn/a/202012/09/WS5fd068fba31024ad0ba9ad1d.html
74. "China's Free Trade Agreements Along the Belt & Road Initiative," *Silk Road Briefing*, February 26, 2021, https://www.silkroadbriefing.com/news/2021/02/26/chinas-free-trade-agreements-along-the-belt-road-initiative/
75. Lu Yang, "BRI, RCEP best solution for South Asia and Southeast Asia recovery," *Global Times*, December 23, 2021, https://www.globaltimes.cn/content/1210800.shtml
76. "Working Together to Deliver a Brighter Future For Belt and Road Cooperation," Keynote Speech by H.E. Xi Jinping President of the People's Republic of China At the Opening Ceremony of the Second Belt and Road Forum for International Cooperation, *Ministry of Foreign Affairs, the People's Republic of China*, April 26, 2019, https://www.fmprc.gov.cn/mfa_eng/zxxx_662805/t1658424.shtml

77 孙敬鑫, "绿色丝绸之路的动力与挑战," *China Today*, October 9, 2020, http://www.chinatoday.com.cn/zw2018/bktg/202010/t20201009_800222969.html

78 携手打造"绿色丝绸之路" *China Economic Net-Economic Daily,* May 8, 2019, http://www.ce.cn/xwzx/gnsz/gdxw/201905/08/t20190508_32021090.shtml

79 Ibid.

80. 以绿色金融促进绿色丝绸之路建设, *Tsinghua Financial Review*, November 28, 2017, http://www.thfr.com.cn/post.php?id=73913
81. Ibid.
82. Adam S. Posen, "The End of China's Economic Miracle," *Foreign Affairs*, October 3, 2023, https://www.foreignaffairs.com/china/end-china-economic-miracle-beijing-washington
83. Ibid.
84. Ibid., also see Adam S. Posen, "The End of China's Economic Miracle," PIIE, September 7, 2023, https://www.piie.com/sites/default/files/2023-09/2023-09-07posen-ppt.pdf

85. Michael Pettis, "Inherited Trauma," *Foreign Affairs*, October 3, 2023, https://www.foreignaffairs.com/responses/who-killed-chinese-economy#inherited-trauma
86. Ibid.
87 Koh Ewe, "Amid Rising Joblessness, China Stops Publishing Its Youth Unemployment Rate, *Time*, August 15, 2023, https://time.com/6304881/china-stops-publishing-youth-unemployment-statistics/
88 Laura He, "China's economy will be hobbled for years by the real estate crisis," *CNN*, October 6, 2023, https://edition.cnn.com/2023/10/06/economy/china-economy-real-estate-crisis-intl-hnk/index.html#:~:text=Absorbing%20this%20%E2%80%9Cexcess%20capacity%E2%80%9D%20in,%2C%20according%20to%20Garcia%2DHerrero.&text=%E2%80%9CExpect%20China%20to%20be%20shaving,until%202026%2C%E2%80%9D%20she%20added.
89. "Paid late, or never – painters, builders and brokers hit by China's property crisis," *The Business Times*, September 3, 2023, https://www.businesstimes.com.sg/international/global/paid-late-or-never-painters-builders-and-brokers-hit-chinas-property-crisis
90 Keith Bradsher, "How China's Property Crisis Is Testing Its Too-Big-to-Fail Banks," *New York Times*, September 30, 2023, https://www.nytimes.com/2023/09/30/business/china-evergrande-banks-property.html
91. Ibid.
92. "Exclusive: China tells banks to roll over local government debts as risks mount-sources," *Reuters*, October 17, 2023, https://www.reuters.com/world/china/china-instructs-banks-roll-over-local-government-debt-sources-2023-10-17/#:~:text=BEIJING%2C%20Oct%2017%20(Reuters),risks%20in%20a%20faltering%20economy.
93. Alexandra Stevenson, "China Bet It All on Real Estate. Now Its Economy Is Paying the Price," *New York Times*, October 16, 2023, https://www.nytimes.com/2023/10/16/business/china-evergrande-country-garden.html#:~:text=on%20Real%20Estate.-,Now%20Its%20Economy%20Is%20Paying%20the%20Price.,housing%20market%20and%20economic%20future.
94. Yuke Xie, "China's local governments step up plans to issue refinancing bonds to tackle LGFV debt," *South China Morning Post*, October 11, 2023, https://www.scmp.com/business/banking-finance/article/3237511/chinas-local-governments-step-plans-issue-refinancing-bonds-tackle-lgfv-debt
95. "Two sessions: China sets 5 percent growth target, boosts military budget," *Al Jazeera*, March 5, 2024, https://www.aljazeera.com/economy/2024/3/5/china-sets-5-percent-growth-target-for-2024-amid-economic-headwinds
96. Ann Cao, "China's chip imports decline 15% in first nine months of 2023 as the country braces for a new round of US tech export controls," *South China Morning Post*, October 14, 2023, https://www.scmp.com/tech/techwar/article/3237914/chinas-chip-imports-decline-15-cent-first-nine-months-2023-country-braces-new-round-us-tech-export
97 "Tech war: US eyes more AI chip curbs on Chinese companies abroad to close loophole," *South China Morning Post*, October 13, 2023, https://www.scmp.com/tech/tech-war/article/3237797/tech-war-us-eyes-more-ai-chip-curbs-chinese-companies-abroad-close-loophole

98 "U.S. updates policies to stop China from getting advanced computer chips," *The Hindu*, October 17, 2023, https://www.thehindu.com/sci-tech/technology/us-updates-policies-to-stop-china-from-getting-advanced-computer-chips/article67430773.ece#:~:text=The%20updates%20also%20introduce%20new,to%20manufacture%20advanced%20chips%20abroad&text=The%20U.S.%20Commerce%20Department%20on,the%20equipment%20to%20manufacture%20them.

99. Philip Blenkinsop, "EU plans anti-subsidy probes to secure steel deal with US," *Reuters*, October 10, 2023, https://www.reuters.com/markets/commodities/eu-plans-anti-subsidy-probe-into-chinese-steelmakers-ft-2023-10-10/

100 Laurie Chen and Philip Blenkinsop, "Borrell says EU to manage ties with China in 'constructive' manner," *Reuters*, October 13, 2023, https://www.reuters.com/markets/eus-borrell-warns-china-de-risking-may-speed-up-if-imbalances-persist-2023-10-13/

101. Alexandra Prokopenko, "The Risks of Russia's Growing Dependence on the Yuan," *Carnegie Endowment for International Peace*, February 2, 2023, https://carnegieendowment.org/politika/88926

102. Amanda Lee, "China has 'rare opportunity' to accelerate yuan internationalisation, but 'scope limited'," *The South China Morning Post*, May 13 , 2023, https://www.scmp.com/economy/china-economy/article/3220355/china-has-rare-opportunity-accelerate-yuan-internationalisation-scope-limited

103. Li Xuanmin, "Myanmar accepts yuan as official settlement currency for border trade with China," *The Global Times*, December 15, 2021, https://www.globaltimes.cn/page/202112/1241577.shtml#:~:text=Myanmar%20has%20accepted%20the%20Chinese,the%20matter%20told%20the%20Global; also see "Pakistan, China agree to trade in yuan," *Anadolu Agency*, November 6, 2018, https://www.aa.com.tr/en/energy/investments/pakistan-china-agree-to-trade-in-yuan/22190#:~:text=Pakistan%20on%20Monday%20announced%20an,information%2C%20told%20reporters%20in%20Islamabad.

104. Chelsey Dulaney, Evan Gershkovich, and Victoria Simanovskaya, "Russia Turns to China's Yuan in Effort to Ditch the Dollar," *The Wall Street Journal*, February 28, 2023, https://www.wsj.com/articles/russia-turns-to-chinas-yuan-in-effort-to-ditch-the-dollar-a8111457

105. Xi Jinping,"Building an Open, Inclusive and Interconnected World For Common Development," *ECNS*, October 18, 2023, https://www.ecns.cn/news/politics/2023-10-18/detail-ihcuappp4691649.shtml

106. "China's trade with BRI countries exceeds 14 trillion yuan in first 3 quarters," *China SCIO*, October 19, 2023, http://english.scio.gov.cn/m/pressroom/2023-10/19/content_116760218.htm#:~:text=In%20the%20first%20three%20quarters,of%20China%27s%20total%20foreign%20trade.

107. Michael Safi and Amantha Perera, "'The Biggest Game Changer in 100 Years': Chinese Money Gushes into Sri Lanka," *The Guardian*, March 26, 2018, https://www.theguardian.com/world/2018/mar/26/the-biggest-game-changer-in-100-years-chinese-money-gushes-into-sri-lanka

108. Dinakar Peri, "China, Pakistan Navies to Hold First Joint Maritime Patrol," *The Hindu*, November 13, 2023, https://www.thehindu.com/news/international/china-

and-pakistan-navies-hold-drills-in-arabian-sea-to-conduct-first-maritime-patrols/article67528374.ece

109. "After asking India to withdraw troops, Maldives signs free military assistance deal with China," *Mint*, March 5, 2024, https://www.livemint.com/news/world/maldives-to-get-free-military-assistance-from-china-signs-agreement-to-bolster-bilateral-ties-11709606653655.html

110. "On China's Belt and Road, how Jaishankar reiterated India's longstanding, consistent position," *The Indian Express*, November 2, 2022, https://indianexpress.com/article/explained/china-belt-and-road-initiative-india-position-explained-8244276/

111. "What is China's Belt and Road Initiative and why was S Jaishankar critical of it at SCO meet?" *First Post*, November 2, 2022, https://www.firstpost.com/explainers/what-is-chinas-belt-and-road-initiative-and-why-was-s-jaishankar-critical-of-it-at-sco-meet-11558711.html

112 "专家：印度不是中国在马尔代夫和斯里兰卡的对手," *Sputnik News*, June 11, 2019, http://sputniknews.cn/opinion/201906111028728329/

113. S Y Surendra Kumar, "China's Footprints in Maldives: Concern for India?" *Artha Journal of Social Sciences*, 15, 4 (2016), pp. 15-29

114. "English Translation of Press Statement by Prime Minister Shri Narendra Modi During the visit of Prime Minister of Nepal," *PIB*, June 1, 2023, https://pib.gov.in/PressReleasePage.aspx?PRID=1929243#:~:text=The%20first%20Cross%2DBorder%20Petroleum,MW%20of%20power%20from%20Nepal.

115. "India Nepal rail link becomes operational: Check distance, stations, and other key details," *CNBC*, July 17, 2023, https://www.cnbctv18.com/travel/india-nepal-rail-link-becomes-operational-check-distance-stations-and-other-key-details-17237961.htm

116. "India, Nepal sign pact to link UPI, NPI for faster remittances," *The Hindu*, February 15, 2024, https://www.thehindu.com/business/india-nepal-sign-pact-to-link-upi-npi-for-faster-remittances/article67849371.ece

117. "India-Nepal enhance financial cooperation; digital payment to be inaugurated soon," *The Economic Times*, March 2, 2024, https://bfsi.economictimes.indiatimes.com/news/industry/india-nepal-enhance-financial-cooperation-digital-payment-to-be-inaugurated-soon/108160287

118. Rishi Ranjan Kala, "India, Nepal & Bangladesh working on a first-of-its-kind tripartite electricity trade deal in South Asia," *Business Line*, August 7, 2023, https://www.thehindubusinessline.com/news/india-nepal-bangladesh-working-on-a-first-of-its-kind-tripartite-electricity-trade-deal-in-south-asia/article67168538.ece#lnisj5nmpsa1vjqv7t

119. Constantino Xavier, "Sambandh as Strategy," *Brookings India Policy Brief*, January 2020, https://www.brookings.edu/wp-content/uploads/2020/01/Sambandh-as-Strategy-India%E2%80%99s-New-Approach-to-Regional-Connectivity.pdf

120. Saptaparno Ghosh, "The Agartala-Akhaura Rail Link," *The Hindu*, November 9, https://www.thehindu.com/news/national/explained-the-agartala-akhaura-rail-link/article67516621.ece

121. Rezaul H Laskar, "India, Bangladesh launch three major connectivity, energy projects," *The Hindustan Times*, November 1, 2023, https://www.hindustantimes.

com/india-news/india-bangladesh-launch-three-major-connectivity-energy-projects-101698824665267.html

122. Abhishek Law, "Shipping Ministry Enlarges Ambit of Indo-Bangla Protocol Route," *The Hindustan Times,* December 23, 2023, https://www.thehindubusinessline.com/economy/logistics/shipping-ministry-pitches-for-stronger-co-op-with-bangladesh-on-waterways-enlarges-ambit-of-indo-bangla-protocol-route/article67668493.ece

123. "Prime Ministers of India and Bangladesh to jointly inaugurate three development projects on 1st November," *Ministry of External Affairs, Government of India,* October 31, 2023, https://www.mea.gov.in/press-releases.htm?dtl/37218/Prime+Ministers+of+India+and+Bangladesh+to+jointly+inaugurate+three+development+projects+on+1st+November

124. "Joint Virtual Inauguration of the India-Bangladesh Friendship Pipeline by Prime Ministers of India & Bangladesh," *PIB,* March 16, 2023, https://pib.gov.in/PressReleasePage.aspx?PRID=1907711

125. "Promoting Connectivity, Catalysing Prosperity: India-Sri Lanka Economic Partnership Vision," *Ministry of External Affairs, Government of India,* July 21, 2023, https://www.mea.gov.in/bilateral-documents.htm?dtl/36864/Promoting+Connectivity+Catalysing+Prosperity+IndiaSri+Lanka+Economic+Partnership+Vision#:~:text=Air%20connectivity%3A,b.

126. "Brief on India - Sri Lanka Relations," *Ministry of External Affairs, Government of India,* July 1, 2021, https://www.mea.gov.in/Portal/ForeignRelation/Brief_on_India_for_website.pdf

127. "Launch of construction of 1300 houses under Indian Housing Project in 45 Estates across 10 Districts of Sri Lanka," Press Release, High Commission of India, February 19, 2024, https://www.hcicolombo.gov.in/press?id=eyJpdiI6IjJPQUpUS25uOExmZjh4b01IaU1SUUE9PSIsInZhbHVlIjoiMDA5c0NGdTR5T1RMeW1PSTZsaVVJUT09IiwibWFjIjoiYjd1NThiZGUwYmIzZmQxNGJkOWU0MjdkNjRhM2E4MTc3MjliY2Q5MWMyY2E5MmU5YmNlMzNjNzhjNDVjYWQ4MSJ9

128. "Honorable Prime Minister of India, Honorable Prime Minister of Mauritius and Honorable President of Sri Lanka witnessed the launch of India's RuPay/UPI connectivity with Mauritius and Sri Lanka," *RBI Press Release,* February 12, 2024, https://www.rbi.org.in/Scripts/BS_PressReleaseDisplay.aspx?prid=57308

129. Keshav Padmanabhan, "Jaishankar urges Indians to visit Sri Lanka, Lakshadweep mentioned in Budget amid row with Maldives," *The Print,* February 1, 2024, https://theprint.in/diplomacy/jaishankar-urges-indians-to-visit-sri-lanka-lakshadweep-mentioned-in-budget-amid-row-with-maldives/1949026/

130. "'Blood is thicker than water': S Jaishankar on India-Sri Lanka Relations," *ANI,* March 18, 2023, https://www.hindustantimes.com/india-news/blood-is-thicker-than-water-s-jaishankar-on-india-sri-lanka-relations-101679090180927.html

131. "Indian Bank Extends $400 Million Credit for Greater Male Connectivity Project," *The Indian Express,* October 12, 2020, https://indianexpress.com/article/india/greater-maldives-connectivity-project-6721899/

132. "India's Assistance Programme for Afghanistan's Reconstruction," *Embassy of India Kabul, Afghanistan,* https://eoi.gov.in/eoisearch/MyPrint.php?0356?000/0001

133. "India and Afghanistan: A Development Partnership," *External Publicity Division, Ministry of External Affairs,* https://www.mea.gov.in/Uploads/PublicationDocs/176_india-and-afghanistan-a-development-partnership.pdf
134. Ibid.
135. "Training Institutions," *Embassy of India, Yangon, Myanmar,* https://embassyofindiayangon.gov.in/pages/MTYw
136. C. Raja Mohan, "Raja Mandala: A Silk Road for the Heavens," *The Indian Express,* April 23, 2019, https://indianexpress.com/article/opinion/columns/india-china-silk-route-beijing-belt-and-road-initiative-big-earth-data-5689184/
137. Akihiko Tanaka, "BIG-B toward Growth beyond Borders," *JICA,* June 16, 2014, https://www.jica.go.jp/Resource/english/about/president/speech/140616_02.html
138. "Mekong India Economic Corridor Development," ERIA, March 1, 2009, https://www.eria.org/research/mekong-india-economic-corridor-development/
139. "Indo-Pacific Economic Framework for Prosperity (IPEF) Supply Chain Agreement signed by the 14 IPEF Partners," *PIB,* November 17, 2023, https://pib.gov.in/PressReleaseIframePage.aspx?PRID=1977529#:~:text=IPEF%20was%20launched%20jointly%20by,%2C%20Thailand%2C%20Vietnam%20%26%20USA.
140. "Fact Sheet: Partnership for Global Infrastructure and Investment at the G7 Summit," *The White House,* May 20, 2023, https://www.whitehouse.gov/briefing-room/statements-releases/2023/05/20/fact-sheet-partnership-for-global-infrastructure-and-investment-at-the-g7-summit/
141. Rajeswari Pillai Rajagopalan, "India Noncommittal on the Partnership for Global Infrastructure and Investment," *The Diplomat,* August 9, 2022, https://thediplomat.com/2022/08/india-noncommittal-on-the-partnership-for-global-infrastructure-and-investment/

Index